We Have Not a Government

We Have Not a Government

THE ARTICLES OF CONFEDERATION AND THE ROAD TO THE CONSTITUTION

George William Van Cleve

THE UNIVERSITY OF CHICAGO PRESS
Chicago and London

George William Van Cleve is research professor in law and history at Seattle University School of Law. He received his PhD from University of Virginia and his JD from Harvard Law School.

The University of Chicago Press, Chicago 60637
The University of Chicago Press, Ltd., London

Published 2017
Printed in the United States of America

26 25 24 23 22 21 20 19 18 17   1 2 3 4 5

ISBN-13: 978-0-226-48050-3 (cloth)
ISBN-13: 978-0-226-48064-0 (e-book)
DOI: 10.7208/chicago/9780226480640.001.0001

LIBRARY OF CONGRESS CATALOGING-IN-PUBLICATION DATA

Names: Van Cleve, George, 1952– author.
Title: We have not a government: the Articles of Confederation and the road to the Constitution / George William van Cleve.
Description: Chicago; London: The University of Chicago Press, 2017. | Includes bibliographical references and index.
Identifiers: LCCN 2017015706 | ISBN 9780226480503 (cloth: alk. paper) | ISBN 9780226480640 (e-book)
Subjects: LCSH: United States. Articles of Confederation. | Constitutional History—United States—18th century. | United States—Politics and government—1775–1783. | United States—Politics and government—1783–1789. | United States—History—1783–1815.
Classification: LCC KF4508 .V353 2017 E302.1 | DDC 342.7302—dc23
LC record available at https://lccn.loc.gov/2017015706

♾ This paper meets the requirements of ANSI/NISO Z39.48-1992 (Permanence of Paper).

In memoriam Foster Osgood Chanock, beloved friend

For my wife and children and our fellow citizens,

now and in the years to come

Those who cannot remember the past are condemned to repeat it.

George Santayana, *The Life of Reason*

CONTENTS

PRINCIPAL CHARACTERS

CONFEDERATION OFFICIALS

John Adams (1735–1826). Born Braintree, Massachusetts. Attorney. Negotiator, Paris Treaty of Peace, 1782–83. Ambassador to England, 1785–88. Husband of Abigail Smith Adams.

Josiah Harmar (1753–1813). Born Philadelphia, Pennsylvania. Revolutionary War soldier. Army commander on Ohio frontier, 1783–91.

John Jay (1745–1829). Born New York, New York. Attorney. Negotiator, Paris Treaty of Peace, 1782–83. Secretary of Foreign Affairs, 1784–89.

Thomas Jefferson (1743–1826). Born Albemarle County, Virginia. Slave-plantation owner, attorney, and author. Congressman, 1783–84. Minister (trade), 1784. Minister to France, 1785–89.

Henry Knox (1750–1806). Born Boston, Massachusetts. Bookseller. Army major general, Revolutionary War. Secretary of War, 1785–94.

Arthur Lee (1740–1792). Born Stratford Hall, Virginia. Doctor and attorney. Revolutionary War diplomat. Member of Virginia House of Delegates, 1781–83, 1785, 1786. Congressman, 1782–84. Indian commissioner, Treaties of Fort Stanwix and Fort Mcintosh. Member, Board of Treasury, 1785–89. Brother of Richard Henry Lee.

Benjamin Lincoln (1733–1810). Born Hingham, Massachusetts. Army major general, Revolutionary War. Secretary at War, 1781–83. Led Massachusetts troops against Shays's Rebellion, 1786–87.

Robert R. Livingston (1746–1813). Born Clermont, Columbia County,

New York. Attorney and major landowner. Secretary of Foreign Affairs, 1781–83.

Robert Morris (1734–1806). Born Liverpool, England. Philadelphia international merchant. Superintendent of Finance, 1781–84. Member of Pennsylvania Assembly, 1785–87. Annapolis Convention delegate, 1786. Philadelphia Convention delegate, 1787.

CONGRESSMEN*

Elbridge Gerry (1744–1814). Born Marblehead, Massachusetts. International merchant. Congressman, 1783–85. Member of Massachusetts House of Representatives, 1786–87. Philadelphia Convention delegate, 1787.

William Grayson (1736?–90). Born Prince William County, Virginia. Attorney. Member of Virginia House of Delegates, 1784–85. Congressman, 1785–87.

David Howell (1747–1824). Born Morristown, New Jersey. College professor, mathematics and natural philosophy. Congressman for Rhode Island, 1782–85.

Rufus King (1755–1827). Born Scarborough, Maine (then part of Massachusetts). Attorney. Member of Massachusetts legislature, 1783–85. Congressman, 1784–87. Philadelphia Convention delegate, 1787.

Henry ("Light-Horse Harry") Lee, Jr. (III?) (1756–1818). Born Prince William County, Virginia. Revolutionary War officer. Congressman, 1786–88.

James Madison (1751–1836). Born King George County, Virginia. Heir to slave plantation. Career politician and political theorist. Congressman, 1780–83, 1787. Member of Virginia Assembly, 1784–86. Annapolis Convention delegate, 1786. Philadelphia Convention delegate, 1787.

James Monroe (1758–1831). Born Westmoreland County, Virginia. Attorney. Member of Virginia Assembly, 1782, 1786. Congressman, 1783–86.

* Throughout this book, the terms "member of Congress," "congressman," and "delegate" are used interchangeably to mean persons elected by the states to represent them in Congress.

STATE LEADERS/INFLUENTIAL CITIZENS

Abigail Smith Adams (1744–1818). Born Weymouth, Massachusetts. Managed family farm and investments in Braintree, 1776–85. With husband, John Adams, in Paris and London, 1785–88.

Samuel Adams (1722–1803). Born Boston, Massachusetts. Revolutionary statesman. Member of Massachusetts Senate and Governor's Council during the 1780s.

George Clinton (1739–1812). Born Ulster County, New York. Revolutionary soldier and statesman. Served seven terms as governor of New York, including 1783–89.

Tristram Dalton (1738–1817). Born Newburyport, Massachusetts. Merchant. Member of Massachusetts House of Representatives, 1782–85. Member of Massachusetts Senate, 1785–88.

Nathaniel Gorham (1738–96). Born Charlestown, Massachusetts. Merchant. Congressman, 1782–83, 1785–87. Member of Massachusetts legislature, 1781–87. Active in suppression of Shays's Rebellion. Philadelphia Convention delegate, 1787.

Alexander Hamilton (1755?–1804). Born Charlestown, Nevis, West Indies. Revolutionary War officer; staff aide to General Washington. Congressman, 1782–83. Annapolis Convention delegate, 1786. Member of New York legislature, 1787. Philadelphia Convention delegate, 1787.

Patrick Henry (1736–99). Born Hanover County, Virginia. Attorney. Member of Virginia legislature, 1782–84, 1787–88. Five-term governor of Virginia, including 1785–86.

Stephen Higginson (1743–1828). Born Salem, Massachusetts. International merchant. Congressman, 1783. Served as lieutenant colonel in forces opposing Shays's Rebellion, 1786–87.

Richard Henry Lee (1732–94). Born Stratford Hall, Virginia. Slave-plantation owner, career politician. Congressman, 1784–85, 1787. Member of Virginia legislature, 1785.

Daniel Shays (ca. 1747–1825). Born Hopkinton, Massachusetts. Revolutionary War soldier and officer. Farmer. A main leader of the 1786 insurgency against Massachusetts government.

George Washington (1732–99). Born Westmoreland County, Virginia. Slave-plantation owner, land and canal investor. Revolutionary War army commander in chief, 1775–83. President, Philadelphia Convention, 1787.

FOREIGN AND NATIVE AMERICAN DIPLOMATS AND LEADERS

Joseph Brant (Thayendanegea) (1743–1807). Born Ohio Country. Mohawk military and political leader. Revolutionary War officer (British ally). Slave-farm owner. Among the principal leaders of postwar Native American tribes' Western Confederacy.

Bernardo de Gálvez, Viscount of Galveston and Count of Gálvez (1746–86). Born Macharaviaya, Spain. Spanish general in Revolutionary War. Governor of Cuba, 1784. Viceroy of New Spain, 1785–86.

Don Diego María de Gardoqui (1735–98). Born Bilbao, Spain. Spanish envoy to the United States, 1785–89.

Alexander McGillivray (Hoboi-Hili-Miko) (1750?–93). Born Little Tallassee (near present-day Montgomery, Alabama). Revolutionary War officer (British ally). Slave-plantation owner. Main leader of Upper Creek (Muscogee) tribes, 1782–87. Attempted to create Native American tribes' Southern Confederacy.

Esteban Rodriguez Miró (1744–85). Born Reus, Spain. Spanish Army officer. Acting governor/governor of Spanish provinces of Louisiana and Florida, 1782–91.

Louis-Guillaume Otto, Comte de Mosloy (1754–1817). Born Kork, Baden. French chargé d'affaires ad interim to the United States, 1785–87.

Charles Gravier, Comte de Vergennes (1719?–87). Born Dijon, France. Foreign minister of France, 1774–87.

THE CONFEDERATION'S FINAL YEARS: A CHRONOLOGY

1783

JANUARY 6	Congress receives army petition seeking pay arrears and retirement pay.
JANUARY 10	Congress secretly authorizes Robert Morris to write bad checks to pay army.
CA. MARCH 15	Preliminary peace with Great Britain announced in United States.
MARCH 22	Congress adopts "commutation" proposal for army officers' retirement: full pay for five years.
APRIL 18	Congress requests Confederation tax powers—5 percent "impost" (i.e., import duty) and supplemental state tax—to pay Confederation debts.
JUNE 8	George Washington sends circular to the states, advocating stronger central government, including Confederation tax powers.
JULY 2	Great Britain imposes major restrictions on American trade.
SEPTEMBER 3	Final peace treaty (Treaty of Paris) signed, ending Revolutionary War.
CA. SEPTEMBER 8	George Washington recommends a 2,500-troop peacetime military.
NOVEMBER 23	British army evacuates New York City.

1784

MARCH 1 — Congress accepts Virginia's cession of its claims to western lands north of the Ohio River.

APRIL 30 — Congress proposes giving Confederation limited commerce powers for fifteen years.

JUNE 2–3 — Congress orders discharge of all but eighty Continental troops, and *recommends* that four states raise seven hundred militia for Confederation service. Its action effectively rejects George Washington's peacetime-army proposal.

JUNE 26 — Spain orders Mississippi River closed to Americans.

JULY 1 — Massachusetts agrees to give Confederation limited commerce powers.

— Barbary Coast pirates attack American shipping, including capture of the *Betsey*.

— Many commodity prices fall; shipbuilding and fishing decline sharply; widespread reports of specie money scarcity; very high exchange rates.

1785

MARCH — Pennsylvania issues paper money to pay public creditors and fund loans to public.

MARCH 28 — Congress receives report proposing greatly expanded Confederation commerce powers; takes no action on it.

MAY 20 — Congress adopts ordinance to begin western land sales.

JUNE — Massachusetts legislature proposes national convention to reform Confederation.

JUNE — Massachusetts adopts retaliatory trade legislation against Great Britain and others.

SEPTEMBER — Pennsylvania repeals charter of Robert Morris's private Bank of North America.

SEPTEMBER 3 — Massachusetts congressional delegation objects to national constitutional convention requested by legislature; seeks reconsideration.

OCTOBER — South Carolina issues paper money and passes debt-relief laws.

— Many business failures in Boston, New York, Philadelphia; Georgia and North Carolina issue paper money; debt suits skyrocket.

1786

JANUARY 21 Virginia legislature proposes national meeting of states to discuss harmonizing states' commerce powers in Annapolis, Maryland, in September 1786.

FEBRUARY 15 Congressional committee reports that Confederation faces a financial "crisis" that will "hazard . . . the existence of the Union."

FEBRUARY 28 Great Britain formally refuses to comply with Treaty of Paris requirement that it evacuate its northwest forts.

SPRING New York, New Jersey, and Rhode Island issue paper money.

MAY 16 Governor Patrick Henry of Virginia writes to Congress protesting Confederation inaction on Virginia-Indian frontier warfare.

AUGUST New York rejects Congress's 1783 impost proposal.

AUGUST 7 Grand Committee of Congress proposes major Confederation reforms; Congress takes no action on them.

AUGUST 29 Majority of states vote in Congress that United States will accept Spanish bar on Mississippi River navigation by Americans, to obtain treaty with Spain.

AUGUST 29 First court blockage by Shays's insurgents in Massachusetts.

SEPTEMBER 11–14 Annapolis commerce convention attended by representatives from five states. Proposes national constitutional convention in Philadelphia in May 1787.

SEPTEMBER 15 Baltimore newspaper report of Shays's Rebellion court blockage.

OCTOBER 11 Congressman Rufus King addresses Massachusetts legislature and opposes 1787 Philadelphia Convention.

OCTOBER 16 Resolution introduced in Virginia legislature authorizing delegates to Philadelphia Convention.

OCTOBER 20 Congress authorizes raising troops to fight western Indians (and Shays's rebels).

NOVEMBER	Connecticut and Virginia defeat paper-money issuance by large majorities.
NOVEMBER 18	George Washington writes that he will decline to serve as a Philadelphia Convention delegate.
NOVEMBER 24	New Jersey chooses delegates to Philadelphia Convention.
DECEMBER 4	Virginia chooses delegates to Philadelphia Convention.
DECEMBER 21	George Washington formally declines appointment as Philadelphia Convention delegate.
DECEMBER 30	Pennsylvania chooses delegates to Philadelphia Convention.

1787

JANUARY 6	North Carolina authorizes delegates to Philadelphia Convention.
JANUARY 25–CA. FEBRUARY 10	Massachusetts troops defeat Shays's rebels.
FEBRUARY 3	Delaware appoints delegates to Philadelphia Convention.
FEBRUARY 10	Georgia appoints delegates to Philadelphia Convention.
FEBRUARY 17	New York legislature again rejects Congress's impost proposal.
FEBRUARY 20	New York effort to block Philadelphia Convention fails. State senate agrees by one-vote margin to instruct states' delegates in Congress to recommend its support of Philadelphia Convention.
FEBRUARY 21	Congress passes resolution acceding to Philadelphia Convention.
FEBRUARY 22	Massachusetts authorizes delegates to Philadelphia Convention but imposes major restrictions on their powers to reform Confederation.
FEBRUARY 26–28	New York legislature appoints delegates to Philadelphia Convention after efforts to severely restrict delegates' and Convention's powers fail.

MARCH 7	Massachusetts legislature secretly removes all restrictions on its Philadelphia delegates' powers to agree to Confederation reforms.
MARCH 8	South Carolina authorizes delegates to Philadelphia Convention.
MARCH 28	George Washington reverses position and agrees to attend Philadelphia Convention.
MAY 17	Connecticut appoints Philadelphia Convention delegates.
MAY 25	Philadelphia Convention achieves a quorum.

Introduction

It appears, sir, that in all the American provinces there is more or less tendency toward democracy; that in many this extreme form of government will finally prevail.

The result will be that the confederation will have little stability, and that by degrees the different states will subsist in a perfect independence of each other.

This revolution will not be regretted by us. We have never pretended to make of America a useful ally; we have had no other object than to deprive Britain of that vast continent. Therefore, we can regard with indifference both the movements which agitate certain provinces and the fermentation which prevails in congress.

Secret instructions about American affairs and possible Confederation collapse from the French royal government to Louis-Guillaume Otto, French chargé d'affaires in the United States. Sent during the Philadelphia Constitutional Convention, August 30, 1787[1]

This is a history of the final years of the Confederation—America's first continental government—from 1783 until its collapse in mid-1787. It had begun as a Revolutionary War alliance between the thirteen American states, operating through the Continental Congress. By 1775, Congress started to manage the war effort closely. But the Confederation's governing instrument, the Articles of Confederation—America's first constitution—was not finally adopted by all states until 1781, late in the war. Due principally to their harsh experience as colonists under the British monarchy, many Americans feared that they would be oppressed by any powerful central government. The Confederation's limited powers—primarily over war and peace—reflected those strong fears and wartime divisions and pressures as well.

The Confederation's last years were a marvelous peacetime experiment in republicanism—representative government by popular consent—at both the state and continental levels.[2] Perhaps because of that, the mid-1780s battles over the Confederation's future resembled those of the American Revolution itself. The revolution began as a tax revolt. Similarly, the true heart of the controversy over the Confederation's collapse was whether Americans were willing to transfer sovereignty—tax and law enforcement powers—to a central government.

Like the revolution, the Confederation's final years were marked by deep divisions about whether and how two fluid, potentially conflicting ideas—empire and republicanism—should be embodied in any new central government. Should a new government be made powerful enough to enable America to become a continental empire? Or should it remain a government of tightly limited powers—like the Confederation—that many thought was more consistent with revolutionary principles protecting liberty? Should majority power be unlimited in a republic, or should minorities instead receive constitutional protection under some circumstances? Answering those questions required Americans to weigh anew the competing claims of liberty, equality, power, and order in the harsh light of postwar realities.

The book opens as Americans achieved their independence after eight years of struggle against the world's most powerful empire, Great Britain. Americans' futures in an expanding country seemed extraordinarily bright. Most people had no inkling that their lives would soon be heavily burdened by the war's legacies. But to their dismay, over the next several years Americans found that there was a massive gap between the promises of the peace and its realities.

After conducting a victorious war, the Confederation had majority public support. But by 1783, America's revolutionary leaders were already divided over its future. Some, such as George Washington, advocated changes to create a much more powerful central government. Others, such as Virginian Richard Henry Lee, fervently opposed them. The Confederation faced massive war debts. Soon it encountered punishing trade restrictions and strenuous resistance to American territorial expansion from powerful European governments. Bitter sectional divisions that deadlocked the Continental Congress arose from exploding western settlement. Efforts to strengthen the Confederation met repeated defeats. A deep, long-lasting recession led to sharp controversies and social unrest across the country over greatly increased taxes, debt relief, and paper money. In sum, during the Confederation's final years, America confronted severe external challenges while facing growing socioeconomic class and sectional conflicts. Those remarkable stresses transformed the Confederation into a stalemate government, which could not make changes needed to withstand them. That in turn led to its loss of public confidence—in other words, its political collapse (as opposed to its imminent financial collapse).

The Confederation's collapse first became publicly visible when Congress voted in February 1787 to support a constitutional convention that May in Philadelphia. Congress's action was a definitive "no confidence" vote on the Confederation. James Madison wrote that both its friends and its enemies regarded it as a "deadly blow." By the eve of the convention, it had become evident that many, though by no means all, Americans had lost confidence in the Confederation. This book tells the story of how and why that confidence was undermined. It concludes by exploring how the convention's proposed 1787 constitution would end stalemate government through a dramatic—some thought shocking—"grand bargain." The rest of this introduction provides an overview of the book, and then contrasts its perspective with the views of earlier historians.

Overview

The Articles of Confederation explicitly preserved the "sovereignty, freedom and independence" of the Confederation's thirteen constituent states. In the Articles, the states delegated narrowly limited powers to the central government they created. The Confederation's powers primarily concerned waging war, conducting external diplomacy and making treaties, judicial resolution of interstate grievances, and related matters. It had no power to tax, and no commerce powers (except as to Indian tribes and under its limited treaty authority). The states retained broad powers of local self-government, affecting most aspects of Americans' daily lives only if and as their citizens chose. New Confederation powers had to be agreed to unanimously by the states.[3]

The Articles envisioned that the Confederation would be governed by a one-house Congress. Each of the states had one equal vote in Congress. All Confederation fiscal and military legislation needed to be adopted by a supermajority vote of at least nine states. The Confederation's structure and supermajority voting requirements greatly strengthened the hands of those who wanted to prevent changes in central-government political and economic powers. During the postwar years, the Confederation faced a series of divisive challenges that were principally legacies of the war. It reached stalemates on all of them.

Though America emerged victorious from the war, it was a deeply traumatic, costly conflict that shattered many Americans' lives and altered society. Soon after its end, the country experienced a severe, lengthy economic recession. New evidence leads recent historians to think that it may have been the worst in American history before the 1930s Great Depression. Debtors all over America were being hard-pressed to pay debts and increased taxes precisely when they had the least ability to pay them. As they searched for remedies, Confederation and state leaders increasingly realized that the economic interests of various states and sections sharply conflicted. Chapter 1 describes the turbulent postwar economic and political landscape they encountered.

The Confederation's overarching problem was the morass of debt left by the Revolutionary War. To fight it, Congress had printed paper money and borrowed millions of dollars from France, Spain, and the Netherlands. And it had issued "enormous" amounts of promissory notes for debts. States and private citizens also had large debts. But the Confederation had no power to tax to pay either its debts or its operating expenses. Instead it depended entirely on state compliance with requests for money made through "requisitions." Compliance was voluntary, because the Confederation lacked any practical means of enforcing it. Its efforts to cope with the problems of debt and taxation are the subjects of chapters 2 and 3. After the war, it encountered several other major problems as well.

The Confederation's lack of any substantial powers to regulate foreign or domestic commerce quickly became an acute concern. In the summer of 1783, Britain prohibited American ships from trading to the British West Indies. Soon American shipping in the Mediterranean Sea came under attack by North African state–sponsored pirates. European governments, including America's wartime allies France and Spain, also imposed postwar trade restrictions. Efforts began in Congress to give the Confederation trade powers to enable it to retaliate and to pay off the pirates. Sectional and interstate struggles over possible Confederation commerce powers and trade policy are the subjects of chapter 4.

America's western expansion also caused sharp conflicts over financial, commercial, and military policy. After the war, Americans began to move west in record numbers. Leaders such as Elbridge Gerry of Massachusetts insisted that sales of America's massive western lands could pay the Confederation's debts, making most Confederation taxation unnecessary. Congress passed ordinances in 1784 and 1785 to enable land sales. It remained deadlocked on territorial government, however, especially the deeply divisive issue of slavery extension. Many leaders opposed or wanted to discourage western expansion, which raised a host of concerns, including likely wars with Native Americans.[4] The Confederation's response to western emigration, and British, Spanish, and Native American resistance to expansion are the subjects of chapter 5.

Spain's concerted effort to contain America's western expansion caused a pivotal clash over Confederation policy as well. In the mid-1780s, as part of its strategy, Spain offered to negotiate a trade treaty with the United States. New England and other northern states pressed Confederation secretary of foreign affairs John Jay to agree to Spain's proposal. It would have handsomely benefited New England's shipping and fisheries. But southern states vehemently opposed it because they thought that it wholly sacrificed their strong interest in western expansion. The treaty clash also raised fundamental questions about America's postwar military establishment. In 1786, it became the most divisive sectional dispute of the entire decade. That controversy and its far-reaching implications for the Confederation's future are considered in chapter 6.

America's severe recession also caused bitter social conflicts. One profound effect of the Revolutionary War was that to pay for it, many states sharply increased postwar taxes. From South Carolina to Vermont, the harsh economic conditions of the mid-1780s, including increased taxation, led to sporadic and in some cases serious social unrest. As a result, legislation to protect debtors against creditors—British, domestic, or both—was passed in a number of states. Seven states also adopted laws authorizing paper money. In Pennsylvania, its issuance was followed by an exceptionally divisive struggle over revoking the charter of the private Bank of North America. That contest raised the vexing question whether popular majorities should have to respect vested property rights. State struggles over paper money and debt relief and their effects on the Confederation are the subjects of chapter 7.[5]

The period's most striking social unrest was an armed insurgency led by Revolutionary War veteran Daniel Shays and others that broke out in 1786 in Massachusetts. The rebels focused their initial efforts on obstructing courts and sheriffs, to prevent the collection of tax and private debts. Their other demands included political reforms, the issuance of paper money, tax relief, and debt relief. Chapter 8 analyzes the rebellion and its effects on the Confederation.

By the end of 1786, majorities (sometimes slim ones) in many states concluded that time had run out for the Confederation. They expected it to collapse financially, which they anticipated would be followed by the Union's dissolution. Deeply dismayed by chronic Confederation weakness, and often disturbed by the actions (or inaction) of their own states as well, many Americans for the first time became willing to risk strong central government. In late 1786, Virginia called for an unlimited national reform convention to be held in Philadelphia in May 1787. Chapter 9 discusses the long and winding road to the convention. It analyzes why critical states finally agreed to it despite intense opposition, and how it set the stage for a constitutional "grand bargain." It also considers how major leaders, including George Washington and James Madison, viewed it.

The book's conclusion explores how the Constitution resolved the Confederation's underlying problem of stalemate government. It transferred sovereignty to the national government and adopted a far more powerful and flexible decision-making process. But it did so by creating an intersectional elite power-sharing agreement, a "grand bargain" that had profound long-term economic and political consequences.

Historians on the Confederation's Collapse

Prior historians have largely fallen into one of two camps that hold dramatically different views of the Confederation's final years. For some late-nineteenth- and early-twentieth-century historians, those years were a "critical period" during which a political and economic crisis occurred. America's state and Confederation governments behaved in what historians saw as dysfunctional ways when tested by those crises. In their view, that led to the creation by the 1787 convention of a more powerful new government.[6]

Many twentieth-century historians, however, deny that there was a real crisis during the mid-1780s.[7] For Charles Beard, the idea that the 1780s were a "critical period" is a "phantom of the imagination produced by some undoubted evils which could have been remedied without a political revolution."[8] Another leading historian, Merrill Jensen, derides the earlier view as the "chaos and patriots to the rescue" conception of

Confederation collapse.[9] In Jensen's view, during the Confederation's final years America was recovering economically, and moving toward a vibrant, decentralized, egalitarian democracy.

Jensen and others accordingly conclude that fundamental reform of the Confederation was unnecessary. They contend that cooperation between the states was successful in resolving important national problems during the 1780s. They claim that such cooperation would have continued had the Confederation not been needlessly destroyed. At most, they think, minor amendments to the Articles could have permitted the Confederation to function well as a national government while preserving state and popular freedom.[10] From their point of view, the Constitution was a "conservative counter-revolution" by an elite determined to protect its wealth and its control of national politics, thwarting rising popular democracy.[11]

This book offers an alternative view that does not fall squarely in either camp. The sources suggest that earlier historians did exaggerate in describing the late Confederation period as one of "chaos," but it was nevertheless a period of extraordinary economic and political stresses. Some governments responded far more effectively to those strains than others did. The sources show that many leading contemporaries thought that there was a political crisis. The book contends that that view was not merely a pretext for class aggression or a delusion. There was an objective basis in the country's circumstances for such a belief.

Ultimately, this book will show that Confederation reform was driven most heavily by the perceived need to create a sovereign national government that could preserve American independence, protect western expansion, combat foreign trade aggression, provide unified continental government and law enforcement, and maintain internal order. The Confederation lacked every one of those capabilities. Reform efforts were also motivated by a desire to protect wealthy conservatives' property against popular economic redistribution demands, but such concerns played a subsidiary role.

We can begin our analysis with an undeniable fact: as historian Gordon Wood concludes, there is strong evidence that by 1786 many

Americans believed that a crisis existed. They believed, he writes, that "the course of the Revolution had arrived at a crucial juncture."[12] As Congressmen Rufus King of Massachusetts reported to Elbridge Gerry that year, "The People generally throughout the Confederation remark that we are at a crisis."[13] But what did contemporaries think that a "crisis" was? What kind of crisis did leaders believe existed?

"Crisis" did not have the same meaning for Americans in the eighteenth century that it typically has for us today.[14] Most commonly then, a "crisis" was an irreversible turning point, or what we would today call a fork in the road, toward which events were thought to be moving. A crisis could therefore change the course of history decisively for better or worse, just as the "crisis" of an illness could lead to recovery or death.[15] Decisions made when events were moving toward a crisis could in some cases avert it and change the course of events that would otherwise foreseeably result from it.[16] That sense of "crisis" is employed here in discussing contemporaries' attitudes.

In the mid-1780s, the sources suggest that most leaders did not think that there was an economic crisis, though there were exceptions. The times were unquestionably hard. There now appears to be an emerging consensus that actual domestic and foreign-trade economic conditions in most of the country during that period are best described as a continuing severe recession, contrary to the more optimistic view of earlier historians such as Merrill Jensen.[17] And there is no doubt that economic recession and related social unrest such as Shays's Rebellion significantly contributed to the collapse of confidence in the Confederation—in some parts of the country.[18] But although to varying degrees leaders supported economic policy changes, such as giving the Confederation commerce powers, failure to obtain them was not at the heart of what many leaders had in mind when they described the Confederation's situation by late 1786 as a "crisis." Instead, the sources suggest that by then many leaders thought that there was a political crisis.[19]

By 1786, the Confederation had undeniably become both insolvent and chronically stalemated. The intractability of the Confederation's problems stemmed principally, I argue, from growing sectional and interstate conflicts, often based on economic interest, as it confronted the massive challenges to America posed by the burdensome legacy of the Revolutionary War. Given the rigid political fractures caused by these exceptionally divisive issues, there is no sound reason to think that the Confederation could have resolved them absent fundamental reform. As the book shows, historians who argue otherwise are compelled to support their claims by defining the Confederation's problems away or by proposing "solutions" to them that had large unavoidable costs and tradeoffs that made such "solutions" unacceptable to many contemporaries. The pivotal controversy over Confederation war debt and taxation is a good example.

The Confederation's inability to pay its massive war debts appeared to many thoughtful contemporaries to be an urgent national political problem by late 1786. Recent historians argue that the Confederation's debt was not a serious problem, however.[20] They contend that the Confederation's foreign debt could have been paid by voluntary state contributions or minor new taxes. They argue that the states could individually have paid their assigned shares of its domestic war debt, including repaying it with state paper money. These untenable views were rejected by contemporaries for reasons explored in chapters 2 and 3. Unless the Confederation received adequate tax and enforcement powers, it was not going to be able to pay its debts. In that event, most leaders, whether they supported the existing Confederation or not, expected that the Union would dissolve.

For many leaders, the prospect of Confederation dissolution constituted a true political crisis. They were convinced that it would be followed inevitably by separate confederations, which in turn would lead to civil war, dictatorship, or foreign intervention.[21] George Washington held that view, and expressed it repeatedly. Washington and others held such views by the end of the war, long before mid-1780s social unrest began. Washington's opinions, and those of others who saw the situation similarly, were based on strongly held conclusions drawn from their understanding of earlier political history. They were not merely expedient or self-interested rationalizations based on current political conditions.[22]

Historians have had a tendency to dismiss the idea that there was a Confederation political crisis. But the sources show that Washington, John Jay, and others had concerns, justified by events, that went well beyond class or self-interest. These included the concerted efforts of the major European powers to limit the trade and territorial growth of the United States after the war. They also included the powerful centrifugal pressures facing the Confederation by late 1786, such as western settlement and the Spanish treaty, not to mention Shays's Rebellion. All these developments manifested the country's pressing need for central government tax, military, and economic powers. Such powers could not be obtained by the existing Confederation, nor could it have wielded them effectively in any event.

As will become clear, economic motives lay behind many of the political decisions made during the period, as well as behind controversies over Confederation reforms. I agree entirely with historian Charles Beard that "whoever leaves economic pressures out of history . . . is in mortal peril of substituting mythology for reality."[23] The sources suggest, though, that Beard and his followers nevertheless sometimes overstate the significance of directly economic class-related motives (or, in a variant view, dislike for egalitarian democracy) in shaping political change. Their view of the Confederation's collapse fails to account sufficiently for the insurmountable governance problems contemporaries thought it faced, including deep sectional divisions, and leaders' grave concerns about the disastrous consequences they believed would follow its dissolution. Those concerns led to increased demands for structural reforms that could protect and support America's expansion to become a continental empire, not reforms merely intended to protect existing wealth or to reward speculation (though some reformers sought them as well).

The prolonged debate among historians over the reasons for the Confederation's collapse has often strongly resembled a modern continuation of the eighteenth-century debate between Federalists and

Anti-Federalists over the adoption of the Constitution.[24] To advance our understanding, we need to escape what is essentially an irresolvable ideological—and even, one might say, quasi-theological—debate of that kind. To do that, we need to explore as precisely as possible what led to a loss of public confidence in the Confederation's ability to govern. Many Americans did not lose confidence, of course; but enough people did to enable the movement for the Philadelphia Convention to succeed. Massachusetts congressman Rufus King's evolving views provide a good example of how opinions changed.

King had been a fervent opponent of holding the Philadelphia Convention as recently as late 1786, when he opposed it in a speech to the Massachusetts legislature during Shays's Rebellion. Yet he had written to Theodore Sedgwick, a Massachusetts colleague, in May 1786, months before Shays's Rebellion, of the gravity of the Confederation's problems:

> The British ministry will not consent to any commercial treaty . . . they know our disjointed system, and despise us. Mr. Adams demanded the evacuation of the [western] Posts, and has been officially refused. . . . Eighty thousand dollars were appropriated for the Barbary [pirate] Treaties—the sum is too small, 150,000 Guineas being the least sum necessary. There is no money in the federal Treasury—the civil list is in arrear—the troops in service mutinous for pay—the loans abroad exhausted . . . and the payments made by the four Eastern and three Southern states for 15 months past not equal to 4 thousand Dollars. Adieu.[25]

King reluctantly changed his mind about the Philadelphia Convention after the suppression of Shays's Rebellion, and became one of Massachusetts's leading delegates there. He slowly and very grudgingly accepted that creating a more powerful central government was an unpleasant necessity. Others whose opinions changed during this period, such as Virginia leader Patrick Henry, became powerful opponents to stronger central government. This book considers the causes and weighs the effects of pivotal changes in opinion in both directions.

Ultimately, the Confederation's abject failures, and the major state weaknesses and sectional divisions they exposed, played the predominant role in the movement for strengthening the Confederation. But postwar economic conflict between wealthy conservatives on the one hand, and middling and ordinary citizens on the other, also played a limited though significant role in increasing support for strengthening central government.

A final note to readers. This book is not a comprehensive history of the period 1783–87. It does not, for example, give extensive consideration to the emerging struggle against slavery, changes in women's roles, or the reintegration of Loyalists into American society after the war. It explores the events that led to the Philadelphia Convention in detail and considers the 1787 Constitution's major implications for curing the Confederation's defects as contemporaries saw them. But it does not discuss in depth the events of the convention or those of the constitutional ratification debate. This book is about why the Confederation became a stalemate government and failed in the eyes of many contemporaries. And it is about why it did so just a few years after America emerged victorious from the Revolutionary War.

PART I

The Search for National Identity

I
War's Aftermath

By early 1783, the United States was nearing independence after its eight-year war against Great Britain. Over the next several years, Americans struggled to rebuild their country and to engage with the wider European imperial world. In doing so, they faced a series of formidable economic and political obstacles.

Although America emerged victorious, the war had been deeply traumatic, and it had fundamentally altered American society. Tens of thousands of soldiers had been killed, wounded, or disabled. Many innocent civilians' lives had been shattered. America's economy was severely damaged. Many people's fortunes had been altered dramatically. Soldiers, women, artisans, and the "middling sort" (people situated between the gentry and the poor) increasingly viewed themselves as entitled to equal participation in politics. Several states' political cultures had become more democratic.

The war's end left the Confederation with heavy burdens and facing significant threats. To fight Britain, it had been forced to go deeply into debt. By early 1783, many creditors were pressing it for payment, especially its disgruntled army. American leaders were sharply divided over the Confederation's wartime performance and about how much peacetime power and resources it needed. The 1783 Treaty of Peace greatly expanded the United States' boundaries, causing many people to dream that it would become a continental empire. But the peace terms had strong enemies in Britain, other major European powers, and Native Americans. The treaty's apparently liberal terms concealed important threats to American expansion at home and abroad.

Adding to the Confederation's troubles, after the war America experienced a severe and long-lasting economic recession. Export incomes slumped drastically below prewar levels. Americans endured sharply falling prices for goods, land, and commodities, skyrocketing interest rates, and extreme money scarcity. Thousands of people lost their jobs, farms, or homes. Thousands migrated westward under economic duress. This divisive economic maelstrom became a prominent feature of the environment in which the Confederation and the states were forced to govern.

***

Poor America is prepared for peace, indeed it may be said that she is prepared for nothing else.

Congressman Abner Nash to James Iredell, January 1783[1]

War, Economy, and Society

Philadelphia merchant Robert Morris was one of America's most prominent and wealthy international businessmen during the revolutionary era. Many of the Revolution's leaders saw him as an opponent of republican popular government and regarded him with distrust at best. Despite that, his strong financial reputation had led Congress in 1781 unanimously to appoint him as the Confederation's superintendent of finance. As superintendent, his most important responsibility during the Revolutionary War was to obtain funds to supply and pay America's army.[2]

In January 1783, Morris faced a problem that threatened to destroy the Confederation. On January 6, the army's representatives presented a petition to Congress demanding payment of a large amount of money owed to it. Morris had no money to pay the army, and knew that if the troops were not paid, they might revolt. On January 10, he met secretly with a congressional committee. He admitted that he had already written checks for 3.5 million French livres (more than $600,000) that the Confederation did not have.[3] That had been a profound violation of Morris's strongly held principles, one that threatened to damage severely both his and the Confederation's credit. Now he felt he had no choice but to take an even more desperate step for which he wanted Congress's approval. Morris told the committee that despite having no funds, he planned to write additional checks for large sums to pay the army some of what it was owed. He hoped that they might be covered by a new European loan before they came due, but could give no assurances. Seeing no alternative to avoid disaster, the committee approved Morris's plan.[4] Since taking office in 1781, Morris had been forced to finance the Revolutionary War largely on credit. Now he had been reduced to hoping that the government might obtain more credit, though it already had at least $35 million in war debts.

The Confederation's growing debt problem was an important sign that the war had inflicted major damage on the United States. It had exacted a large, long-lasting human toll, and caused significant economic damage. In another wholly unexpected series of developments, the war also set in motion a substantial democratization of American government and society, and caused critical political divisions.

THE RAVAGES OF WAR

The land war had been fought all across America, from the seacoast to the western frontiers. To fight it, America mobilized what one historian regards as the first modern popular army.[5] An estimated two hundred thousand Americans, or about one-third of the military-age free male population, served in the Continental army or state militias. The army mixed social classes. Most officers were men of the gentry, including substantial landowners, or of the middling sort. Common soldiers, on the other hand, were often conscripts. They were typically poor, landless young men who often came from recent immigrant groups such as the Irish. Some five thousand African Americans, including slaves, also served. At least twenty thousand women worked to support the Continental army. Historians estimate that twenty-five to thirty-five thousand American soldiers died in battle and in prison, of disease or of wounds. By way of comparison, that would represent a loss of about three million American lives today.[6]

British troops captured major cities such as Charleston and New York. They burned others, including Norfolk (with American help), New London, Groton, and Falmouth, as well as homes and plantations. A British officer justified the burning of Fairfield, Connecticut, including its churches, as a way to cause "a general Terror and despondency."[7] British forces captured more than eleven hundred American ships, while American privateers captured more than twenty-three hundred British ships. From 1777 to 1781, roughly one hundred thousand British and American troops lived off of firewood, crops, and livestock that were requisitioned, or in some cases plundered, from farmers around the country.[8]

The war caused widespread misery. By its end, thousands of families had had their lives permanently disrupted by its harsh realities, including death, disability, rape, separations, flight, and impoverishment. Some families lost more than one member. Mary Jones wrote from South Carolina to her brother in 1785 that she had been forced away from her plantation for two years "by means of the Enemy" and that she had lost two sons. "One was taken prisoner and murdred and other died with his Wounds. . . . I was very much Distresd before I was drove away." In 1782, John Barnam sought furlough from his Connecticut regiment to help his aged parents with the harvest. He supported his request by saying that his two sisters' husbands had both apparently died in service.[9]

The Revolutionary War was also a civil war. Popular opinion on the war was split between ardent American patriots, neutralists, and Loyalists to varying degrees in different parts of the country. Friends and families were sometimes divided. Historian Patrick Griffin describes the war in South Carolina in 1780 and 1781, for example, as a series of "skirmishes, raids, and appalling violence and humiliation," where battles often involved neighbors. Forces on both sides often gave no quarter, relentlessly executing their vanquished opponents.[10]

The war at times descended into utterly lawless torture and murder that made a mockery of the idea that war could ever be civilized. In the West, American vigilantes brutally massacred Native Americans, some of whom were neutrals with no British connection (several tribes did fight with Britain). In reprisal, Native Americans murdered settlers.[11] General Henry Knox provided assistance in 1782 to twenty-two American women and children from the Virginia and Pennsylvania frontiers whose husbands and fathers had been murdered, and who had then been taken prisoner. He euphemistically described them as "having experienced horrors unutterable" during captivity, a phrase intended to convey that they had been gravely abused.[12]

Loyalist and British atrocities in certain parts of the country caused enormous, long-lasting bitterness. Hugh Williamson, a doctor and member of Congress, wrote to an acquaintance in England after the war that when he served in the army, "I have seen the Enemy hang up our people in Dozens . . . I have seen them destroy with the Bayonet multitudes of cripled men & men who had surrendered, and have . . . seen them treat hundreds of prisoners in such a manner as to secure their Death." American diplomat John Jay described the "greater part" of the Tories as "inhuman, barbarous wretches." Tens of thousands of Loyalists fled America by war's end. They reportedly removed more than £1.5 million from New York alone as they left.[13]

But the war's ravages were felt unevenly across the country. As historian Stephen Conway concluded, there were whole areas of the United States that either were lightly touched by war or escaped its ravages completely.[14] Rhode Island, for example, was occupied by British forces for three years, and its shipping was essentially destroyed. In 1774, Newport sent out nearly 140 vessels; in 1782, it sent out "not more than 5 or 6." Pennsylvania, on the other hand, was unoccupied between mid-1778 and 1783, as was much of the North. Some backcountry areas, such as those in Virginia, were also comparatively insulated. Two Virginia entrepreneurs, John Lewis and John Oliver, in 1779 created a seven-year partnership to run a plantation and a public house to entertain travelers who "resort the Baths for the use of the waters" at Warm

Springs in the Blue Ridge Mountains. When the British made their ill-fated invasion of Virginia in 1781, they never got near the resort or most of the state's western half.[15]

Still other areas suffered severe, comparatively long-lasting damage. A British observer, James Simpson, reported two months after Charleston's capture that he could only believe so much devastation had occurred so quickly in a previously wealthy area because he had seen it personally. One historian concludes that destruction and impoverishment in South Carolina were so great that the state was "nearly submerged by the British tide." Perhaps twenty thousand slaves fled masters, mainly from southern plantations. Overall, another historian concludes, the South suffered considerably greater losses than the North, and they came later in the war.[16] In addition to physical infrastructure damage, the war caused a variety of other economic losses.

During the war, American exports plummeted, reducing incomes significantly, especially in coastal areas. Chesapeake tobacco exports fell roughly 90 percent from prewar levels by the early 1780s, and Carolina rice exports to Britain had dropped 80 percent by then. Philadelphia shipping tonnage dropped more than 90 percent by 1779. Before the war, America's four largest cities—Boston, New York, Philadelphia, and Charleston—had 5.1 percent of the country's population. In 1790, those cities had less than 3 percent of the population, indicating that their relative prosperity had declined compared to the prewar period.[17]

The war caused other significant economic disruptions. The Confederation issued about $241 million in paper money (the opposite of "specie" or "hard money," i.e., gold or silver coin). One historian estimates that that amount was larger than the entire American gross domestic product at the time.[18] The unintended result of issuing large quantities of paper money at a time of widespread shortages of goods was massive inflation. In Maryland, for example, the price of foodstuffs went up between 1,900 percent and 5,000 percent between 1777 and 1780.[19] Samuel Adams paid $2,000 in Boston in 1779 for a suit of clothes. A single horse was sold for $12,000 in 1781 in North Carolina.[20]

Ultimately, the total Confederation paper issue was exchanged for roughly 20 percent of its face value in specie equivalent before becoming worthless. The states also issued more than $200 million in paper money, and by late 1780, most of it was essentially worthless as well. Maryland currency, for example, traded at one hundred Maryland dollars for one Spanish dollar by then. In some cases, despite such depreciation, paper money was required by law to be accepted at its face value, no matter what it was actually worth on the market in specie (i.e., it was made "legal tender").[21] Merchants complained that wartime paper-money and legal-tender laws had had unfair results.

Leading Philadelphia merchant Stephen Collins explained in disgust to a London correspondent after the war that a Pennsylvania estate for which he was the executor had been sharply reduced in value because he had been forced by law to accept paper money worth little in full payment of far larger debts to it. To another British correspondent he wrote that "the War has been a disagreeable and ruinous affair to the trading Interest of this Country, as well from the great Risque, and many captures at Sea, as the destructive Consequences arising from the great and rapid Depreciation, and next kin to a final Destruction of the paper Money, by which many are greatly injur'd, & some totally ruined." In addition to numerous merchants who suffered losses, several other groups had reason to be unhappy about the war's costs to them by the time peace arrived.[22]

One important disgruntled group was America's returning veterans. The Confederation had supported its army poorly during the war. One historian concludes that "soldiers and officers received virtually nothing" in pay in 1781–82. He says that that "relieved" the Confederation of an expense of at least $3.5 million a year, which he thinks was "necessary to maintain solvency in other areas."[23] Soldiers' families had to shift for themselves. George Washington described the army to his fellow general, Nathanael Greene, as "composed of Men oftentimes half starved; always in Rags, without pay, and experiencing, at times, every species of distress which human nature is capable of undergoing." He said that future historians would have trouble believing that an army in that condition could possibly have won the war.[24]

General Greene would undoubtedly have agreed with Washington's description. He later explained that he had spent $40,000 on clothing for his troops in 1782 because several hundred "had been as naked as they were born . . . for more than four months, and the enemy in force within four hours march of us all." In 1782, North Carolina's congressmen had written to Governor Alexander Martin that "never was an army worse paid than they have been and are, to say nothing of their cloathes & rations." Because they were paid poorly or not at all, many soldiers became involuntary "public creditors" of the states and the Confederation. As we will see, the parsimonious treatment that ordinary soldiers received during and after the war led many of them to become discontented with both the Confederation and their own state governments.[25]

Another unhappy group consisted of farmers who had been unwilling participants in the war. They supplied the American army or militias and were promised repayment, thus also becoming public creditors. Later they often felt that they had received little real compensation. In Virginia, Shenandoah Valley farmers alone supplied at least 232,000 pounds of flour and 566,000 pounds of beef to the government between 1781 and 1783. In exchange, they received state debt certificates that were usually worth only a small fraction of their face value on the market. In 1784, some of these farmers petitioned the Virginia legislature, complaining that they had not been paid for their livestock and crops, which were "our only dependance for the support of ourselves and familys." Instead, for their goods and personal services they had been given "a Species of paper—Specie which will pay nothing but the Redemption of itself and of consequence No Restitution at all." Unable for lack of hard money (i.e., actual specie) to pay either "private debts or publick Tax," they requested that they be able to use the state debts owed to them (i.e., their state debt certificates) to pay both. Not surprisingly, other farmers, such as those in New Jersey, hid their cattle from the army rather than have them exchanged for government debt certificates of far less value. Still others, notably from Connecticut, engaged in traitorous smuggling to sell goods to New York British forces who would pay hard money for them, defying army interdiction efforts.[26]

THE WAR AND SOCIAL AND POLITICAL CHANGE

The war had important effects on social structure as well. It changed the relative economic positions of many individuals.[27] It did so by shifting many economic risks, creating windfalls, and providing new opportunities. Some people, including war privateers, military contractors, urban artisans and manufacturers, newly established Whig merchants, and those able to buy confiscated or abandoned lands cheaply, grew prosperous and often rich. One privateer owner wrote to his business partner that his ships had taken prizes worth more than £15,000 on one day in the spring of 1783.[28] Others became poor, such as merchants or real estate owners who could not conduct business or collect debts, planters whose plantations were destroyed or whose crops could not be exported, or Tories whose homes and businesses were confiscated.

Conditions in Norfolk, Virginia, illustrate these changes. In 1785, an Irish visitor, John Joyce, wrote to his uncle describing them. He said that "such a vast heap of Ruins and Devastation, are almost impossible to have any Idea of unless seen." A 1777 official report valued the war damage in Norfolk to 1,331 houses and personal property at more than £175,000. Norfolk's inhabitants both before the war and in 1785 were almost all Scottish, but they were not the same people. "I have been Informed there are not over 30 or 40 [people] in it now, who possessed it before the War," wrote Joyce. Many Scottish merchants had fled Norfolk. Other merchants there and elsewhere had few remaining assets other than large stacks of unpaid debts owed to them. These debts were worth little because they were going to be unable to collect them for years, if at all. Joyce's interviews led him to conclude that during the war, "people of any property suffered in general exceedingly, many of them [reduced] from Wealth & affluence almost to Beggary."[29]

The war also affected women's social roles. It made unprecedented demands on them. They suddenly became the heads of households, managers of businesses and farms, members of patriotic organizations that tried to help meet war needs, and real estate and securities investors.[30] Probably in consequence, many thoughtful women believed after the revolution that politics was within their sphere, so that they should have the right to voice political opinions and perhaps even to participate directly in shaping public policy.[31]

A moving 1782 letter from Abigail Adams to John Adams illuminates what women thought justified that change. Women, she said, are excluded from government, and from control of their own property: "is it not sufficient to make us indifferent to the publick Welfare? Yet all history and every age exhibit Instances of patriotick virtue in the female Sex; which considering our situation equals the most heroick of yours."[32] She continued, "When you offer your Blood to the State, it is ours. In giving [the state] our Sons and Husbands we give more than ourselves. You can only die on the field of Battle, but we have the misfortune to survive those whom we Love most."

It was a very short step from Abigail Adams's stout assertion of women's patriotism to concluding that they had a right to political opinions and participation. There is evidence that suggests that other women shared such views. But for reasons that are not entirely clear, these changed sentiments and new roles did not translate into substantial postwar changes in women's rights. Other groups, however, successfully asserted new rights after the war. It caused significant social and political democratization in several areas.[33]

Perhaps the war's most important democratizing influence was that as a result of their efforts in it, many soldiers and urban workers came to believe that they had a right to participate in both the economy and politics on an equal level with their former gentry superiors. This is well-illustrated by a description of the 1783 Philadelphia elections by Peter S. Du Ponceau. Writing to New York leader Robert R. Livingston, Du Ponceau reported that the Pennsylvania state party called the Republicans had won the election for two reasons. The first was that an incumbent politician named Meredith had refused to present a petition to the Pennsylvania legislature on behalf of a mechanic who was a steel maker in Philadelphia. The mechanic said that without limits on the importation of foreign steel, "all the steel makers must in a short time be absolutely ruined." Du Ponceau reported:

> Mr. Meredith answered that commerce should be by no means restrained for the sake of a few tradesmen. That the war had suddenly enriched too great a number of them, & that they should return to their former way of living; You mechanics, added he, are now the richest people in the city, you live better even than the merchants, for my part I know very well that if I go ever so early to market, I can never get supplied with a good turkey, tradesmen run away with them all.... The conversation was fatal to Mr. Meredith. This speech was repeated about town in a thousand different manners, & it was at last asserted, that Mr. M. had moved in the House that a law should be enacted to prevent tradesmen from eating turkies.

The Republicans decided to "pay their court" to the mechanics, and Meredith was replaced on the Republican ticket by a silversmith. The Republicans also benefited because their opponents had tried to prevent men under twenty-one and soldiers from voting. They said the soldiers "had no will of their own," "upon which they were told by one of them: You had no objection some time ago to our fighting, & now you have some to our voting; this is not just; we have fought for the right of voting, and we will now exercise it. The soldiers voted, & some say that they actually did gain the victory to their party."[34]

The war's democratization also extended to the social and economic class composition of state legislatures and to states' wartime constitutions. Historian Jackson Turner Main shows that before the war most state legislators came from the colonial upper class, and were either well-to-do or wealthy. During and after the war, he finds, nearly all state legislatures had many more members who were not merchants, lawyers, or large landowners, but instead were yeomen, artisans, or men of moderate means, that is, of the middling sort. In New York, for example, this new legislative "middle class" was large enough that its members controlled the legislature throughout the 1780s.[35] Such changes in social class composition made several legislatures in the 1780s considerably more responsive to popular opinion.

The increased prominence of the middling class also played a role in shaping the new constitutions adopted during the war by nearly all states. The wartime constitutions moved generally in the direction of much more popular control of state government by increasing legislative power. For example, they commonly provided for weak governors who usually lacked both veto and appointment powers. But there were important differences between them, and many unequal colonial-era divisions of political power remained.

The new constitutions of Pennsylvania and Massachusetts, for example, embodied clashing ideas of republicanism.[36] The Pennsylvania constitution of 1776 established very broad suffrage by abolishing property qualifications (other than tax paying) for voting. It established a one-house legislature. The legislature's authority was supreme. Overall, the constitution was designed to provide for the greatest possible popular government. One Baltimore merchant described it as "an unlimited democracy (the most horrid of all governments)" where "no one can be secure of personal safety," and contrasted it to Maryland's constitution, which was "stable . . . and opposite to every principle of anarchy and *levelism*."[37] Pennsylvania leader Benjamin Rush described it this way: "They call it a democracy—a mobocracy in my opinion would be more proper. All our laws breathe the spirit of town meetings and porter shops."[38] Judged by the extent of popular power, the Pennsylvania constitution was the most radical of any state. Disputes over it divided Pennsylvania politics into warring parties throughout our period. Not surprisingly, Robert Morris became one of its leading opponents.

The conservative 1780 Massachusetts constitution, in sharp contrast, was clearly intended to maintain rule by property holders. It restrained popular influence by maintaining property qualifications for voting and office-holding, and by creating two equal houses in its legislature (a house of representatives and a senate). Under it, seats in the Massachusetts Senate could be held only by relatively wealthy men.

Senate seats were allocated among various parts of the state on the basis of the amount of public taxes paid by those areas. It was thus heavily biased toward maintaining the strong political influence of eastern Massachusetts (including Boston), which was far wealthier than western Massachusetts. John Adams was heavily involved in drafting the 1780 constitution, and became one of its most vocal advocates. We will see that after the war, just as these sharply conflicting constitutional structures might suggest, Pennsylvania and Massachusetts pursued very different economic policies.

WAR AND DIVIDED POLITICAL LEADERSHIP

A final and exceptionally significant effect of the war was to divide American leaders into two broad ideological camps whose members from different parts of the country frequently were postwar political allies. Their members saw both America's political needs and the reasons for its success in the war very differently. (Of course, there were differences of opinion within these camps as well; not all leaders fit neatly into either camp; and both groups had supporters across the country.) That led them to view postwar government and the country's needs in sharply opposed ways, with important effects on the Confederation.

The first group of leaders will be called federalists, a term chosen to avoid the label "Anti-Federalist" that some prefer for them, since that label can be both loaded and confusing here. Federalists saw the war as having been fought principally for the purpose of establishing independent republican state governments in America. For them, the Confederation was solely an instrument or agent of the thirteen state republics. They believed that its original structure was an ideal republican structure, because in it all states had equal powers and because states could not be compelled to increase the Confederation's carefully limited powers without their unanimous consent. They saw the war as a victory for republican popular government enabled by the Confederation's successful performance as an instrument for state cooperation.[39]

Federalists believed that to protect liberty, government power needed to be limited to the absolute minimum necessary. For them, any centralization of power in the Confederation was anathema because it threatened to destroy republican government and replace it with aristocracy or monarchy.[40] Officials of a central government endowed with sovereign powers such as taxation would inevitably use them to make the central government and themselves more powerful by various means, including most dangerously the creation of a peacetime standing army. Richard Henry Lee summarized their longstanding belief: "For, give the purse, & the sword will follow."[41] Federalists fervently opposed creation of a standing army as the inevitable death of freedom. As Massachusetts political leader Tristram Dalton wrote, "Can it be supposed that the People of the Northern States . . . can ever admit, without horror, the idea of consequences naturally flowing" from a standing army? He continued, "If any of the United States acquiesce in this scheme [of a peacetime army], they are formed for Slaves."[42]

For federalists, the predictable chain of events that would follow any centralization of power flowed from human nature's unchanging tendency aggressively to seek and to abuse power.[43] As a leading republican theorist wrote, "The love of power is natural, it is insatiable; it is whetted, not cloyed, by possession. . . . Power is of an elastic nature, ever extending itself and encroaching on the liberties of the subjects."[44] As Congressman David Howell of Rhode Island expressed this: "Avarice, ambition or the lust of power . . . are so much more active & prevalent than the virtues . . . that . . . the Government of this World [is] commonly in the hands of the vilest men in it. . . . How restless are many of our rulers to engross more power?"[45] As of 1783, federalist leaders included men active during this period, such as Samuel Adams, Elbridge Gerry, and Tristram Dalton in Massachusetts; Richard Henry Lee, Arthur Lee, and Theodorick Bland in Virginia; and David Howell in Rhode Island.

The other major political camp by war's end was the nationalists, again a term chosen to avoid potentially misleading labels.[46] Virtually all of its members also supported republican popular government. But they were convinced that the Confederation had been a failure in managing the war. They often bitterly blamed it for having made the war both longer and more expensive than necessary. As George Washington wrote to Alexander Hamilton, "No man in the United States is, or can be more deeply impressed with the necessity of a reform in our present Confederation than myself . . . for to the defects thereof, and want of Powers in Congress, may justly be ascribed the prolongation of the War, and consequently the Expences occasioned by it. More than half the perplexities I have experienced in the course of my command, and almost the whole of the difficulties and distress of the Army, have their origin here."[47]

In the nationalists' view, the Confederation lacked a power that was fundamental to all others: the ability to enforce its decisions over state opposition. As Connecticut leader Oliver Ellsworth wrote, without enforceable Confederation powers, it "will be impossible to support . . . national existence." In the same vein, Major Samuel Shaw wrote to John Eliot in 1783, "Unless there is a power vested in some supreme head sufficient to enforce a compliance with such regulations as are evidently calculated for the general good adieu to all government—I mean that species of it which alone deserves the name."[48]

Nationalists saw no inherent threat to republican liberty from an expansion of Confederation powers. In a republican government, the governors were also the governed, and laws would apply equally to them. George Washington wrote in spring 1783 to Governor Benjamin Harrison of Virginia: "Congress are in fact, but the People; they return to them at certain short periods; are amenable at all times for their conduct, and subject to a recall at any moment. What interest therefore can a man have, under these circumstances distinct from his Constituents; Can it be supposed that with design, he would form a junto, or pernicious Aristocracy that would operate against himself . . . I cannot conceive it."[49]

Nationalists were convinced that the country could not survive unless the Confederation was strengthened by being given powers commensurate with its national responsibilities. If not, it was only a matter of time until it would collapse. In the letter just quoted, Washington warned Harrison that "if the powers of Congress are not enlarged, and made competent to all *general purposes*, . . . the Blood which has been spilt . . . will avail us nothing; and . . . the band, already too weak, which holds us together, will soon be broken; when anarchy and confusion must prevail."[50] He wrote to another correspondent in 1783:

> Certain I am, that unless adequate Powers are given to Congress for the general purposes of the Federal Union that we shall soon moulder into dust and become contemptible in the eyes of Europe, if we are not made the sport of their Politicks . . . when the band of Union once gets broken, every thing ruinous to our future prospects is to be apprehended; the best that can come of it, in my humble opinion is, that we shall sink into obscurity, unless our Civil broils should keep us in remembrance and fill the page of history with the direful consequences of them.[51]

If the Confederation collapsed, nationalists thought that the country would break up into smaller confederations. They would engage in civil war that might give rise to a dictatorship or be at the mercy of foreign powers seeking to take over the continent. Washington described these undesirable outcomes with the shorthand phrase "Anarchy and Confusion." For the nationalists, these predictions about the future were not speculative; they were based on what they saw as the indisputable lessons of political history.[52]

By 1783, George Washington led the nationalist camp. It included Alexander Hamilton, James Madison, and many of the generals and Confederation officials, such as Benjamin Franklin and John Adams, who had led America during the war. It also included leading international businessmen such as Nathaniel Gorham of Massachusetts and Robert Morris of Pennsylvania. Federalists and nationalists had had no choice but to cooperate during the war. But after it ended, intense political strife broke out as they fought over how to deal with its legacies, particularly over taxation, commercial, and military policy. As we will see, after the war the nationalist reform agenda evolved. Various state leaders supported some reforms to strengthen the Confederation advocated by nationalists, but opposed others. Those leaders, such as Patrick Henry and Rufus King, could be thought of as occupying a fluid middle ground between the two camps. For the next several years, federalists and their allies had the upper hand in the state legislatures, successfully resisting efforts by Congress to strengthen the national government and ensuring that the Confederation had little influence on events. The mid-1780s might therefore be thought of as a peacetime experiment in federalism at the state and national levels.

The Treaty of Peace and Postwar Prospects

In February 1783, news of King George III's December 1782 speech to Parliament conceding American independence arrived in Philadelphia. James Madison noted that it had "produced great joy except among the Merchants." Madison continued, however, that there was a "great diminution of joy" among the "most judicious" members of Congress "from the impossibility of discharging . . . the claims of the army & . . . new difficulties from that quarter." A few days later, Congressman Hugh Williamson wrote, "I would rather take the field in the hardest military service I ever saw, than face the difficulties that await us in Congress within a few months."[53]

When Congress announced publicly in mid-March that preliminary articles of peace with Great Britain had been signed, there was again considerable rejoicing. Many Americans included France's king and its soldiers in their victory toasts, because they knew that their help had been essential to America's victory.[54] Numerous wartime leaders soon let friends and families know that they were planning to retire from government and politics.[55] Many ordinary Americans would probably have agreed with Abigail Adams's sentiments. Writing to Mercy Otis Warren in 1784, she said, "As to politicks, the world is at peace and I have wholly done with them." Exhausted by war's cares, people wanted to return to their former lives, and be left alone to follow their private pursuits.[56]

In March, Congress received detailed information about the preliminary articles of peace. They conceded America's independence. And they greatly expanded the United States' boundaries, moving them westward to the Mississippi, northward to the Great Lakes, and southward to the thirty-first parallel (an east-west line running just north of present-day Florida). They granted America extensive Atlantic-coast fishing rights, and the right to free navigation of the Mississippi River.[57] The articles utterly ignored the interests and concerns of Native Americans. More than half the new lands granted to the United States were "Indian country" (i.e., areas claimed and occupied by Native Americans).[58]

But the articles also imposed significant obligations on the Confederation and the states. All British creditors had to be permitted to recover "the full value in sterling money of all bona fide debts" owed to them. And Congress was required to "earnestly recommend" to the states that they make restitution of "all estates, rights and properties" confiscated from "real" British subjects and from former Americans (Tories or Loyalists) who had fled during the war but had not fought for the British. Still, Congress saw the articles as on balance quite favorable to the United States. The final Treaty of Paris signed in September 1783 incorporated the preliminary articles without material change.[59]

On paper, the treaty looked very advantageous to the United States. But the reality was to prove different. The treaty was not self-enforcing. If either country decided not to honor its provisions, the offended party would be unable to enforce them without military action, but could respond by ignoring other treaty requirements. Over the next several years, both sides chose to violate the treaty. Americans violated both of the main obligations imposed on them. One historian concluded that Congress's recommendation that states should comply with the provisions concerning Loyalist property and protection was treated with "open contempt" across the country. Another historian concludes that "in virtually every state of the Union" the treaty provisions on Loyalists were "flagrantly ignored." The treaty requirement for unobstructed recovery of British prewar debts also was quickly flouted (see chapter 2).[60]

As will be discussed in later chapters, these violations had an entirely unintended but very significant influence on the fate of the Confederation. The treaty also created substantial postwar conflicts with the interests of Europe's major powers and those of Native Americans.

America's expansive new boundaries encouraged many Americans to dream that their country would become a powerful continental empire. In a sermon given before all of Connecticut's government officials in May 1783, the Reverend Ezra Stiles, the president of Yale College, predicted that

> [o]ur population will soon overspread the vast territory from the Atlantick to the Mississippi, which in two generations will be a property superior to that of Britain. . . . It is probable that within a century from our independence the sun will shine on fifty million of inhabitants in the United States. This will be a great, a very great nation, nearly equal to half Europe. Already has our colonization extended down the Ohio and to Koskaseah [Kaskaskia] on the Mississippi. . . . Before the Millennium, the English settlements in America, may become more numerous millions than the greatest dominion on earth, the Chinese empire.[61]

But the treaty's apparent liberality concealed fundamental problems that would soon threaten Americans' glorious visions of western settlement and increased foreign trade. Both France and Spain actually opposed significant parts of the treaty because they opposed America's expansion. During peace negotiations, they had jointly proposed that the United States accept far smaller boundaries than Britain ultimately agreed to.[62] Native Americans denied that the United States had any right to expand into Indian country. And European powers had added reasons for opposition. Spain believed that it possessed the right to control the navigation of the Mississippi River. France had opposed the grant of Atlantic fishing rights to the United States. Finally, both France and Spain had existing colonial interests to protect against increased American trade.[63]

The treaty also failed to protect American trade with Britain's empire, which had been a major contributor to its prewar prosperity. American negotiators had repeatedly attempted but failed to gain inclusion in it of a provision for reciprocal free trade between the United States and Great Britain. From 1783 onward, major European powers and Native Americans were strongly interested in preventing America from receiving many of the central benefits promised by the Treaty of Peace.

The American Economy, 1783–87: A Look Ahead

America experienced a severe economic recession during the mid-to-late 1780s that became a major feature of the climate in which state and Confederation political controversies were fought out. Americans mired in the recession were primarily concerned about and motivated by what was happening to them in the short term. Many did not have the luxury of basing decisions on views about the country's long-term prospects.[64] Later chapters examine the ways in which the Confederation and the states sought to address these economic problems. This next section provides an overview of economic conditions. It has two parts. The first part describes them in general terms. The second looks at examples of how Americans observed them in daily life.

MID-1780S ECONOMIC CONDITIONS: AN OVERVIEW

In the 1780s, more than 90 percent of America's population of about three million lived on farms; the rest lived in small towns or cities. Economic historians think that the economy had two tiers, higher-income coastal areas that depended on exports and poorer "subsistence-plus" hinterland farming areas that did not rely on them significantly.[65] There was relatively little overlap between the major exports by various sections (i.e., regions).[66] For example, nearly half of New England's prewar exports were from fishing and whaling, while about 70 percent of the upper South's exports were of tobacco.[67] That meant that economic or political forces that harmed one region's exports might have little or no impact on another region's exports.

The major coastal cities in each region typically served as export centers, but their residents also engaged in (often related) specialized activities. For example, Boston and Philadelphia built ships; merchants, artisans, and professionals there provided many high-value goods and services. Exports provided added income for many Americans, but also paid for most of America's large goods imports. Prior to the revolution, America usually ran only a small negative balance of trade with Britain (i.e., imports were slightly higher than exports). That meant that usually only small amounts of specie needed to be exported to make up the difference between imports and exports.[68]

One major postwar economic (and, we will see, political) problem facing the country was whether it could rebuild its exports.[69] The sources suggest that the United States was unable to rebuild its exports fully until at least the early 1790s. Overall, it appears that America's exports were probably more than 24 percent lower in the early 1790s than in 1768–72. For the first few postwar years at least, American imports greatly exceeded exports. The resulting large negative trade balance meant that large amounts of specie had to be exported. That was one major reason why throughout this period people refer repeatedly to their inability to pay debts or taxes in hard money (or even paper money) as due to a "scarcity of specie," "the lack of a circulating medium," or many equivalent expressions.[70]

Another equally, if not more, significant postwar problem America faced was a "liquidity crisis." A liquidity crisis is a period during which economic assets become completely unsalable, or can only be sold for far less than their "normal" value, due to widespread price declines (i.e., deflation). In other words, the assets have become increasingly "illiquid" because they can be turned into money only at a very high discount compared to earlier prices (i.e., in today's colloquial terms, a "fire sale" must occur). (For example, the severe United States recession that began in 2008 was a liquidity crisis that particularly affected assets such as people's homes.)

During the mid-1780s, the American economy as a whole experienced extreme illiquidity. Prices for goods and land declined sharply.

By 1788, consumer prices for a wide range of goods and commodities had on average fallen more than 16 percent from 1783 levels.[71] Property prices and farm rental rates fell as well. Interest rates skyrocketed, reflecting a scarcity of credit throughout the entire country. There was little American capital available to invest, because "one large portion of the wealthy men of colonial times had been expatriated, and another part impoverished" by the war.[72] Foreign capitalists largely declined to invest.

During this liquidity crisis, hard money became quite scarce. But that was actually only another way of saying that it was extremely expensive to purchase it using other assets such as goods, land, or state paper money, since their prices had fallen sharply relative to specie. Hard money's scarcity meant that demands for payment in it were very difficult for most people to meet without suffering. In a fair number of cases, meeting such demands meant economic disaster. A small farmer who had no choice but to pay taxes or debts in specie might well be forced to sell his or her farm to pay them. Liquidity was so low that even major landholders had difficulty raising cash to pay debts and taxes.

Historians form two broad schools in their views about economic conditions in the mid-to-late 1780s. The first argues that the Revolutionary War and its aftermath were only temporary economic setbacks. These historians accept that a brief, relatively severe postwar recession occurred. But they contend that recovery from it had begun by 1786 or 1787 as Americans made various successful adjustments to new economic realities.[73]

More recently, however, historians think that the mid-to-late 1780s were part of a severe recession that rivaled the Great Depression of the 1930s.[74] Historian Allan Kulikoff concludes that, compared to 1774, per capita income in the United States had fallen by two-fifths in 1790, "equal to the early years of the Great Depression." Other historians place the drop in per capita income at between one-fifth and one-third.[75] That sharp income drop alone suggests that the country experienced severe economic stress in the 1780s. Note, however, that whether the Confederation or the states were somehow responsible for economic recession; whether their policies made it better or worse; and whether it actually led to the demise of the Confederation, are entirely separate questions.

Following are examples from contemporary sources describing economic developments that Americans observed after the war. Their assessments highlight some of the major problems and their effects.

ECONOMIC CONDITIONS IN CONTEMPORARIES' EYES

Signs of hard times were evident across the country. They included westward migration, business and industry failures, and explosions in tax delinquencies and debt litigation. In October 1784, Philadelphia merchant Joseph Reed wrote to London merchant Dennis de Berdt that poor economic conditions there were forcing westward emigration. He said, "Multitudes of People crowd to the back Country & I apprehend will experience much Distress. The Streets here swarm with Servants and Persons seeking menial employment."[76]

There were also concerns in Virginia about increasing emigration and its effects. In November 1784, Caroline County residents warned its legislature that they expected state revenues to be "greatly diminished by the emigration to the Western country taking place." They asked that it ensure emigrants paid their taxes so that remaining residents did not have to pay them.[77] Virginia leader Richard Henry Lee shared their concerns, writing to James Madison in November: "The accounts that we daily receive of the powerful emigrations from our State to Georgia, to North & South Carolina, & from the interior parts to Kentucky, are very alarming. The causes assigned, are two—the desire of removing from heavy taxes, and the search after [fertile, inexpensive] land."[78]

According to historian Bruce Mann, after Pennsylvania passed a bankruptcy law in 1785, creditors filed bankruptcy petitions against 184 business debtors over the next four years. Many Philadelphia merchant firms begun after the war, as well as many of the city's less nimble established merchants, failed in the mid-1780s. Failures occurred at the rate of more than one a month. Similar levels of business failures in New York were reported.[79]

During this period, state governments faced continuing difficulties in collecting taxes, and in some areas there were high levels of delinquencies (see chapter 3). In January 1785, Congressman William Grayson wrote to Governor Patrick Henry of Virginia asking him to provide relief to the Prince William County sheriff for £692 he owed the state in uncollected taxes. Grayson explained that the failure to collect them was not the sheriff's fault. Local citizens faced an "extreme scarcity of corn" and had spent their money to buy it instead of paying taxes. Although the sheriff had conducted fifty "distresses" (i.e., involuntary property auction sales to collect overdue taxes), they had "no effect as no person would attend to purchase, as in the next instance it might be his fate."[80] Sheriffs all over Virginia reported similar collection difficulties. Around the country, there were popular tax and debt boycotts during the mid-1780s (see chapters 2 and 3).

In September 1785, in a sure sign of desperate times, Hannah North, a Lancaster, Massachusetts, woman, wrote secretly to Boston merchant Caleb Davis. She pleaded with him not to take action against her husband who was "largely indebted" to Davis (possibly by imprisoning him for debt). She said she was going "out of my sphere" by writing, but was doing so out of concern for her several children. They had had to leave school, "like flowers nipt in the Bud, which gives me the greatest un-Easyness." She told Davis that her husband could not pay him because he had taken pity on a veteran and been unable to collect other debts. She offered land that she owned to Davis if he would accept it in payment of her husband's debt.[81]

A month later, John Adams's brother-in-law, Richard Cranch, reported to him on the Massachusetts economic situation. Cranch wrote that excessive debt due to imports and widespread price drops have "brought many of our Country People into very difficult Circumstances, and rendered them unable to pay their Debts and Taxes with Punctuality: the Consequence of which has been a great increase of Law-suits,

Failures, Abscondings & c. in all our Counties, to the great Distress of Families and sowering of their Minds with respect to public measures."[82] As Cranch noted, there had been an explosion of Massachusetts debt litigation. For example, in Hampshire County alone in 1784, there were nearly 3,000 debt cases, a 262 percent increase over the period 1770–72.[83]

In 1787, conditions were still poor in Virginia and much of the South. In May, a legal notice announced that more than 20,000 acres of land in Bedford County, Virginia, would be sold for unpaid taxes.[84] In July, merchant James Duncanson wrote to his business partner James Maury in England describing dire conditions in Virginia:

> I think this country was never more distressed . . . a prodigious number of Judgments have been obtained since the quarterly courts commenced . . . & property sold by Execution [for] less than one fourth of its value . . . the People are getting exceedingly restless, and have threatened in many counties to stop the courts. King William Courthouse was burned down the night before the last quarterly court, & all the Records destroyed, in short it appears to me that some desperate measures will be adopted in a little time. . . . [A] good many Judgments obtained, but no money to be got, indeed the People cannot pay.[85]

Duncanson's assessment would have applied equally well to conditions in several other states at the time. A 1788 letter from South Carolina leader David Ramsay describing South Carolina conditions reported very similar conditions. Ramsay wrote, "Our sufferings here as to money matters are greater than in the time of the war or just after its close." There is enormous indebtedness, Ramsay wrote, but "houses and lands will not sell for a fourth of their former value."[86]

International Trade Declines. In the mid-1780s, debt increased while export markets sharply declined. There was a surge in American goods imports in 1783 (and probably part of 1784), particularly from Britain. According to historian Curtis Nettels, American merchants bought on credit between three-fourths and four-fifths of the goods they purchased in England. But since American importers in turn "commonly supplied American dealers, retailers, and consumers on credit," this meant that "a network of [new] debt soon covered the country."[87] As a result of these imports, debt climbed, prices of goods fell, and scarce specie drained out of the country.

In June 1783, Stephen Collins wrote to London merchants that the United States had seen an "amazing influx of Goods from almost every part of the World . . . by numberless Speculators in Europe under an Idea of the Countries' being [in] great want of Goods, when in fact the Country was full at the end of the War." Soon, Collins wrote that goods prices were "low, they will not sell for cash." As a result, exporters were being forced to sell newly arrived goods as much as 40 percent below cost.[88]

Nor were American exports strong enough to pay for the massive postwar imports. In 1784, for example, Pennsylvania wheat exports were more than 80 percent lower than 1774 levels. Flour exports had fallen nearly 24 percent from earlier levels. Indian corn exports were 59 percent lower than in 1774.[89] Growing debt, lack of credit, and limited exports meant many city and country merchants would fail in time. In November 1784, merchant John M. Nesbitt wrote to Nicholas Low, a prominent New York City merchant, reporting that he had tried to collect £3,000 of business debts owed by people in Baltimore and could not collect "a halfpenny" despite repeated efforts.[90]

The South also had sharply reduced export income during the mid-1780s. From 1783 to 1786, the United States exported only 46 percent as much rice as it had in 1770–73. The income received by southern rice planters dropped by about half from the earlier period.[91] Income from tobacco exports also dropped dramatically. Although postwar export levels remained relatively stable, tobacco prices declined significantly. By early 1786, London tobacco merchant Joshua Johnson's collection list of money owed his firm by American debtors had grown to more than £50,000.[92] By 1787–88, prices for Virginia tobacco had declined more than 25 percent from levels just a few years earlier. The resulting loss of income to planters was about £200,000 annually, or roughly the size of the entire Virginia state budget.[93]

Land-Price and Rental-Income Drops. Agricultural land prices seem to have declined throughout the mid-1780s as their value was hit by dropping export prices, competing government land sales, and western emigration. By 1784, low prices for land transactions—and sometimes complete inability to sell for cash—indicated that the land market was glutted. In April 1784, to pay debts Virginia slave-plantation owner Ralph Wormeley, Sr., offered to sell three thousand acres of land on credit. His son wrote the next year that Virginia land could not be sold for cash. And in 1788, he wrote that that was still true even if prices were cut by 50 percent.[94]

In mid-1784, Pennsylvanian William Hamilton, one of the state's largest landowners, told his attorney Jasper Yeates that he needed to raise £2,000 to pay debts during a planned trip to England. He pleaded with Yeates to raise the money from his properties, particularly by trying to collect debts. He thought his tenants were in arrears £4,300 to him, but he had only been able to recover a small fraction of that amount over several months. Hamilton later wrote to Yeates in dismay that "during the present scarcity of cash it seems almost impossible to obtain a sufficiency" needed to pay his debts.[95]

In August 1784, a sale of several thousand acres of Kentucky frontier land was made for about $0.70/acre.[96] During November 1784, more than nine thousand acres of lands were advertised for sale in one Virginia newspaper. At nearly the same time, Baltimore's leading merchants, Samuel Purviance and his brother Robert, advertised thirty-seven thousand acres for sale. These two advertisements, published within one month, offered forty-six thousand acres for sale. At the same time, various states were beginning to try to sell state lands, often at very low prices, in order to raise money. As the market was flooded, land prices fell further.[97]

An April 1785 letter written to a family member in Ireland by John Joyce, an emigrant to Virginia, said that extensive migration into Kentucky had "lowered the price of [Virginia] lands much, and made taxes more severe [because there are fewer people to pay them]." Virginia landowners don't have tenants, Joyce continued, and could not get any because "land is too plenty; there are Thousands of Acres lying uncultivated . . . consequently not the fourth or the 8th of [these lands] can . . . serve to bring in any Money Yearly."[98] Joyce's report is amply corroborated by a September 1785 letter from Virginia slave–tobacco planter Ralph Wormeley, Jr., to his London brokers. He described the economic situation in Virginia in terms that would apply equally well throughout the South and probably just as well (mutatis mutandis) to most of the country:

> What will become of us, if tobacco fall I know not; little money in the country, no price for land, none for Negroes [i.e., slaves], except on credit, and laws of so little stability, that every action of political and judicative affairs is suspended, till some promise of permanency may be given. Men who have property, and who honorably and speedily wish to pay their debts by parting with some of it, cannot at present effect their purposes, so extremely scarce is money, and so precarious and loose are things, that there is little reliance on future payments—property may be disposed of, and nothing gotten [because credit buyers then fail to pay their debt].[99]

Although large landowners like Wormeley might have been wealthy on paper, many were cash poor and often unable to pay debts. In February 1787, major landholder William Hamilton wrote that over seven months he had received only £267 income from his "whole Estate," part of which was from the sale of property.[100] In June 1787, Fairfax Bryan in Virginia wrote to Dr. Denny Fairfax in England. He reported on the status of the Manor of Leeds owned by Fairfax, a 150,000-acre estate in northern Virginia. Bryan wrote that the current income from it was supposed to be about £600, "which if paid very little exceeds the taxes on it." But, he noted, "the Payments have been very short for many years. . . . I have heard it supposed that there may be three thousand pounds due for Arrears of Rents and vastly more for Quit Rents . . . I heard in Conversation more than once of Many of the Tenants refusing to pay."[101] The next year, Wormeley wrote that extreme illiquidity had continued. He explained that Virginia lands would not sell because people who want "fresh lands emigrate to the Country of Western Waters by thousands. This circumstance renders it impossible to sell land, even if one would take for it half its value."[102]

Interest Rates and Credit Scarcity. During this period, high interest rates prevailed, so that credit was exceptionally scarce; indeed, it was often unavailable to ordinary citizens. Historian Winifred Rothenberg concludes that although during this period maximum lawful interest rates were 6 percent, interest rates began in 1785 to climb to 7, 8, or 9 percent.[103] But interest rates for some investments available primarily to the wealthy were potentially far higher than that. By the end of 1783, Abigail Adams was discovering that speculating in tax-free Massachusetts state notes (government debt) was a much better investment than buying more land around Boston.[104] Her choice was an early sign of what became a booming speculative market in Confederation and state securities. By 1787, certified interest-bearing claims against the Confederation were worth less than fifteen cents on the dollar. That meant that the effective interest rate on such claims was more than 26 percent if they were ultimately honored.[105]

Meanwhile, credit provided by foreign investors was virtually unavailable. By the mid-1780s, most Europeans were unwilling to invest in private businesses in America if offered land as security. In July 1786, London merchant Joshua Johnson reminded his business partners that very prominent Americans with major landholdings such as Pennsylvanians James Wilson and Robert Morris had already tried to borrow in Europe and "not one Shilling could be procured" there using lands as security.[106] As a practical matter, that meant that most Europeans were unwilling to invest at all. In March 1787, Scottish New York merchant Collin McGregor wrote to his partner John McKenzie advising him against getting involved in the dry goods business—or any other business—in America. He said, "I have been looking round, and really it does not appear to me to be a time to risk much in this country."[107]

DEBTORS AND CREDITORS IN THE 1780S

Since debt-related issues arise throughout this book, it will be useful to describe creditor-debtor relations in the 1780s. Debtors faced a far harsher world than they do in modern America. Credit was generally both scarce and expensive (i.e., interest rates were relatively high). Creditors had far more power than today. While it is sometimes said that creditors were often debtors as well, in reality those who were wealthy were typically wealthy because they were large net creditors, whatever debts they owed. The economic and political interests of creditors as a class and debtors as a class normally conflicted, as we will see later.

Most debtors were ineligible to file for bankruptcy (where such laws existed at all). Very few legally acceptable excuses existed for failure to pay debts. Debtors could instead be forced into prison by creditors for failing to pay them. Failure to pay debts was widely regarded as deeply immoral. The availability of credit was often seen as a profoundly dangerous invitation to extravagance that would corrupt republicanism. Thomas Jefferson wrote, for example, that good would arise from the destruction of America's credit because "nothing else will restrain our disposition to luxury, and the loss of those manners which alone can preserve republican government."[108]

In the 1780s, even governments that borrowed money were usually required to do so on a "secured" basis. That meant that they were expected to establish a dedicated fund of future revenue (e.g., specific taxes, mortgage loan payments) as a source of repayment, as opposed to giving a bare promise. Attitudes toward debt and economic failure were beginning to become more modern and instrumental, but in the years just after the war, debt repayment was still widely deemed a moral and legal necessity. During the war, however, governments had suspended many creditors' rights. During that long debtors' holiday, prewar debts increased substantially as interest accumulated. Meanwhile, governments, and hence taxpayers—many of whom were already in substantial debt—accumulated major new debts.[109]

Conclusion

The United States emerged victorious from the Revolutionary War only at a high cost in lives and property. Postwar conditions made recovery very difficult. The country faced a daunting task of reconstruction. It was burdened by a large private and public debt overhang. Society and politics had become less hierarchical, diffusing authority. Leaders were sharply divided over the future of the Confederation. Great Britain, France, Spain, and Native American tribes feared and had considerable power to obstruct America's expansion both at home and abroad.

Moreover, the United States was destined to suffer through an economic maelstrom over the next several years. During its severe recession, prices for goods and land fell sharply. There was a severe credit crunch. Specie money was remarkably scarce. Export incomes were considerably, in some cases greatly, below prewar levels. Thousands of people lost their jobs; thousands of others lost their property, farms, or homes. These harsh conditions forced many poor and middling Americans to sell assets in "fire sales" for a fraction of their value. Poor conditions also led large numbers of people to migrate westward. And as we will see, they led to repeated social unrest.

How the Confederation, the states, and the American people tried to cope with the war's legacies as they struggled to rebuild America and engage with the wider world as an independent country are the subjects of much of the rest of this book.

2

Americans and Postwar Debts

PUBLIC FAITH OR ANARCHY?

By far the most momentous problem facing both American leaders and many ordinary citizens after the war was a giant overhang of debt. The Confederation owed millions of dollars to foreign creditors and to Americans. And in 1783, it agreed to increase its debt to the army. Americans also owed British prewar private creditors an amount nearly one-third as large as the Confederation's entire debt.

The Confederation wanted to maintain national "public faith" by paying its debts. The Articles of Confederation required each state to pay its share of them at Congress's direction. Over the next four years, the states failed to pay most of their debt shares. Meanwhile, Pennsylvania and two other states decided to pay only those Confederation debts held by their own citizens; New Jersey threatened not to pay any Confederation debts. Under the Articles, Congress had no power to force states to pay. None of the popular "solutions" to compensate for the states' failures were workable—including dividing up Confederation debts among the states or selling western public lands. The Confederation ran a large deficit from 1783 onward. By early 1786, it became clear that the Confederation was permanently insolvent and might well collapse. By 1787, it had defaulted on major loans. Many leaders feared anarchy would result, possibly followed by civil war, foreign intervention, or both. Even some very strong opponents of added Confederation powers now reluctantly agreed they were needed.

The states also had to decide whether they should compel their citizens to honor prewar British debts as required by the Treaty of Peace. The states whose residents owed the vast majority of those debts refused to require their payment. The Confederation was powerless to compel them to obey the treaty. Great Britain retaliated by refusing to evacuate its western forts, seriously threatening western expansion.

***

> We shall talk forever in vain, My Friend, about the Dignity of our Country, and Federal Systems, if the Feelings of our Countrymen are not more sensibly affected at the sound of those Sacred Words, "Public Faith." If the Faith of the Nation cannot be depended on . . . it will never be respected nor confided in at home nor abroad. If the People cannot be convinced of the indispensable Importance and Necessity of this Principle, all must be given up to the Guidance of Chance and Accident, factious rage, insidious selfishness and delirious enthusiasm.
>
> *Ambassador John Adams to Congressman Rufus King, June 14, 1786*[1]

> And how short sighted a politician must he be who does not see of what importance it is to establish a good character & reputation [for keeping public faith] among the other nations of the earth? The loss of this oftimes occasions oceans of blood & millions of treasure.
>
> *Secretary of Congress Charles Thomson to Pennsylvania president John Dickinson, January 20, 1785*[2]

When Americans decided whether to preserve their "public faith" by paying America's debts, they were inevitably determining America's power as a country and its identity on the world stage, John Adams and Charles Thomson agreed. This chapter argues that Americans chose to manage postwar debt problems not collectively as a nation but instead as thirteen state republics acting cooperatively through the Confederation, and failed completely.[3]

The Need for Public Faith

At war's end, Americans agreed that the creation of virtually all of the Confederation war debt had been inevitable. No one thought that it would have been politically possible to pay for the war by raising taxes. American leaders of widely differing political views uniformly agreed that nearly all Confederation war debt should be repaid. They thought that both moral and prudential reasons supported their view.

Prominent revolutionary leaders such as Samuel Adams thought that keeping public faith was essential to just government. As the word "faith" implies, governments could not be compelled to pay their debts except by force; no law then could compel a sovereign to pay its debts. But debt repayment was thought to be a fundamental moral duty for governments, just as honoring debts was for individuals. As Adams put it, "States & Individual Persons are equally bound to fulfill their Obligations, and it is given as Characteristick of an honest Man, that 'though he sweareth (or promiseth) to his own hurt he changeth not.'"[4]

In asking the states for new powers to pay Confederation debts, Congress invoked Americans' shared sense of this moral duty when it wrote "we call upon the justice and plighted faith of the several states."[5] George Washington urged in the same vein that the country needed to adopt "such a system of Policy, as will ensure the future reputation, tranquillity, happiness and glory of this extensive Empire; to which I am well assured, nothing can contribute so much, as an inviolable adherence to the principles of the Union, and a fixed Resolution of building the National faith on the basis of Public Justice—without which all that has been done and suffered, is in vain."[6] Congress also told the states that the Confederation's ability to pay its debts would be regarded around the world as a key test of republican government.[7] Many believed that such popular governments were not stable enough politically to honor burdensome long-term obligations such as public-debt repayment. But there were also compelling policy reasons that many American leaders thought justified debt repayment.

In 1783, Congress appealed to the country's future need for credit and political support as a central justification for debt repayment by the states. It said, "A wise nation will never permit those who relieve the wants of their country, or who rely most on its faith, its firmness and its resources, when either of them is distrusted, to suffer by the event."[8]

Congress was politely but clearly warning the states that they could not count on creditors—foreign or domestic, including the army—to support the country in the future if they were not repaid. The concern that America would need credit and support in order to fight future wars was widespread. Before the war ended, Alexander Hamilton had urged public credit's importance to national military strength.[9] George Washington wrote to Pennsylvania leader Joseph Reed in 1780 that "in modern wars, the largest purse must chiefly determine the event."[10] Even leaders of opposing political philosophies such as Virginia congressman Richard Henry Lee agreed with him on this point.

In his capacity as president of Congress, Lee wrote seeking Confederation funds to the governors of all the states in January 1785. Lee told the governors that American public credit abroad was precarious because the Confederation was having difficulty obtaining revenues to pay its bills. America needed to do justice to its friends abroad such as France, who had assisted it in its distress, by repaying them, he said. Lee made clear to the governors that America might again need their help in the event of future wars. In his usual oblique yet blunt style, Lee reminded them of the "close connection that subsists between national safety and national faith, that the loss of the latter will ever have the most malignant effects upon the former."[11] Washington later wrote in the same vein to Thomas Jefferson that "were we without credit, we might be crushed by a nation of much inferior resources but possessing higher credit."[12] Because in all likelihood America would be unable to raise taxes on its people to fight future wars, its leaders agreed that they needed to pay both domestic and foreign war debts (i.e., debts owed to Americans and debts owed abroad). Otherwise, they would be unable to obtain essential future financial help.

But although Confederation leaders agreed on the compelling reasons to repay America's debts, they had sharply clashing ideas about how that should be done. There were disputes about whether certain debts should be classified as Confederation debts or instead as state debts. There were disagreements about how to raise the needed money. The two main proposals were to use the existing Confederation requisition system (discussed below), or to create new Confederation tax powers (discussed in chapter 3). Many congressional leaders believed that by selling its western lands, the Confederation could pay its debts without need for either requisitions or taxes. Finally, a few leaders advocated turning most if not all of the Confederation debt over to the states for repayment. Some historians claim that transferring the domestic debt to the states and land sales would have solved the Confederation's debt problem without any need for requisitions.[13]

During the period from 1783 to 1787, however, most of Congress's energy was devoted to vigorous efforts to make the existing Confederation requisition system work. Because federalists were the primary source of political support for continuing the requisition system, using it to manage Confederation debts can be thought of as a peacetime experiment in federalist finance.

The Failure of the Requisition System

The Confederation requisition system worked as follows. Under the Articles of Confederation, Congress had the power to make expenditures on behalf of the United States, such as those for the war. It could pay for its expenditures either by spending funds it received, or by borrowing. In either event, to raise the necessary money to pay its bills, Congress was required to adopt a requisition to the states. The requisition allocated Congress's total expenditures for a particular period or purpose between the states for payment. The states could raise their shares of their requisition in any way they chose, including borrowing, taxation, or sales of state property.

The inescapable conclusion from the evidence below is that the requisition system was a complete failure during 1783–87 because states were either unwilling or unable to pay their shares of requisitions. The states paid only 31 percent of the requisitions Congress made to them from 1781 to mid-1787, based on the most generous possible assumptions.[14] That represented an average annual per household contribution by the free population of the United States of about $1.40 in specie and "indents" (certificates of interest) over that period. Through mid-1787, the states paid only 16 percent of the requisition amounts Congress had called for with respect to the domestic debt.[15]

The states' repeated failures to comply with requisitions were due to state politics, contemporaries thought, and not in most cases to inability, as today's historians often argue.[16] As Virginia congressman William Grayson observed in 1787, "Congress annually vote requisitions for the foreign & domestic interest which are totally disregarded. It appears to me that there is a considerable party in every State against the payment of the domestic debt." Grayson then remarked sarcastically that based on the Confederation's experience with the states, "upon the whole it seems to be the current opinion that however excellent democratical governments may be in some respects, the payment of money & the preservation of the public faith is not among their good qualifications."[17] Grayson's comments suggest that in this respect, things had not changed much since 1783. Confederation secretary of foreign affairs Robert R. Livingston had written then to George Washington expressing concern that Americans would not obey the Treaty of Peace, especially its debt-repayment requirements, because "national faith, and national honor are considered things of little moment" by "the mass of the people" and by state legislatures.[18]

Other leaders reached conclusions similar to Grayson's. South Carolina congressman Charles Pinckney spoke as a representative of Congress when he addressed the New Jersey legislature in March 1786 regarding its outright refusal to pay requisitions. Pinckney blamed much of "our present disorders" on "the refractory and inattentive conduct of the states; most of whom have neglected altogether the performance of their federal duties." He described the states' failure to honor Congress's decisions as "licentiousness" that could lead to anarchy, "the fate of all the ancient . . . and . . . without great care . . . probably the fate of all the modern republics." By "anarchy" Pinckney said he meant a government "where the laws lose their respect . . . where no permanent security is given to the property and privileges of the citizens; and no measures pursued, but such as suit the temporary interest and convenience of the prevailing parties."[19]

Because the states failed to pay their requisitions, the Confederation had no choice but to engage in large-scale deficit financing throughout the period 1783–87 (see table 2.1). It ran its overall finances as though it had a modern credit card with a low minimum monthly payment and no credit limit. However, it did seek to control its direct expenditures for current services. In 1790, the United States had both a larger foreign debt, and a larger domestic debt, than it did in 1783 (see table 2.2).[20] The total debt had increased by about 25 percent. In that context, historians' claims that the Confederation maintained a balanced budget, raised almost enough to cover its expenses, reduced its domestic debt, or otherwise improved its finances have very little significance, as contemporaries plainly agreed by 1786 (see below).[21] Under the Articles, there was no prospect whatsoever that Confederation finances would have improved.

By early 1786, the Confederation's financial position was unsustainable. The states had repeatedly failed to follow Congress's decisions about debt repayment. Congress approved a report in February 1786 concluding that there was an "utter impossibility of maintaining and preserving the faith of the federal Government, by temporary requisitions on the States." Further reliance on them, it said, would be "dangerous to the welfare and peace of the Union." The report pointed out that in 1787, about $1.8 million would come due in interest and principal on French and Dutch loans. Nearly $1 million would then become due on them annually for the next nine years. Yet during the preceding fourteen months, the Confederation had received from the states only about $400,000, "a sum short of what is essentially necessary for the bare maintenance of the federal government." The Confederation had so little income that it was not even covering its normal operating costs, and it had no income whatsoever to pay any of its impending debts, foreign or domestic, in 1787 or thereafter. The report concluded that the continued existence of the Confederation was doubtful.[22]

TABLE 2.1. Average annual Confederation expenses and deficit (1783–87) and state-requisition deficit (1781–86)

AVERAGE ANNUAL EXPENSES AND DEFICIT, 1783–87	
Peacetime operating expenses[a]	$430,000
Foreign-loan interest[b]	$346,000
Domestic-loan/debt interest[c]	$1,370,000
1. Total average annual expenses	$2,146,000
2. Average annual requisition income from states (including indents)[d]	$631,700
Average annual Confederation deficit[e] (1–2)	$1,514,000
STATE REQUISITIONS AND DEFICITS, 1781–86[f]	
3. Total congressional requisitions to states, 1781–86	$11,977,000
4. Total state payments on requisitions (including indents), 1781–mid-1787	$3,790,000
Total state-requisition deficit (3 – 4)	$8,187,000
Average annual state-requisition deficit, 1781–86	$1,364,000

Note: Numbers in this table have been rounded and are intended as order-of-magnitude approximations rather than precise figures.

[a] Estimated using data from Charles J. Bullock, *The Finances of the United States from 1775 to 1789, with Special Reference to the Budget* (Madison: University of Wisconsin, 1895), 183; and E. James Ferguson, *The Power of the Purse: A History of American Public Finance, 1776–1790* (Chapel Hill: University of North Carolina Press, 1961), 236–37.

[b] This conservative estimate was created by choosing a midpoint between Ferguson's data (*Power of the Purse*, 235) and the average of interest schedules found in two 1785 congressional documents, *JCC*, 29:543–44; and "Minutes of Congressional Grand Committee on 1785 Requisition," Peter Force Collection, ser. 9, microfilm reel 107, LOC. It very likely understates the Confederation's obligation. See Bullock, *Finances of the United States*, 187.

[c] Data taken from the interest schedules found in a 1785 congressional report, *JCC*, 29:543–44. Includes all forms of domestic debt. See Bullock, *Finances of the United States*, 187, for a similar estimate.

[d] This average is 31 percent of requisition amounts. Indents were worth much less than their face value on the market, but are treated as equal here since contemporary government accounts do so. Treasury of the United States, Register's Office, September 25, 1787, "Schedule of Requisitions on the Several States by the United States . . . ," PHK, microfilm reel 18. Although one could argue instead for indent accounting based on reducing indents to specie value, the conservative result of the approach here is to overstate state contributions to the Confederation, and to understate its actual average deficit.

[e] Bullock's data for 1784–89 support an average annual deficit of about $1.6 million. Bullock, *Finances of the United States*, 187.

[f] Data computed from Treasury of the United States, Register's Office, September 25, 1787, "Schedule of Requisitions on the Several States by the United States . . . ," PHK, microfilm reel 21. Includes indents through mid-1787; see note 14.

TABLE 2.2. Estimated national debt, 1783–90

DATE	FOREIGN DEBT	DOMESTIC DEBT	TOTAL DEBT
April 1783[a]	$7,885,000	$34,115,000	$42,000,000
January 1785[b]	$8,960,000	$35,743,000	$44,703,000
June 30, 1787[c]	$9,507,000[d]	$38,770,000	$48,277,000
January 1790[e]	$11,710,378	$42,414,085	$54,124,463

Note: The estimates presented here, other than that for 1790, are intended solely as order-of-magnitude approximations.

[a] *JCC*, 24:285–86. The Confederation's debt consisted of three major categories as of early 1783: (1) foreign debt (roughly $8 million); (2) voluntary loan debt (roughly $11 million); and (3) involuntary loan debt, such as debts to the army and suppliers (roughly $23 million).

[b] "Minutes of Congressional Grand Committee on 1785 Requisition," Peter Force Collection, ser. 9, microfilm reel 107, LOC.

[c] Estimate added the average interest due per year on foreign loans and domestic debt to the January 1785 indebtedness, and then deducted interest paid on Dutch loans (see Ferguson, *Power of the Purse*, 235–37) and all indent payments to date (see note 14). The data found in Charles J. Bullock, *The Finances of the United States from 1775 to 1789, with Special Reference to the Budget* (Madison: University of Wisconsin, 1895), 181–87, are generally consistent with the interest estimates used here. Bullock's figures suggest, however, that the total domestic debt was about $2 million less than that shown here.

[d] The foreign debt was probably somewhat higher by this time due to additional borrowing. Ferguson, *Power of the Purse*, 235–38.

[e] United States Secretary of the Treasury, "Report on the Public Credit," January 1790, in Congress of the United States, *American State Papers, Finance Series* (Washington, DC: Gales and Seaton, 1832), 1:22, 27–28.

The Confederation's financial condition continued to worsen. By June 1786, Massachusetts congressman Rufus King wrote to Elbridge Gerry that "you may depend on it, that the Treasury now is literally without a penny."[23] Arthur Lee, a fervent opponent of Robert Morris and now a member of the Confederation Board of Treasury, also wrote to Gerry in June 1786 acknowledging that the Confederation would have to abandon requisitions due to state failures. Lee wrote, "The last advices from the Ohio represent an Indian war as inevitable, & yet the treasury has not been able to supply the Secretary at War with 1000 dollars to transport to Pittsburg the ammunition required for the troops." He continued, "I am grieved to see that the confidence reposed in the several Legislatures by the Confederation, proves so unmerited in the Trial; & produces a necessity of increasing the powers of Congress, to prevent the Union from dissolving in its own weakness. Increase of powers may be dangerous, but Anarchy is more so. The conduct of the States, has left us only a choice of evils."[24]

Lee's letter shows how desperate the financial situation of the Confederation had become. His concession that Congress would need more powers due to the failure of the requisition system was remarkable indeed. Since 1783, he had been one of the staunchest opponents of conferring broad tax powers on the Confederation. Four years of bitter experience had convinced him that however unpleasant it was, change was necessary. As we will see later, Lee was not alone in that conviction.

The states' failure to comply with Confederation requisitions became the first item on James Madison's list of "Vices of the political system of the U. States," which he wrote to identify problems that needed to be addressed by the 1787 Philadelphia constitutional convention. Examination of the Confederation's vain attempts to manage its debt supports his view that the requisition system was inherently flawed, "radically and permanently."[25] We can usefully begin by looking at Congress's 1783 debate over the expansion of the Confederation debt, its first significant postwar debate on such issues.

Commutation and Public Faith

In January 1783, the army sent representatives to Congress to make a series of financial demands, including provisions for officers' retirement pay. In making them, the army acted without outside influence, so far as is known. Its representatives told Congress that the desperate troops thought that peace was imminent and believed, as Washington wrote, that "the prospect of compensation for past services will terminate with the war." On March 22, 1783, Congress made its first major decision about the army's demands.[26]

Congress agreed to grant "commutation" retirement pay to army officers who served through the end of the war—that is, full pay for five years. (This was referred to as commutation because it reduced benefits that would otherwise have been payable under Congress's 1780 officers' retirement pay ordinance, which had provided half-pay for life.)[27] Groups of officers were collectively given the right to accept or opt out of commutation, allowing them to seek state compensation instead if they chose. Congress's action increased the total Confederation domestic debt by an estimated $5,000,000, or more than 15 percent. It soon met with intense opposition, primarily in the New England states. Historians have long recognized that the political stakes of commutation were far greater than whether or how much the officers were paid.

Most historians view the commutation debate as a relatively minor part of a much broader controversy over Confederation taxation powers (considered in chapter 3). That is understandable. Congress was debating new tax powers at much the same time it was considering commutation. The army's demands certainly added pressure on Congress to create tax-based funds to pay the army debt.[28] But Congress's tax debate was inevitable before the army's demands were ever made. The rest of the Confederation debt needed to be funded through taxes unless Congress was willing to accept the requisition system as its sole means of obtaining revenue. As early as 1781, Congress had refused to do that, and sought Confederation tax powers. Moreover, the army's demands could have been resolved separately from the taxation debate. Congress ultimately decided the commutation issue on its own merits. It is useful to consider the commutation debate separately, because it tells us a good deal about how the country felt about the war and its soldiers, and about its future as a republic.

When Congress agreed to commutation in 1783, for many Congressmen the decisive issue was whether Congress would keep public faith with veteran army leaders. Even Congressmen such as Massachusetts's Samuel Holten, who represented states that had strongly opposed Congress's more generous 1780 retirement pay ordinance, now accepted that that ordinance had been necessary to avoid the army's collapse. Contemporaries believed that there were important fairness considerations supporting commutation as well, as Samuel Adams's views show.[29]

Adams had opposed the 1780 ordinance while a Massachusetts congressman. Later he reversed his position and supported commutation. He wrote to Noah Webster during a Connecticut dispute over it that because "the Opportunities of the Officers of the Army of acquiring moderate fortunes or making such Provision for their Families as Men generally wish to make, were not equal to those of their Fellow Citizens at home," it would be "but just & reasonable that an adequate Compensation should be made to them." Many officers had served in their prime earning years, and often were about to return to civilian life with skills of limited use there. Congress's failure to provide commutation would defeat many officers' legitimate expectations. And in debating it, Congress also decided another important issue—should commutation be a national (i.e., Confederation) debt, or should responsibility for paying it be transferred to the states?[30]

Had paying army officers' commutation become a state responsibility, strong opposition to commutation in several states might well have meant that army veterans previously promised substantial retirement benefits would receive either nothing or dramatically smaller amounts. As James Madison later explained, "The opposition in the N. England States to [commutation] . . . has increased to such a degree as to produce almost a general anarchy. . . . Those who are interested . . . look forward with very poignant apprehensions. Nothing but some continental provision can obtain for them this part of their reward." Moreover, due to states' differing financial capacities and fluctuating paper-money values, officers residing in different states would almost certainly have been paid significantly differing amounts, even if Congress agreed that they were entitled to be paid the same amounts. All these differences in treatment would have occurred solely because retired officers lived in different states, creating potential bitterness and division.[31]

Moreover, unequal payments would have conflicted with the principle of equal compensation for equal military service. Even more importantly, such inequalities would have been inconsistent with the idea that the revolutionary army had been an army of the nation, as opposed to an assemblage of troops sent by, paid by, and responsible to the states. In deciding that commutation should be a Confederation debt, Congress was not simply deciding an abstract dispute about central versus state governing authority. Instead, it was reaffirming the country's view of the army's national identity.

Congress's creation of the army in 1775 was one of the country's most fundamental acts in making the revolution, constituting in British eyes both treason and a de facto declaration of war. Throughout the war, Congress insisted that the army was its army, responsible to it and under its control, and not responsible to or under the control of individual states. Congress exercised extraordinarily tight direct control over the army, from choosing its leadership to directing its conduct of specific military campaigns, much to the dismay of army leaders.[32] When it adopted the 1780 half-pay ordinance, it explicitly did so on a nationwide basis that ignored officers' state origins. As one historian concludes, for supporters of the revolution, "the Continental Army came in time to symbolize the new nation." Without it, "they could not hope for deliverance."[33] Treating the army after the war instead as if it had been nothing more than a congeries of state armies would have been a dismal precedent for achieving national unity in future wars.

In the event, a proposal to make payment of commutation a debt of the states was soundly defeated in Congress, receiving the support of only two states. Nine of twelve states voting then supported commutation as a Confederation obligation. Unlike 1780, all of Massachusetts's and Connecticut's congressmen supported commutation, and their states' votes provided the needed supermajority.[34] But the fight on commutation did not end there.

In July 1783, the Massachusetts legislature sent Congress a letter attacking commutation. It contended that commutation violated the "spirit and general design" of the Confederation, because it was "a grant of more than adequate reward" for officers' services and was "inconsistent with that equality which ought to subsist among citizens of free and republican states . . . to raise and exalt some citizens in wealth and grandeur, to the injury and oppression of others." The legislature implied that Confederation dissolution might occur if Congress did not change its position. A congressional committee responded sharply in September 1783 that if dissolution of the Confederation occurred over the issue, it would be Massachusetts's fault for having abandoned the Confederation requirement that states comply with Congress's decisions.[35]

A bitter controversy over commutation broke out in Connecticut as well. In Connecticut, citizens claimed that commutation would subvert republican government by throwing "excessive Power, the constant attendent of property, into the Hands of the Few," and lead to "a proper Aristocracy." They began to hold popular county conventions to organize opposition to commutation.[36] But for Samuel Adams, who was asked for his views on their actions, Congress was "and must be the cement of the union of the states."[37] Federalists like Adams thought that Congress's decisions must be followed by the states for the Confederation to survive. As we have seen, however, many states gave little more than lip service to the Articles' requirement that they follow Congress's decisions. That meant that they were violating an essential principle at the heart of the federalist conception of the Confederation.[38]

Why Requisitions and Alternatives to Them Failed

By the war's end, it was apparent that the requisition system could never work unless the states cooperated with it voluntarily. It could not be enforced against violators. By 1783, leaders such as Congressman Oliver Ellsworth of Connecticut had concluded that if Congress could not enforce its decisions, the Confederation could not function effectively as a government.[39] Members of Congress such as James Madison quickly came to understand that there was no way to enforce the requisition system against states that chose not to pay. Madison was so frustrated by this realization that he proposed giving the Confederation the power to take military action against recalcitrant states. Similar proposals had been made by the Hartford Convention of 1780. No such proposals were ever approved.[40] In fact, no one ever proposed a workable method of forcing states to comply with requisitions, through proposals continued to be discussed through mid-1786.

The Confederation's inability to enforce its requisitions was that system's fatal flaw.

State noncompliance became so widespread that by 1786, New Jersey was confident that it could openly refuse further contributions without being penalized. It announced that it would not pay any further requisitions unless the Confederation forced New York to stop practices such as taxing imports into New Jersey. While Congress sent a delegation to New Jersey that succeeded in changing the legislature's position, it did so by persuasion alone (including some blunt political threats). Everyone understood that no means of compulsion was available.[41] Voluntary cooperation was the only way that the requisition system could conceivably work. But there were unfortunately very strong incentives for states and different sections not to comply voluntarily. Instead, states could continue to be what economists call free riders, gaining Confederation benefits without paying for them, just as they had during the war.[42]

Normally, to comply fully with a requisition, a state would have had to raise its taxes. In many states in the 1780s, there were serious fights occurring about supposedly unfair and burdensome state taxes, even without such increases. Moreover, compliance with requisitions benefited or burdened states in various parts of the country quite differently, because different sections of the country held dramatically different amounts of Confederation debt. These sectional disparities influenced Congress's debt management, caused it to manipulate the requisition system, and seriously reduced states' incentives to pay requisitions.

As contemporaries knew, nearly all of the Confederation domestic debt (i.e., loan debts and debts to the army and suppliers) was held by residents in the eight states north of Maryland. Only about 16 percent of that debt was held in the southern states.[43] This serious fiscal imbalance adversely interfered with Congress's debt management. First, in 1784, the southern states unsuccessfully tried to have the loan-certificate debt—about one-third of the entire domestic debt—removed as part of the Confederation debt, because their citizens held only 10 percent of it. They thought that it was unfair that they should be required to contribute disproportionately to its repayment.[44]

Second, states outside the South had sufficient strength in Congress to force a key 1784 change in the requisition system that gave them a sectionally discriminatory discount on their debt-repayment obligations. Since the northern and middle states held nearly all of the domestic debt, most of the interest payments due on it were owed to their residents. The Confederation issued paper certificates (known as indents) as evidence of interest payments due periodically on that debt, since it could not pay it. The indents were worth far less than their face value on the market; they were essentially a form of heavily depreciated paper money.[45] But the northern and middle states used their influence in Congress to provide that indents returned to the Confederation would nevertheless be counted at full face value toward each state's share of the Confederation debt. The southern states unsuccessfully opposed this proposal because it would force them to pay a significantly larger share of their portion of requisitions in specie, rather than in indents.

All in all, the sectional imbalance in domestic-debt holdings markedly lessened the enthusiasm of the southern states for making requisition payments on that debt. Four out of five southern states—Maryland, North Carolina, South Carolina, and Georgia—made no payments on domestic-debt requisitions at all through mid-1787. However, some smaller northern states—New Hampshire, Rhode Island, and New Jersey—also made no payments on the domestic debt. As a result, the states as a whole paid only 16 percent of that requisition debt as of mid-1787. Ninety percent of those payments were made by northern and Mid-Atlantic states.[46]

Another important factor that interfered with states' requisition compliance was that as contemporaries understood, the foreign and domestic debt could not be separated without causing a "great clamor." As Massachusetts merchant Elbridge Gerry explained to John Adams in February 1785, if the foreign and domestic debts were separated, the southern states "would gladly accept the measure and perhaps would then avoid contributions to pay the domestic interest because they have very little in the federal funds, but the citizens of the other States would probably be so dissatisfied as to withhold taxes or apply them to the payment of the interest due to themselves."[47] In other words, Gerry thought that if the foreign and domestic debts were separated, the southern states would no longer pay any part of the domestic debt, owed primarily to the northern states. In response, the northern states would refuse to pay their share of the foreign debt or Confederation expenses. The Confederation foreign and domestic debts were thus bound together in a political Gordian knot that could not be untied without finally destroying the requisition system. Due to these irreconcilable sectional conflicts, Congress took no steps to divide the domestic from the foreign debt.

There were, however, two alternatives to the requisition system that either avoided the need for states to grant any Confederation tax powers or sharply reduced it. Both had some popular appeal. The first was transferring the Confederation domestic debt to the states. Historian Merrill Jensen claims that the federalist position at the time was that the domestic debt should be divided among the states and paid by them.[48] The second alternative was paying the debt by selling the Confederation's western lands.

Because the domestic debt was not being paid by the Confederation (except by interest indents worth comparatively little), creditor pressure on the states to pay it instead increased in the mid-1780s. In response, three Mid-Atlantic states voluntarily assumed responsibility for paying interest on much of the federal domestic debt both issued to and owed to their own residents—but not for such debt issued or owed to nonresidents. These states were discriminatorily treating their own residents as preferred federal creditors without any justification under the Articles of Confederation. That limitation subjected Pennsylvania, one assuming state, to charges of "ingratitude, selfishness & want of faith & national honor."[49] When Pennsylvania initially proposed to assume Confederation debt in 1784, Congress objected that doing so would violate Confederation fiscal principles and breach public faith. But Congress was powerless to prevent Pennsylvania and other states from assumption.[50]

Historian E. James Ferguson estimates that these three states assumed about $9 million worth of Confederation domestic debt. He concludes that this was about one-third of the total domestic-debt principal. He claims that the remainder of the domestic debt could have been assumed by the states in the same way, and that they would have done so over time, eliminating the need for most if not all requisitions. Essentially, Ferguson claims that every state should have been able to decide unilaterally how much of the Confederation domestic debt owed to its residents it would honor. If a state chose to repay only 25 percent of the domestic debt owed to its citizens, that would have been just fine. Of course, that did not happen, and Congress never even proposed it.[51] There are good reasons to think that it would not have happened had the Confederation survived, and that it would have permanently damaged the Confederation as a national government even if it had.

The main reason to think that voluntary assumption of Confederation debt would not have happened in other states is that where it did occur, it usually occurred only as part of expedient political bargains. In them, public creditors typically agreed to support the issuance of new state paper money, but only if part of the new money was reserved for payment of debts owed to them. In Pennsylvania, for example, nearly two-thirds of the new paper money issued by the state in 1785 was reserved not for borrowing by needy debtors but instead for payments to public creditors, including Confederation debts assumed by the state.[52] In states such as North Carolina, on the other hand, where paper-money supporters were politically strong enough to persuade legislatures to issue paper money without creditors' support, federal domestic debts were unlikely to be assumed. And in the six states where no paper money was issued during the 1780s, such debts were equally unlikely to be assumed. For that reason alone, most of the states were unlikely to have been willing to assume federal debts to their residents.

There is another strong reason to think that widespread state assumption of Confederation domestic debt would not have occurred. Had states done so, they would have had no choice but to increase taxes. The tax increases would have been proportionately larger in northern states, where more of the debt was held. Many poorer and middling residents in those states who did not own federal debt securities would have faced significant tax increases without receiving any benefit in return. All of the available evidence suggests that in the 1780s legislatures already embroiled in disputes over allegedly oppressive state taxes would have been unwilling to adopt such unquestionably unpopular new taxes to pay Confederation debts owed mostly to wealthier residents.

Moreover, debt assumption would have damaged the Confederation's reputation and destroyed its future credit. The reason is that in some states, the assumed Confederation debt actually repaid would have been sharply reduced or "written down" by being paid back using paper money or state securities that were worth only a small fraction of the value of the Confederation debt. Events in Rhode Island show what would probably have happened. Rhode Island issued paper money in 1786, and it rapidly declined in value (see chapter 7). The state then decided to eliminate its state debt.

With what Ferguson describes as "remorseless consistency," the state required most debt holders to present their state securities and receive in return one-fourth of the debt principal in state paper money. If debt holders did not present them, they were forfeited. This process was repeated over several years, as the state's paper money continued to decline in value. It effectively reduced or "wrote down" the total amount of debt Rhode Island actually repaid to its creditors by 75 percent or more below its face value. By using steadily depreciating state paper money to pay debts, the state was really paying only about 20–25 cents in value for every dollar of state debt it forcibly retired.[53]

Ferguson notes approvingly that as a result of the state's debt-retirement program, "by the time Rhode Island entered the new federal union in 1790, she was practically debt-free." He argues that Rhode

Island's "procedure was not as arbitrary as it may appear" because creditors had "probably" bought their securities on the market at a discount. If so, they were not actually losing money when repaid only a fraction of the debt's face value. Further, he writes, its legislature defended its action on the grounds that other states had "sanctioned tender laws and revalued debts during the war."[54] At the time, however, many Americans utterly detested Rhode Island's actions. They thought that its peacetime compulsory debt retirement using heavily depreciated paper money to write down the debt was nothing more than a form of state-sanctioned theft. Whether allegedly similar state actions might have been wartime necessities was an entirely different matter, they thought.[55]

But the overriding point here is that if Confederation debts had been divided among the states, all of them would have been free to treat Confederation debts the way Rhode Island treated its state debt. Ferguson contends that Congress should have allowed individual states to write down Confederation debt whenever popular majorities deemed it inconvenient to repay it. In all likelihood, some would have done just that because it would have avoided tax increases. It was precisely because they feared that that would occur that creditors in some states opposed assumption.[56] As Secretary of War Henry Knox wrote, "as soon as this shall happen, the public creditors will be ruined, because if the public debt is to be provided for at the pleasure of the local [i.e., state] governments, they will never please to provide for it."[57]

Ferguson describes Rhode Island's actions with apparent approval as a "cheap and easy" method of debt redemption, and suggests that many Americans preferred this approach. He thinks that if the Confederation debt had been divided, "most of the states would probably have retired the bulk of the debt by cheap methods" like those Rhode Island employed.[58] States such as Massachusetts, on the other hand, would probably have repaid Confederation debts at nearly 100 cents on the dollar, based on past practices. So the states would probably have been split, with some repaying former Confederation debts in full, while a number of others repaid them at an enormous discount.

Such repayment disparities would have created unfairness and bitterness, as identically situated creditors—such as army veterans and farmers—received very different treatment based entirely on where they lived.[59] More importantly, the entirely unpredictable results of such a policy would have successfully dissuaded domestic or foreign creditors from ever voluntarily lending money or supplies to the Confederation in the future, because they would have had absolutely no way to know what repayment they would receive.

Thus the superficially appealing idea of dividing the Confederation's domestic debt up among the states had insurmountable flaws. It is not difficult to see why Congress rejected it.[60] Instead, both during and after the administration of Robert Morris, Congress consistently took the position that all creditors should receive full payment. In its view, drastic debt write downs either by the Confederation or by the states would have violated public faith.

The other popular panacea for eliminating debt outside the requisition system was for the Confederation to sell its western lands. Many Confederation leaders devoutly hoped that the Confederation would be able to pay its debts by selling the western lands that had been ceded to it by various states. Most of them continued to think that land sales were a practical alternative until at least late 1785, when the system failed its first important test. Most of these lands were Indian country, occupied and claimed by Native Americans. They vehemently opposed American western expansion, and they were willing to fight to protect their historic homelands.

After finally agreeing on a general system for land sales in 1785, Congress sent surveyors to the West to begin that process. However, Delaware and Wyandot tribal representatives demanded they stop work. In late 1785, Congress learned that the chief surveyor's emissary to the tribes agreed because he believed that "had the Surveyors . . . continued surveying the Lands in the Western Territory, they would have either been made prisoners, or killed and Scalped."[61] The survey's obstruction caused Congressman David Ramsay of South Carolina to conclude that "our expectations from the western territory have failed us."[62] By mid-1786, many in Congress realized that profitably developing the West would be far more difficult than previously thought, if it were possible at all. (That issue is discussed further in chapter 5).

Moreover, the western lands proved to be worth little in the 1780s. They were being offered for sale before there was enough market demand. By 1787, Congress had managed to sell about five million acres of land, but it had received only about ten cents an acre in return. Competing state and military grant lands were selling at similarly low prices. Land sales returned an income to the Confederation of only about $760,000 through 1788. These types of depressed-market sales would not be sufficient to pay off a debt of more than $50 million unless absolutely massive quantities of lands were sold, and that was not possible.[63] By 1787, few leaders regarded western land sales as a realistic means of paying off the Confederation debt.

The complete failure of the requisition system in meeting Confederation debt obligations led a majority of Congress to continue to advocate new tax powers for the Confederation long after the resignation of Superintendent of Finance Robert Morris, the allegedly "aristocratic" mastermind of the plan for such powers. That controversy is considered in chapter 3. But at the same time, Americans had to contend with another critically important debt issue, the problem of prewar British debts. Here again, the states wholly failed the Confederation, with important consequences for its future.

States' Dishonor of Prewar British Debts and Its Consequences

One of the most significant problems created for America by the 1783 Treaty of Peace was article IV's unequivocal requirement that Americans impose no lawful impediment to the collection of massive prewar private debts owed to British creditors. Before the war, Americans owed those creditors about £3 million, or an amount nearly one-third the size of the entire Confederation debt as of 1783. If wartime interest were also due on those debts as Britain claimed, as of 1783 the British private debt would have been nearly 40 percent of the size of the Confederation debt.[64] Perhaps most important politically, however, the burdensome debt was not owed equally by all Americans. Rather, 84 percent of the total debt was owed by people in the five southern states, while New England residents and people in the middle colonies each owed less than 10 percent.[65]

In ratifying the treaty, Congress had accepted its requirement that British prewar debts be repaid. Under the articles, the Confederation's agreement should have bound the states. John Jay, the Confederation's secretary of foreign affairs, concluded flatly in a legal opinion that treaty ratification bound them.[66] However, many of the states refused to honor this provision of the treaty, while in others, the treaty was honored on paper but dishonored in practice.

During or shortly after the war, many states had adopted laws that adversely affected either the value of British debts or British creditors' ability to collect them, or both. As an example, Virginia's courts were entirely closed to British creditors, though its citizens alone owed more than 45 percent of the total British debt.[67] Some states, such as Massachusetts, had adopted laws that prevented British creditors from recovering any wartime interest on debts. If such laws were valid, they would reduce the claimed value of British debts as of 1783 by about 40 percent. Other state laws provided that debts could be repaid in a series of installments beginning several years after the war, and sometimes stretching for as many as four years beyond that, as in South Carolina. There were other restrictive laws as well.

Some states passed laws designed to make it nearly impossible for British creditors to sue state residents, by imposing preconditions to any suit on a debt that creditors could not actually meet. Finally, some states, such as South Carolina, passed laws permitting debtors to tender property rather than money in payment of debts and requiring creditors to accept it (or in some cases, to accept state paper money instead). British creditors claimed that such laws forced them to accept property that was actually worth much less than their debts.[68]

Secretary Jay concluded that laws in Massachusetts, Pennsylvania, South Carolina, and Virginia violated article IV of the treaty.[69] Together, these states' residents may have owed as much as 80 percent of the total British private debts due. But there was nothing the Confederation could do to compel states to honor that treaty provision, for the same reasons that made requisitions unenforceable. And their state legislatures were under intense pressure not to change their laws in ways that would assist British creditors.

The southern states imposed the greatest barriers to British debt repayment. But repayment was a divisive issue even there. As early as May 1783, George Mason wrote to Patrick Henry advocating repayment. He told Henry that "in conversation upon this subject, we sometimes hear a very absurd question: 'If we are now to pay the debts due the British merchants, what have we been fighting for all this while?'" Obviously, though, many Virginians did not agree that that was an absurd question. For Mason, neither British actions in the war nor independence justified nonpayment. And, he said, any effort to evade treaty restrictions would be "highly dangerous and imprudent," possibly risking a new war or seizure of Americans' property abroad.[70] Mason's views could be regarded as special pleading. As a major slaveholder and tobacco planter, he wanted good British commercial relations maintained.

Other Virginia and southern planters, however, were angry about the fact that departing British military forces had taken away several thousand slaves whom they viewed as their property. They claimed that the slaves had been taken in violation of an explicit provision of the 1783 treaty. In mid-1784, using slave removals as its pretext, the Virginia legislature defeated efforts by James Madison and others to repeal laws that blocked British creditors.[71] Actually, though, most of the Virginia debt to the British was not owed by Virginians who had lost slaves, but instead by small debtors and small farmers.[72] Virginia's Patrick Henry became the small farmers' and debtors' champion in repeatedly opposing efforts to permit collection of British debts. Under popular pressure, Virginia's courts were closed to British creditors until 1792.[73]

The British were not without recourse in the face of America's treaty violations. Britain retaliated by refusing to evacuate its western American forts as required by the 1783 treaty. The forts were strategically important for several reasons. First, they were economically and militarily important to the British (as well as to the Native American tribes, as we will see in chapter 5). As long as the British held them, they could decide whether to support Indian attacks on American western settlers, impede them, or ignore them. Second, the British themselves had good reason not to alienate the Indians, since their traders and merchants derived very large profits from the Indian fur trade, which the forts allowed them to control. It is estimated that the 1780s British fur trade had revenues of about £200,000 a year—or around $700,000–$800,000. British merchants wanted to monopolize it, and some historians think that that was the primary motive behind Britain's retention of the forts. After the war, Britain's on-scene military commanders at first dragged their feet about evacuating the forts, and were then quietly instructed by London authorities to retain them.[74]

Eventually, John Adams, America's ambassador to England, demanded possession of the forts. Britain then informed the United States that it would not relinquish them until the United States complied with the peace treaty's provisions on British debts and Loyalists. In early 1786, Britain's foreign minister, Lord Carmarthen, provided a detailed account of alleged American treaty violations. As discussed above, Secretary Jay then informed Congress that in his view the United States had in fact violated the treaty. And because its violations pre-dated those by the British, they were justified in retaining possession of the forts.[75] Perhaps more importantly, the Confederation had no power to force Britain to give them up, both because doing so would risk a new war, and because it had no money to pay for an extended military action in any event. It became clear to Americans by 1786 that if the United States wanted Britain to give up the forts, the states would have to comply with the treaty, particularly the British debt provisions.

Conclusion

In conclusion, the Confederation's requisition system utterly failed to provide funds to pay its debts. States' actions showed that, as Madison thought, it was radically and inherently flawed. State "free riding" and sectional economic conflicts meant that voluntary full compliance with the requisition system would never occur. And the Confederation lacked any workable means to enforce requisitions against noncompliant states, despite years of efforts to devise one. Historians' contentions that requisitions or taxes could have been avoided by dividing up the Confederation domestic debt between the states repeat a position rejected by Congress at the time and are implausible even as counterfactuals. Sales of western lands could not have paid off the Confederation debt. The Confederation was also wholly incapable of compelling the states to honor the 1783 treaty's British debt and Loyalist provisions, which allowed Britain to justify its treaty violations. British occupation of the western forts would continue unless they were forced out. But without reliable revenues, the Confederation would never be able to field an army to force British evacuation.

While the country's debt crisis worsened, Congress and the states had been conducting a desultory six-year debate about whether the Confederation should be given tax powers to meet the country's needs and allow it to keep the public faith. That critical debate is the subject of chapter 3.

3

Republic and Empire

THE STRUGGLE OVER CONFEDERATION TAXES

In 1781, Congress asked the states to grant the Confederation power to impose an import tax. Its primary purpose was to create a dedicated fund of revenue independent of the states to pay Confederation debts, particularly those to foreign creditors. During the war, eleven states agreed to grant some form of that power; then Rhode Island flatly rejected Congress's request in late 1782. Extensive debate and what some historians think was successful strong-arming of Congress by the army and public creditors followed. Ultimately, Congress decided in April 1783 to seek expanded tax powers to pay both the Confederation's expenses and interest on all its foreign and domestic debts. Many major political figures, including wartime leaders such as General Washington, took sides in the ensuing contest over those proposals during the next several years.

The Confederation tax controversy concerned the heart of America's political identity. It was the central chapter in the postwar struggle over the proper limits of Continental government authority in a country committed to republican popular government. Federalist leaders firmly believed that granting the Confederation taxation powers would lead inevitably to the creation of a British-style aristocracy or monarchy, destroying republican freedom. Nationalists thought that if the Confederation continued to lack them, the insolvent Union would soon dissolve. And they were certain that if the Union ceased to exist, European imperial aggression, civil war, or both would again engulf the country. Among other things, the controversy revealed powerful sectionally inflected disagreements about postwar American national defense policies. But under the Confederation, the states were the ultimate arbiters of such disputes, and state leaders had their states' discrete and often opposing interests to protect.

***

There must, sir, be a revenue somehow established that can be relied on and applied for national purposes . . . independent of the will or views of a single state, or it will be impossible to support national faith, or national existence.

Connecticut congressman Oliver Ellsworth to Governor Trumbull, July 1783, supporting Confederation tax powers[1]

Sure I am that if our State parts with its advantage in point of revenue from [taxing import] trade, it must soon succumb under its [resulting increased direct tax] burdens & dwindle into insignificance.

Rhode Island congressman David Howell to Deputy Governor Jabez Bowen, April 1784, opposing Confederation tax powers[2]

This chapter concerns two topics: the reasons that the states did not pay Confederation requisitions, which would have eliminated any need for Confederation tax powers; and the six-year debate over granting such powers. It concludes that the states chose not to pay requisitions primarily because they were politically unpopular, not because the states or their people could not afford to pay them. And it shows that the long struggle to obtain tax powers for the Confederation failed principally because it conflicted with the economic and political interests of various states, not because opponents won the war of ideas. To put these subjects in context, it helps to begin by looking briefly at taxation in the American colonies and its place in the revolution.

The American Revolution began as a tax revolt. Ironically, it occurred principally because Great Britain had gone heavily into debt while winning the Seven Years' War. Afterward, it tried to shift some of the costs of its expanded empire to Americans by taxing them more heavily.[3] Britain's desire to allocate these burdens more equally came as a rude shock to colonists, who paid less than 2 percent of their income in taxes on average. Indeed, colonial Americans were among the most lightly taxed people in the world. Yet an overwhelming majority of them resented paying even these low taxes, according to one careful study.[4]

Although the revolution started as a dispute about the British parliament's taxing powers, most Americans did not want it to fundamentally alter their own local tax systems. In breaking with Britain, they insisted that what they objected to was taxation "without representation" in Parliament. But even assuming that they were properly represented in the Confederation Congress, most people wanted to keep their traditional decentralized system under which local legislatures that they controlled imposed nearly all taxes.[5] Nor did most of them expect that they would pay higher taxes, or that government costs would grow significantly, as a result of the revolution. It was intended to end imperial taxation, but it was not, most thought, intended to alter American taxation.

In the American colonies, the power to tax and the power to appropriate—to determine what tax revenues were spent on—had been inseparable powers of colonial legislatures. But under the Articles of Confederation, they were deliberately separated. The power to determine how much money should be raised for national purposes and how it should be spent was reserved to Congress. But the power to tax to obtain the necessary revenues for those purposes was reserved to the individual states.

Why State Taxation Failed to Meet National Needs

After the war, Americans received another extremely unpleasant shock when their state taxes skyrocketed. Tax levels increased by roughly three to six times over prewar levels.[6] Most of the new taxes were imposed to pay state or Confederation Revolutionary War debts. An estimated 50 to 90 percent of total postwar tax revenues were spent on debt repayment.[7] Yet, as we saw in chapter 2, the states paid less than one-third of

Congress's total requisitions to them. To understand why, we need to consider the politics and economics of postwar state taxation.

To say that postwar tax increases were unpopular would be a gross understatement. They were strongly resisted in most states. As a study by historian Roger Brown has shown, the result was the same nearly everywhere: state authorities caved in to popular pressure. Although they had authorized taxes they thought both necessary and within people's ability to pay, they failed to collect them when faced with resistance.[8] In Pennsylvania, for example, when the state tried to collect unpaid taxes by auctions of delinquent taxpayers' property, residents in several counties seem to have agreed that no one would bid at them. Yet the responsible county boards would not seize the property of delinquent tax officials, as they were supposed to do if taxpayer auctions failed. By 1784, state treasurer David Rittenhouse informed state leaders that "there seems to be almost a total stop in the Collecting of Taxes."[9] The states' collection failures limited revenues, so they chose to prefer in-state creditors, many of whom had their debts paid, to Confederation creditors, many of whom did not.

There are disagreements about why states did not tax effectively. Some historians claim that postwar taxes were simply beyond most people's ability to pay.[10] They claim that elite nationalists such as John Jay and Congressman James Wilson of Pennsylvania mistakenly thought that people could pay taxes because they equated people's failure to pay taxes with personal irresponsibility or immorality, and overlooked their difficult economic circumstances. However, the evidence suggests that although the depressed economy played a role, Americans' strong desire to pay as little in taxes as possible and their widespread lack of support for paying Confederation creditors' debts led state politicians to collect only enough taxes to pay more influential in-state creditors.

Let's look first at the evidence about whether taxpayers could afford to pay postwar taxes. In his study of postwar taxation, Roger Brown concedes that the absolute amounts of the state taxes do not seem large, but argues that people could not obtain the specie needed to pay them. Contemporaries frequently made similar claims. But the evidence instead suggests that many Americans could have paid these taxes, which were fairly modest by today's standards. And they could have done so even though their postwar incomes had been significantly reduced. As table 3.1 shows, in the four major states studied by Brown, the amounts of specie taxes ranged from 0.9 percent to 6.3 percent of the average household's estimated income as of 1783, which has been adjusted downward to reflect recession conditions.[11] Specie and paper taxes together ranged from 3.9 to 9.0 percent of average household income, depending on the state.

TABLE 3.1. Taxes as a percentage of 1783 average estimated household income in selected states

STATE	AVERAGE TAXES PER HOUSEHOLD[a]	AVERAGE ESTIMATED HOUSEHOLD INCOME 1783[b]	PERCENTAGE OF HOUSEHOLD INCOME PAID IN TAXES[b]
Massachusetts	$11.60 specie/paper $5.80 specie only	$189.70	6.1% specie/paper 3.1% specie only
Rhode Island	$9.60 specie/paper $9.18 specie only	$196.23	5.3% specie/paper 5.1% specie only
Pennsylvania	$20.16 specie/paper $14.10 specie only	$224.57	9.0% specie/paper 6.3% specie only
South Carolina	$20.05 specie/paper $4.37 specie only	$511.52	3.9% specie/paper 0.9% specie only

Note: This table is intended as an approximation only.

[a]Data from Roger H. Brown, *Redeeming the Republic: Federalists, Taxation, and the Origins of the Constitution* (Baltimore: Johns Hopkins University Press, 1993), 35, table 3. Brown's table uses a source of population data that probably understates 1783 population; therefore it probably somewhat overstates the tax burden per household. Nevertheless, I used Brown's data here for conservatism.

[b]Household income derived from Peter H. Lindert and Jeffrey G. Williamson, "American Incomes Before and After the Revolution," *Journal of Economic History* 73, no. 3 (2013): 742, table 3. Lindert and Williamson's 1774 per capita income data is used as a basis, and then adjusted to an average household income for different regions using Brown's household-size numbers (Roger H. Brown, *Redeeming the Republic*, 35, table 3 note). That income is then reduced 40 percent to reflect depressed 1783 economic conditions. Some estimates of income reduction are significantly lower than 40 percent (see Lindert and Williamson, "American Incomes," 753), which implies that taxes were a lower percentage of income than shown here.

Another way of viewing the tax burden from Confederation requisitions is that during 1781–86, Congress's requisitions requested an average of $4.43 per year from each free household. That amount seems quite manageable for all but the poorest of them. (Residents' total tax burden included payments on state expenses and debt, and both are included in table 3.1.) It follows that paying the Confederation debt by itself would clearly have been manageable for most Americans.[12]

The claim that specie was too scarce to enable these taxes to be paid is flawed. During the mid-1780s, specie was unusually "scarce"—everyone agreed. But that did not mean it was unobtainable. There is evidence that sufficient specie to pay taxes or debts could be obtained by anyone willing to pay a high enough price for it.[13] What specie scarcity actually meant was that someone who needed it would have to sell a larger amount of some asset to get it than they would have had to sell if it had been plentiful.

For that reason, it is most useful to interpret claims that specie was so scarce that people "could not afford" to pay specie taxes instead as an assertion that people should not have been forced to liquidate assets at large losses to obtain it. This is very similar to claims that today's American homeowners should not have been forced to sell their "underwater" homes (that is, homes that had market values less than the amount of mortgages owed on them) at depressed prices during the 2008 US recession in order to pay debts or taxes. During the mid-1780s liquidity crisis, many people agreed that government policy should not compel major asset liquidations. So the view best supported by the evidence is that a significant majority of Americans could have afforded to pay postwar specie taxes, but that many who could pay thought that it would be unfair for them to have to do so.

However, recent income data also show that there were unquestionably some people during the 1780s who could not have paid their taxes without disastrously large asset liquidations, or even after liquidating all they owned. For them, paying taxes often amounted to losing their cattle, homes, or farms. The evidence suggests that such people were a minority, though in some parts of the country perhaps a sizable one.[14]

Most were farmers, and they lived primarily in depressed rural areas isolated from major markets, such as western Massachusetts. Such particularly depressed areas shortly became centers of social and political rebellion in several states (see chapters 7 and 8).

People who owed significant debts would also probably have had a difficult time paying taxes. In Virginia, for example, postwar British private debts amounted on average to roughly $14.00 per capita, or $130 per household. The interest alone on that average debt would have amounted to a significant percentage of the average household tax burden shown in table 3.1.[15] Virginia's decision to block British debt collection thus effectively enabled other creditors to be paid instead. The state's preferred creditors, whose debts did get paid, were its state officials, its own citizens, and, to a far lesser extent, Confederation creditors. Other states followed Virginia's approach, preferring with limited revenues to pay their own citizens first and, as a distant second if at all, Confederation creditors.

None of the states responded to discovering that postwar taxes were unaffordable for some taxpayers by large-scale, overt redistribution of tax burdens to wealthy taxpayers. That would certainly have enabled states to pay their Confederation requisitions. Income data suggest that wealthier taxpayers could have paid most if not all of the taxes appropriately regarded as unaffordable for their fellow citizens, though their taxes would have increased markedly as a result.[16] But redistribution based purely on ability to pay was either politically unthinkable or unlikely to have succeeded politically. Instead, in the face of tax protests, the states made a variety of accommodations.

In Virginia, for example, the state legislature postponed tax deadlines several times. It periodically allowed taxes to be paid in commodities such as tobacco, or by using depreciated debt certificates that could be purchased for a fraction of their face value and then used to pay taxes at their full face value.[17] And it permitted local sheriffs required by law to collect taxes not to collect them for years after they were due without suffering the loss of their own property instead. By 1789, sheriffs from more than twenty-five counties located throughout much of Virginia owed the state hundreds of thousands of dollars in uncollected taxes for tax years 1783 to 1786. In at least one case, for more than five years the state failed to enforce a court judgment in its favor against a delinquent sheriff for thousands of dollars in taxes due.[18]

All of Virginia's accommodations effectively amounted to tax cuts, because they reduced the specie value of taxes collected and cost the state lost interest revenue as well. Not surprisingly, given its willingness to cut taxes under popular pressure, Virginia actually raised only part of the money it attempted to raise. It paid only 30 percent of its Confederation requisitions through mid-1787. But some Virginians probably got to keep their farms as a result.

Tax delinquency levels were relatively high in a number of other states studied. Some of the largest defaults were harbingers of coming social unrest. By 1784, western Pennsylvania counties owed more than 90 percent of taxes assessed from 1778 to 1783, while Philadelphia and surrounding eastern counties had paid most of their assessments. Eastern and western Pennsylvania divided over key political issues throughout most of the 1780s, including the 1787 Constitution. By 1785, Worcester and Berkshire counties in western Massachusetts, which became the heartland of Shays's Rebellion in 1786, had paid only 28 percent of taxes imposed from 1778 to 1782, while the state average was roughly half.[19]

In sum, in the mid-1780s, state demands for increased taxes were met with various popular calls for what amounted to tax cuts or nonenforcement. Such demands were very often successful, and large levels of delinquencies were often tolerated. But there were still significant numbers of people who lost their property for failure to pay taxes or private debts. With limited revenues, states chose to pay Confederation debts last, if at all. Public unwillingness to pay taxes to meet Confederation requisitions was often justified by attacking them as unjust demands that were anti-republican or unfairly benefited the rich or speculators, as historian Woody Holton's studies have shown.[20]

Throughout New England, taxpayers attacked the Confederation debt created by granting army commutation. They argued that their states should refuse to pay it or to authorize Confederation taxes to do so. And they attacked requisitions intended to repay Confederation debts at face value even if the debts were held by speculators who had purchased them at far below face value.[21] As discussed in chapter 2, southern taxpayers saw little reason to pay Confederation domestic-debt requisitions that would primarily benefit northern-state debt holders. All in all, many taxpayers saw little reason to repay various Confederation domestic debts.[22] Because Confederation debts were widely unpopular, most of the states chose not to pay most of the amounts of Confederation requisitions made by Congress to them.

There are two additional reasons to think that state taxpayers could have paid Confederation requisitions had they chosen to do so. First, as we saw in chapter 2, in the 1780s three Mid-Atlantic states decided temporarily to assume $9 million worth of Confederation debt principal owed to their own residents and to pay interest on those debts. Even though this added debt increased state taxes, none of those states faced a serious revolt like that which later occurred in Massachusetts. Peace prevailed even though they were paying debts, often to wealthy speculators, that they could have avoided paying without facing sanctions. Their citizens were demonstrating their capacity to pay their state's full share of both state and Confederation debts. Yet none of these states actually paid their full Confederation requisitions for the 1781–86 period.

Second, after the war several states apparently paid down their own state debts. Although exact figures are unavailable, historians think that New Hampshire and Connecticut may have reduced their debt by a total of nearly $2 million, while Virginia later claimed that it had redeemed a "large proportion of the [state] debt . . . by the collection of heavy taxes."[23] Again states were voluntarily preferring their resident creditors to nonresidents, since the money used to pay down state debts could in most cases have been paid to the Confederation instead.

The states gave preference to their residents' debts because only their residents had power to choose their state legislatures, and tax policies could be decisive in the outcomes of elections. The Confederation, on the other hand, had only a thin base of postwar political support. It consisted primarily of its public creditors, a group that usually could be "divided and conquered." In New York, for example, when the state decided to assume Confederation debts for its residents and pay interest on them, it assumed only the kinds of debts widely held by residents who supported Governor George Clinton and his allies. It deliberately chose not to assume the Confederation debts held only by a comparatively small number of wealthy New Yorkers who generally opposed Clinton. Confederation debt-repayment choices in New York and elsewhere were determined by state politics, not by Congress's decisions.[24]

Several prominent leaders concluded after the war that Americans could afford to pay taxes, but were unwilling to do so. Nationalist John Jay reluctantly decided in 1786 that Confederation requisitions had not been paid voluntarily because "too much has been expected from the virtue & good sense of the people. . . . [T]he Treasury is empty tho' the Country abounds in Resources, and our people are far more unwilling than unable to pay taxes."[25] Tristram Dalton, a Massachusetts legislator, agreed with Jay. Dalton wrote in late 1785 to John Adams that "our Farmers must cease complaining of Taxes, which they can pay with ease—our Trade [merchants]—of duties and excises—that are not felt. . . . The people of these states are well able to pay *regularly* the interest, and, in a very short time, the principal [of the national debt]—but they seem to think that Independency being obtained, their Liberty is secured without paying the Cost, or bestowing any more care upon it—A Stock, that we can draw upon at pleasure."[26]

Pennsylvania congressman James Wilson also concluded that Americans could afford to pay Confederation taxes. He told Congress that the people of the United States had demonstrated a "peculiar repugnance" to paying taxes because before the war, citizens had paid "indirectly & insensibly" an average of 10 shillings (about $2.00) per head, and "insensibly borne" higher burdens through wartime paper-money depreciation. But as of early 1783, Congress had received only about one-tenth of that amount from the states in the previous year.[27] Massachusetts leader James Sullivan reached a similar conclusion. He wrote to John Adams in 1785, "Did our people content themselves with living as well as they did before the revolution or three times so well as common people in other Countries live, they might pay taxes enough with ease to discharge in a short time our public debt."[28]

Nor were nationalists the only ones who concluded that Americans could afford to pay taxes, but were choosing not to do so. After the war, some Confederation leaders—such as Virginia federalist Arthur Lee—believed that states were not paying requisitions because their residents were then unable to pay taxes, but that they would pay them once peace had a chance to heal the wounds of war.[29] Lee described the 1783 impost proposal as a Tory plot to subvert the revolution. But three years later, based on his experience as a member of the Confederation Board of Treasury, he had changed his mind, and now believed that the states simply could not be trusted to pay requisitions, no matter what conditions were.[30]

At the same time that the states were failing to pay Congress's requisitions, they were refusing to give the Confederation the necessary powers to collect taxes of its own to pay Confederation debts. We turn next to that part of our story.

The Futile Six-Year Fight over Confederation Taxation

THE 1781 IMPOST

In February 1781, Congress made its first effort to obtain tax powers so that it would no longer have to rely on requisitions to pay Confederation debts. It proposed that the Confederation be given power to impose a 5 percent "impost," or import tax. At the time, most congressmen, and Confederation officials such as Superintendent of Finance Robert Morris and Benjamin Franklin, were convinced that without a stable, dedicated fund independent of the states that they could rely on for repayment, many if not all foreign lenders would be unwilling to make further loans to the United States. Most states seemingly agreed during the war, and by late 1782, eleven states had adopted some form of

Congress's proposal. But then Rhode Island's legislature unanimously rejected the impost. It is worthwhile to understand that controversy, because the arguments made during it framed much of the debate over Confederation taxes between 1783 and the Philadelphia Convention.

The strongly federalist Rhode Island delegates to Congress saw the impost dispute as an apocalyptic sovereignty struggle between the states and Congress.[31] David Howell wrote, "The pretensions of the particular States to Sovereignty after they have parted with the controul of their purses will be no less ridiculous than the claim of the man in the Fable to enjoy the Shadow after he had sold his Ass, alledging that altho he had parted with his Ass, he had not parted with his Shadow."[32] The impost was a violation of basic liberties for which Americans had fought the revolution, they claimed. The exclusive right to impose taxes was reserved to the states by the Articles of Confederation. That limitation on Congress's powers was one of the revolution's central achievements.[33]

Public debate on the impost continued into early 1783. It was attacked as a measure that "contains the seeds of slavery, because it places in the hands of the Supreme Executive of the States, a permanent revenue, which they can hold independent of the people." Independent revenues "hath in all countries . . . been the foundation of tyranny; it is this that hath ruined Britain."[34] It was condemned as "insensible" taxation, "founded in a supposition incompatible with the principle of a free and popular state, viz. that there is not virtue enough in the people to grant knowingly sufficient for the necessary expenses of government."[35]

Other writers insisted that Confederation tax powers would permanently corrupt republicanism. Massachusetts congressman Samuel Osgood spoke for many Americans when he explained to John Adams, "Our Danger lies in this—That if permanent Funds are given to Congress, the aristocratical influence, which predominates in more than a Major Part of the United States will finally establish an arbitrary Government in the United States."[36] Osgood explained to a leading federalist that the southern state governments were inherently aristocratic. "It is impossible in the Nature of Things, that their Governments should be democratic," he wrote, and "if they vary from [aristocratical principles] it will be to monarchical ones."[37] Another writer claimed that creating a powerful continental government by granting it tax powers would inevitably result in dictatorship or monarchy, an American Caesar or Cromwell.[38]

Moreover, opponents argued, the contention that Congress had sovereign power to impose the impost was exactly the same kind of claim made by the British government before the revolution to authorize it to tax Americans. The exclusive method authorized for raising revenue under the Articles was to make requisitions to the states based on the relative value of land, buildings, and improvements in each state. These provisions protected the states' freedom and equality, and granting Congress tax powers would be inconsistent with them.[39]

Impost supporters responded that Congress had authority and a duty to pay the country's debts, and that Confederation taxation was the only means available to ensure that they would be paid. Congress could be trusted with added powers because its members represented the states and the people. A Boston observer wrote that "the members of it can in no instance exempt themselves from a share of the burthens necessary for the defence of the country, in common with their constituents."[40] Other nationalists, such as Charles Pinckney, argued that state failures to pay requisitions ordered by Congress were "licentiousness" and "anarchy." In his view, republicanism was not intended to allow such untrammeled or "pure" democracy, in which Congress's decisions could be unilaterally disregarded by individual states.[41] But despite both sides' ideological arguments, the 1781 impost debate was most decisively influenced by state political and economic factors.

The Rhode Island delegates also advanced pragmatic reasons for their opposition. They contended that the impost would add the expense of "numerous Tribes of Officers, concerned in the revenue." They claimed it would "draw a larger proportion of the public debt from [Rhode Island], as a Commercial State . . . than any other State." The impost would bear harder on the "poor and laborious" and "those who have large families." It would "require a Military, force to execute it, and bring in Standing Armies."[42] What the Rhode Island delegates did not say publicly was that Rhode Island could impose its own state import tax that would generate enough revenue to help keep its other state taxes low. To them, low taxes seemed necessary to the state's survival. One wrote privately, "Sure I am that if our State parts with its advantage in point of revenue from trade, it must soon succumb under its [increased direct tax] burdens & dwindle into insignificance."[43]

Rhode Island's rejection of the impost came as a grave shock to Congress. Some congressmen believed that its rejection would damage America's credit standing abroad, making it difficult, if not impossible, to obtain foreign loans. Others believed also that if foreign loans could not be obtained because the impost was defeated, states would inevitably face the "irksome Task of laying immediate, and *direct* taxes upon their citizens."[44] In late 1782, Congress decided to send a delegation to Rhode Island to persuade its leaders to change their minds.

But just as the delegates began their journey, they learned that Virginia had revoked its approval of the impost. That was an enormous blow to supporters. According to James Madison, "the most intelligent members [of Congress] were deeply affected & prognosticated a failure of the [tax] scheme, & the most pernicious effects to the character, the duration, & the interest of the confederacy."[45] To put this more plainly, Madison and his nationalist allies believed that without the impost, the Confederation would not be able to pay its debts and would eventually collapse. George Washington was so unhappy about what Virginia had done that he wrote a remarkably uncharacteristic vehement letter to Governor Benjamin Harrison, arguing that its action could not possibly be justified.[46]

Virginia leaders such as Arthur Lee argued publicly in Congress that granting tax powers to the Confederation was inconsistent with the idea of the Confederation itself and would have "dangerous consequences to the liberties of the confederated states." It was an "established truth," Lee said, "that the purse ought not be put in the same hands with the Sword; that like arguments had been used in favor of Ship money in the reign of Charles I." ("Ship money" referred to a notorious effort by King Charles I to impose taxes without Parliament's consent.) Lee argued, in other words, that as long as Congress had power to make war, it should never be given the power to tax. Lee also contended that it would enrich large Confederation-debt-holding states like Pennsylvania at Virginia's expense.[47] James Madison noted privately, however, that Virginia also opposed Confederation tax powers because it wanted to impose state import taxes that would be paid by out-of-state consumers, particularly those in North Carolina. Other congressmen viewed Virginia as having acted in its self-interest. One wrote that Virginia "has paid little, or no part of the Requisition of 1782, had not one Soldier in the great Army last Campaign, and only a few hundreds in the seperate, southern Army, and still with unexampled Perverseness, continues her futile Claim to the immense Western Region."[48] As in Rhode Island, federalist principles and parochialism had combined to frustrate Congress's proposal.

Madison reported that on December 24, 1782, "it was at length, notwithstanding [the widespread sense of despair and gloom over the failure of the 1781 impost], determined to persist in the attempt for a permanent revenue."[49] Congress resolved to continue to seek new tax powers before learning several weeks later that the army planned to demand the payment of debts to it backed by a revenue fund. Just as Congress had originally decided in 1781 to seek Confederation tax powers for reasons unrelated to army demands, it decided to continue its effort to obtain such powers for reasons independent of them.[50]

Many congressmen remained convinced of the necessity for an impost. Congressman Nathaniel Gorham of Massachusetts wrote to a leading Boston merchant that he believed that states such as Massachusetts, which had been "forward"—that is, more willing to pay war expenses and requisitions than other states—"will never obtain justice until funds are established—and Unless such establishments are made or some alteration in the articles of confederation takes place the union must ere long dissolve."[51] Virginia's inconsistency showed that the requisition system would never work. Unless Congress was given tax powers, debts owed to Massachusetts would never be paid, and the Confederation would collapse.

Just days before Gorham's letter, Superintendent of Finance Robert Morris had written to the governor of Delaware harshly condemning that state's failure to pay requisitions. He wrote, "Your Citizens sir while they Witness the condition of those Veterans who yet remain from the bloody sickly Plains of Carolina will present to View an equal Inattention to their Sufferings and to those Rights for which America has contended."[52] Morris's strident language reflected his sense of desperation about the states' continued failure to pay Confederation requisitions, which he thought created a pressing need for tax powers.

Throughout the mid-1780s, a majority of Congress supported granting the Confederation tax powers. Although the army's demands and the pleas of public creditors certainly played a role in Congress's 1783 tax decisions, those decisions were very consistent with Congress's earlier actions. Congress never reconsidered its decision to seek such powers before the 1787 Philadelphia Convention, even after Robert Morris resigned and fervent federalist opponents of his power and financial policies became a majority in Congress.

CONGRESS'S 1783 TAX PROPOSAL

Congress's April 1783 tax proposal had two main parts: an impost or import tax, and a "supplemental" tax to be paid by the states.[53] The debate over it lasted for almost four years. Because nearly all the states ultimately adopted the import tax part of the proposal, some historians claim that all the states would ultimately have agreed to the import tax if the Confederation had not collapsed. Several have gone further and argued that this shows that the 1787 Constitution's far broader tax powers were unnecessary overreaching.[54] These are mistaken claims. The view best supported by the historical evidence is that the full 1783 proposal never had any realistic chance of adoption. Nor do the facts show that the Confederation would actually have received even import tax powers. Indeed, the early history of the 1783 proposal foreshadowed its eventual failure.

Nationalist leaders in Congress felt that they could not accept the defeat of the 1781 impost, because if they could not pay the Confederation debt, "the Union would break up under the strain."[55] James Madison deplored the idea that the new American government would be founded on debt repudiation. He told Congress in early 1783 that "the idea of erecting our national independence on the ruins of public faith and national honor must be horrid to every mind which retained either honesty or pride."[56] By the time the tax debate resumed in early 1783, Madison had given a great deal of thought to the relationship between Confederation debts, tax powers, and the Union.

In Madison's view, the cement of the Union was the common war debt, which should be paid by Confederation taxes. If each state paid only its own debts owed to its residents, Madison asked Congress, "What then would become of the Confederation? . . . What [would be] the tie by which the States could be held together?"[57] During the war, it had been obvious that the states had no choice but to cooperate for the common defense, or they would almost inevitably face defeat. But in peacetime, why should states cooperate except when they chose to do so? In effect, Madison was asking why the states would have any reason to cooperate on national concerns if they were not engaged in paying a common debt to build the nation's reputation and strength for their common benefit.

But based on the fate of the 1781 impost, Madison also knew by early 1783 that the states would be unlikely to accept Confederation tax powers on their own merits. His confidential memoranda show that he thought that some states would be better off financially if they kept tax powers in their own hands. And he thought that many others had important concerns that might interfere with their willingness to grant such powers.[58]

To begin with, individual states had sharply conflicting views about whether the Confederation owed them money for war expenses. Some believed that the Confederation owed them a larger amount than their share of the Confederation debt; if so, why should they be required to pay Confederation requisitions or taxes? States also had their own views about whether their residents would benefit from Confederation taxes or whether they would lose financially. And many "landless" states such as Rhode Island were unhappy that "landed" states such as Virginia claimed ownership of vast western lands that they thought should be held for the Union's benefit. Western lands could be used to pay debts so that landless states could avoid imposing taxes on their residents instead.[59] Madison saw that Confederation tax proposals would not be considered on their own merits, but would instead inevitably be considered in the light of these other sharply divisive issues.

Therefore he told Congress that he wanted it to enact a fiscal "grand bargain" to encourage the states to agree to its tax proposals. It was necessary for the Confederation to enact such a comprehensive fiscal plan because it would "be the only one that would cut off all sources of future controversy among the States." In addition to the taxes that Congress was considering, he proposed that the plan include state cessions of western lands to the Union; basing state tax quotas not on land values but on population (which would impose a heavier relative burden on the southern states); and Confederation assumption of the states' Revolutionary War debts, including equitable claims and abatements.[60] Unfortunately for Madison, however, Congress was unwilling to adopt all the elements of his proposed grand bargain, especially the adjustment and assumption of the states' war debts. That meant that Congress's 1783 tax proposals were ultimately considered by the states largely without the political inducement of Madison's other proposals. As a result, the states made their decisions on them based primarily on their perceptions of their interests as individual states, which often conflicted with Congress's decisions.

In late January 1783, as a first step, Madison moved that Congress resolve that "the establishment of permanent & adequate funds to operate generally throughout the U. States is indispensibly necessary for doing complete justice to the Creditors of the U.S., for restoring public credit, & for providing for the future exigencies of the war."[61] Madison's motion ran into opposition on both practical and theoretical grounds.

Congressman Theodorick Bland of Virginia argued that the states could not afford to pay congressional requisitions. That concern was dismissed by congressmen such as James Wilson of Pennsylvania. As we saw earlier, Wilson offered calculations demonstrating that the states were providing the Confederation with only a small fraction of what Americans had paid in prewar taxes.[62] Some congressmen objected in principle to Confederation as opposed to state tax collection, while others insisted that the Confederation could never successfully collect taxes without federal collectors. Relatively few congressmen challenged the basic principle that permanent tax funds should be established to pay Confederation debts. Those that did argued that the Confederation had never been intended to be a separate government with power to tax. Madison's colleague from Virginia John Francis Mercer said, for example, that he would do his best to destroy the Confederation if it were given tax powers.[63]

Madison defended his position on various grounds. Reflecting the army's influence on the debate, he argued that it would not be "just or politic" to fail to provide strong security for the army's debts and instead to "leave them to seek their rewards separately from the states to which they respectively belong."[64] He denied that state sovereignty would be impaired by Confederation taxes. He argued that the Confederation already had the power to obligate states to raise money to pay Confederation debts. All that authorizing taxes would do would be to change the mode for getting the states to pay their shares. That argument implied that Congress had inherent tax powers, so however valid theoretically it might have been, it was politically tone deaf and entirely unpersuasive. Eventually, Congress began to consider the specifics of a tax proposal.

It was obvious to Confederation tax supporters that the 1781 impost could not simply be re-proposed, or it would fail again. Four out of five southern states had ultimately refused to accept the 1781 impost, and it was unpopular in various parts of the North as well. A new, more politically appealing proposal had to be developed. In April 1783, Congress sent to the states a proposal for two taxes: a 5 percent import tax (also called an impost), and a "supplemental tax."[65]

By itself, a 5 percent import tax was expected to raise about $500,000 to $1 million per year.[66] That would have covered the Confederation's operating expenses and some of its foreign-loan debt payments. Robert

Morris had originally proposed creating a series of additional taxes, so that the Confederation's expenses and interest on both its foreign and domestic debts could be paid. The additional taxes Morris proposed included a land tax, a poll tax, and potentially, excise taxes on items such as liquor. After months of debate, and after agreeing to pay army commutation, Congress agreed that enough taxes should be proposed to pay all Confederation expenses and foreign and domestic debt interest. But it could not agree on any specific new taxes beyond the import tax. To replace them, it proposed instead a "supplemental tax," which was a fixed obligation for each state that would raise a total of $1.5 million per year.[67]

Congress also explicitly provided that neither the impost nor the supplemental tax would go into effect until both of them "shall be acceded to by every state."[68] The primary reason that the two taxes were directly linked was that delegates from some states such as Massachusetts would not have supported the impost if it had not been linked to the supplemental tax. They expected that the supplemental tax would bear most heavily on the southern states, so in theory it would compensate other states for lost revenues or disproportionate burdens from import taxes.[69] They also believed that the southern states were wealthier than the northern states, so they should pay a proportionately larger share of taxes.[70]

The supplemental tax was to employ a radical new allocation formula, using relative state population rather than land values to establish state quotas. That formula became known as the three-fifths rule, because in it, slaves were counted as three-fifths of a person for the purposes of counting population. Under the new formula, the southern states' tax quotas would increase about 15 percent. They would pay about 47 percent of total supplemental taxes, though they contained only 41 percent of the estimated free population.[71] The southern states' willingness to bear a disproportionate share of the supplemental tax provides substantial evidence that they were significantly more interested in having a Confederation tax package adopted than were the northern states.

Virginia in particular had a strong reason for desiring Confederation tax powers. Madison explained in a confidential analysis that Confederation taxes were of interest to Virginia primarily because it and other southern states were "likely to enjoy an opulent and defenceless trade," and Confederation military power created with tax revenues would "secure to her the protection of the Confederacy against the maritime superiority of the E[astern] States."[72] Madison's examination of the national defense issue went much deeper, however.

Madison wrote that if the Confederation could not pay its debts, in the future "the most respectable people" might ally with Great Britain to preserve political stability. There would be "danger of convulsions from the army." And the states could be expected to have calamitous disputes, because many of them believed that other states owed them money due to the war. The result of such disputes "would be a rupture of the confederacy." "Foreign aid would be called in" in the event of such interstate disputes, he wrote.[73] For Madison, paying Confederation debts was not just about justice in the abstract; it was essential to strengthen national defense and political stability. Because of Virginia's military vulnerability, Madison saw national defense as the primary motive for Virginia to support Confederation tax powers.

For George Washington as well, providing for national defense was the primary reason supporting Confederation tax powers. He profoundly desired to keep faith with the army by seeing debts to it paid, which would also improve unity and morale in future wars. But Washington was also acutely aware of Virginia's own military weaknesses in the event of a future war.[74] Northern leaders such as Massachusetts congressman Nathan Dane shared Washington's view that the southern states were militarily weak. Dane believed that that weakness could be exploited by northern states to gain their Confederation objectives by threatening to dissolve the confederacy.[75]

Washington openly described himself as a "warm friend to the impost," and expressed grave concern that if the states did not enable Congress to pay Confederation debts, the Union might dissolve and "anarchy and confusion" would follow.[76] In a widely publicized June

1783 letter to the states criticizing their failure to comply with congressional requisitions and to give Congress needed powers, Washington expressed his concern that their licentious behavior—that is, refusing to honor Congress's decisions except when they chose—might dissolve the Union and be followed by a dictatorship. He wrote that "there is a natural and necessary progression, from the extreme of anarchy to the extreme of Tyranny; . . . arbitrary power is most easily established on the ruins of Liberty abused to licentiousness."[77] In reaction, there were claims that he had stepped outside his proper sphere by becoming involved in civil government. Others such as Stephen Higginson of Massachusetts saw Washington's actions as raising serious questions about his commitment to republicanism.[78]

Meanwhile, federalist opponents of Confederation taxes were convinced that they would be used to establish an oppressive standing army. That was one of the main reasons why federalists such as General James Warren, Tristram Dalton, and Elbridge Gerry of Massachusetts, Richard Henry Lee of Virginia, and David Howell of Rhode Island opposed them.[79] Congressman David Howell wrote that "the Confederation gives Congress no power to make any military establishment in time of peace."[80] He wrote to Rhode Island's deputy governor that "imposts & excises in the hands of the Sovereign power & standing armies have grown up together & yielded mutual support to each other."[81] Massachusetts congressman Samuel Osgood wrote that instead of the impost, the Confederation debt should be divided among the states because "a standing debt, well funded" "will be the Parent of" "a standing Army."[82]

In Virginia, George Mason attacked the 1783 tax proposal as an effort to obtain the kind of arbitrary power exercised by the hated seventeenth-century Stuart kings, including Charles I in England.[83] One of the most detested features of Stuart rule had been their efforts without Parliament's approval to impose royal taxes and then use the revenue to maintain standing armies. Mason's attack went to the heart of the fears many Americans, particularly those in New England, had about Confederation taxation. They thought that it would support a powerful central government that would inevitably become the basis for an aristocracy or monarchy backed by armed force, crushing popular freedom. Massachusetts representatives such as Gerry believed in the unconquerable prowess of their state's militia and saw no need for a standing army. They congratulated each other on the defeat of Washington's proposal to create a peacetime standing army in late 1783.[84] Thus, underlying the divisive tax debate were views on sections' differing military strength and a related sharp, sectionally tinged disagreement about America's national defense policies.

The Fate of the 1783 Tax Proposal

During 1783–84, at least eight states adopted the impost part of the 1783 proposal. In gaining its adoption in Virginia and Massachusetts, vocal public support by Confederation leaders such as John Adams and George Washington played an important role. Many Massachusetts federalists, such as former general James Warren and Stephen Higginson, opposed it as a tool of Robert Morris and an "aristocratic junto."[85] Morris's strong advocacy of central government tax powers, combined with his extensive official authority, high-handedness in pressing states for requisition payments, and perceived conservatism, made ad hominem attacks on him a plausible political device for federalists opposed to Confederation tax powers. Massachusetts accompanied its approval of the impost after a sharp legislative contest with instructions to its congressional delegates to seek the abolition of the office of superintendent of finance.[86]

In other states such as North Carolina, Connecticut, and New Jersey, leaders supported the import tax primarily for defensive reasons. The harm being done by state import taxes to other states was significant. For example, New Jersey announced in 1786 that it would not pay future Confederation requisitions as long as it was required to pay import taxes to New York or any other state. These states' leaders believed that if the Confederation received import tax authority, import taxes could not be imposed by neighboring states on their residents.[87]

Unfortunately for the 1783 tax proposal's supporters, it quickly became clear that while many states were willing to grant the import tax, very few were willing to grant the supplemental tax. The basic political logic behind the supplemental tax proposal was fundamentally flawed. State politicians did not see the supplemental tax as compensation for losses from the import tax. Instead, within various commercial states, merchants and coastal residents often favored the impost, while inland farmers opposed either the supplemental tax or both the import tax and the supplemental tax.[88] It was well understood that the supplemental tax would be used to pay interest on the Confederation domestic debt, and as we have seen, many states' residents had no interest in paying such debts.

For these reasons, adopting both parts of Congress's 1783 proposal—while it might have increased tax equity between various states and regions—was internally divisive in most states. Most of them therefore failed to adopt the supplemental tax. By August 1786, only five states had adopted it. Three major states, New York, Virginia, and South Carolina, had failed to adopt. And in Massachusetts, one of two large adopting states, the supplemental tax was extremely unpopular, and became one of the issues that led to Shays's Rebellion. There was no chance whatsoever that the supplemental tax proposal would be accepted by all states, so the Confederation would never have obtained the revenues needed to pay even the interest on its domestic debt.

Congressional leaders gave up hope for the supplemental tax by 1786. They began to argue that states' approvals of the import tax were sufficient to allow it take effect even though the supplemental tax effectively had been defeated. But Pennsylvania, in adopting the supplemental tax, had decided that its approval of the import tax would not become effective unless all states approved both taxes (which Pennsylvania legislators probably knew would never happen). It refused to alter its stance despite urgent pleas from congressional representatives.[89] So there is reason to think that the import tax would never have become effective even if New York, the final holdout by 1786, had approved it. But it was New York's refusal to adopt the impost, despite repeated pleas from Congress and its members, which ultimately persuaded even hopelessly optimistic politicians that the Confederation would never receive tax powers. Ironically, New York's refusal was completely foreseeable as early as 1784 in light of its state politics.

During the mid-1780s, the New York state legislature was dominated by Governor George Clinton's supporters, most of whom represented rural areas whose residents rabidly opposed higher direct taxes. As Alexander Hamilton told the legislature, "There is not a farmer in this state who would not pay a shilling in the voluntary consumption of articles on which a[n import] duty is paid, rather than a penny [one-twelfth as much] imposed immediately on his house and land [in direct tax]."[90] The governor and his allies therefore went to considerable lengths to find state revenue sources that would allow them to avoid imposing direct taxes. During 1784–85, about 60 percent of New York's revenue was derived from either state import taxes or revenues from Loyalist property forfeiture. In 1786–87, 55 percent of the state's actual new receipts (other than newly issued state paper money) came from import taxes alone.[91]

Clinton's forces had no desire whatsoever to give up the more than $100,000 in annual revenues the state received from its import tax, since everyone was convinced that that would require an increase in direct taxes. As one supporter of New York's impost wrote during the fight over ratification of the 1787 Constitution: "What hath kept taxes so low in this state . . . the reason is obvious, our impost duties . . . our landed property will ever sell according to the conveniency of it; the lighter the tax, the higher the land [prices]; . . . Let our impost and advantages be taken from us, shall we not be obligated to lay as heavy taxes as Connecticut, Boston, etc." Connecticut and New Jersey residents paid more than a third of all the import taxes imposed by New York, so taxpayers there were effectively being coerced into paying a significant part of New York's government's costs. That was bitterly resented. But it made no difference, because neither state was in a position to force New York to abandon its tax—and the Confederation certainly had no way to do so.[92]

After the New York legislature in 1785 initially defeated Congress's import tax proposal, in 1786 it adopted another proposal that supposedly met Congress's requirements. However, New York's action was widely regarded as inconsistent with Congress's proposal. The reasons for that included its provisions for state-appointed collectors and for permitting use of New York paper money to pay the tax. Congress asked that it be reconsidered. New York's final rejection of the impost occurred in February 1787.[93]

During the 1787 New York legislative debate, Alexander Hamilton appealed for adoption of Congress's 1783 impost proposal in an impassioned speech regarded as one of his greatest. He ridiculed the idea that Congress would become a tyrant to the states. He made the point that New York's insistence that its citizens be allowed to pay the Confederation impost with reasonably sound New York paper money would destroy the impost's financial value. Other states would insist that their citizens be allowed to do the same thing, but those citizens would use badly depreciated paper money instead. He argued that New York was actually losing financially because it was paying its Confederation requisitions while other states were not. And he admitted that using national tax collectors would impair New York's sovereignty, but argued that New York would benefit. Clinton's forces answered Hamilton by voting his position down by a substantial margin. A distinguished historian concluded, "It was truthfully said that 'the impost was strangled by a band of mutes.'"[94] After New York's rejection, no one could claim that the impost (or realistically, any other confederal tax) would ever be adopted by the Confederation. Conflicting state interests were simply too powerful, and could be pursued without any serious cost.

Conclusion

Confederation tax-power proposals fundamentally threatened state sovereignty, opponents claimed. Many Americans familiar with Britain's past controversies over taxation and royal power feared the consequences of changes that would increase central government power. English monarchs had indeed historically sought to control the power to tax in order to thwart Parliament's authority and support royal armies. As federalist taxation opponents repeatedly observed, those kings had sought to combine the purse and the sword.

Their nationalist opponents such as George Washington thought from 1783 onward that the nation needed a more powerful central government, because America's strength and reputation depended on its ability to act in unison. As Washington wrote to the governors of the states, "It is only in our United Character, as an Empire, that our Independance is acknowledged, that our power can be regarded or our Credit supported among foreign Nations."[95] That meant that America needed to be able to finance its national government, including national defense, and to be able to borrow abroad, without being subjected to the vetoes of individual states. It also required that war debts be paid by the nation, not as individual states saw fit. As Connecticut leader Oliver Ellsworth wrote, "There must, sir, be a revenue somehow established that can be relied on and applied for national purposes, as the exigencies arise, independent of the will or views of a single state, or it will be impossible to support national faith, or national existence."[96] To meet these needs required national tax powers.

It was clear by 1786 that Confederation expenses and debts would never be paid unless they were paid through Confederation taxation. The nationalists argued their case largely from that unpleasant necessity. They did not offer a clear alternative theory of government, but instead painted a dark vision of possible disunion and its consequences. They claimed that a more powerful Congress could not possibly impair state powers. But many Americans feared that if Congress became more powerful, it might seek to control the states in the interest of an aristocratic elite or a new king. So on an ideological level, there was no basis for rapprochement. And during 1783 to 1785, in any event, the nationalists' vision of Confederation collapse was not compelling enough to sway opponents.

Once the need to pay war debts nationally was accepted, however, tax opponents had a much weaker practical position. They had to concede that foreign debts must be fully paid and paid in specie, so ultimately they had no choice but to agree that the Confederation should have at least an impost. By 1787, many of its formerly diehard opponents, including Richard Henry Lee, grudgingly accepted that.[97] Some argued that the domestic debt should be divided among the states to avoid Confederation taxation. But there was inadequate support for that alternative throughout the mid-1780s, so Congress never proposed it.

In the final analysis, though, it was the self-interest of the states and their citizens that destroyed the 1783 proposals for Confederation taxation. Many Americans had little desire to pay the Confederation's domestic debts voluntarily. Their state governments understandably would not force them to pay taxes in order to pay debts that popular majorities or even powerful, disruptive minorities were fundamentally opposed to paying. And the state governments themselves were internally divided on tax issues, so that most were incapable of agreeing to provide the Confederation with tax powers sufficient to permit it to pay such debts instead. Nothing in the Confederation's structure required or even encouraged the states' leaders to consider anything other than their individual state's economic and political interests. On that basis, many decided that they would be worse off rather than better off if the Confederation were given tax powers, so they declined to grant them.

Nearly all states approved the three-fifths population-based formula for allocating the supplemental tax, showing that they thought that it was fair. Their unwillingness also to approve the supplemental tax meant that they were effectively declining to pay the domestic debts that it was intended to pay. And the fact that Pennsylvania and New York both effectively declined to authorize even the impost shows that the Confederation, after six years of inconclusive struggle, was incapable of agreeing on any meaningful power to tax. The states would continue to hold the nation's financial future hostage to their individual interests and desires as long as the Confederation survived.

4

Protecting American Commerce in an Imperial World

After the war, America hoped to rebuild its foreign trade, particularly with Great Britain. But the European imperial powers wanted instead to protect their colonial interests and their navies. Even before the 1783 peace treaty was signed, Britain imposed major restrictions on America's trade with its empire. Its action seriously damaged American exporters, shippers, and shipbuilders, especially in New England. Soon new restrictions by France and Spain further harmed trade. Individual states retaliated by imposing import duties and, in a few cases, even by prohibiting foreign nationals' exportation of American goods. Retaliation often backfired. But it had little effect on America's large negative trade balance or on foreign-government policies.

In 1784, Congress requested that states give it trade-retaliation authority. It proposed that Congress have power to prohibit imports and exports, and to protect American shipping. Congress's proposal failed to gain needed approval from all thirteen states. Many thought that it probably would not have worked in any event.

Commerce advocates therefore proposed in 1785 that Congress be given far broader, "radical" powers to regulate and tax both foreign and domestic commerce. That proposal was rejected by Congress and by states that considered similar ideas, largely due to sectional jealousies. In both Massachusetts and Virginia, opponents were fearful that if Congress received such broad powers, their states would be harmed by other sections with conflicting interests. Massachusetts's legislature instead initially advocated a national convention on Confederation reform, but the state's congressional leaders persuaded it to drop its proposal. Virginia's legislature asked states to meet in Annapolis, Maryland, in September 1786 to discuss harmonizing states' trade regulations. That convention was fully attended by only a handful of states. Leaders there concluded that no interstate commerce agreement could be reached without a general convention on Confederation reforms. They called for a convention to be held in Philadelphia in May 1787. Later events would show, however, that that recommendation was not what caused pivotal states to change their positions on the need for Confederation reforms and to attend the Philadelphia Convention.

***

Unless the United States can act as a nation and be regarded as such by foreign powers . . . they can never command reciprocal advantages in trade and without such reciprocity our foreign Commerce must decline and eventually be annihilated.

Congressional committee report, April 1784, supporting Confederation commerce powers[1]

So great is the Jealousy of the States and so excessive their attachment to local and partial interests, that there is no probability of their giving very soon to Congress the necessary powers . . . [to regulate or tax trade]—nothing short of severe sufferings and sad experience will teach them the necessity of doing it.

Stephen Higginson to John Adams, August 1785[2]

Foreign trade was reasonably important to the health and growth of the American postwar economy as a whole, but it was vitally important to America's coastal cities. Together, America's four largest such cities—Boston, New York, Philadelphia, and Charleston—were probably larger in population than Rhode Island and Delaware combined. Their economies—and those of the states and subregions in which they were located—depended very heavily on trade.[3] Their citizens very much hoped to rebuild them.

But the major European empires pursued postwar policies intended to prevent American trade's growth. This chapter emphasizes the ensuing trade controversy with Britain, America's major colonial-era trading partner. What is said about America's response to Britain can, however, apply equally well to its ability to respond effectively to restrictions by other European powers, particularly France and Spain. (Chapters 5 and 6 consider in detail America's response to Spain's efforts to contain American expansion and trade.) The sources suggest that the United States was unable to rebuild its exports fully until at least the early 1790s. Overall, it appears that America's exports were probably more than 24 percent lower in the early 1790s than in 1768–72.[4]

Recent historians have often placed insufficient emphasis on postwar struggles over trade. Some are convinced that commercial regulation was an issue about which everyone agreed; others think state commerce regulations were effective.[5] But contemporary sources support an alternative view. They show that in the mid-1780s, state and sectional interests on significant aspects of commercial policy sharply conflicted. The Confederation's inability to resolve those conflicts made it impossible to respond effectively to severely harmful actions by European powers. They also shed further light on Confederation politics. Leaders in major commercial states opposed their own citizens' demands for effective Confederation commerce powers because they feared the political and economic consequences of such powers.[6]

Imperial Mercantilism and Confederation Trade Diplomacy

At the war's end, most European nations regarded it as normal that both their own borders and their colonies should be closed to foreign trade. In classic mercantilist fashion, they wanted to monopolize trade with their Atlantic colonies, not to face potentially powerful American competition. They thought that American expansion would inevitably harm their economic and military interests. Adam Smith's classic work *The Wealth of Nations* had recently been published. But as of the

1780s, many, perhaps most, European leaders still disagreed with its advocacy of free trade.[7] One European even wrote dismissively, "Dr. Smith, who had never been in trade, could not be expected to write well upon that subject any more than a lawyer upon physick."[8] European empires' willingness to permit foreign trade with their countries and colonies usually depended on their receipt of reciprocal benefits such as military alliances. By European standards, the United States had little military power. Unless it could use power to control economic markets as a bargaining tool, it could not expect to reach significant trade agreements with most major foreign governments. But under the Articles, the Confederation had only very limited powers over commerce.

Despite its limited authority, the Confederation had made efforts to advance American commerce by negotiating trade treaties, beginning during the war. It advocated free trade with low trade barriers, which was then viewed as a revolutionary idea.[9] By the mid-1780s, US diplomats had negotiated trade treaties with France, Sweden, the Netherlands, and Prussia. Several of these were with relatively minor trading partners or had limited effects. One historian concludes that the Prussian treaty, for example, had little effect on the previous pattern of limited trade between the two countries. Congress sought to negotiate a treaty with Portugal that could have led to increased trade, but was unsuccessful. The states sometimes treated American treaties with indifference; Sweden, for example, protested against states' treaty violations.[10]

By early 1786, the list of countries with which treaties had been attempted but failed was a good deal longer than the list of those with whom treaties had been agreed. Many years later, the accomplished diplomat John Quincy Adams described the dismal results of American foreign negotiations: "All the shores of the Black sea, of the whole Mediterranean, of the islands of the African coast, of the southern ports of France, of all Spain, and Portugal, were closed against our commerce, as if they had been hermetically sealed."[11] But while a few European governments were willing to enter commercial treaties with the United

States, the remaining major European powers pursued the opposite course. They sought to restrict American trade. Britain's actions were the most immediately harmful.[12]

Great Britain's Trade Restrictions

On July 2, 1783, two months before the Treaty of Peace was signed, Britain's Privy Council issued an order closing the British West Indies colonies to American ships and sailors. It also barred many major American exports to them.[13] The order was a bruising defeat for John Adams and his fellow peace negotiators. They had earnestly sought inclusion of an agreement permitting American free trade with the British Empire in the final treaty. But it was a triumph for British merchants and imperialists, whose most prominent spokesman was the Earl of Sheffield. Britain's "temerity" came as an "electric shock" to Congress. Many of its members had expected that Britain would agree to open trade.[14]

Prior to the Privy Council's West Indies decision, Lord Sheffield had published a widely disseminated pamphlet advocating restrictions on American trade.[15] James Madison summarized it in an August 1783 letter to Virginia leader Edmund Randolph. He said that Sheffield urged strenuous adherence to the principles of Britain's Navigation Act. That law protected and encouraged Britain's huge merchant marine (and indirectly, its naval power) by requiring that imperial trade be conducted in British ships sailed by British seamen. Sheffield argued that even if Britain restricted American trade, British goods would continue to be preferred in the United States. They met American needs. More importantly, though, British merchants would provide American merchants and consumers with credit to purchase them, while other European countries would not provide credit.[16]

Sheffield then made the pivotal claim that "the interests of the States are so opposite in matters of Commerce," and that the authority of Congress was "so feeble that no defensive precautions need to be feared on the part of the U.S." Finally, he contended that in the unlikely event that retaliation did occur, Britain could respond by imposing further trade restrictions that would destroy the US "carrying" trade (i.e., export shipping). In sum, Sheffield argued that Britain could restrict American trade to further its interests without facing any penalty in lost British trade.

John Adams thought that the Privy Council's order showed that Sheffield's position had prevailed. He wrote to Secretary of Foreign Affairs Robert R. Livingston a few days afterward that "this Proclamation is issued in a full confidence that the United States . . . cannot agree to act in a Body as one Nation."[17] Congress then learned that British prime minister William Pitt, previously thought to be a strong friend of free trade with America, instead strongly supported both the Navigation Act and the Privy Council order.[18] British trade experts feared that permitting any American shipping in British trade would eventually destroy the British merchant marine, leading to "the absolute destruction" of its navy.[19]

This course of events suggested that Britain was unlikely to change its position unless it could be forced to do so. As Adams ultimately concluded, that would depend entirely on whether the United States could develop profitable new trading partners such as France, manufacture goods domestically, or retaliate effectively.[20] Trading and retaliation were by far the two most promising alternatives, despite contemporary debates over, and some steps toward, increased manufacturing.[21]

Historians generally agree that the Privy Council's order hit New England hardest, especially Massachusetts. Exports and related high-value services such as shipping and insurance had historically made up a large, profitable share of the entire New England economy. As historian Forrest McDonald pointed out, the order "almost paralyzed the New England carrying trade." New England was prevented from supplying fish, one of its largest exports, to the British West Indies. Britain also levied a prohibitive duty on American whale oil, another major New England export. Moreover, by the end of 1783, American ships trading in the Mediterranean, many of them from New England, had come under sustained attack by Barbary coast state-sponsored pirates. They seized vessels and enslaved sailors, and held them for ransom or sold them. Together, these actions decimated Massachusetts's and New England's export markets.[22]

Some historians contend that the British West Indies trade restrictions had little or no actual effect because they were circumvented by smuggling.[23] There is no doubt that smuggling occurred, but it is a mistake to overstate its importance. Studies by several historians document substantial decline and dislocation in West Indian trade during this period.[24] Those conclusions are supported by a mid-1785 report by prominent Massachusetts businessman Stephen Higginson to John Adams, attacking British restrictions and suggesting that they were primarily responsible for depressed conditions in the Massachusetts fishery.[25]

New England was able to develop some replacement markets during the 1780s, but British restrictions hurt both its exports and shipbuilding. In 1785, Massachusetts had fifteen vessels engaged in whaling, a 90 percent decline from the period just before the war. Its fleet declined by two-thirds between 1775 and 1789.[26] In 1785, Massachusetts built 15 or 20 ships, as opposed to 125 per year in the 1770s.[27] Employment in the Massachusetts cod fishery during 1786–90 declined 25 percent from prewar average levels, a loss of more than one thousand jobs.[28] During the period 1785–87, 97 percent of the fish imported by the British West Indies came from Britain's Canadian colonies instead.[29] Throughout the Confederation's postwar life, Massachusetts artisans, merchants, and political leaders were at the forefront of vigorous, repeated efforts to encourage commerce by political means. If American smuggling to the West Indies had been widely successful, there would clearly have been far less political impetus than there was in New England to obtain or exercise retaliatory trade powers.

Other states felt the effects of the British West Indies restrictions as well. In mid-1785, Virginia planter Ralph Wormeley, Jr., complained to a London businessman that "the restrictions on the West India trade are very injurious to us."[30] A newspaper account published in Richmond, Virginia, in August 1785 concluded, "Various accounts from the West India islands cannot leave a doubt of their determination rigorously to abide by their navigation system. Our trade feels the effects of these illiberal measures."[31] British and French trade restrictions affected the Mid-Atlantic states as well. In November 1785, Philadelphia's leading merchant Henry Drinker and a fellow trustee wrote to London merchant Frederick Pigou that they could not remember any time during their thirty years in business when conditions had been as bad. They reported that Philadelphia had almost completely lost its shipbuilding business and carrying trade. In 1786, only thirteen ships were built in Philadelphia.[32] Still, there would be limited support in other parts of the country for some of New England's more ambitious goals to advance commerce through political means, primarily due to sectional conflicts.

As contemporaries understood quite well, New England had interests in trade far different from those of the rest of the country, particularly the southern states. New England's major exports, such as fish, whale products, and livestock, had little overlap with other regions' exports. More importantly, it dominated American prewar shipping and shipbuilding. One leading Massachusetts politician described the "carrying Trade" as being of "vast essential consequence to the United States, & of the last [i.e., utmost importance] to New England."[33] New Englanders wanted these activities protected against foreign competition. Some advocated their protection through an American version of the British Navigation Act, that is, a law requiring American international trade goods to be shipped in American-owned bottoms.

Prominent Massachusetts leaders such as retired general James Warren worried that "other states will be indifferent" to the damage to "the Transport Trade." Warren thought that southern exporters had interests that conflicted with New England's, because they would prefer to use the cheapest shipping to get their goods to market. They would want free competition, not navigation-act protection.[34] Many southern state leaders, such as Richard Henry Lee of Virginia and James McHenry of Maryland, shared Warren's view that sectional interests conflicted.[35] As chapter 1 showed, southern states' markets for major products such as rice remained seriously depressed, indicating that they had not developed successful replacement markets. In the circumstances, they had little incentive to support protection for New England shipping.

There were also reasons why after the war some Americans opposed any growth of American commerce. Some were opposed to the growth of commerce itself. Many believed that increased commerce would allow the spread of luxury, which they thought inevitably corrupted republican virtue. Others saw it as harmful to domestic manufacturing. Some opposed it because they believed that trade caused money scarcity. Others thought merchants were greedy, unpatriotic monopolists. Indeed, Robert Morris, one of America's most capable merchants, believed that "a merchant, as such, can be attached particularly to no country." Finally, many farmers did not produce primarily for export markets. Particularly if they farmed for subsistence, as many did, they had only an indirect interest at best in protecting or expanding them. But as historian Merrill Jensen observes, economic realities prevailed.[36]

Congress's 1784 Trade Proposal

By late 1783, prompted in part by Britain's restrictions, Congress had considered America's international trade situation. A committee reported that France and Great Britain "hath discovered the utmost jealousy of the commercial Prosperity of America." In a clear-eyed assessment of political realities, its report added, "It is clearly not the interest of any maritime European Power, to promote rapidly our encrease in numbers and in wealth." It proposed that Congress create a committee to consider retaliatory legislation.[37]

In April 1784, Congress proposed that the states grant the Confederation economic market powers to enable the United States to retaliate against foreign countries that refused US citizens access to their markets.[38] In support of its proposal, it argued that "unless the United States can act as a nation and be regarded as such by foreign powers . . . they can never command reciprocal advantages in trade and without such reciprocity our foreign Commerce must decline and eventually be annihilated."[39] As Congress's statement reflected, in the imperial world of the 1780s, international trade was regarded as a matter of strategic national concern, not as private enterprise whose conduct should be left to free markets.

Congress proposed that the states grant it authority for fifteen years to prohibit the importation or exportation of goods in ships owned by foreign nationals, unless their country had a commercial treaty with the United States. It also proposed that foreign nationals be prohibited from importing goods to the United States from countries other than their own, unless their country had a treaty with the United States. These powers had the potential to protect both America's export-import trade and its shipping industry. Neither of them could be exercised with the consent of less than nine states. Thus, any significant group of states, or even one section of the country, could block their use. Congress's proposal faced two important obstacles.

The first hurdle was that many merchants and state leaders quickly concluded that Congress's proposals were too weak to work. They were powers only to prohibit, not to regulate. Flat prohibitions were blunt instruments; Congress might be unwilling to use them. The omission of regulatory power caused most people to think that Congress was unable to tax imports or exports. Even more importantly, states were not prevented from taxing or regulating them.

While Congress would continue to approve future trade treaties, merchants and foreign governments alike recognized that under the Articles it had no power to force states to implement them. The 1784 proposals would not have changed that. States could frustrate Confederation trade treaties by imposing prohibitively high taxes on imported or exported goods. In the mid-1780s, the states had differing import-export profiles and potential foreign markets. They had little incentive to engage in uniform taxation or to avoid protectionism. Why, for example, should South Carolina agree to protect Pennsylvania manufactures? Why should New York promote South Carolina's indigo exports?[40] The overarching problem facing Congress was very similar to its problem with Confederation requisitions: it had no authority to enforce its decisions, and states had positive incentives not to cooperate voluntarily. That led to a movement seeking far more comprehensive commerce powers for Congress, which will be discussed shortly.[41]

The second hurdle facing the 1784 proposals was doubt that they would be adopted by all thirteen states. If not, as Massachusetts state legislator Tristram Dalton wrote to John Adams, "the court of G. Britain may look on the Confederation as a rope of sand" that could not enforce restrictions.[42] By mid-1785, Massachusetts businessman Stephen Higginson reported to Adams that "so great is the Jealousy of the States and so excessive their attachment to local and partial interests, that there is no probability of their giving very soon to Congress the necessary powers . . . [to regulate or tax trade]—nothing short of severe sufferings and sad experience will teach them the necessity of doing it."[43]

By the spring of 1786, Congress's 1784 proposals had been adopted by a slim majority of states. Four states had adopted them as proposed, while three others had adopted them with problematic duration limits. Two others had declined to permit Congress to regulate exports. Another state had conferred much broader powers than requested but suspended them until all states agreed to such powers, which was highly unlikely ever to occur. In 1786, Congress renewed its plea to the states to adopt these proposals. Several responded favorably, but they were not adopted unanimously by the states as required to become effective.[44]

State Efforts to Control Trade

In the absence of Confederation commerce powers, individual states undertook varying forms of trade regulation. Some imposed import duties, and some of them were discriminatorily higher on British shipping, goods, or both. As we saw in chapter 3, import duties were so politically appealing that some states used the revenues to fund a major part of their state government budgets. But while such import duties were "profitable" to the states that imposed them, they often were costly to citizens of other states. A substantial part of New York's impost revenues came from citizens of Connecticut and New Jersey, who received no discernible benefits in return. Rhode Island's and Virginia's import duties similarly beggared their neighbors. But these self-interested policies achieved no significant change in British trade policy or improvement in America's massive negative balance of trade with Britain.[45]

Some states also imposed import duties in order to protect local industries rather than merely for revenue. Historian Allan Nevins concludes that by the mid-1780s, states in nearly the entire northern half of the Confederation imposed significant protective duties. Massachusetts imposed some tariff rates as high as 25 percent, and passed a 1786 law that banned the importation of fifty-eight separate articles. Pennsylvania passed a protective tariff that contained rates as high as 19 percent, and included special protections for refined-iron manufacturers, shipbuilders, and joiners. These tariff laws often also applied to goods imported from other states. Then as now, not everyone was happy about high duties that protected politically influential businesses at the expense of merchants and consumers. But although both domestic and foreign merchants complained about them, their imposition did nothing of substance to alter the trade policies of European powers.[46]

New European Imperial Trade Restrictions and Barbary Coast Piracy

Instead, by 1785 several foreign countries had actually increased restrictions on American trade. In June 1784, America's former ally Spain announced that it had an exclusive right to control navigation of the Mississippi River. It would be closed to thousands of Americans who wanted to use it to export goods unless and until a suitable treaty with Spain was negotiated. Spain's restrictions seriously threatened western expansion and outraged many Americans, causing enormous political harm to the Confederation itself (discussed in chapter 6).[47]

France imposed major new commerce restrictions as well. In 1784, it barred major American exports such as wheat and flour to the French

Caribbean, and prohibited Americans from importing those colonies' major products, such as sugar. Those restrictions were especially harmful to the Mid-Atlantic states such as Pennsylvania because they affected key exports. In 1785, France granted large bounties to French subjects who shipped codfish into the French West Indies or major European ports. It imposed taxes on codfish imported by foreign subjects. These restrictions gave substantial advantages to French competition against New England. John Adams said that he thought France deserved to be retaliated against for its trade restrictions just as much as Great Britain. Congressman Elbridge Gerry wrote to a colleague that "France has been evidently averse to our being powerful by land or sea, and this edict strikes at the foundation of our naval establishment." Meanwhile, despite American minister Thomas Jefferson's efforts to liberalize trade, France continued to insist on buying American tobacco through a French monopoly, depressing tobacco prices.[48] Neither Confederation actions nor state protectionism had any discernible influence on the colonialist policies of France and Spain.

The Barbary coast pirates continued their attacks on American shipping and seamen. America made futile diplomatic efforts to persuade European countries to join them in combating piracy. Benjamin Franklin wrote to Robert R. Livingston that in London he had heard a cynical merchants' maxim that "*if there were no Algiers* [a major pirate base] *it would be worth Englands while to build one*" to prevent American competition.[49] Congress rejected as impractical Jefferson's proposal that America declare war on the pirates.

Congress eventually realized that the United States would have to come to terms with the pirate states or give up Mediterranean trade. That meant it would have to pay large tributes, as other countries including Britain did. Congressman William Grayson of Virginia described the $80,000 an insolvent Congress authorized for tribute as "Contemptable," but it had no way to raise more. Most Barbary coast piracy continued. Faced with growing restrictions, American commercial interests sought more aggressive political action.[50]

"Radical" Commerce-Power Proposals, Sectional Conflicts, and Taxation

Recognizing that Congress's 1784 proposals were unworkable, supporters of strengthened Confederation commerce powers began developing a far stronger proposal in late 1784. It granted Congress perpetual power over all foreign and domestic interstate commerce (exports as well as imports), and the power to prohibit, regulate, or tax such commerce. In an important concession to states, the proposal provided that any tax would be collected by and accrue to the use of the state in which it was payable. As originally proposed, such powers could have been exercised only with the consent of at least nine states (later versions required eleven states' consent, a sure sign of sponsors' political desperation).[51]

That far-reaching proposal is referred to for convenience as the Monroe proposal, because one of its most prominent advocates was Virginia congressman James Monroe. Monroe recognized that his proposal was a dramatic increase in Congress's powers, a "radical change" "in the whole system of our government." Monroe wrote Thomas Jefferson that it would "put the commercial OEconomy of every state intirely under the hands of the union."[52] An accompanying report was presented to Congress in March 1785. It argued that permitting individual states to act through taxation and regulation would make it impossible for Congress to negotiate effective treaties. And it made it clear that one of the main purposes for which Congress sought powers was to enable it to protect the American carrying trade, which it contended was a national asset.[53] Not surprisingly, the proposal ran into a buzz saw of opposition.

When the Monroe proposal was debated in Congress in July, the principal opposition came from the southern states. Congress's ability to protect the carrying trade became the main bone of contention. Virginia congressman Richard Henry Lee was the main opposition spokesman. Monroe later summarized Lee's arguments: (1) It was dangerous to liberty and national security to concentrate power as this proposal did. (2) Different sections had conflicting interests. In particular, eight northern states would act together to protect American shipping, which would "shackle and fetter the others" (i.e., the five southern states) by preventing competition. (3) All attacks on the Confederation's existing structure were dangerous, and would weaken it.[54]

The possibility of much stronger commerce powers also raised concerns in areas other than the South. Monroe himself seems to have recognized that the dramatically larger powers conferred by the proposal frightened even the "Eastern people" who stood to benefit most from it.[55] An example of these concerns is found in the May 1785 letter from Samuel Bryan to his father George Bryan, a leading Pennsylvania judge and Constitutionalist Party politician. Bryan wrote that there was general sentiment in favor of commercial regulation in Pennsylvania. A report that a London ship that had been turned away from Boston was "in the River" had "raised a great ferment among the Mechanicks and indeed the Merchants [seem?] to have caught a spark of the patriotic flame which has ever been kindled in New England." Bryan said that Congress "undoubtedly" ought to have "efficient powers for the regulation of Commerce."[56]

However, Bryan was apparently concerned that proposals like Monroe's would completely destroy state authority. He wrote, "The difficulty is, how to regulate such powers with the individual importance of the several States to prevent Congress in that event absorbing all power and influence within their vortex." Pennsylvania never adopted legislation similar to the Monroe proposal. Bryan's letter contains his own commerce-power proposal, though, which shows he accepted that to be effective, Confederation commerce powers needed to include the power to impose import taxes.[57]

For better or worse, by mid-1785, the debate over commerce powers had become increasingly linked to the debate over trade taxation. Several states were concerned that even Congress's original 1784 proposals might be interpreted to encompass the power to tax imports. New York approved those proposals in April 1785, but made any duties imposed by Congress or revenue collected in New York subject to the state's approval.[58] New Jersey, on the other hand, made such revenues available to the Confederation to pay its debts.[59] The resistance to Monroe's proposal during congressional debate persuaded him that it might be defeated or damaged in Congress. He recommended that supporters instead seek to have it adopted by the state legislatures. It is illuminating to see how that recommendation fared, beginning with developments in Massachusetts.

Commerce Powers and Confederation Politics

As of May 1785, economic conditions in Massachusetts were dismal. To protect jobs, artisans there organized to seek trade protection from the legislature for domestic goods such as shoes. Manufacturers of twenty types of goods also met and resolved to seek protection. And agitated merchants began a vigorous campaign to get Massachusetts and other states to take action to improve conditions by granting new Confederation commerce powers or by tougher state legislation. These groups coalesced in support of each other's efforts.[60] By then, John Adams had lost hope that there would be a British commercial treaty in the absence of unified American action.[61]

Massachusetts politicians responded to the increasing agitation for commerce legislation in two ways. First, the legislature passed the most draconian trade legislation adopted by any state. Its state navigation act barred ships not just from England but from all foreign countries from exporting goods from Massachusetts. It was accompanied by new discriminatory, and in some cases prohibitively high, duties on a long list of foreign goods and foreign vessels.[62] State leaders and citizens were optimistic that other states would join what they saw as their patriotic efforts.

However, Massachusetts soon discovered to its dismay that despite stirring rhetoric, few states were actually willing to follow its lead. Instead, vessels that could not or did not want to enter Massachusetts under its new laws simply entered other American ports. Only two other states, both in New England, adopted legislation similar to Massachusetts's navigation law. They repealed or suspended it by mid-1786. By then, Massachusetts was willing to give up the fight. It suspended its retaliatory law until all other states adopted similar legislation, which was virtually certain never to happen. Massachusetts governor James Bowdoin wrote to Governor Nicholas Van Dyke of Delaware in July 1786 informing him of Massachusetts's suspension and complaining bitterly that other unnamed states had taken advantage of Massachusetts's efforts.[63] As Massachusetts's experience shows, individual state retaliation could not be effective because it was in the interest of other states to undercut it and reap the benefits of the trade lost by the state engaging in retaliation. As one historian concluded, "It appeared that the British were correct in assuming that their policy was secure because of the 'Interference of Commercial Interests among the States, and mutual jealousy arising therefrom.'"[64]

But the Massachusetts legislature was not content just to adopt new commerce regulations. It wrote to its congressional delegation in mid-1785 instructing them to seek Congress's support for a general convention for Confederation reform. The legislature—or, at least, its promerchant majority led by Governor James Bowdoin—seemed to think that a general convention was necessary in order to gain agreement on strong federal commerce powers. Such a convention would, of course, bypass Congress, which had been unwilling to adopt the Monroe proposal. Remarkably, however, after several months delay, the Massachusetts congressional delegation objected to the legislature's instructions.

In early September 1785, its members asked the legislature to reconsider what the delegation strongly implied was a dangerously misguided proposal. The delegation—led by Elbridge Gerry, and including Rufus King and Samuel Holten—shared federalist views on many issues. They began by arguing that if any new Confederation commerce powers were desirable, the Monroe proposal was not acceptable because it was perpetual. They contended at tedious length that temporary powers could be tested by experience, but that perpetual powers could only be revoked by unanimous consent. They were therefore especially dangerous incursions on state power.[65] And then the delegation dropped a bombshell on the legislature.

The delegation argued that holding a general convention would be likely to lead to an aristocratic takeover of the Confederation. They began by challenging the idea that a convention could ever be a desirable means of altering the Confederation, because it would bypass Congress. Next, they argued that earlier there had been "artfully laid" plans that were "vigorously pursued," "which had they been successful, We think, would inevitably have changed our republican Governments, into baleful aristocracies." The government sought by the aristocrats "will afford lucrative Employments, civil & military. Such a government is an Aristocracy, which would require a standing Army, & a numerous train of pensioners & placemen to prop & support its exalted Administration."[66] As we have seen, Gerry and other Massachusetts leaders such as Samuel Osgood had strenuously opposed both proposals for many types of Confederation tax powers and proposals for a standing army, which they thought that such tax powers would both support and require. It is apparent that the delegation's letter was referring to such nationalist proposals and condemning them as the primary goals of aristocratic government that would inevitably result from a general convention.[67]

In a letter to incoming Massachusetts congressman Nathan Dane, Rufus King spelled out the basis for the delegation's concerns about the legislature's general convention proposal. A general convention would result in "a confederation less republican than the present one. The larger States when the present Confederation was adopted, objected to the admission of the smaller ones upon equal rights with themselves." The "surrounding dangers at that period" convinced them to give up their objections. "But at this time, was the question again open to decision, the same objections would be made, the real inconvenience experienced, and the increasing principles of aristocracy, would strengthen them, and I think we should by the measure be thrown into total disunion."[68] Later, King wrote to prominent merchant and Massachusetts leader Caleb Davis that if the states were given authority to generally revise the Confederation, "farwel to the perfect Republican plan."[69]

The Massachusetts delegation seems to have believed that maintaining the Articles' rule for equal state voting in Congress was essential to preserving republicanism at both the state and national levels. In their view, a general convention would almost certainly change that rule, and doing so would permit aristocratic forces—a combination of southern state aristocrats and their allies in the Mid-Atlantic states, such as Robert Morris—to take majority control of the Confederation government. The aristocrats would use that control to transform the government in fundamental ways that would harm the states and destroy republican liberty. In sum, as of late 1785, Massachusetts federalists thought that although granting the Confederation commerce powers would be desirable, it was not desirable enough to grant permanent Confederation powers or to obtain broad powers through a convention that would inevitably open the door to oppressive "aristocratic" government.

After receiving the delegation's letter, the legislature reversed itself and dropped its call for a general convention in late 1785. However, its request for a general convention was reported in newspapers around the country.[70] For the time being, Massachusetts was content to let state legislation be the only means of combatting British trade restrictions. But southern resistance to the Monroe proposal was so frustrating to Rufus King that he began privately to advocate the formation of a separate northern sub-Confederation for commerce as the only remedy for economic distress there.

In July, King wrote to a close friend in Massachusetts, Daniel Kilham, that the southern states were convinced that free trade, including unregulated shipping, was the best policy for them. He continued, "The eastern states will consent to vest powers in Congress competent to a regulation of foreign commerce, but the southern states will never consent to regulations which will effect what the northern States desire."[71] By November, he wrote to John Adams that the "Eight Eastern states" "*are competent* to form, and in the event must form, a sub confederation remedial of all their present Embarrassments" if the "southern states" "*decline*" to vest "adequate powers on Congress to regulate external and internal commerce." In King's view, such a sub-Confederation would "rely upon her own ships, and her own mariners, to exclude those of all other nations."[72] He thought, in other words, that to avoid southern states' objections, northern states should confederate and adopt a navigation act to protect New England's carrying trade against competition.

The Monroe proposal also led to a very significant exchange of correspondence between George Washington and one of his closest wartime aides, James McHenry. McHenry, now a Maryland congressman, had written to Washington in early August 1785, decrying Monroe's proposal as damaging to the southern states. Washington's response captures exceptionally well his strongly majoritarian views of decision making in the national interest. It contrasts sharply with McHenry's (and the Massachusetts delegation's) restrictive positions based on state and sectional interests.

Washington wrote that if some states benefited more from commercial regulation than others, that concern "applies to every matter of general utility." He continued, "We are either a United people under one head, & for Foederal purposes, or, we are thirteen independent sovereignties, eternally counteracting each other. If the former, whatever such a Majority of the States, as the Constitution requires, conceives to be for the benefit of the whole, should, in my humble opinion, be submitted to by the Minority." Continual attention to differences of interest between states and sections caused "unreasonable jealousies . . . which are continually poisoning our minds, and filling them with imaginary evils" that could lead to disunion. He thought that it was unlikely that the northern states would permanently monopolize the carrying trade. But if they did, that would be a price worth paying, since to deprive Congress of needed commerce powers would be to "stand . . . in a ridiculous point of view in the eyes of the Nations of the Earth; with whom we are attempting to enter into Commercial Treaties without means of carrying them into effect. . . . In a word we are one Nation today, & thirteen tomorrow—Who will treat with us on such terms?"[73] Washington strongly favored the national-government unity and power afforded by deciding commerce issues by majority rule, despite possible costs to minorities. But a majority of Virginia's elected leaders strongly disagreed with his views.

In October 1785, a drama similar to that in Massachusetts was played out in Virginia. When the Virginia legislature met, James Madison asked the legislature to support a much stronger federal commerce power. The legislature had received petitions from Virginia's major port cities complaining of poor commerce conditions and demanding action by the legislature, so there was some public support for reform. The legislature began by debating whether it should try to remedy commercial problems through purely state means such as a navigation act like that of Massachusetts. After debate, it concluded that new federal powers were needed instead, and authorized a committee to propose them.[74]

The committee's proposals were limited to foreign commerce. It proposed that Congress be empowered to prohibit or tax vessels and cargoes from countries that had no trade treaty with the United States. Such duties would be for the benefit of a state. It proposed that the duties include Congress's proposed 5 percent impost, thus linking commerce regulation and Confederation taxation. And it proposed that no state be able to impose duties on merchandise imported from another state. However, any action by Congress would require consent of at least two-thirds of the states, and Congress's power would be limited to a term of years, not perpetual.[75]

As the legislature considered the report, however, it dropped the authorization for import duties to include the 5 percent impost. According to James Madison, at first the rest of the committee proposal was opposed on its general merits, including attacks on protection of the carrying trade. Several legislators suggested that it would be better to encourage British shipping than the "eastern marine."[76] But opponents then realized that it would be easier to defeat the proposal entirely by limiting the powers' duration, and they proposed a thirteen-year limit. Supporters, who had sought perpetual powers for Congress, were so disheartened by the legislature's willingness to limit the term to thirteen years that they abandoned the proposal completely. Richard Henry Lee's views had triumphed.

Madison later defended supporters' abandonment decision in a letter to George Washington. He wrote, "I think it better to trust to further experience and even distress, for an adequate remedy, than to try a temporary measure which may stand in the way of a permanent one."[77] Opponents had persuaded the legislature that temporary powers would be sufficient because they could be renewed if they were working. In effect, the Virginia legislature took the same position as the Massachusetts congressional delegation: permanent Confederation commerce powers were unacceptably dangerous to the states.

Madison thought that the opponents' true position was that no effective commerce powers should be granted to the Confederation. He bitterly told Washington, "And as to the hope of renewal, it is the most visionary one that perhaps ever deluded men of sense. Nothing but the peculiarity of our circumstances could ever have produced those sacrifices of sovereignty on which the foederal Government now rests. If they had been temporary, and . . . required a renewal at this crisis, pressing as the crisis is, and recent as is our experience of the value of the confederacy, sure I am that it would be impossible to revive it."[78] As we have seen, Madison's views were amply confirmed by rampant state noncompliance with Congress's decisions under its existing treaty and requisition powers. State leaders' opposition to making commerce powers perpetual was, in reality, a pretext for opposition to conferring effective commerce powers on the Confederation at all.

However, the Virginia legislature's majority still apparently wanted to be seen as taking some action on commerce. Virginians were aware from news reports that Massachusetts had asked its congressional delegates to support a general convention for Confederation reform.[79] Virginia legislator John Tyler proposed a narrower plan instead. He moved that Virginia invite the other states to send commissioners to meet in convention in Annapolis in September 1786 to discuss "the trade of the states . . . and consider . . . a uniform system in their regulations." James

Madison later explained to James Monroe that the legislature would have "revolted" against giving broader powers than that to its Annapolis delegates.[80] The legislature adopted Tyler's proposal, which led to what is usually called the Annapolis Convention.

Thus, as of early 1786, both Massachusetts and Virginia had rejected granting any Confederation commerce powers beyond Congress's ineffectual 1784 proposals. Supporters of stronger federal powers had been defeated by state leaders concerned that adopting such proposals would lead to permanent Confederation changes that they deemed unacceptable. Those leaders preferred to support what Madison thought were unworkable temporary powers instead, giving themselves a political fig leaf but blocking real change.

The Annapolis Convention

The Annapolis Convention met from September 12 to 14, 1786, to discuss commerce issues. The brief meeting reached no agreement except to recommend that a general constitutional convention be held in Philadelphia in May 1787. Notably, that recommendation was made before news of court blockages by Shaysite insurgents in Massachusetts reached Annapolis, so the revolt did not cause or influence it.[81]

The Annapolis Convention has served many historians as the endpoint of a superficially plausible "historical genealogy" for the 1787 Philadelphia Convention. They observe that Virginia and Maryland had successfully negotiated an agreement about their respective rights in the Potomac River through an interstate convention. As a result, they claim, the proposal for an Annapolis convention seemed like a natural extension of interstate commerce negotiations. When the Annapolis Convention met, its members supposedly suddenly realized that it wasn't possible to resolve commerce issues without reaching agreement on a wide range of other issues, so instead they proposed holding the Philadelphia general convention. Since that recommendation in turn seemed to be a "natural" extension of the interstate negotiation process, the states agreed to it, so the story goes. That genealogy is a convenient but misleading historical fiction. Here is what the sources show about the Annapolis Convention and its influence.[82]

After receiving Virginia's invitation to attend the Annapolis Convention, states had at least six months to decide whether to attend and make arrangements. But it turned out to be a "rump" convention, fully attended by only three states and by unofficial observers from two others that lacked a delegate quorum.[83] A total of twelve delegates attended. Several of them were distinguished men, including Alexander Hamilton, John Dickinson, and Edmund Randolph. But no one from the New England states, or from the southern states (including Maryland, the host state) except Virginia, attended. There were contemporaneous claims that northern state delegates who missed the meeting had "tarried several days at New York, in order to retard their arrival."[84] One historian concludes that "those opposed to increased federal power had boycotted the meeting."[85] The remarkably poor attendance strongly suggests that few states had any real interest in trying to reach interstate agreements on commercial issues, at least in isolation from other issues.[86]

The Annapolis commissioners also reached a conclusion that was completely predictable before they ever met. It was that national agreement on commerce issues could not be separated from agreement on other major unresolved Confederation issues, including most particularly Congress's taxation powers. That was not a new conclusion: the intimate connection between commerce regulation and taxation had already become apparent to many people during state and congressional debates over federal commerce powers throughout 1785–86. The debates in the Virginia legislature showed that supporters of stronger federal commerce powers wanted to link them to Confederation taxation powers. Meanwhile, the Massachusetts delegation had opposed a national convention precisely because they thought it might open up core Confederation issues such as state representation and voting in Congress.

Under these circumstances, the Annapolis Convention's recommendation cannot in any meaningful sense have "caused" twelve states to agree to attend the Philadelphia Convention in May 1787, and it was not the reason that they decided to do so. The timing of the Annapolis recommendation was a coincidence, as we will see when we discuss in chapter 9 why the states actually chose to organize and attend the Philadelphia Convention. In fact, many states' leaders had clearly had serious misgivings about the Annapolis Convention before it ever began.

From the beginning, convention preparations were dogged by suspicions about its sponsors' intent. Ironically, James Madison was widely believed to have been behind the proposed convention. Yet there is reason to believe that it was not Madison's idea and that he was unenthusiastic at best about it. Despite that, Massachusetts merchant Stephen Higginson wrote to John Adams in July 1786 that considering "the source from whence the proposition was made, I am strong to think political Objects are intended to be combined with commercial." After listing the attendees he knew of, including Madison and Robert Morris, Higginson said, "The Men I have mentioned are all of them esteemed great Aristocrats." His derogatory language implied that federalist Massachusetts leaders should not agree to any proposals such men might make.[87]

Still another new Massachusetts congressman, Theodore Sedgwick, insisted to another Massachusetts leader that the purpose of the Annapolis Convention was to prevent a grant of strong Confederation commerce powers: "Of this I have the most decisive evidence." Rufus King agreed that "this is certain, that" the Annapolis Convention proposal came "from those, who in Opposition to" Confederation powers "have advocated the particular Regulations of individual states."[88] Sedgwick was so unhappy with what he saw as the southern states' unwillingness to grant needed commerce powers that he wrote to prominent Massachusetts attorney Caleb Strong that the northern states should seriously consider breaking completely with the southern states and setting up a separate general confederation (not one limited to commercial issues).[89] On the other hand, Massachusetts merchant Nathaniel Gorham, a strong nationalist who had recently become a Massachusetts congressman, urged state leader Caleb Davis to ensure that "men of good Federal ideas" (by which Gorham meant men interested in increasing Confederation powers, not federalists) were appointed to attend the convention.[90]

Meanwhile, Congressman William Grayson of Virginia strongly cautioned Madison months before the Annapolis Convention met against reaching any agreement with Massachusetts there. He explained that if Massachusetts got a commerce-power agreement that satisfied it, it would not agree to any other Confederation reforms.[91] Grayson's comments are very illuminating. They accurately portrayed the Massachusetts congressional delegations' actual posture. And they made clear that Virginia's congressmen had other Confederation reforms such as taxation powers in mind, as indeed Virginia's past and future conduct would show that they did. Madison himself acknowledged that "many Gentlemen both within & without Congs. wish to make" the Annapolis meeting "subservient to a Plenipotentiary Convention for amending the Confederation." But in August 1786, Madison did not think that that was possible, even though he favored the idea.[92]

After the Annapolis Convention's conclusion, French interim chargé d'affaires in the United States Louis-Guillaume Otto reported to French foreign minister Vergennes that it had been a pure pretext. It had been created as a surreptitious device by merchants in order to gain support for a new national government with "powers extensive enough to compel the people to contribute" taxes for the purpose of paying its debts. The Annapolis Convention's sponsors expected it to fail: "The authors of this proposition had no hope, nor even desire, to see the success of this assembly of commissioners, which was only intended to prepare a question much more important than that of commerce."[93] Otto may well have been wrong about the pretextual nature of the convention, and offered no evidence for his view. But he did have a very accurate perception of the political goals behind the Annapolis Convention's recommendation.

As Otto pointed out, the Annapolis commissioners

> employ an infinity of circumlocutions and ambiguous phrases to show to their constituents the impossibility of taking into consideration a general plan of commerce and the powers pertaining thereto, without at the same time touching upon other objects closely connected with the prosperity and national importance of the United States. . . . In spite of the obscurity of this document, you will perceive, my lord, that the commissioners were unwilling to take into consideration the grievances of commerce, which are of exceeding interest for the people, without at the same time perfecting the fundamental constitution of congress.[94]

The Annapolis Convention's position was that since commerce issues could not be resolved without addressing other national issues, a general reform convention should be held. That recommendation was the nationalist response to federalist unwillingness to open the Confederation to general reform by means of a convention. A convention would occur outside of Congress, which by September 1786 was quite evidently incapable of reaching agreement on reforms. But the Annapolis recommendation also was the opposite of the position taken about a year before by both the Massachusetts and Virginia legislatures. Their majorities were unwilling to advance commerce powers if that risked limiting state powers. Not surprisingly, Massachusetts congressmen Rufus King and Nathan Dane blocked the adoption of the Annapolis recommendation in Congress, and then went to Massachusetts and opposed its adoption there (see chapter 9).[95]

Remarkably, despite that, both Virginia and Massachusetts soon accepted the Annapolis recommendation and sent delegations to Philadelphia in May 1787. The willingness of these two influential states—main pillars of the revolution—to participate at Philadelphia was essential to that convention's success. The question is why their leaders changed their minds, and decided to take the large risk of wholesale Confederation reform after rejecting it as unacceptable at the end of 1785. We can answer it only by considering other developments, including the intense political strains caused by western expansion and 1780s popular reform movements. These are the subjects of subsequent chapters.

Conclusion

Under the Confederation, the United States was utterly incapable of protecting American commerce in an imperial world. Despite concerted efforts, both the Confederation and individual states proved unable to take any meaningful steps to combat trade restrictions by Britain and other European powers, or to end the outrages perpetrated by the Barbary pirates. Yet major states such as Virginia and Massachusetts proved unwilling to give the Confederation the powers needed to permit it to take effective action because they feared the effects of Confederation reform on the powers of their states and the liberties of their citizens. Their citizens' confidence in the wisdom of maintaining their states' sovereignty by keeping the Confederation weak would soon be sorely tested.

PART 2

Western Expansion Strains

5
"Astonishing" Emigrations and Western Conflicts

The Treaty of Peace opened a massive territory between the Appalachians and the Mississippi to American settlement. Thousands of new settlers surged west every year. But conflicting claims to the West had to be resolved before settlement could occur peacefully. It had long been occupied by Native Americans. Several states had large western land claims that conflicted with US claims.

The Confederation created the national domain. But it then failed to control or benefit from its settlement, often paralyzed by sectional disputes. In treaties, Native Americans yielded much of the Ohio River valley, but several tribes later repudiated the treaties. Congress attempted to limit settlement. But to leaders' dismay, it accelerated. When settlers violated Indian tribes' rights, the Confederation was unable to respond effectively.

The Confederation's western land sales yielded little revenue. It failed to agree on any workable territorial government system until after the 1787 Philadelphia Convention began. It provided settlers with scant protection against Indian attacks. Spain and Britain provided some tribes with secret aid to resist settlers' encroachments. Britain continued to hold its strategically important western forts. Many westerners seriously considered secession from their states and the Union.

By 1786, Virginia governor Patrick Henry was complaining bitterly about Congress's failure to protect its Kentucky settlers against Indian "Murders and Depredations." Congress refused Virginia's request for military aid there, primarily because of sectional disagreements. Virginia went to war against the Wabash and other tribes in Ohio. By the end of the year, a widespread western Indian uprising forced Congress to triple the army's size. But it had no money to pay the new troops, and its efforts to raise money failed.

Confederation weakness in the face of Indian attacks and British policy supporting tribes' resistance to expansion led to profound changes in Virginia public opinion. Many western Virginia citizens moved toward support for a markedly strengthened Confederation government.

***

People feel that things do not go well. . . . The principal [reason], I take to be the rage for emigration & the establishment of new States. The consequence is, that the old ones are in a fluctuating situation . . . the imposition of taxes becomes difficult, the collection desultory, & the produce precarious.

Virginia leader Arthur Lee to John Adams, March 1785[1]

The lawless . . . conduct of the inhabitants of Kentuckey towards the Indians . . . [west of] the Ohio, has lately occasioned the loss of a number of valuable lives. . . . The Governor & Delegates of Virginia clamour for war against the Indian Towns . . . I am decidedly against any such war . . . at present.

Massachusetts congressman Rufus King to Elbridge Gerry, June 1786[2]

The Flood of Western Settlement and Its Effects

The peace treaty's opening of the West led Yale College president Ezra Stiles to predict confidently that America would create an empire there. Fifty million Americans would people the continent from the Atlantic to the Mississippi within a century, he claimed. Stiles's bold prediction soon received apparent support from what leaders and foreign observers agreed was an "astonishing" westward emigration. It flowed "from all parts of the continent" during the mid-1780s toward "these happy countries."[3] Western population grew about two to four times as fast as America's total population between 1783 and 1790. By 1786, a newspaper account estimated that there were more than thirty thousand settlers in Kentucky alone. The writer reported that thirty-four boats had arrived at Fort Finney on the Ohio River with at least one thousand new settlers headed to Kentucky within a forty-day period; many others were coming there "through the wilderness from Virginia." He concluded, "It will be as practicable to turn a torrent of water backward, as to prevent the amazing emigration to this country."[4]

But remarkably, during the same period, the West was the scene of ruthless conflict and terrorism. Though the Treaty of Peace had utterly ignored this reality, more than half the landmass it covered was Indian country.[5] Settlers and Native Americans competed desperately for sovereignty over lands and resources, often engaging in brutal warfare beyond the control of any legitimate government. Settlement continued unabated despite Indian attacks that killed 1,500 whites in Kentucky alone between 1783 and 1790; no one knows how many Native Americans were killed there or in other parts of the West during those years.[6] The "winning" of the American West had begun.

Where did the western emigrants come from, and who were they? Some ten to twenty thousand people migrated away from New England each year. One historian thinks that a total of nearly one hundred thousand people left there in the 1780s, about 10 percent of the region's entire 1790 population.[7] Europe contributed immigrants. Virginia and the Carolinas also experienced substantial out-migration.

Some of the southwest's remarkable growth came from emigrant journeys like that of the Wallace family of Virginia. In late October 1784, Rosanna Wallace wrote from Viney Grove, Kentucky, to her sister Anne Fleming in western Virginia. She was very happy with the farm that she now lived on after her family's recent move to Kentucky. There had been serious Indian troubles during her family's move, she said. Some people traveling near them had been killed. But her family had joined others headed west, and "before we passed Rock Castale [Castle] there was near three hundred people with us." Wallace's move was part of a flood of southwestern settlement. By 1790, the frontier areas that now comprise Kentucky and Tennessee had more than one hundred thousand residents, or a population nearly as large as that of Rhode Island and Delaware combined. About fifteen thousand of them were slaves.[8]

In the mid-1780s, few emigrants were wealthy leading citizens like George Washington. Washington had western claims to some sixty thousand acres (mostly rewards for military service), but though he wanted to profit from them, he had no intention of moving. Some emigrants were middle-class families seeking a new start in life, like Rosanna Wallace's family. They had traded Virginia land for a larger Kentucky tract in mid-1784. But many others were landless adventurers. They were seeking cheap, fertile land, and often hoping to escape "heavy" taxes, according to Virginia leader Richard Henry Lee. Others fled debts they could not pay, sometimes to avoid debtors' prison. Many settlers were squatters, who had no legal title to lands they occupied. Some were very poor. Elizabeth House Trist described the condition of an emigrant family she met while traveling west from Pittsburgh: "A Man and his Wife, their father and mother, and five children . . . had not had a morsel of bread for the last three months. . . . The poor little children, when they saw us, cry'd for some bread."[9]

From the outset, some national leaders saw emigrants as "the least worthy subjects in the United States," and thought that they were "little less savage than the Indians."[10] Even before the war was over, army officials who met with emigrants believed that some wanted to form "new states," and that "neither the U.S. nor any particular State will reap much advantage from them."[11] Others were openly hostile to government efforts to control settlement. In early 1785, US Army lieutenant colonel Josiah Harmar wrote from Fort McIntosh (western Pennsylvania) to Pennsylvania president John Dickinson that if the fort did not continue to be manned by troops, "immediately upon my marching from hence, it will be demolished by the Emigrators to Kentucky."[12] Lawlessness persisted. By early 1785, there were already several thousand squatters on Confederation lands.[13] Uncontrolled, mushrooming western expansion had a series of economic and political effects that deeply concerned American leaders throughout the period.

As early as 1783, Confederation officials were particularly worried that unrestrained western settlement would renew Native American warfare. During the Revolutionary War, several tribes of the Iroquois Six Nations Confederacy, including the Mohawk, Onondaga, Seneca, and Cayuga, had fought as British allies.[14] White western settlers were primary targets of their attacks. Most of the time, settlers had had to defend themselves because the United States could not aid them. There was enormous and lasting bitterness and hostility between many settlers and Indians as a result of the war's often heartbreaking atrocities. Those included "massacres of whole communities, including women, children, and the aged; of fiendish tortures of prisoners [and] the burning of prisoners to death at the stake."[15] The situation was little better after the war. Native Americans had not been parties to the 1783 Treaty of Peace, and none believed that America's victory meant that they had lost their historic right to occupy and use Indian country. White settlers were dangerous foreign trespassers in their eyes and could be dealt with violently if necessary.[16]

Over the next several years, the Confederation made a series of efforts to control and benefit from western settlement in a climate of rising concern about its effects on the original states and the country as a whole. These consisted primarily of its settlement policy, its land ordinances, and its treaties with Native Americans.

Western Settlement and the Creation of the National Domain

By September 1783, the Confederation had declared that settlement on lands "inhabited or claimed by Indians" outside the limits of any state was illegal.[17] At that time, Congress intended to purchase or otherwise peacefully acquire title to lands from Native Americans before permitting white settlement. But settlers and various states often utterly disregarded what the Confederation declared to be natives' rights. That same month, Congress received a report from Fort Pitt commander General William Irvine that about four hundred men from Virginia had crossed the Ohio to establish a settlement on the Muskingum River.[18]

The Muskingum settlers had crossed into territory occupied by Native Americans. Irvine feared that "an immediate Indian war, will be among the first of the many evil consequences that must result from such lawless measures."[19] Reports said that the Virginians had "committed many wanton & unprovoked acts of cruelty that had in some measure produced retaliation."[20] The Confederation's small army was powerless to stop settlers' violations of Indian country such as this one. Soon after Irvine's news arrived, George Washington told a Massachusetts congressman that unless Congress carefully governed the West, "in five years from this time, there would be a severe war in that part of the country."[21] Meanwhile, some states were encouraging settlement in Indian country. In November 1783, Georgia entered into a treaty with Creek Indians that purportedly ceded a large amount of Creek lands. It was repudiated shortly afterward. According to a recent study, "Creeks began to call Georgians *ecunnaunuxulgee*, 'people greedily grasping after the lands of the red people.'"[22]

The settlers' illegal crossing of the Ohio in the fall of 1783 helped force resolution of one long-standing Confederation dispute. For years, the states had disagreed over whether the United States or individual states owned large areas of western lands. "Landed" states such as Virginia claimed ownership of western lands, while the six "landless" states (e.g., Rhode Island) believed, among other things, that they were at a competitive disadvantage to them. Landless states had to tax comparatively more heavily because they had no lands to sell instead. That drove people out of their states: "the depopulation of stretches of the seaboard loomed as an unpleasant possibility."[23] Disparities in state size had become a chronic source of friction between the states. By late 1783, one of the largest remaining major "landed" state claims was Virginia's. In 1780, it had agreed in principle to cede certain lands to the Confederation, but only on various conditions.[24]

In September 1783, New York's congressmen wrote Governor George Clinton that they had accepted Virginia's "hard terms" for its proposed cession because "there is now left as the undoubted Right of the United States an immense Tract of Country which is daily overrun by lawless men (who endanger by their Rashness a new Indian war)."[25] Virginia congressman John Francis Mercer wrote in the same vein that "above all the accounts we have receiv'd from the back Country of a banditti [i.e., white settlers] having already in great numbers repair'd to those Theatres of violence, rapine & villainy at length got the better" of other states' resistance to Virginia's conditions.[26]

On March 1, 1784, Congress approved Virginia's cession of its claims to all the US territory northwest of the Ohio River. That created the national domain.[27] But it did little or nothing to enable orderly western settlement or to allow the Confederation to benefit from it. In 1784, Congress adopted an ordinance intended to govern territories, but it never operated. It then adopted a 1785 land-sales ordinance that produced almost no results. During the 1787 Philadelphia Convention, the insolvent Confederation agreed in desperation to sell millions of acres to large land-speculation syndicates at bargain basement prices.[28] Congress did not create any new state or even any politically feasible government for new territories until July 1787, in the middle of the Philadelphia Convention. By then, years of conflict had shown that to pave the way for white western settlement it would be necessary to fight a war against Native Americans that the Confederation could not afford to fight.

Confederation Western Land Policy

In 1784, Congress took a two-pronged approach to expanding western settlement. It attempted to plan for the government of new territories, and it sought to use treaties to move Native Americans peacefully out of the path of settlement. In the spring, it adopted the so-called Ordinance of 1784.[29] Written primarily by Thomas Jefferson, it was intended to provide for the government of new national territories and their eventual statehood. Congress seems to have had two main goals in adopting it. It wanted to raise money to pay the national debt, and it wanted to control the course of western emigration.[30]

To enable peaceful settlement, the ordinance provided that lands would be "purchased of the Indian inhabitants" before they were settled by whites. The ordinance divided the Northwest into ten potential new states. They were to start out as self-governing territories (after Congress's initial approval and subject to certain requirements). If a territory was later admitted to statehood, it would become a state on an "equal footing" with the original states, that is, one having equal rights and responsibilities. That "anticolonial" provision meant that new states would govern themselves; Congress would exercise no control over their legislation.[31] However, during the ordinance's consideration, Jefferson proposed that after 1800, slavery be banned in the Northwest. His proposal lost narrowly. Leaders had other fundamental concerns about the 1784 ordinance even after its adoption, however.

The 1784 ordinance was politically "dead on arrival" and never went into operation. The main reason for its demise was that the idea of creating as many as ten new states on liberal terms proved unacceptable to many leaders. It threatened to upset the existing sectional balance of power. Alarmed congressmen pointed out that the new states would eventually take control of government away from the East. That meant that the nation's policies would be dictated by frontier agricultural interests. Some historians think that some eastern interests, such as land speculators, also disliked Congress's decision to allow new territories and states to engage in self-government. Finally, the 1784 ordinance was also adopted in a climate where leaders had increasing concerns about the effects of emigration and western settlement.[32]

French officials in America were reportedly "astonished at the policy, or rather impolicy, of congress in thus promoting the settlement of interior states" by adopting the 1784 ordinance. They thought that it would allow people to flee their creditors and justice, and would hurt land values and tax revenues in the eastern states.[33] Others shared such concerns. By late 1784, Virginia officials received complaints from dozens of citizens in Caroline County. Prominent residents there, such as Edmund Pendleton, feared that they would face increased tax burdens when large numbers of emigrants ceased to pay Virginia taxes.[34] Some contemporaries agreed that eastern states might be harmed by emigration, but anticipated potentially offsetting benefits from expansion.

As Virginian Arthur Lee explained to John Adams, the main reason that things were not going well in the United States by 1785 was "the rage for emigration & for the establishment of new States. The consequence is, that the old ones are in a fluctuating situation . . . the imposition of taxes becomes difficult, the collection desultory, & the produce precarious."[35] But like a majority of Congress, Lee nevertheless thought that the West should still be opened. Settlement could not be prevented unless Congress had "absolute powers." But if emigration could be properly controlled, the revenues from Confederation land sales could pay the national debt, Lee hoped.[36] Still other observers saw a much greater danger from settlement, however.

Leaders such as George Washington thought that western settlement could be dangerous because settlers might separate from the United States and ally with foreign powers. By late 1784, Washington had had firsthand experience that significantly influenced his views. He had toured most of his western lands in September. At one Pennsylvania tract he visited, he had had a disturbing encounter with thirteen families who were squatting on his lands. They insisted that they had a right to remain, though they had no title to properties for which he had held grants for many years. They refused to pay him any rent. Washington decided to sue them because, as he later told his lawyer, "I viewed the defendants as wilful and obstinate Sinners, persevering after timely & repeated admonition, in a design to injure me." He won his suit two years later. By then some of the defendants had left, without paying him a penny.[37]

But the most important result of Washington's tour was political, not personal. The settlers' attitudes convinced him that the Confederation needed to find a way to retain their political allegiance. Instead of trying to control or limit settlement, which he saw as futile, he wanted to find ways to cure the problems it created. To do that, Washington thought that it was essential to link eastern areas such as Virginia and western regions commercially. He decided to advocate the building of a Potomac River canal, joining the Potomac to the Ohio River, a distance of nearly 175 miles. As a recent historian concluded, "It was an endeavor that only a supreme risk taker and visionary would contemplate." Washington quite probably thought that if it succeeded, it would enhance the value of his western lands. But for him the project had a far more important objective: preventing the defection of western settlers from the United States.[38]

In October 1784, Washington wrote to Virginia governor Benjamin Harrison recommending that the state authorize the canal project. The West would "settle faster than any other [area] ever did, or any one would imagine." Virginians, he wrote, needed to accept that commerce was part of the nation's future. Virginia needed to connect itself to the West. That link was essential because foreign powers flanked the United States, and because there were no ties whatsoever that presently bound western settlers to it. Using careful language that emphasized how strongly he felt, Washington told Harrison, "The Western settlers, (I speak now from my own observation) stand as it were upon a pivot—the touch of a feather, would turn them any way."[39] Without commercial ties, they would either be "*driven* into the arms of, or be made dependant upon foreigners," which would bring on separation or war. If they seceded, the United States would lose the revenues from their lands, their commerce, and the military buffer zone that settlements offered against foreign governments and Native Americans.[40] Washington expressed these economic-realist views to others, including political opponents such as Richard Henry Lee, repeatedly over the next several years.[41]

Washington was farsighted in appreciating western settlers' lack of firm ties to the Confederation. Strong separationist movements arose in the mid-1780s in the areas that became Tennessee and Kentucky, and even in western Pennsylvania's Wyoming Valley. The Kentucky separation movement ultimately failed because Virginia agreed to a peaceable separation, if approved by the Confederation. The Tennessee movement to create an independent "state of Franklin" eventually collapsed when settlers chose to remain part of North Carolina. But separationist sentiments remained strong throughout this period. Many settlers wanted to permanently sever ties to the Union, which they thought provided them with no assistance. Many others were ready to join them if the Confederation took any action that harmed their interests. But instead of adopting Washington's approach by binding settlers to the United States, Congress continued its policy of permitting settlement only on its terms, while seeking to avoid Indian warfare.[42]

In 1784, as the second part of its approach to settlement, Congress began trying to extinguish Native American claims to the Ohio Country. Confederation officials including former Virginia congressman Arthur Lee "negotiated" three treaties between 1784 and 1786. In the 1784 Treaty of Fort Stanwix, the United States forced the tribes of the Iroquois Six Nations Confederacy, including America's wartime allies, the Oneida and Tuscarora tribes, to relinquish their claims in the northwest.[43] Lee asserted that, contrary to the Iroquois's position, they were not a "free and independent nation" but instead a "subdued people" who had lost the war.[44] The United States provided no compensation to the tribes. It claimed that the ceded lands were reparations for Indian actions when they fought on the British side during the war. Collectively, the three treaties purported to extinguish tribal claims to much of the Ohio River valley. On paper, they provided a basis for United States sales of northwest lands. But by 1786, several tribes had repudiated them, and were claiming the entire Ohio Country.[45]

Meanwhile, conflict continued between trans-Appalachian white settlers and Native Americans. In late 1784, the trans-Appalachian counties that composed the "Kentucky district" of Virginia held a convention. Its delegates resolved that the fact that the Virginia court for the Kentucky district wasn't deciding suits brought there was a grievance. The court responded to the convention: "We need only suggest that two of the Judges having been slain by the Savages and another having declined to accept the Office has occasioned repeated delays."[46] In March 1785, Governor Patrick Henry received a letter from veteran Indian agent Colonel Joseph Martin. Martin told him that western North Carolinians had set up an independent state of Franklyn. They intended to "lay off" (that is, to measure off boundaries for) a new county encompassing lands reserved by North Carolina for Native Americans, including towns in which natives were currently living. Martin's letter predicted that Indians would retaliate for settlers' actions, including what he described as the murder of an Indian, committed by one of the settler leaders. He then described several incidents in which a half-dozen settlers were murdered and scalped by various tribes, some of whom he thought were trying to start a war with Virginia. Settlement conflicts were continuing in Ohio as well.[47]

In April 1785, Congress sent Confederation troops to the frontier to remove squatters who had crossed the Ohio into Indian country in violation of Congress's settlement policy. The troops burned squatters' cabins, but the squatters returned and rebuilt them. An army officer in charge of removing the settlers, John Armstrong, described them as "banditti whose actions are a disgrace to human nature." But the squatters remained defiant. When Armstrong read settlers the Confederation's instructions against settlement north of the Ohio River, they laughed at him. One published a statement saying that "all mankind, agreeable to every constitution formed in America, have an undoubted right to pass into every vacant country, and to form their constitution." The Confederation had no power to prevent the exercise of those rights, he said.[48] But whether or not the Confederation had theoretical power to prevent squatters from crossing the Ohio, it clearly lacked any practical authority to do so. As these persistent conflicts in Kentucky, Tennessee, and Ohio suggest, to have any realistic chance of controlling the flow of settlement, avoiding war, and obtaining sorely needed revenues, Congress badly needed a new land policy. It therefore debated and approved a new land ordinance in the spring of 1785.[49]

In April 1785, Virginia congressman William Grayson wrote to George Washington explaining the eastern states' position on the proposed land ordinance then before Congress. Congress was divided: some members wanted to raise revenue without losing their states' inhabitants and "thereby prevent the lands in the original states from depreciating." Part of the "Eastern Gentlemen" wanted lands "sold in such a manner as to suit their own people who may chuse to emigrate, of which I believe there will be great numbers." Other "Eastern Gentlemen" "are apprehensive of the consequences . . . from the new States taking their position in the Confederacy. They perhaps wish that this event may be delayed as long as possible."[50]

Washington responded to Grayson in late April that "under the rose" it looked to him as though the ordinance "disguises a disclination to add new States, to the confederation, westward of us." Unlike the eastern states' leaders, Washington thought that the creation of new states would be "the inevitable consequence of emigration to, & the population of that territory." It was futile to try to limit the pace of settlement by adopting the ordinance's cumbersome land-sales process. Trying to restrain emigration would be like trying to "prevent the reflux of the tide, when you had got it into your rivers."[51] The provisions of the May 1785 land ordinance showed that Congress rejected Washington's views, and hoped to limit settlement.

The 1785 ordinance was a compromise between the northern and southern states. In most respects, it favored the settlement views of the northern states and the interests of wealthy land speculators. It used a "checkerboard" approach, making some lands available for sale and settlement, while reserving other lands for specific purposes and still others for the United States. It required that lands be surveyed before sale. Some historians think that the survey process that the ordinance required inevitably meant that selling large amounts of lands would take years. It seems likely that many supporters saw that delay as a desirable way to limit settlement.[52] Surveyed lands were to be sold in 640-acre minimum-sized parcels, an amount of land that many poorer settlers could not afford to buy. That made land-speculator acquisition and corporate settlement far more likely than individual settlement.[53]

The 1785 ordinance addressed only the process of selling western lands, not western government. One extraordinarily divisive issue Congress avoided as a result was the legality of territorial slavery. Although Massachusetts congressman Rufus King attempted during consideration of the 1785 ordinance to get Congress to bar it, Congress refused even to consider the issue. Despite King's continued efforts, it remained unresolved until after the 1787 Philadelphia Convention began, due to southern-state resistance.[54] That disagreement played a major role in preventing Confederation agreement on any territorial government framework until July 1787.[55] Even as Congress finished work on the 1785 ordinance, settlement conflicts continued.

In late May 1785, retired brigadier general William Irvine wrote a report on Indian affairs to Pennsylvania president John Dickinson from Fort Pitt in western Pennsylvania. Irvine had been sent to the area to explore "donation Lands." He told Dickinson that there were Indians "of the [Iroquois] six nations, and detachments from other tribes" "actually planting Corn" in areas he believed had been ceded by treaty to Pennsylvania. When Irvine told an Indian chief of his belief, the chief replied that "none of his friends who are now settled at Vinango was at the Treaty nor had they received any of the goods." Irvine added, "He has departed apparently sullen and dejected." Irvine then added that "authoritative accounts have arrived of murders having been committed at Siota, Canetucki, and sundry persons being attacked on their passage up and down the River." Irvine observed that "the lawless manner in which the Whites of this Country conduct themselves is sufficient alone to bring about a new War." He predicted that unless Confederation land policy changed quickly, western settlers would not provide any revenues to the United States. And, he said, "the governments will also go into other hands—who may probably, not be in union with the old States."[56]

Irvine's prediction seemed confirmed by a letter Pennsylvania president Dickinson received later that summer from Kentucky adventurer James Wilkinson about secession by Kentucky. Wilkinson, a retired army major general, was shortly to become a Spanish double agent working to separate Kentucky from the Union (if he had not already become one). He told Dickinson that Kentucky's late-1784 convention, "unprotected by any efficient regulation and irritated by the continued depredations of the savages," had asked voters there to consider applying to Virginia "for a separation." He reported that "our neighbors the Savages, notwithstanding treaties, & a professed pacific disposition, are perpetually depredating & murdering in our interior Settlements;

and yet our Settlements expand, with incredible rapidity, and the Earth brings forth an unexampled abundance."[57] As the Confederation began the process of selling western lands in the national domain, it faced the risk that settlers there would also want to separate. But the land-sales process itself proved unworkable.

After the 1785 ordinance's adoption, the Confederation began surveying western territory. For reasons to be discussed shortly, very little surveying was completed before the 1787 Philadelphia Convention. The first Confederation auction sales of surveyed lands were held in New York in September and October 1787, and resulted in sales of $176,090 in depreciated currency.[58] A financially desperate Congress agreed to sell large tracts to a land-speculation syndicate outside the surveyed area, contrary to the 1785 ordinance's requirements, but these too yielded little revenue. In 1787, Congress sold or gave options on a total of several million acres to a land syndicate, the Ohio Company, at an effective price of 8–9 cents an acre, though the 1785 ordinance called for a minimum price of $1 an acre. By comparison, at roughly the same time, land in Massachusetts often sold for $20–30 an acre.[59] There was little prospect that the Confederation debt would be paid any time in the foreseeable future by such bargain-basement discount sales.

But by 1786, northern leaders had become even more concerned about settlement as Indian-settler conflicts intensified sharply. During congressional debates on a controversial treaty in the summer of 1786, one prominent Pennsylvania congressman, retired general Arthur St. Clair, said that he thought that emigration "has injured us much already." He added that if his support for the proposed treaty would "stop the Emigration to the westward it is an event devoutly to be wished." Settlement was dangerous, because settlers "find themselves a distinct People that has little connection with and no defence upon any of the Atlantic States. They are fit instruments ready to be laid hold of by their Ennemies." St. Clair asked a Virginia congressman rhetorically to tell him whether Virginia's treasury had ever received "one Shilling" in taxes from Kentucky, saying "I believe not Sir and farther I believe their [treasury] never will."[60] He wrote privately that the possible secession of western settlers was "a strong reason against the formation of such settlements . . . if they are not under the general Controul the sooner exterminated the better."[61] St. Clair's views were probably shared by a significant part of Congress's members. By the fall of 1786, Rufus King, for example, was reportedly opposed to further emigration.[62] But desperate for revenue, Congress soon concluded that settlement must go forward, even in the face of widening Indian warfare against western settlers.

Native American and Imperial Resistance to American Expansion

After the war, the Spanish and British governments hoped that with their support Indian tribes would contain American western settlement. Spain's North American leaders were convinced that Indian alliances were critical to maintaining their positions in Louisiana and Florida by blocking American expansion. Louisiana governor Bernardo de Gálvez wrote to the Spanish government that his experience had "demonstrated that the conservation and prosperity" of Spain's territories "depend primarily on the friendship of the Indian nations who inhabit them, and this can only be done by means of gifts and a well established trade."[63]

In June 1784, as part of its containment strategy, Spain secretly entered into a quasi-military and trade treaty with Creek tribes at the Pensacola Congress. Esteban Miró, acting governor of Louisiana, and other high officials signed the agreement for Spain. The main negotiator for the Creek nation was the ambitious Scottish-Creek leader Alexander McGillivray (Hoboi-Hili-Miko). McGillivray's unusual background made him ideally suited to forge Native American political alliances with European powers because he could bridge cultures. While growing up, he had lived first in a Creek village, but he had also lived in Georgia and received a British-style colonial education there. He had left Georgia early in the war when his Tory father's slave plantations were confiscated. He and other Creeks had fought the war as allies of the British, so there was no love lost between them and the United States.[64]

Under the Pensacola agreement, in return for exclusive rights to receive Creek hides, furs, and other products, Spain provided "a huge amount" of goods to the Creeks. Included were three hundred guns, more than eight thousand knives, six thousand gunflints, and "large volumes of powder and musket balls." Historian Kathleen DuVal finds that "the Spanish assured the Creeks that the bounty would continue. The crown substantially increased its budget for Indian presents, including guns, powder, and ball."[65] The Spanish government, in other words, was committing to continuing military support for the Creeks. Spain also agreed that if the Creeks lost their lands to any "enemies of [the Spanish king's] crown," Spain would grant them lands elsewhere in its empire. However, Spain was unwilling to agree to defend the Creeks' borders, as they had hoped.[66]

Spain's unwillingness to defend the Creek nation's borders shows that it was willing to oppose American expansion as long as the political and economic cost of doing so could be contained. For the same reason, by 1786, when the Creeks declared war on Georgia, Spanish officials were instructed by their superiors to continue providing weapons to the Creeks "with the greatest secrecy and dissimulation."[67] They were to say falsely that the weapons were for hunting, not warfare. When it became inexpedient for Spain to encourage further Creek warfare with Americans in the spring of 1787, Louisiana governor Esteban Miró cut off their military supplies. Spain's true policy was to keep the Creeks as "dependent vassals," but to employ them as long as possible in resisting American expansion.[68]

Britain's overall containment policy was similar to Spain's. After the war, Britain took several steps in pursuit of its goal of limiting American expansion. It refused to give up its western forts and supported the creation of an Indian western confederacy to oppose expansion. In 1784, the governor of Quebec, General Frederick Haldimand, made a substantial land grant to Britain's wartime Iroquois Six Nations allies led by Mohawk leader Joseph Brant (Thayendanegea). Roughly half the members of the Iroquois nations that had been British allies chose to live there. Like Alexander McGillivray, Brant had received a British-style colonial education before the war, and had fought as a British ally. He has been described by a recent historian as "an inspiring leader, a tactical genius, and a strategic thinker," who had led "devastating raids," one of which was "especially brutal," during the war. Brant's raids terrified frontier settlers.[69] Brant became one of the driving forces behind the creation of a Native American Western Confederacy. Its leaders hoped to defend the Ohio River as a border with the United States.[70]

Britain's strategic western forts, also under Haldimand's control, provided important military and economic support to various Indian tribes. They were central to economic life in the area between the Great Lakes and the Ohio River.[71] The tribes engaged in lucrative fur trading and other business at the forts. That commerce enabled the tribes to purchase arms and ammunition as well as other needed goods.[72] Britain also continued to provide Native American tribes with military aid such as guns and ammunition.[73] The forts strongly reinforced the tribes' defensive capabilities. The support provided by the British through the fort system was so important to the tribes that several historians believe that Britain feared that if it withdrew from them, an Indian revolt would result.[74]

Britain's forts symbolized its refusal to give up claims to the American West, a message not lost on either Americans or Indians. By 1786, lieutenant colonel Josiah Harmar had received "truly alarming" intelligence that tribes were conducting military reconnaissance in Ohio against the United States, using a British fort as an operations base. Colonel Harmar expressed his strong concern that there were far larger implications of the British forts' use by the Indians. He wrote, "I am well convinced that all their [Indians'] treaties are farcical, as long as the British possess the posts."[75] Harmar's view was that northern Native Americans would not honor treaties because they would continue to believe that resistance to American expansion was possible as long as Britain held the forts.[76] Britain's aid to the tribes supported that belief as well.

Britain's and Spain's western strategies were made less costly by the fact that federalists in Congress had prevented the creation of a significant Confederation standing army. As a result, the United States had only a few hundred troops in the West after 1783. For the Confederation to undertake offensive military action against Native Americans, Congress would have to approve raising new troops. That issue came to a head when Virginia sought Confederation diplomatic and military assistance for its western citizens, particularly the counties in its Kentucky district, during 1785–86.

Confederation Conflict over Native American Resistance to Settlement

In April 1785, Virginia governor Patrick Henry wrote to the state's congressional delegation complaining that no Confederation treaty had been negotiated with western tribes such as the Wabash. In Henry's view, those tribes were the most dangerous to Virginia's interests. He pointedly asked the delegation to let him "know by the earliest opportunity the particular situation and progress of this affair, in order that measures calculated for public safety may be adopted if found necessary."[77] The same day, Henry wrote to Indian agent Colonel Joseph Martin, urging him to maintain Virginia's neutrality in the event of an Indian war with Tennessee settlers: "I wish you to consider an Indian war as a fatal evil, to be avoided if possible." Henry gave Martin two reasons: the "cruel suffering" of individuals, and war expenses that must "produce total derangement, confusion, and final ruin of [Virginia's] public credit." Virginia did not want and could not afford a needless Indian war.[78] Later in 1785, Henry received a report that western Virginia militia had been called out in response to an Indian uprising. But upon discovering that some of the Virginians who had been murdered had crossed the Ohio, he declined to defend them. At the time, Henry was willing to respect Confederation settlement policy.

Then, in April 1786, Governor Henry's brother-in-law, Colonel William Christian, a prominent Kentucky settler, was killed in a battle with

Indians near the Ohio River. He had been a soldier and a Virginia state legislator, and had worked in Henry's law office. The sources suggest that Christian had been killed by Wabash tribe members while leading a party of Kentucky settlers pursuing them. Christian's force had gone after them because its leaders believed that they had stolen settlers' horses near present-day Louisville. In following them, the settlers had crossed the Ohio River into Illinois Country (now southern Indiana).[79]

Other Virginians' families were then suffering from Indian hostilities in Kentucky as well. The diary of Colonel Francis Taylor of Orange County, Virginia, for May 9, 1786, records his conversation with a Major Madison. Madison said he had seen "T. Brown" from Kentucky "who told him that the Indians were very troublesome [and] had killed a schoolmaster at E. Taylors [a Taylor relative who lived in Kentucky]. That E. Taylor had ten men for a Guard."[80] By this time, Creeks had also begun a war against Georgia settlers who were encroaching on tribal lands. Georgia sought Confederation help, but none was forthcoming.[81]

Governor Henry was deeply affected by Christian's death. On May 15, he wrote a moving letter to his sister consoling her:

> I am at a loss how to address you, my dear sister. Would to God I could say something to give relief to the dearest of women and sisters. My heart has felt in a manner new and strange to me; insomuch that while I am endeavoring to comfort you, I want a comforter myself. I forbear to tell you how great was my love for my friend and brother. I turn my eyes to heaven, where he is gone, I trust, and adore with humility the unsearchable ways of that Providence which calls us off this stage of action.[82]

On May 16, Henry wrote to the Virginia congressional delegation with details of attacks by Wabash tribes on the "Eastern, Southern & Western Borders" of the Kentucky district. Henry asked the delegation to seek Confederation military assistance for the settlers.[83] He closed his letter with a pointed reminder that the proper management of Indian affairs "may be justly reckoned amongst the capital advantages of federal government to Virginia." The clear implication of Henry's statement was that if the Confederation could not or would not protect Virginians against Indians, it would lose much of its value to them.

The same day, Henry wrote separately to the president of Congress that "much property and many valuable Lives have been lost [in Kentucky]." He told the president that he expected that "the necessity of the case will enforce the people, for the purpose of self preservation, to go against [attack] the offending [Indian] Towns."[84] Henry then complained bitterly that Congress had not seen fit to conclude a treaty with the Wabash, or to notify him that they had refused to enter into a treaty, since "with them such a Refusal is another name for War." Congress's Indian agents had "passed by several tribes near our Frontiers, & went on to the Southern [Indian] Department" without explanation. Henry accused Confederation officials of "seeming inattention" to Indian problems. He claimed that his first "intimations" that there were problems with the Indians occurred from "Murders & Depredations committed on our citizens." To emphasize his disappointment about Confederation inaction, Henry added that "it appears to me that [Virginia] has more at Stake as to Indian Affairs, than any, or perhaps all, the States of the Union besides."[85] He was remarkably unhappy about what he felt was the Confederation's failure to protect Virginians, and demanded relief.

Virginia congressman William Grayson took the lead in seeking Confederation military aid for Kentucky residents. Grayson wrote to James Madison that he and the delegation intended to request that Congress order "Colonel Harmar with 400 Continental troops and such a number of Kentucki Militia as may be necessary, march to their towns & destroy them if they do not make concessions & deliver hostages as security for their good behav[i]our in future." A committee reported in favor of Virginia's request on June 6. It proposed to authorize two companies of Continental troops to unite with up to one thousand Virginia militia for the purpose of either "treating with the said Indians, or of making war on them, as circumstances may require."[86]

Congress's action on the report was delayed by lack of state attendance (nine states were needed to approve such action), but most importantly by the opposition of northern congressmen to providing assistance. On June 8, Congress learned from General George Rogers Clark that several tribes of Indians, in conjunction with the Wyandots, had declared war against the United States.[87] That same day, Massachusetts congressman Rufus King wrote to Elbridge Gerry: "The lawless, and probably unjust, conduct of the inhabitants of Kentuckey towards the Indians bordering on the western side of the Ohio, has lately occasioned the loss of a number of valuable lives on the Frontiers of Virginia. . . . The Govr. & Delegates of Virginia clamour for war against the Indian Towns . . . I am decidedly against any such war, as I at present understand the situation."[88] King and most of New England's representatives continued to oppose making war on Indians across the Ohio to protect Virginia settlers.

On June 29, Congress considered the committee's main "peace or war" recommendation. Pennsylvania congressman Charles Pettit, seconded by Massachusetts congressman Theodore Sedgwick, attempted to defeat it. Pettit proposed that Congress instead reorganize the Indian Department. His motion lost on a sectional vote.[89] Voting on sectional lines, Congress then narrowly voted down Grayson's compromise proposal to make the decision to go to war subject to the authority of Congress's Indian commissioners.[90] The army commander's ability to ask for up to one thousand Virginia militia in support was also defeated on a sectional vote.

Finally, and most importantly, Congress gutted the report's basic proposal to force the Indians to make peace or face war. Instead, the report's authorization to the army for military action was left entirely to the discretion of the army commander: "such operations" as may be "necessary for the protection of the frontiers."[91] Congress agreed to send two companies of infantry (about two hundred troops) under the command of Colonel Harmar to the vicinity of Virginia to assist the settlers. It asked Governor Henry to mobilize Virginia militia to support them. Henry agreed to provide militia on July 12.

But Congressman Pettit interpreted Congress's action as, in reality, the denial of Virginia's original request. He wrote to Pennsylvania leader James Wilson that "after various Manouvres" the whole June 6 "Report was negatived by a large majority as being more hostile than we conceived existing Circumstances would warrant. A soothing answer however is ordered to be given to the Gov. of Virginia, requesting him to hold the Militia of Kentucky in readiness to cooperate with the Troops to repel invasion if necessary." In short, Pettit saw Congress's decision as negating any requirement that the army either negotiate a treaty with the Wabash, or make war on them, as Virginia had originally requested.[92]

On July 5, a deeply frustrated Governor Henry wrote an irate letter to the Virginia congressional delegation informing them that Indian attacks appeared to be spreading. Henry said that Georgia was under attack and additional tribes appeared to be ready to join in attacking Kentucky and Virginia. Henry then demanded to know whether Congress would "defend & protect our Frontiers." If not, he needed to take steps to defend Virginia. He said that people expected that the Confederation would make treaties and protect them. But if not, "are not all the western people driven into a separation from us, and of course the States having settlements on the Western waters bro't to the Dilemma, of abandoning them or the present Confederation?" Henry's implication was clear: there was no reason for westerners, or even states like Virginia whose citizens wanted to move west, to stay in the Union if it would not protect them.[93] In light of Henry's growing opposition to strengthening the Confederation in other respects (discussed in chapter 6), it is especially noteworthy that he believed that Confederation military support was critically important to Virginia.

Remarkably, Henry's July 5 letter conceded that "I know it is urged by some, & with too much Truth, that our own people [i.e., settlers] are the Aggressors." Even more remarkably, he continued by saying that settlers were often people likely to end up fighting with the Indians: "The Character of such Americans as usually frequent the Indian Borders, coming into co-operation with that of the Indians themselves, necessarily produces contention." But, he argued, Congress should have known that and have acted to anticipate problems.[94]

In effect, Henry was trying to shift all the blame for the Kentucky settlers' predicament to Congress, thus absolving the state under his administration from any responsibility.[95] To understand Henry's actions, it helps to recall that he thought Virginia could not afford Indian wars. As we have seen, Virginia's leaders were also divided about the desirability of western emigration. These considerations suggest that Henry sought to shift responsibility for defending Kentucky because he wanted to avoid a fight in Virginia's legislature over raising troops to assist settlers there. Raising troops would have required unpopular tax increases. Eastern Virginians would have been forced to pay increased taxes to support western Virginians who themselves were paying little or nothing in state taxes. Henry might well have lost such a fight, and he detested losing. On July 17, the Virginia delegation responded to Henry that his letter had been read in Congress, but that its majority declined to take any action beyond that already agreed upon.[96]

Henry's authorization of Virginia militia to assist the army's forces was not the end of the controversy, however. Indian hostilities continued, and caused increased concern in Congress. By mid-August 1786, western army officials had informed Secretary of War Henry Knox that Virginia planned direct military action against Native American tribes in Ohio, particularly the Wabash. Virginia's campaign was conducted by Kentucky militia under the command of General George Rogers Clark.[97]

In mid-September 1786, Congressman St. Clair submitted a motion to Congress to prohibit states from warring against Native Americans in violation of treaties. His motion was aimed quite explicitly at prohibiting Virginia's actions. A motion made at nearly the same time by Virginia congressman Henry ("Light-Horse Harry") Lee, Jr., and supported by several states, protested some of the recent Confederation–Native American treaties.[98] But just before Congress considered these dueling motions, the political situation unexpectedly changed. Congress learned that Native American attacks were spreading around the country and that its land surveyors' work had been blocked by threatened attacks.

By 1786, the insolvent Confederation was desperate for the revenues that many congressmen hoped land sales would bring in. But the process of surveying western lands for sale had proved agonizingly slow. Only minor surveying had been done before 1786. Surveying was delayed for various reasons, but Congress's inability to provide adequate funds slowed work, particularly because Indian resistance to it required military protection for the surveyors.[99] A larger survey effort began in the summer of 1786, but the army's few hundred western troops could not provide enough protection to deal with Indian hostilities that had become widespread by then.

In October 1786, a Pennsylvania newspaper quoted a September 13 letter written by "an officer commanding at Fort McIntosh" to a Philadelphia private citizen. The army officer reported that Ohio settlers with whom he had met "say the Indians are in general disposed for war, and there are 700 warriors collected at the Shawona towns, and more expected." The settlers said that they had been told by two other men who had apparently been present in the Indian camp that "they had brought in 13 scalps and 4 prisoners, 2 men, and a Mrs. Moor and daughter; the two latter they burned before the men, and told them that was to be their lot in a few days." The Fort McIntosh commander said that the settlers had told him "that the Indians are determined to strike at Capt. Hutchins, [chief Confederation] surveyor, and those with him." He expressed the hope that General Clark's 1,500 Virginia men would "cut them out some other work than the butchering our defenceless inhabitants." He added that "the Indians say they will not disturb the whites, if they will confine themselves within the bounds of Pennsylvania, and on this side of the Ohio."[100]

By October 10, Lieutenant Colonel Josiah Harmar had written to Secretary of War Knox to report that because of Indian hostilities, Captain Hutchins had declined to continue surveying work and retired to the Ohio River.[101] Shortly after that, Congressman Rufus King wrote to Massachusetts governor James Bowdoin that Congress was now "deeply impressed with the Danger arising from a very extensive combination of savages from Georgia to the Frontiers of Pennsylvania."[102] King also wrote to Elbridge Gerry explaining that "the Indians now appear to have united to oppose the survey and settlement of" the "Western Lands." He complained, "This combination is most unjust since we have fairly and bona fide extinguished their claims."[103]

Massachusetts now reversed its position and supported military action against Indians across the Ohio. King wrote to Governor Bowdoin, "[W]e willingly acceded to the wishes of Congress" to "augment the federal troops to a legionary corps to consist of two thousand men including artillery and cavalry."[104] Congress's purposes, he told Gerry, were "to do ourselves justice and protect the frontiers together with the surveys of the Indian cessions."[105] But Congress had no funds to pay these troops; it then tried to raise the money, but failed. Shortly after Congress approved troop increases, a committee chaired by Congressman Henry Lee, Jr., reported on the St. Clair and Lee motions.[106]

The Lee committee concluded that Virginia's Clark expedition "preparations in the district of Kentucky for offensive operations against sundry Indian tribes" showed "the most profound respect to the sovereignties of the United States" and were "in perfect conformity with the Confederation." It found that the "offensive operations commenced by the inhabitants of Kentucky are authorized by self preservation and their experience of the imbecility of the foederal government." It is striking that the committee recited the Confederation's "imbecility"—that is, its inability or unwillingness to take military action in Confederation territory across the Ohio—as a justification for offensive military operations there by Virginia.[107] That was the diametrical opposite of Congressman St. Clair's position.

Equally importantly, the committee also found that the "inimical disposition" of the Indian tribes "north west and south adjoining the territory of the U. States" stemmed from the inability of the Confederation to compel British withdrawal from the western forts. It concluded that no change "in the minds of the savages" could "be effected but by the

British troops abandoning the territory of the U. States." That conclusion agreed with the long-standing views of senior army officials such as Lieutenant Colonel Josiah Harmar. The committee recommended that federal troops on the Ohio be repositioned "to accomplish this."[108]

Congress never acted on the Lee report, which probably represented a minority view. The Virginia congressional delegation wrote to Virginia's new governor, Edmund Randolph, in December 1786, saying that "we are fully in sentiment with your Excellency that our [Virginia's] Western troubles demand, in their nature, the interposition of the Arms of the Union, but Congress have been tried upon this point, & have determined differently."[109] Congress had refused to use the army to protect Kentucky settlers.

After their experiences in 1785–86, Virginians were acutely aware that the Confederation would not or could not protect their western frontier. It was equally clear to Virginians that if the British gave up their forts, the Indians would be greatly weakened. The Confederation's failure to achieve either goal had profound political consequences. Many Virginians now decided that they wanted the Confederation strengthened so that it would have a military force to assist them against Native Americans, the British, and other possible enemies. That important shift in Virginia opinion affected state policy in fundamental ways explored in chapter 9.

Conclusion

In May 1787, just days before the beginning of the Philadelphia Convention, Lieutenant Colonel Josiah Harmar reported to Secretary of War Knox from Fort Harmar (near present-day Marietta, Ohio) that in the past seven months, "one hundred and seventy seven boats, two thousand six hundred and eighty-nine souls, thirteen hundred and thirty three horses, seven hundred and sixty six cattle . . . have passed Muskingum bound for Limestone and the Rapids. If Congress should be of opinion that it will be expedient to shut the navigation, I think a respectable post . . . will be necessary; otherwise, from all appearance, the people will become so strong, in the course of a little time, as to force a trade at all events."[110]

Harmar thought that settlement was rapidly nearing the point where the army would no longer be able to prevent it. But its spiraling growth increased Native Americans' resistance and desire for war to protect native lands. By the spring of 1787, Congress belatedly realized that a war would be needed before the Northwest was safe for settlers.[111] But it was a war that an insolvent Confederation could not afford to fight. Nor could it prevent the dangerous, costly flood of uncontrolled settlement or reap any benefit from it.

The Confederation had wholly failed to meet the challenges posed by the flood of white settlers moving westward and Native Americans' defense of their homelands. It had equally failed to develop effective methods either of governing its new western lands or of deriving significant revenue from them. And it faced a graver challenge still from Spain's effort to maintain its North American territorial possessions by blocking US expansion using the Mississippi River. That extraordinarily divisive struggle, which threatened to shatter the Confederation itself, is the subject of chapter 6.

6
The Spanish-Treaty Impasse and the Union's Collapse

Shortly after the war, the Spanish Empire made clear that it was implacably opposed to America's western expansion. In July 1784, Spanish officials suddenly closed the Mississippi River to American navigation. Over the next three years, Americans disagreed vehemently about how to respond to Spain's closure and its North American territorial claims. Negotiations between Spain's envoy Don Diego de Gardoqui and Confederation secretary of foreign affairs John Jay played an important role in that controversy. Congress engaged in a bitter sectional clash over a proposed Spanish treaty that resulted from their negotiations. It became permanently deadlocked over that issue. Spain's edict was still in force when the 1787 Philadelphia Convention met.

The Confederation's public support was seriously weakened by its inability to resolve the impasse. During the controversy, for the first time many Americans came to view the Confederation as a dangerous tool for sectional aggrandizement. Influential leaders across the country began to ask seriously whether it would be preferable to secede from the Union to form sectional confederations. The contest also played a very important role in convincing prominent Americans such as Virginia governor Patrick Henry that they must firmly oppose efforts to strengthen the national government. And it led many western Americans to consider abandoning their allegiance to the United States.

James Madison came to believe that Spain's policy was deliberately intended to divide and conquer Americans, weakening the United States in order to protect its North American empire.[1] *If so, it had succeeded admirably. The 1787 Philadelphia Convention delegates had little choice but to negotiate an agreement that would finesse the sectional impasse on western expansion.*

***

> Mr. Lee . . . was sorry to find gentlemen talk so lightly of a separation & dissolution of the Confederation; he considered our existence as a nation to depend on our Union. . . . [I]f this measure [the Spanish treaty] was pursued farther . . . the people west of the moun[tains] would be severed from their brethren on the East, & either set up for themselves or put themselves under the protection of Great Britain or Spain and in either case become formidable enemies to the US.
>
> *Virginia congressman Henry Lee, Jr., on the Spanish treaty, speaking during congressional debate, August 1786*[2]

> It well becomes the eastern and middle States, who are in interest one, seriously to consider what advantages result to them from their connection with the Southern States. They can give us nothing, as an equivalent for the protection which they derive from us but a participation in their commerce. This they deny to us.
>
> *Massachusetts congressman Theodore Sedgwick, privately advocating creation of a separate northern states' confederacy, August 1786*[3]

Spain's Containment Strategy

The right to navigate the Mississippi River was regarded by many Americans as critical to the future of western settlement. Most western crops and products could not be commercially profitable unless they were shipped down the river for sale. Many Americans believed that the United States possessed Mississippi navigation rights even before Britain agreed to them in the 1783 Treaty of Peace. If Spain knew about that provision of the treaty while it was being negotiated, as seems very likely, it deliberately stood by without objecting. Less than a year after the treaty was signed, however, Spain chose to close the Mississippi to

Americans, part of a containment policy that one historian concludes was intended to "strangle the American west."[4]

Spain acted to protect its important North American interests. At the end of the war, it held considerable territory below the United States' southern border. And it asserted that it owned very large areas of western lands that were also claimed by the United States. They included much of the Mississippi River and surrounding territory at least north to the Ohio River.[5] Spain had been concerned for years about contraband trade by non-Spanish subjects on the Mississippi. Such trade harmed its ability to profit from its mercantilist exclusive trade relations with its American colonies.

The surge of western emigration toward the end of the Revolutionary War, especially in 1783, alarmed Spanish colonial officials such as Louisiana's intendant Martin Navarro and acting governor Esteban Miró. They realized that demand to use the river for potentially damaging trade would intensify enormously as settlement expanded. American settlement would also threaten Spain's American territorial claims and its ability to govern its colonies. They wrote warning letters to Spanish central government officials, which eventually reached Spain's chief minister, Count Floridablanca. He has been described as the Spanish counterpart of Britain's exceptionally able prime minister, William Pitt the Younger.

Floridablanca agreed to order the Mississippi River's closure to Americans in mid-1784. He planned that after the closure Spain would convince the United States to renounce its Mississippi navigation claims in return for other commercial and political benefits. After carefully developing instructions to guide him, Spain sent Don Diego de Gardoqui, a very capable Spanish diplomat, to the United States to negotiate a treaty to that end. It was intended primarily to ratify Spain's decision to close the river, though imperial boundaries adjacent to the United States were also at stake.[6]

Spain's closure policy should have come as no surprise to America's more realistic Revolutionary War leaders. They knew that Spain and France had opposed American expansion toward the Mississippi during peace negotiations. Remarkably, however, it did come as a shock to James Madison. In 1784, Madison wrote to Thomas Jefferson that he had concluded for various reasons, including "the general rights of humanity" and the "usage of nations," "that Spain will never be so mad as to persist" in its policy.[7] In retrospect, Madison seems to have been in denial about the reasons for Spain's actions and their likely consequences.[8]

At first, it looked as though Americans from different sections of the country would unite in opposition to Spain's ban. By March 1785, both the Massachusetts and Virginia legislatures had passed resolutions instructing their congressmen to secure the reopening of the Mississippi River.[9] To pursue that goal, Congress agreed to have Secretary of Foreign Affairs John Jay negotiate with Gardoqui over Spain's closure and other disputed issues. In August 1785, Congress unanimously instructed Jay that he must insist that Spain allow free navigation of the river as a condition of any treaty.[10]

Jay was an experienced diplomat who had been one of the leading American negotiators of the 1783 peace treaty with Britain. He was an eminent lawyer whose strong opinions were often based on his "deep piety and unbreakable religious faith of a strong Protestant persuasion."[11] Both Jay's legal training and his principles seem to have interfered at times throughout his career with his ability to appreciate when politics required pragmatic compromises. He has been aptly described by a leading historian as a "powerful personality with intense convictions . . . one of those righteous men in action who are so often wrong in fact."[12] He was described by another distinguished historian as personally vain, ponderous, and having a "rather over-confident appreciation of his own merit. 'Mr. Jay's weak spot is Mr. Jay,' said a close student of him at that period."[13] In Gardoqui, he seems to have met a worthy adversary. The Spanish diplomat eventually returned to Spain to become minister of finance, and has been described as "the ablest and most active minister in the Spanish Council of State" during his later career.[14]

Gardoqui's approach to the negotiations combined substance with diplomatic charm and a cash offensive. He had been instructed that under no circumstances would Spain agree to reopen the Mississippi to Americans. To gain American acceptance of that ultimatum, Gardoqui offered Jay a laundry list of other concessions—most importantly for our purposes, a trade treaty. As Gardoqui was well aware, the trade agreement he proposed had very large potential economic benefits for New England. It would be able to sell fish and naval timber to Spain, probably carried there in American ships. That would give the New England economy a badly needed long-term boost. The proposal would also have significantly aided Mid-Atlantic states' exports. But the proposed treaty would have provided little or no benefit for the southern states, primarily because it specifically excluded tobacco from its provisions.[15]

Gardoqui also assiduously courted Americans whom he thought he could influence. Before leaving Spain, he made suggestions regarding his own instructions to his superiors. Based on his prior experience with Jay, he described him as a "very self-centered man." Jay's wife, he said, "dominates him and nothing is done without her consent, so that her opinion prevails, though her husband at first may disagree." He recommended a charm campaign against the Jays. Gardoqui received enough Spanish secret service money to enable him to use various forms of persuasion such as gifts, and even what may have been bribery, to gain Spain's objectives. Among other things, during the negotiations, the king of Spain sent a gift to George Washington, a jackass shipped across the Atlantic to provide him with mule breeding stock. Gardoqui lent $5,000 to Virginia congressman Henry Lee, Jr., who was sympathetic to Spain's position and close to Washington. He accommodated Jay's request for a royal license to import a Spanish stallion by making him an outright gift of one, which Jay got Congress to approve. And he ingratiated himself enough with Jay and his family that he escorted Mrs. Jay to dinner parties and dances in New York.[16]

Meanwhile, however, Gardoqui's position on the navigation of the river remained inflexible: it would remain closed to Americans. Despite the trade treaty's sharply disproportionate benefits for northern states, Jay felt strongly that it should be agreed to. That would require accepting Spain's decision to close the river, at least for several decades, but that did not bother him. He chose, however, to make a misguided effort to try to end-run treaty opponents in Congress. In late May 1786, Jay asked Congress to create a special committee to direct his treaty negotiations.

Congressional Action on the Spanish-Treaty Proposal

Jay's request for a directing committee was intended to allow Congress to override his 1785 instructions insisting on Mississippi River access without admitting that that was his goal. Jay's strategy seems to have seriously underestimated both the extent of his opposition and its effectiveness. But it succeeded brilliantly in persuading opponents that he lacked candor. Virginia congressman James Monroe immediately concluded that Jay's request was designed to release him from his restrictive instructions. Congress approved Jay's request. Massachusetts congressman Rufus King, Pennsylvanian Charles Pettit, and Monroe were appointed to the committee.[17] Fortunately, we have good information about how various leaders reacted to Jay's strategy and the proposed treaty.

Almost immediately, Rufus King shared his views on the treaty with leading Massachusetts politician Elbridge Gerry. King's letter suggests that he and Jay had been working closely together.[18] He argued strenuously that if the Mississippi River were opened, the United States could never benefit from the increased western settlement that would result. There was no way for the United States to get western settlers to agree to any "paper engagements, or stipulations" that will "insure a desirable connection" between east and west. Western settlers would not want eastern protection; they would be protected from "all foreign hostility"; and their trade would be "wholly confined to the Mississippi." As a result "entire separation must eventually ensue," and the United States would never "receive a penny of revenue from the Inhabitants." King would therefore "consider every emigrant to that country from the Atlantic states as forever lost to the Confederacy."[19] And King had another major reason for supporting the treaty.

King thought that a treaty with Spain would have very large sectional economic benefits as well. He asked rhetorically, "Would not such a treaty be of vast importance to the Atlantic States?" The treaty would significantly improve the United States' ability to sell fish and flour to Spain—that is, principal export products of New England and the Mid-Atlantic states. King acknowledged that "popular opinion throughout the U.S. is in favor of the free navigation of the Mississippi." He discussed the objection that the treaty would require the United States to "forbear to use the navigation of the Mississippi for 20 to 25 years." He argued that the United States was utterly incapable of asserting its right to use the river over Spain's objection. He contended that attempting to do so would require a war against Spain that Spain would win, and that would greatly damage New England. It "would terminate in the loss of the Fisheries, and the restriction of [American territorial] boundaries."[20]

James Madison's reaction to the intelligence about Jay's treaty plans differed radically from King's. At the end of May, James Monroe had written Madison that he thought that Jay planned to agree to the "occlusion" of the Mississippi River by Spain. If that occurred, "we seperate those people I mean all those westward of the mountains from the federal government and perhaps throw them eventually into the hands of a foreign power," Monroe said.[21] Strongly agitated, Madison wrote back to Monroe in painstakingly prepared code even though he was to see him in person shortly. He said that he wrote to Monroe because he could not "forbear in the meantime expressing my amazement that a thought should be entertained of surrendering the Mississippi."[22]

Madison roundly condemned the idea that America would agree to accept Spain's closure of the Mississippi. He wrote that "the measure in question would be a voluntary barter in time of profound peace of the rights of one part of the [American] empire to the interests of another part. What would Massachusetts say to a proposition for ceding to

Britain her right of fishery as the price of some stipulations in favor of tobacco. . . . can there be a more shortsighted or dishonorable policy." Madison seems to have believed that Congress would quickly reject Jay's proposal, again suggesting he was in denial on the treaty issue.[23]

George Washington had also been approached about his views on the navigation of the Mississippi by Virginia congressman Henry Lee, Jr. Lee was strongly inclined to favor policies that would delay the use of the Mississippi by western settlers as long as possible because he thought that emigration harmed the Atlantic states.[24] Washington responded that he agreed that delay would be desirable, but with one very important qualification. Washington thought that the United States should avoid directly addressing the issue with Spain for as long as possible, and that its policy should be "<neither to> relinquish, nor to push our claims to the navigation." Meanwhile, he wanted to strengthen commercial ties between eastern and western states through navigation projects like the Potomac River canal. When the western states grew large enough so as "*really* to need it, there is no power that can deprive them of the use of the Mississippi."[25] Washington would have preferred that the treaty be removed from Congress's agenda. Unfortunately, most if not all of the other parties involved in the dispute felt that they had no choice but to fight. Lee responded to Washington's letter by urging support for a Spanish treaty, saying "I do not think you go far enough."[26]

Most western settlers didn't think Washington's position went far enough either. They were seriously considering using armed force against Spanish interests, and in some cases actually using it. By the spring of 1786, some were calling for war against Spain over the river. They claimed that they were entitled to attack the Spanish because the United States had treaty rights to its navigation.[27] By mid-1786, westerners were outraged by the possibility that it would be closed with the consent of northern states.[28] Many Americans knew that that summer Thomas Amis had been arrested by the Spanish commander at Natchez. Amis's trade cargo had been confiscated, including several hundred iron cooking vessels and fifty barrels of flour. Westerners were infuriated, and an armed band of Virginians led by George Rogers Clark retaliated that September against Spanish settlers at Vincennes.[29] Unfortunately, given the size of the Confederation's army, which was far smaller than the number of armed western settlers, the Confederation would be unable to prevent settlers from starting a war against Spain if feelings became further inflamed. Many congressmen felt that they had to resolve the treaty issue to avoid having the country be dragged into such a war. By July 1786, the congressional committee appointed to "assist" Jay in treaty negotiations stalemated, and the issue came before the full Congress.

In early August, Jay appeared personally before Congress to make the case that his free navigation instructions should be repealed.[30] One foreign diplomat who knew Jay well described him as being "the most zealous partisan" of the northern states in supporting the treaty.[31] Jay claimed that the treaty did not harm the southern states or western settlement because the limited extent of existing settlement meant that Mississippi River navigation was unimportant to the United States, and would be for decades.[32] Jay told delegates that they had only a few real options. The United States could either agree that the river must remain closed for at least twenty-five years to Americans, go to war with Spain, or be disgraced.[33]

Jay made plain that he thought that war was not a realistic option. The United States was "not prepared for a War with any power" and "many of the States would be little inclined to a War with Spain for that object at this day."[34] Even southern congressmen generally agreed that the Confederation could not afford a war with Spain. Virginia congressman Samuel Hardy agreed that Spain's closure was "a National Outrage" but that "our Situation at present . . . seems to proscribe every idea of war."[35] James Monroe, Jay's most ardent opponent, conceded that the United States "may not be in a situation, nor even think of it for the present, to contest" Spain's position.[36] After Jay's presentation, in August Congress debated whether to repeal Jay's instructions.

Congress's debate over free Mississippi navigation laid bare the exceptional strains that were stretching the Confederation to the breaking point. It had enormous implications for the future of American territorial growth in the west, as perceptive observers like Thomas Jefferson knew. He had written from Paris to Archibald Stuart in early 1786 about American expansion, saying that "our confederacy must be viewed as the nest from which all America North & South is to be peopled." To make that possible, Jefferson said, "the navigation of the Mississippi we must have."[37] And from the outset, thoughtful leaders understood that the fight would have inescapable implications for the survival of the Confederation itself. Henry Lee, Jr., wrote to Washington that the ultimate problem the Confederation faced was "the inefficiency of the foederal government." But stronger federal powers "already in every state . . . have too many enemys." The treaty would make matters worse by giving "such a tent for popular declaimers, that the great object viz bracing the foederal government may be thwarted." Lee's concerns would prove remarkably well-founded.[38]

After Jay's presentation, Congressman Charles Pinckney of South Carolina opened the debate in a long, scathing reply. He began by attacking Spain's usefulness as a political or commercial partner. He denied that the proposed treaty went much beyond existing trade relations between the two countries. Yielding on the closure of the Mississippi based on limited existing western settlement would also justify accepting Britain's retention of its western forts, he observed. Pinckney painted the Spanish treaty as a sectionally biased project sponsored by a commercially desperate New England. He claimed that Spain was trying to divide the Confederation and to separate the eastern and western United States. Pinckney pointed out that the treaty would almost guarantee that southern states would be unwilling to give the Confederation any new powers. He closed by observing ominously that Congress could not enforce the treaty against the states even if it agreed to it. The distinguished diplomatic historian Samuel Bemis described Pinckney's speech as "entirely conclusive" against Jay's position even "to the reader today."[39]

Congressman William Grayson of Virginia then argued that Spanish trade would not be especially beneficial. But to the extent that it was, it would largely help the eastern states, both in increased commerce and in selling their state lands. Grayson reportedly said that "the occlusion of the river would destroy the hopes of the principal men in the Southern States in establishing the future fortunes of their families—that it would render the western country of no value . . . that it would separate the interest of the western Inhabitants from that of the rest of the Union & render them hostile to it—that it would weaken if not destroy the union." What Congress needed instead, Grayson said, were tax and commerce powers. But if the northern states pursued the treaty, those powers would never be granted by the southern states. Grayson added a few days later that the treaty amounted to the dismemberment of some of the states by other states, which would "endanger the existence of the Union."[40]

Rufus King defended the proposed treaty. He pointed to the "distressed state of the Eastern States" and their need for a Spanish market for their fish. "They had an ungrateful soil & no staple but what they drew from the sea. . . . That therefore a treaty with Spain was of the utmost consequence to the Eastern states in particular, but the terms which were mentioned were beneficial to all the states," King claimed. He denigrated the western interest in expansion, saying that "refusing to treat on the terms proposed is sacrificing the interest & happiness of a Million to promote the views of speculating land jobbers." He argued that if there were no treaty, the western settlers would attack Spain's river posts and that "the US will be precipitated into a war before they are prepared. That in case of such an event the existence of the Confederation will be endangered." States that would gain no benefits from the war would not support it—and if those states were deprived of the benefits of the treaty, "they are deprived of the only advantages which they could expect from the Union."[41] Here King stated the classic Massachusetts postwar position: it needed to receive only economic benefits from the Confederation, not military defense. An ill-advised Spanish war would destroy the Confederation by prompting secession, King implied.

Congressman Henry Lee, Jr., a distinguished Revolutionary War veteran, said that he thought it was unfortunate that congressmen were "talking so lightly of a separation & dissolution of the Confederation." Another report says that Lee regretted that possible secession of the "Eastern States should be expressed as a reason" why the treaty should be adopted "yet it has been expected that the forming treaty would isolate the Southern States—; they would dissolve the Confederacy."[42] In short, it appears that both sides threatened that if their views did not prevail, they would secede from the Confederation.

In response, Pennsylvania congressman (and retired general) Arthur St. Clair said that it would be desirable if the Spanish treaty slowed emigration, because emigration was harmful to the country in its present situation.[43] St. Clair wrote privately that western secession was "very likely to happen at any rate" and was "a strong reason against the formation of such settlements." He added that if settlements were not under general control of Congress, "the sooner exterminated the better."[44] St. Clair's and King's views make clear how strongly northern state representatives disliked, and hoped they could weaken or even halt, western emigration.

Congress's debate demonstrated that northern and southern states had reached an impasse not just on the treaty but on the viability of the Confederation itself. Both sides threatened secession. Northern states felt that if the Confederation did not enter into the treaty, they had little or nothing to gain from continuing to belong to it. Southern states believed that if the Confederation did enter into the treaty, the western settlers would separate from the Union and their states might well follow them. Southern representatives were unanimous that if the Confederation agreed to the treaty, all efforts to increase its powers would be in vain. If the Confederation continued to lack needed powers, it would remain insolvent and serve no one's purposes, so it would collapse.

Remarkably, however, the northern states decided to force the issue anyway. They either thought that the southern states were bluffing about secession, or they were desperate to enter into the treaty. Both motives may have played a role. According to Congressman Henry Lee, Jr., "The eastern states consider a commercial connexion with Spain, as the only remedy for the distresses which oppress their citizens, most of which they say flow from the decay of their commerce. Their delegates have consequently zealously pressed the formation of this connexion, as the only effectual mode to revive the trade of their country."[45] Rufus King's private correspondence shows that he thought that increasing western emigration meant that the Confederation had no choice but to agree to close the Mississippi. Otherwise, either the settlers would separate or the Confederation would be dragged into a futile, damaging war with Spain on their initiative.[46]

Many of the southern states' representatives were also desperate to prevent the river's permanent closure. During the debate, they proposed a compromise that would permit American exports to travel down the Mississippi and through New Orleans if they paid a small but significant tax, but would prohibit imports up the Mississippi. Their proposal was voted down on purely sectional lines.[47] Southern representatives then met privately in August with French chargé d'affaires Louis-Guillaume Otto, to try to persuade him that France should support their position and intercede with Spain to reach a compromise.[48] Jay had told Congress that France would side with Spain. The fact that southern state representatives nevertheless tried to persuade France to change its position despite its well-known ties with Spain shows how desperate they were. France chose not to intervene.

At the end of August 1786, Congress narrowly agreed in a series of purely sectional votes to allow Jay to agree with Spain that the Mississippi could remain closed to Americans for twenty-five to thirty years. Twelve votes occurred during the debates. On eight out of the twelve, including all of the important votes, the states divided 7–5, and each division was along starkly sectional lines. Although under the Articles of Confederation nine votes were required to agree to a treaty, northern states insisted that Jay's negotiation instructions could be repealed with only seven votes. These were the strongest sectional divisions that had occurred since the end of the war. They had a series of profoundly important political effects that damaged the Confederation's legitimacy.[49]

Sectional Treaty Impasse and Visions of Confederation Dissolution

Most immediately, the sectional divisions significantly increased interest in breaking up the Confederation into several sectional confederations. James Monroe wrote to Virginia governor Patrick Henry about the treaty in mid-August. Monroe believed that northern representatives were so unprincipled and intent on achieving their treaty aims that they were increasingly interested in splitting up the Confederation if necessary to reach them. Monroe told Henry that he believed northern representatives were plotting to partition the Union. Their purposes, he explained, were to "break up . . . the settlements on the western waters, prevent any in future, and thereby keep the States southward as they now are." If there were new settlements, the northern states wanted them designed "so as effectually to exclude any new state [arising] from it, to throw the weight of population eastward & keep it there, to appreciate the vacant lands of New York & Massachusetts."[50] Some well-placed foreign observers actually thought that sectional concerns also motivated southern opposition. They believed that southern states wanted to alter the political balance of power in their favor by adding new western states.[51] In other words, many contemporaries understood the whole treaty controversy as largely a sectional struggle. It was one that both sides knew could permanently change the balance of power in the Confederation. And they saw it as what political scientists refer to as a zero-sum game, that is, one in which if someone wins, someone else must lose.

Many historians believe that Monroe's suspicions of a separate-confederacy conspiracy were exaggerated. But that conclusion misses the point in one critical respect. There is little doubt that northern politicians were interested in the possibility of a northern confederation. In the minds of many leaders there, it would have been a better solution to the Confederation's problems than strengthening the existing Confederation.[52] By the end of 1785, Rufus King was advocating a separate northern commercial confederation. In the midst of the treaty controversy, his colleague Theodore Sedgwick, long-time western Massachusetts attorney-legislator and now congressman, wrote to another leading Massachusetts politician and businessman, Caleb Strong, advocating a separate northern general confederacy.

Sedgwick first cautioned Strong that Massachusetts would not receive any protection from the Confederation against sharply rising social unrest there: "Should Massachusetts fall into anarchy the great prop of the union would be prostrate." He then pointed to the failure of Confederation efforts to protect commerce from the Barbary coast pirates. He claimed that the Annapolis Convention was actually intended to defeat the enlargement of Congress's commerce powers. Because the Confederation was ineffective and near collapse, he said, "It well becomes the eastern and middle States, who are in interest one, seriously to consider what advantages result to them from their connection with the Southern States. They can give us nothing, as an equivalent for the protection which they derive from us but a participation in their commerce. This they deny to us. . . . Even the appearance of a union cannot in the way we now are long be preserved."[53] Sedgwick went on to advocate creating a separate northern confederacy with plenary authority, that is, one not limited to commerce powers. His comments are important for several reasons. They reflect the very widespread northern view that the southern states were militarily weak, and could not offer northern states protection against threats such as social unrest, Indian warfare, or foreign aggression. Sedgwick's comments also reflect that section's prevailing view that the only thing Massachusetts had to gain from the Confederation was stronger commerce powers—or as an alternative, the Spanish treaty. Southern states' opposition to the Spanish treaty had therefore poisoned the Confederation well for many in the northern states.

Monroe was so convinced that the northern states were contemplating breaking up the Confederation that he wrote about the subject to several other Virginia leaders. In a letter to Madison, Monroe claimed that in order to carry the treaty, Jay and other northern representatives were "intriguing with the principal men" in New Jersey and

Pennsylvania to make sure their states supported it. That included, if necessary, splitting up the Confederation by its "dismemberment to the Potowmack [River]." Monroe regarded Pennsylvania's allegiance as pivotal to either section's plans for a separate confederation. He said, "A knowledge that she was on our side would blow this whole intrigue in the air. . . . If a dismemberment takes place that State must not be added to the eastern scale. It were as well to use force to prevent it as to defend ourselves afterwards."[54]

Based on the surviving sources, it is difficult to credit Monroe's view that there was a widespread concrete conspiracy to break up the Union at the time. And it is quite remarkable to see him coolly proposing that Pennsylvania be forcibly coerced into joining a southern states' confederation if a breakup occurred. Still, Monroe was scrutinizing the situation very thoughtfully—and analyzing it in much the same way that Theodore Sedgwick probably would have. They were both thinking seriously about the possibility that the Confederation might break up over the treaty. That suggests that the treaty combatants were calculating the value of the Union to themselves and their regions.[55] They also all seemed persuaded that their own sections could survive as part of a separate sectional confederation if a split occurred. But if they could, why keep the Confederation? And if not, what would happen if it collapsed?

Sectional Impasse and Weakened Confederation Support

The treaty impasse caused significant damage that went well beyond inducing leaders to consider seriously the feasibility of separate confederations. The first was that the divisiveness it caused essentially ended Congress's usefulness as a decision-making body during the year before the Philadelphia Convention. The congressional Grand Committee proposed major Confederation reforms in early August after months of effort. The Grand Committee proposals proved to be Congress's last stab at proposing its own reforms as an alternative to proposals by an outside convention. They were stillborn; Congress never considered them. North Carolina congressman Timothy Bloodworth informed his state that the treaty controversy had ended any prospect that Congress would legislate during the rest of its session. He reported to the governor that "all other business appears out of View, & I do not expect any thing of account will be done by the present Congress."[56] Congress's vote also had important fallout effects across the country. We begin by looking at the reaction of western settlers.

Across the south and southwest, Americans felt as though in supporting the Spanish treaty Congress had betrayed them for sectional gain. Historian Allan Nevins wrote that most Virginians believed that the northern states were deliberately planning "the mutilation and injury of the south to gain a few dollars." They agreed with Jefferson's anguished view that "the abandonment of the Mississippi 'is an act of separation between the eastern and western country.'"[57] A good indication of the changed western political climate is a letter provided to Congress by Secretary Jay in early 1787. It was purportedly sent by a settler at the "falls of Ohio" (present-day Louisville) to a friend in New England in late 1786.

The "late commercial treaty with Spain"—that is, Congress's vote in favor of agreeing to Spain's treaty terms—"has given this Western Country an universal shock," the settler wrote. The letter reported that when goods had been taken for sale to New Orleans, even legally under permits from the Spanish governor, settlers were "obliged to sell at a price he was pleased to state or subject themselves to lose the whole." "Large quantities of Flour, Tobacco, Meal &c. have been taken there the last Summer, and mostly confiscated," it added. In view of Spain's arbitrary behavior, "to sell us and make us Vassals to the merciless Spaniards, is a grievance not to be borne."[58]

The writer went on to threaten war against the Spanish garrisons by western settlers. He described how remarkably fertile and appealing to settlers the western lands were. He then derided eastern efforts to control settlement and settlers' relations with the Spanish. He wrote:

> Do you think to prevent the emigration from a barren Country loaded with Taxes and impoverished with debts to the most luxurious and fertile Soil in the world? Vain is the thought and presumptuous the supposition! . . . Shall one part of the United States be Slaves [under the arbitrary rule of the Spanish] while the other is free? . . . We can raise twenty thousand troops. . . . In case we are not countenanced and succoured by the United States . . . our allegiance will be thrown off, and some other power applied to. . . . You are as ignorant of this Country as Great Britain was of America.[59]

Another well-informed observer of western sentiment, Josiah Harmar, wrote that settlers looked upon the possible closing of the river as "the greatest grievance, as the property of the Western World depends entirely upon this outlet."[60] If the Mississippi River remained closed to Americans, settlers' futures that could have been bright and prosperous would instead be confined to hard labor to eke out meager subsistence.

Another letter from western North Carolina (now Tennessee) published in early 1787 expressed fervent opposition to Spain's closure and any treaty accepting it. The stakes were very high: "every man considers that his all is at stake" if the treaty is adopted. This writer also emphasized Spain's arbitrariness: "the man who takes or destroys one half of your property today, may be capricious enough to claim the other half tomorrow." The author suggested that settlers believed that the original states had interests that conflicted with theirs. Westerners believed that their "claim to the navigation of that river, is as clear and indisputable as any claim [they] ever had to a cow or a horse." They intended to prosecute that claim, by force if necessary, but did not expect "much assistance from your side of the mountain" or from Congress. They knew that "you are not desirous to send colonists to this side of the mountain, because your rents and taxes are better paid while you persuade them to stay."[61] Political controversy surrounding the treaty then spread well beyond serious western discontent and occasional skirmishes with Native Americans.

In late 1786 and early 1787, the Spanish treaty became an issue in both northern and southern state politics. In August 1786, both Pennsylvania and New Jersey congressmen had voted in support of the Spanish treaty. Madison, Monroe, and others began efforts to persuade leaders in those states to force their congressional delegates to change positions. The New Jersey legislature ultimately instructed its congressional delegation to oppose the treaty because it would cost the Confederation land-sales revenues. But the issue was far more divisive in Pennsylvania, threatening to split the state geographically.

In western Pennsylvania, H. H. Brackenridge ran successfully for the legislature on a platform demanding that the state oppose the treaty.[62] Once elected, he offered resolutions committing the state to support free navigation. A letter from leading Philadelphia banker and merchant Thomas Fitzsimons to retired general Samuel Meredith, a merchant and land speculator, shows that Fitzsimons opposed having the legislature take any position in response. He wanted to avoid either giving "Weight to the Spanish proposal" or offending "the people of the western country." Fitzsimons appears to have been aligned, quite unusually, with "the politician from Westmoreland" (probably Constitutionalist Party leader William Findley) on that issue. In spring 1787, the legislature declined by a small majority to adopt any resolution on the treaty or to instruct the state's congressmen about it. That suggests that with the Philadelphia Convention soon to begin, Pennsylvania leaders on both sides of Confederation reform wanted to avoid dividing potential supporters over the treaty.[63]

The Spanish-treaty vote also markedly weakened support for Confederation reforms in the southern states. Southern leaders now saw the Confederation as a potential threat. Reporting to the North Carolina legislature on the treaty, Congressman Timothy Bloodworth wrote, "If seven states can barter any part of the Privileges of the Different States, for any advantage whatsoever, there remains no security for any possession. It is well known that the balance of Power is now in the Eastern States, & they appear determined to keep it in that direction."

In a similar vein, Madison wrote to James Monroe that the treaty was a classic example of an interested majority unjustly plundering a minority, attempting to make "force as the measure of right." These comments represented the emergence of a fundamentally new political fear in the southern states—that they could lose in a zero-sum game if they remained within the Confederation or gave it more power.[64]

The best example of the shift in southern opinion is the changing views of Patrick Henry and the Virginia legislature. As James Madison ruefully admitted, Henry had "been hitherto the Champion of the federal cause," supporting reforms such as the Confederation's import tax proposal, before the Spanish-treaty debate.[65] But Henry personally helped organize western opposition to the Spanish treaty. He is reported to have said that he "would rather part with the confederation than relinquish the navigation of the Mississippi."[66] As we have seen, there were prominent Virginians on the other side of the issue, among whom were Henry Lee, Jr., and, it appears, both Richard Henry Lee and Arthur Lee. Notably, however, no one was foolhardy enough to take their side of the argument in the legislature. It voted unanimously in late November 1786 to condemn the treaty as a dishonorable violation of the basic principles of the Articles of Confederation.[67] Even more importantly, Henry became an enemy of Confederation reforms. As historian Allan Nevins puts it, "a powerful party arose in Virginia, headed by Patrick Henry, which believed that the manifestation of sectional cross-interests and selfishness in this Mississippi question proved that a stronger Union was impracticable."[68]

True, the Virginia legislature had also voted unanimously in November to issue a call to the states to hold the 1787 Philadelphia Convention. But that victory was a temporary one that meant little, because Henry's influence might well prevent any proposals made by the convention from being ratified there. Henry declined appointment as a convention delegate. Madison told Jefferson that this was because "Mr. Henry's disgust [about the Spanish treaty] exceeded all measure and I am not singular in ascribing his refusal to attend the convention to the policy of keeping himself free to combat or espouse the result of it according to the result of the Mississippi business among other circumstances."[69]

In fact, Madison was convinced that the treaty issue could by itself defeat Virginia ratification of any new constitution proposed by the Philadelphia Convention. He wrote to George Washington just after the legislature's votes opposing the treaty and supporting the convention that "I am entirely convinced, from what I observe here, that unless the project of Congress [i.e., agreeing to the Spanish treaty] can be reversed, the hopes of carrying this state into a proper federal system will be demolished."[70] Seeking to prevent further loss of support for Confederation reforms, Madison spent a considerable part of his time before the convention trying to get Congress to modify its treaty position. Events in Massachusetts in late 1786 then changed the controversy's course in unexpected ways.

By the end of 1786, Massachusetts seems to have limited its efforts to push the Spanish treaty forward due to more immediate concerns. By then, an armed rebellion led by Daniel Shays and others had erupted against the Massachusetts state government (see chapter 8). Congressman William Grayson reported to James Madison in late November that "the affair of the Mississippi hangs in suspence. I rather think nothing has been done in it. The M. Bay [Massachusetts] delegation have been more on the conciliatory plan, since the late insurrections in that state. They I believe depend on the foederal aid."[71] But apparently Massachusetts and Grayson disagreed about what conciliatory meant.

To frustrate efforts to change Congress's vote favoring the treaty, Rufus King persuaded Congress to adopt a rule whose practical effect was to prevent it from ever reconsidering its vote. The rule required that twelve states with enough representatives in attendance to be able to cast their state's votes all be present on the floor of Congress before a motion to reconsider could even be made. Twelve states were very rarely present and fully represented in Congress, especially after August 1786. King also led other congressmen to believe that his views against western emigration had hardened further. He told retired general Samuel Meredith, a newly elected Pennsylvania congressman, that "it would prove a happiness to all the settled parts of the Country if the Ohio was to be the boundary for a number of years, as well as be a means of quieting the Indians & Spaniards."[72]

For their part, Virginia delegates met privately with Gardoqui in late March 1787. They tried to persuade him that Spain should change its position on opening the river. Gardoqui flatly refused. They then tried to make a virtue out of weakness. They told him that Spain would be wise to base its policy on the inevitability of western settlement because Congress could not control it through a treaty. Gardoqui responded acerbically that as far as he could tell, Congress was unable to enter into any treaty at all. He added that "he had observed the weakness of the Union and foreseen its probable breach."[73] This remarkably undiplomatic statement strongly suggests that Gardoqui agreed with others, including the French government, who by then expected that the Confederation might well collapse. Only a few months later, in fact, the French government instructed its chargé d'affaires, Louis-Guillaume Otto, that it was entirely indifferent about what it saw as the likely prospect that the Confederation would fall apart. He was told that he should not do anything to encourage or support opposition to Spain's Mississippi River policy. The government's letter plainly meant that if the Spanish-treaty impasse contributed to the Union's collapse, that would be just fine with France.[74]

In early April 1787, Congress agreed to require Secretary Jay to report on the status of his negotiations with Gardoqui.[75] Jay reported that Gardoqui had been unwilling to agree to any statement, or even the implication, that the United States had a right to navigate the lower Mississippi. Jay's new proposal was to have the two countries agree that they could both navigate on the upper Mississippi River, while barring Americans from navigating the lower Mississippi. According to Jay, that provision was neutral regarding both Spain's and the United States' rights on the lower Mississippi. It would, however, explicitly prevent Americans from using the Mississippi to trade goods through New Orleans, thus denying westerners what they most wanted.

Jay also reported to Congress on western settlers' involvement with

Spanish forces and residents. That included the raid on Vincennes led by George Rogers Clark in late 1786 in which Spanish goods were seized. He told Congress that western-settler reprisals against Spain meant that "the period is not far distant" when the United States "must decide either to Wage War with Spain" or to settle the countries' differences by treaty. Jay ended by telling Congress that he wished a pox on both their houses, as the saying goes. He lectured Congress that it would not be possible for the Confederation either to wage a war that was not supported by many of the states, or to enter into a treaty that many states did not support. That meant that there was no road out of the existing impasse.

During the weeks just before the Philadelphia Convention, Madison was still trying to find some way of improving the southern states' treaty position. First, he asked Congress to shift the negotiations to Madrid and to put Jefferson in charge in place of Jay. During the ensuing debate, Congressman Nathaniel Gorham of Massachusetts "avowed his opinion that the Shutting [of] the Mississippi would be advantageous to the Atlantic States, and wished to see it shut." Madison attacked Gorham's position as an unpatriotic violation of revolution principles. Congress declined to act on his motion to displace Secretary Jay, killing it.[76] Madison then moved that Jay be instructed that his proposed suspension of Americans' use of the Mississippi was based on an invalid vote of Congress because only seven states had supported it. King opposed the motion. Congress agreed to postpone (i.e., reject) Madison's motion. Jay remained in control of the treaty negotiations and was still free to agree to yield the navigation of the river in them.

On May 2, 1787, Madison left New York to attend the Philadelphia Convention. Surprisingly, he chose to interpret his complete inability to persuade Congress to alter its August 1786 vote in favor of the treaty as a victory that killed the treaty. He wrote, "It was considered on the whole that the project of shutting the Mississippi was at an end; a point deemed of great importance in reference to the approaching Convention for introducing a Change in the federal Government, and to the objection to an increase of its powers foreseen from the jealousy which had been excited by that project."[77] Note Madison's exceptionally passive phrasing: "It was considered . . . that." He does not tell us who thought that the treaty project was dead—and as it would turn out, there were many people who were not persuaded that it was. But Madison was acutely aware that it was essential for people to believe that "the project was at an end." If they did not, any reform proposed in Philadelphia was likely to run into opposition much tougher than even the strenuous opposition that it was already quite foreseeable it was going to face.

The sources suggest that Madison described the treaty as being dead for reasons of political expediency, not because doing so was accurate. Skirmishing between the states on the issue in Congress continued during the Philadelphia Convention. On July 4, Congress, temporarily dominated by southern states, heard a report favoring free navigation of the Mississippi, but left Jay's instructions unchanged.[78] On July 5, Massachusetts congressman Nathan Dane, a strong supporter of the treaty, wrote to Rufus King, then a delegate in Philadelphia, asking whether "to renew the subject of the S. Treaty."[79] It was entirely possible that the northern states would reopen the issue if an opportunity presented itself. Even more important, state leaders now recognized that the Confederation could be used for sectional aggrandizement on future issues as well. That meant that the Confederation's failure to resolve the Spanish treaty impasse and its implications now formed an inescapable part of the backdrop to the work of the Philadelphia Convention.

But by 1788, there appears to have been a major decline in northern states' support for the Spanish treaty. Congressman John Brown of Virginia's Kentucky district, a leading western politician and strong advocate of Kentucky independence, wrote in January 1788 to his friend James Breckenridge about the status of the Spanish treaty. Brown said, "I think little is to be feared from the Project for ceding the Navigation of the Mississippi to Spain; almost a total change of Sentiment upon that Subject has taken place. The Opposition has acquired great Strength from the Sales of Western Territory; many Inhabitants of the Eastern States of great Influence & powerful Connections have become

Adventurers in that Country & are now engaged in forming Settlements at Muskingum, Miamia &c."[80] Brown's letter suggests that important changes in national life had occurred since Madison left for Philadelphia.

Conclusion

The Spanish-treaty controversy was the most intractable political stalemate of the postwar period. The Confederation was unable to formulate a policy in response to Spain's actions that could command both majority support and minority acquiescence. The highly emotional sectional debate led to threats of secession from the Confederation on both sides. It sharply increased interest in creating separate sectional confederations to replace the United States. It divided some states politically. Most importantly, it markedly increased opposition to strengthening the existing Confederation. Spain had managed, at almost no cost to itself, to find a way significantly to increase American disunity at precisely the time in the life of the Confederation when unity was most needed. It did so by cleverly exploiting the human weaknesses of Confederation officials such as Jay, the greed and ambition of leading western settlers, and the political weaknesses of the Confederation itself.

James Madison was right to see the proposed treaty as a Spanish plot to derail America's efforts to strengthen its government. Spain's stratagem caused substantial political damage and made the task of Confederation reform far more difficult. Many Americans began to envision life without the Confederation and came to see it as a dangerous tool of sectional aggrandizement. The Philadelphia Convention had little choice but to try to cure the damage done by the sectional impasse on the treaty and western expansion created by Spain that the Confederation had failed to resolve.[81]

PART 3

Internal Divisions: State Social Conflicts

7

Economic Relief, Social Peace, and Republican Justice

During the mid-1780s recession, popular movements supporting economic relief erupted across the country. Seven states issued paper money, and several states provided debt relief. But the total amount of money issued was quite small relative to size of the economy. The issues failed to combat deflation. And they often depreciated significantly. Debt-relief laws often postponed payment but did not eliminate most debt; in some cases, debts grew as a result. Economic-relief proposals encountered vigorous opposition and were defeated in several states.

Popular relief forces were, in reality, weaker nationwide than historians have traditionally thought. Relief advocates dominated legislatures in states such as South Carolina. But in Pennsylvania, New York, and New Jersey, paper money's popularity was so limited that public-creditor support was essential to obtaining its issuance. States mostly chose moderate debt relief, rejecting requests for more extensive relief. In most states, popular relief movements were predominantly peaceful (a few states were exceptions, and there was scattered violence in others).

Opposition to paper-money laws and debt relief increased during these controversies for two reasons. Such laws became inextricably bound up in a wider struggle over the proper limits of republican majorities' powers over minorities. They were also badly tarred by what many contemporaries saw as Rhode Island's relief abuses, which were often viewed as having damaging interstate effects.

The 1780s economic-relief controversies had limited effects, however, on *the Confederation reform movement. Elite federalist and nationalist leaders across the country frequently opposed states' economic-relief programs. That did little to bring them closer together on the need for fundamental Confederation reforms such as commerce powers. Nevertheless, the perceived interstate effects of relief policies and broader concerns they raised about potential majority tyranny made it inevitable that they would be on the agenda of the 1787 Philadelphia Convention.**

***

> *Vox Populi Vox Dei* . . . The ends and purposes of government implicitly give . . . a right to modify and supercede such [debt] contracts when the good of the community requires.
>
> *South Carolina Assembly Speaker John Julius Pringle, defending the state's economic relief laws, 1787*[1]

> Among the numerous ills with which this practice is pregnant, one I find is that it is producing the same warfare and retaliation among the states as is produced by the State regulations of commerce.
>
> *James Madison to Thomas Jefferson, describing states' paper-money policies, 1786*[2]

During the mid-1780s, the states responded to the severe postwar economic recession, some far more effectively than others. Popular movements across the country demanded economic relief. Under the Confederation, the states had unrestricted authority to provide various kinds of relief. As we have seen, they controlled taxes and their collection. They had the power to issue paper money.[3] They had authority over laws governing both the extent of debtors' obligations and their

* Portions of this chapter were originally published in George William Van Cleve, "The Anti-Federalists' Toughest Challenge: Paper Money, Debt Relief, and the Ratification of the Constitution," *Journal of the Early Republic* 34, no. 4 (2014): 529–60, and are reprinted by permission.

enforceability. This chapter reexamines the divisive relief controversies in key states. It explains the policies adopted by the states (beyond tax relief, discussed in chapter 2) and analyzes their consequences. And it explores what significance the state controversies had for the fate of the Confederation.

Wartime Economic Relief and Its Effects

The Revolutionary War influenced Americans' views about the desirability of economic relief, whether in the form of paper money or of debt relief.[4] Those two major forms of relief had a somewhat different wartime history, however. During the war, for various reasons creditors often had comparatively little ability to collect debts. In effect, by law or necessity many debtors were granted a debt-collection freeze. Debts did not disappear, however, and in many cases they grew because more interest was owed on them as the war dragged on. After the war, creditors around the country began concerted efforts to collect them, and court actions against debtors spiked. In Massachusetts's Hampshire County alone, for example, there were nearly three thousand debt suits in 1784–86, 262 percent more than in 1770–72.[5] Creditors' actions gave rise to popular clamor for debt-relief laws in nearly every state. Debtors and creditors clashed in legislatures across the country over the next several years.

Unlike debt relief, paper money had played a visible role in the war effort and had had widely observed ill effects. During the war, the Confederation issued about $240 million worth of paper money, which depreciated rapidly. The states had issued about $200 million worth of paper money. Like the Confederation's paper money, it rapidly lost most of its value.[6] Some historians think that it was the bitter experience of paper money's extreme wartime depreciation and accompanying hyperinflation that caused vigorous resistance to its issuance later in the 1780s.[7]

The course of postwar events strongly suggests that most Americans did want to avoid repeating their dismal wartime experience with paper money. Even after widespread popular agitation for the issuance of paper money around the country in 1785–86, total mid-1780s state emissions—very roughly speaking—were on the order of magnitude of one million British pounds sterling equivalent (about $4.5 million then).[8] That total was quite small relative to the size of the overall economy and was minuscule compared to wartime issues. The emissions' small quantity probably explains why they failed to prevent the severe deflation that was occurring.[9] But although the wartime experience was influential, it does not fully explain either the nature or the extent of the vehement opposition to paper money and debt relief after the war. During the mid-1780s controversies, two new issues of fundamental importance came to prominence: Should there be limits on the powers of republican majorities to provide economic relief if it harmed some people as well? What, if anything, should be done about the significant interstate harms that many people thought were caused by some states' economic relief policies?

Economic Relief Policies in Postwar Politics

By the 1780s, many of the arguments for and against paper money and debt relief were familiar to Americans. But instead of being seen as perhaps unfortunate but necessary war measures, these policies were now being discussed in peacetime. Paper money was the most popular economic-relief policy (beyond tax relief), and views about it were often linked to opinions on debt relief. To understand the state economic-relief controversies, it helps to begin with a brief survey of leaders' views about the pros and cons of paper money after the war.

In the 1780s, leaders such as James Madison and George Washington opposed paper money because they were convinced that it would inevitably depreciate in value. Washington wrote wearily that "the wisdom of man . . . cannot at this time devise a plan by which the credit of Paper money would be long supported."[10] Madison and many other leaders thought that specie was actually scarce due to the United States' large negative foreign trade balance (an excess of imports over exports). But rather than leading to desirable changes such as increased exports, specie's scarcity became an unfortunate excuse for demanding economic relief. As Madison wrote, "By draining us of our metals [it] furnishes pretexts for the pernicious substitution of paper money, for indulgences to debtors, for postponements of taxes."[11] Many contemporaries also saw paper money as a form of legally sanctioned fraud. Some insisted that only specie could be legitimate money, since other forms were inherently subject to political abuse.[12]

Paper money was also seen by some leaders as little more than a vehicle for concealed debt relief. Whether or not paper-money supporters intended depreciation to occur, if it did, Washington believed, only debtors would benefit and "in proportion to his gain, the creditor, or the body politic suffer."[13] Secretary of War Henry Knox and Virginia leader William Grayson were both convinced that paper-money supporters saw it as a device to abolish debts through depreciation.[14] Grayson wrote, "The Antients . . . contended openly for an abolition of debts in so many words, while we strive as hard for the same thing under the decent & specious pretense of a circulating medium."[15]

On the other hand, prominent leaders such as Benjamin Franklin regarded paper-money emissions, particularly for land-bank purposes, as successful ways to stabilize colonial economies and foster growth.[16] Franklin viewed paper-money depreciation as a form of taxation. However, he thought that it was a tax imposed largely on the wealthy, so depreciation was perfectly acceptable.[17] When paper-money opponents such as the prominent New Jersey attorney William Paterson condemned it as a form of "levelling," they were essentially opposing such redistributive effects.[18]

As historian Woody Holton points out, wealth redistribution "through currency manipulation was not simply a theoretical possibility, for something very close to that had just occurred during the Revolutionary War."[19] George Washington, Thomas Jefferson, and the wealthy South Carolina merchant Henry Laurens (one of America's peace negotiators with Britain), for example, had all lost large amounts of money. Debtors had repaid debts to them with heavily depreciated "legal tender" paper money. Laurens estimated that he lost 95 percent of the value of the money owed to him.[20] But supporters of paper money made arguments for it beyond assisting economic growth and the desirability (or acceptability) of redistributive taxation.

In the mid-1780s, supporters of paper money also insisted that it was a necessary corrective for the scarcity of specie. Greedy merchants had sent all the specie abroad. Paper money was therefore needed as a "circulating medium," so that they could pay oppressive taxes and debts.[21] Using paper rather than specie money would reduce American dependence on imports and increase domestic manufacturing, so any harm to merchants from it was irrelevant.[22] And paper money would allow taxes that largely benefited public creditors to be more easily paid by non-creditors.[23]

In short, postwar leaders were divided on paper money, though among nationally prominent leaders Franklin's positive views may well have been in the minority. Arguments made for and against issuing paper money tended to correlate closely with support for and opposition to debt relief as well. But as historian Merrill Jensen points out, in the end the outcome of economic-relief conflicts depended on who controlled state legislatures, not on pro and con arguments.

To understand where support for economic relief was concentrated, it is useful to arrange the states' approaches to paper money and debt relief along a spectrum. At one end are several states that issued paper money and provided very broad debt relief. For example, South Carolina issued paper money, and it stayed and stretched out debt obligations and allowed debtors to tender property in payment of money debts. The legislatures of states at that end of the spectrum were dominated by economic-relief supporters. Several states in the middle of the spectrum, such as Virginia and Connecticut, refused to adopt paper money but provided at least some—in Virginia's case, major—debt relief. At the spectrum's other end, Massachusetts steadfastly refused to adopt either type of measure. In the mid-1780s, the Massachusetts legislature was controlled by economic conservatives, many of whom were opposed to granting economic relief on principle.[24]

Broadly speaking, the mid-1780s relief laws were often popular, but that generalization needs careful qualification to be accurate. Historian Jackson Turner Main's data show that on average paper-money and debt-relief laws received support from about 58 percent of legislators in the four to six states he surveyed.[25] These averages suggest that substantial opposition often existed. They also conceal fundamental variations, depending primarily on who stood to gain or lose from such laws. In some states, such as South Carolina, relief laws had a high level of public support, including large cash-poor planters and most merchants. In others, such as North Carolina and Rhode Island, there was majority legislative support for paper money but also vocal minority opposition, often from merchants. In three others—Pennsylvania, New York, and New Jersey—public opinion was sharply divided, and urban merchants were strongly opposed. States that adopted paper money also divided sharply over whether it was made legal tender.[26] Though it would be mistaken to reduce this era's conflicts to debtor–creditor clashes, their important role in economic-relief controversies was quite evident. Main's work shows that states also took significantly different approaches to debt relief.[27]

The following discussion of economic-relief disputes is not intended as a comprehensive survey. Instead, it focuses on important differences between key states. It shows that one of the most important effects of the 1785–86 debates over paper money and debt relief was that new concerns about potential majority tyranny and interstate harms became central to these controversies. Our discussion begins, however, with an extended discussion of events in South Carolina because they shed light on many issues that arose across the country.

Economic Relief in the Lower South

In South Carolina in 1785, more than one thousand men in Camden "gathered to stop the Court of Common Pleas." Governor William Moultrie called a legislative special session, telling legislators that "your courts [are being insulted], your laws set at defiance."[28] Saying that debtors faced potential ruin, he urged relief measures, including issuance of £400,000 in paper money. The legislature agreed as a compromise to issue paper money in the amount of £100,000.[29]

The 1785 South Carolina paper-money law was a "land-bank" law. Government loans would assist both small farmers and large land-rich but cash-poor planters.[30] The money issued was not made legal tender. Land-bank supporters saw it as needed to avoid widespread forced property sales at fire-sale prices.[31] Supporters also sought allies by arguing that paper money would assist "patriotic friends to their country" who held state debts. They were being paid interest in severely depreciated South Carolina "State Indents," and would be better off if paid in state paper money worth more.[32] Not everyone was happy about the state's relief policies. During 1786, one leading Charleston newspaper reprinted a steady stream of bitter attacks on paper money; others attacked debt relief.[33] Historians have traditionally thought that South Carolina paper money held its value against specie reasonably well. But some recent research, though anecdotal, suggests that it may actually have depreciated by 25 percent or so by late 1786.[34]

South Carolina also enacted extensive debt-relief measures. After the war, South Carolina allowed repayment of many debts to be delayed until 1786. Later laws permitted repayment to be stretched out for several more years. The so-called Pine Barren Act went beyond that.[35] By 1786, the act made debtors' property (as opposed to money) a legal tender. Eligible property included unimproved real estate such as western pine forests. Creditors were required to accept property at three-fourths of its appraised value, though its actual market value might be far lower. Appraisals might be unreliable, and the tender process could be manipulated.[36] South Carolina merchant Henry Laurens wrote that the law had been "a compromise, under apprehensions of something worse. . . . In a Word men are determined to get out of debt" using the law.[37]

Laurens denounced the Pine Barren Act as "infamous" and said it violated "every principle of justice." A London writer complained that South Carolina might as well have said "we white wash all debtors."[38] In describing this "unjust" law, a French official wrote that instead of forthrightly demanding abolition of debts, "Americans endeavor to give to the most crying injustice an air of equity, of which no one can be the dupe. They call this law of Carolina the Barren Land Law, and their creditors take good care not to press them, fearing [that the law will force them] to acquire land which they do not want."[39] By late 1786, South Carolina merchants were refusing to pay state taxes because they were unable to collect debts owed to them.[40] In early 1787, Laurens wrote that "all the debts due to my Brother's Estate a considerable Amount & to myself, might as well have been confiscated as to be barred by such laws as have been enacted in this State. . . . I have not received one farthing Principal or Interest of either. . . . Many of these debtors employ our Money in gainful Jobbings & some of them are seen riding in their Coaches."[41] Laurens's comments strongly suggest that South Carolina's debtor-relief laws were susceptible to abuse.

South Carolina leaders justified their economic-relief program on the basis that democratic majorities had power to take necessary actions to protect the public good. The Speaker of the South Carolina House of Representatives, John Julius Pringle, said, "*Vox Populi Vox Dei*. . . . The ends and purposes of government implicitly give . . . a right to modify and supercede such contracts when the good of the community requires."[42] Pringle's statement goes to the heart of the controversy over paper money and debt relief in the 1780s. Conflicts over economic relief often turned on whether legislatures would authorize existing debt contracts to be altered to protect debtors, including by paying specie debts with paper money instead. Such ex post facto laws were described by one contemporary as "engines of oppression."[43] They gave republican majorities unlimited power over both private and public contracts. As we will see, for many Americans that raised concerns about possible majority tyranny over minorities.

Georgia and North Carolina also made paper-money emissions in the mid-1780s. Both states' emissions depreciated sharply. Georgia authorized a £50,000 paper emission in August 1786. It quickly lost value, falling to four-to-one against specie by 1787 (i.e., roughly 75 percent depreciation).[44] Historian Merrill Jensen describes the contest over the North Carolina 1785 paper-money emission as "a clear-cut fight between debtor farmers and planters on the one hand, and the merchants and a few wealthy planters on the other" that resulted in a "sweeping victory for the debtors." The emission's management was a tragedy of errors. For example, the state used a third of the money to buy tobacco, hoping for its profitable resale, but had to resell it for a fraction of what it had paid. Jensen concludes that "the combination of corruption, opposition, and depreciation gave the state's currency almost as bad a reputation as that of Rhode Island." By mid-1786, the paper money had depreciated 25 to 30 percent.[45]

Economic Relief in the Mid-Atlantic States

The politics of paper money was qualitatively different, however, in Pennsylvania, New York, and New Jersey. A conservative estimate is that these states together issued roughly half of the total paper money issued by the states in the mid-1780s. In them, even moderate economic-relief programs could be adopted only by creating coalitions whose members had very different, indeed arguably conflicting, interests. Following is a sketch of those states' paper-money politics.[46]

In Pennsylvania in 1784, there were unsuccessful efforts to legislate for state paper money, but it would not have aided public creditors. In 1785, the Constitutionalist Party–dominated legislature authorized a currency issue of £150,000. The bill created a loan office (land bank) to loan one-third of the paper money to borrowers with land as security. But fully two-thirds of Pennsylvania's total issue was designated to pay interest on the state's securities, including assumed Confederation debts (referred to as certificate debt) owed to residents.[47] In other words, most of the paper-money issue was actually intended to benefit public creditors. For them, state paper money was financially better than the available alternatives, including Confederation indents worth very little.[48]

The Pennsylvania bill's particularly small loan-office funding (roughly one-fourth of New York's emission per capita) led to charges that its main purpose was to enrich public creditors and speculators. It was said that the law's real purpose was not to help poor citizens but was "throwing a tub to the whale, to keep us quiet, and to get hold of the money to pay your own certificate interest."[49] Philadelphia's influential merchants also adamantly opposed the bill.

During its consideration of the paper-money law, one major issue facing Pennsylvania's legislature was whether government-debt speculators should benefit. (Speculators bought debt cheaply [i.e., far below face value] in the hope of either reselling it or ultimately redeeming it at a much higher face value.) John Dickinson, the wealthy conservative president of the state executive council, opposed the bill because, he claimed, it would reward speculators. If all current debt holders including speculators were paid, Dickinson asserted, many speculators would receive returns of up to 50 percent on their investments.[50] But the legislature disagreed. It allowed payment to speculators who held debt owed to a resident, except with respect to military pay or commutation-certificate debts owed to soldiers.[51] Since much of the total outstanding debt was nonmilitary, the law was a "veritable gold mine for speculators."[52]

Across the country, there was widespread public antipathy to rewarding war-debt speculators, as historian Woody Holton's work shows.[53] When citizens sought tax relief, it was frequently at least in part because they opposed paying taxes to benefit speculators. Soldiers, often poorer men who had been forced by necessity to sell their military certificates at low prices, were especially bitter about being forced to pay taxes so that wealthy speculators who had purchased their certificates could profit. In that light, the legislature's decision to authorize payments on large amounts of speculative debt suggests that allowing speculative profits was a necessity to obtain enough public-creditor support to enact the coalition's paper-money program.[54]

Despite these challenges, a coalition of strange bedfellows passed the Pennsylvania paper-money law. One historian concluded that "the legislation . . . represented a deal between creditors, paper money advocates, and land speculators."[55] Pennsylvania would not have adopted paper money without that coalition agreement. Legislators also voted nearly unanimously against making the paper money legal tender. And they rejected efforts to provide broad debt relief like that in South Carolina. By large majorities, they raised taxes and tightened tax collection to ensure that the paper money could be retired. They rejected arguments that Pennsylvania should try to collect an estimated £400,000–£500,000 in delinquent taxes instead.[56]

Pennsylvania's economic-relief program thus occupied what some popular-relief advocates viewed as a sorely disappointing middle ground. It satisfied traditional requirements for financial backing and did not markedly restrict creditors' rights by conferring legal-tender status.[57] Despite that, by mid-1786, Pennsylvania paper money had reportedly depreciated some 15 to 20 percent, and then for about a year, fluctuated between a depreciation of 12 and 20 percent. By 1788–89, it had reportedly declined one-third in value. One historian concludes that by 1788, the money had "fallen so low it had ceased to be a medium." But the state still accepted it at face value for tax payments, so "the State thus lost [money] in receiving them."[58]

Pennsylvania's paper-money emission also profoundly shifted the course of public debate over economic relief. It led to a heated legislative debate over whether to revoke the state charter of the private Bank of North America founded by Robert Morris. That debate in turn caused many people to begin to view the controversy over paper money as part of a broader and more fundamental question. That was whether republican governments should have the power to modify or invalidate (i.e., "impair the obligation of") existing contracts. Revoking the bank charter was one example of that power's exercise. But paper money designated as legal tender was soon seen as another. As a result, the legislature's 1785 revocation of the bank charter significantly widened and reshaped the controversy over paper money and debt relief not just in Pennsylvania, but around the country.

The Bank of North America was a commercial bank whose wealthy stockholders, mostly interstate merchants, were located in virtually every major city from Baltimore to Portsmouth, New Hampshire.[59] It lent money only in connection with short-term commercial transactions in order to limit its risks. Because it refused to make long-term loans, farmers and artisans were usually unable to obtain loans, a source of great political resentment.[60] Bank critics accused it of helping to depress the state's economy by promoting imports, which drained specie from the United States. Some claimed that it dominated the state's economy: "The Junto [Morris and his associates] have actually the command of all the money in the State, by means of their Bank." Critics charged that its high interest rates were unfair to farmers who could not afford them, and that its operations had caused interest rates to skyrocket. Legislator John Smilie charged that "from the establishment of the bank, interest rose from six percent to the enormous degree at which we see it at present. Usury has been coeval with the bank." Moreover, the bank fostered the growth of aristocracy, opponents claimed.[61]

The legislature's decision to issue paper money precipitated the fight over the bank's charter. The bank's opponents saw its operations as a powerful enemy of state paper money, which they believed prevented it from trading at par with specie. Opponents argued that they could revoke its charter in the public interest because "the happiness of the people is the first law." Westmoreland County Constitutionalist Party legislator William Findley had spearheaded the fight for paper money and was a principal leader in the charter attack.[62] He argued that as an institution that created wealth outside public control, the bank was fundamentally incompatible with democracy, not just with state paper money. It was "an unlimited institution . . . for the sole purpose of increasing [private] wealth" and therefore "democracy must fall before it."[63] At least 87 percent of the legislators who supported paper money also supported charter revocation.[64] But before long a major backlash developed.

Thomas Paine, who had written the enormously popular revolutionary tract *Common Sense*, responded vociferously to the charter revocation. He broke ranks with the Constitutionalist Party, with which he had long been allied. Paine had opposed Robert Morris on various issues, and had written as recently as early 1785 that "there may be cases in which paper money may be generally serviceable."[65] Now he attacked both the charter revocation and paper money as blatant violations of cardinal republican principles. Paine argued that a first principle of republican government was that in forming it, the people renounced their right of "breaking and violating their engagements, compacts and contracts" with each other. Interference with contracts such as the charter was therefore unconstitutional. He attacked paper money as an artificial political creation that would inevitably harm honest laborers. He reserved particular scorn for legal-tender laws, a "most presumptuous attempt at arbitrary power."[66]

Paine's essay provided a republican rationale for a constitutional ban on impairment of all forms of contracts. It entirely reframed paper money as a form of government-sanctioned contract abuse. Paine's work was a highly visible riposte to repeated 1780s claims made by advocates from South Carolina to Rhode Island that the will of republican majorities should always govern and that that principle justified all forms of paper money and debt relief. His essay was published in February 1786. Within four months, its attack on paper money was excerpted in at least a dozen newspapers from New Hampshire to South Carolina. They linked Paine's views to his patriotic stature by attributing the essay to the "author of *Common Sense*."[67] It elicited replies from leading paper money advocates in New Jersey, as well as vitriolic attacks on Paine's character, including claims that he had been bought.[68]

A political backlash against the Pennsylvania legislature's actions began almost immediately as well. In the fall of 1785 assembly elections, fifteen out of seventeen members of the Philadelphia area and Chester County delegations were replaced. Unlike their predecessors, nearly all of the new legislators were supporters of Robert Morris and the bank, and opponents of paper money. This trend continued in the 1786 elections, which gave conservatives a narrow legislative majority. A contemporary observer interpreted the results this way: "the late returns of Assemblymen . . . fully evinces that the Bank of North America has recovered its popularity, and that paper money has lost its credit throughout the state. On these two points the late general election turned in every county."[69]

The paper-money controversy in New York strongly resembled that in Pennsylvania. The state assembly rejected a proposal for the issuance of £500,000 in 1785, before it proposed a £100,000 loan-office bill, but even that was blocked by the elite state senate.[70] Merchants hoped that the Bank of New York would instead provide sufficient credit. But as in Pennsylvania, rural interests saw the New York bank as unhelpful if not downright hostile to their interests, because it did not provide credit to them.[71]

In 1786, with Governor George Clinton's support, a coalition persuaded the legislature to approve £200,000 in paper money. As historian John Kaminski concludes, there was some support for paper money throughout the state. But support and opposition were still geographically highly concentrated. Historian E. Wilder Spaulding found that the 1786 voting showed that as in 1785, the "hard-money party was located in the southern commercial and maritime counties [in and around New York City]; and allied with them was Albany County with its little commercial city and, in all probability, its great landholders." Spaulding's conclusion is strongly reinforced by voting patterns for the controversy's most contentious aspect, legal-tender status.[72]

The legislature rejected making the paper money legal tender. New York's Chamber of Commerce merchants had submitted a lengthy memorial to the legislature attacking legal-tender status for it, as a fraud that would be "fatal to commerce." The assembly divided nearly evenly on the issue, with legislators from New York County, its environs, and Albany County voting against it by a 78 percent majority, while 86 percent of those from the remaining, predominantly rural, areas supported it. A proposal like South Carolina's property-tender law was overwhelmingly rejected. Debtors were instead permitted to tender paper money to most creditors who chose to sue them, probably deterring some claims.[73]

Like the Pennsylvania law, the New York legislation was a coalition compromise necessary to win passage. One-fourth of the new issue was to be used to pay interest on public-debt securities, with the remaining three-quarters to be used to fund the loan office that would primarily benefit farmers and land speculators. The state also agreed to assume responsibility for about 30 percent of the total Confederation debt held by New Yorkers. The assumed federal debt was held by about five thousand people, which amounted to "approximately half of the state's voters" in a normal election.[74] Kaminski finds that the remaining $3.6 million in *un*assumed federal debt was "owned by a couple hundred wealthy, and generally anti-Clinton, New Yorkers." He concludes that "Clinton and the paper money men were seeking support for their measures while attempting to divide the interests of the public creditors."[75] New York's paper money seems to have held its value reasonably well.[76]

New Jersey's paper-money politics were similarly divisive, so that coalition compromises were necessary to obtain it as well. Prosperous citizens like leading lawyer William Paterson thought that republicanism meant that there should be "virtue," not "equalizing of property" (i.e., redistributive leveling) through politics, and hence no paper money. "True" republicans, however, thought very differently. As one wrote, in a "republican government . . . the people (the majority of the people) bear rule, and it is for them to determine w[h]ether a proposition is *unjust*."[77] The general assembly paper-money leader, Abraham Clark, wrote that government should "help the feeble against the mighty," and prevent detrimental inequality of property. It should protect land-backed emissions of legal-tender paper, because without them New Jersey would "sink back into poverty and abjection." The people would then be at the mercy of "greedy dogs" (presumably, moneylenders).[78]

New Jersey's farmers were a large majority of the state's voters, and many wanted paper money. Supporters insisted that a loan office would provide a needed "domestic circulating medium." Merchant and financial interests opposed it, arguing that merchants would be "totally ruined" by it. As in New York, supporters argued in response that if paper money ruined merchants because they were unable to trade using specie, that would be good for the state. It meant that domestic manufactures and sales of country produce would grow.[79]

In mid-1786, the loan-office bill was adopted. The legislative council (the legislature's upper house) had initially rejected it before agreeing to it by a one-vote margin. The general assembly had divided sharply before agreeing that the paper money should be legal tender. New Jersey governor Livingston had been burned in effigy before agreeing not to veto paper-money legislation a second time. Virginia congressman William Grayson wrote to James Madison about the law, which he thought was designed to extinguish debts: "This same Jersey bill was one of the most iniquitous things I ever saw. . . . If Lord Effingham is right that an act against the Constitution is void, surely paper money with a [legal] tender annexed to it is void, for it is [*sic:* is it] not an attack upon property, the security of which is made a fundamental in every State in the Union."[80] Governor Livingston's son explained to a French visitor, Brissot de Warville, that paper money was the popular means used to extricate citizens from debt, and that New Jersey representatives had responded to public pressure in agreeing to issue it. New Jersey also adopted but then quickly repealed property-tender legislation akin to South Carolina's. That showed its intense split of opinion on creditor-debtor issues.[81]

The legislature's sharp divisions required compromise between paper-money supporters and public creditors before the law could be passed. The day after passage, the legislature adopted a report proposing added revenues to pay interest on public securities, the "overwhelming bulk" of which were held in northern New Jersey. One historian concludes that that was part of a compromise agreement; another finds that interest on residents' federal securities was paid using state paper money.[82] New Jersey's paper money "depreciated with breakneck speed" after "New York City and Philadelphia treated the new money with contempt," according to one historian.[83] By 1788, it had depreciated about 30 percent.[84]

Rhode Island Economic Relief

The need to assemble disparate coalitions in the Mid-Atlantic states in order to pass economic-relief laws demonstrated the comparative weakness of relief advocates in them. Rhode Island's policies, on the other hand, demonstrated their complete domination of its state politics. Rhode Island's policies in 1786–87 stemmed from the electoral triumph of country-party relief advocates who had campaigned on that issue.[85] Its policies and the reaction to them also lent important support to the view that state paper money and debt relief policies could cause interstate damage.

Rhode Island passed loan-office legislation providing for legal-tender paper money in 1786. On a per capita basis, the Rhode Island paper-money emission of £100,000 substantially exceeded that of every other state. It is estimated to have been twice as large as New York's, and three times as large as North Carolina's.[86] The law included draconian penalties for noncompliance. Heavy fines could be imposed after nonjury trials on anyone who refused to accept paper money. Paper money could be lodged with a court in full payment of debts at face value if a creditor refused to accept it. The law's sponsors apparently believed that if people could be forced by law to accept state paper money, it would maintain its value, but that did not happen. Within a year, Rhode Island's paper money had depreciated to four-to-one against specie (i.e., by 75 percent). The state's policies not only hardened public sentiment across the country against paper money and debtor relief, but did so in uniquely important ways that reshaped the national debate.

Historian Pauline Maier writes that Rhode Island's law was intended to counter deflation and "meant to allow people to pay their taxes and support economic development, not to defraud creditors." Another historian concludes that it nevertheless brought the Rhode Island economy "to a standstill." Some merchants left the state; others refused to sell goods, including food, and closed their stores rather than accept paper money. One leading historian concludes that riots broke out in response to the law; another writes that the disorder was "reminiscent of the opening years of the Revolution." Residents complained that "property is no where secure, houses and stores have been promiscuously broken into, and many persons have been wounded in defending their effects from the depredations of the mob."[87] A newspaper reported that a West Indian vessel originally destined for Rhode Island was diverted to Virginia so that the ship's owners would not be forced to accept payment for goods in heavily depreciated paper money. That avoided the owners' "inevitabl[e] ruin," according to the account.[88] Because of Rhode Island's extensive involvement in interstate trade, its state economic-relief policies had the potential to cause very broad interstate effects.

Rhode Island residents' ability to lodge depreciated paper money with courts to satisfy debts to out-of-state creditors caused outrage. Horror stories concerning that aspect of the law abounded. One that caused widespread disgust was the case of a Rhode Island orphan girl who had inherited £400 in silver and was sent to school in Boston. She was summoned home, where her guardian announced that he had "discharged himself of all future demands on him, as Guardian, by a tender of the nominal sum of £400 in *paper money*" worth far less than her original inheritance, effectively destroying it.[89] An enterprising Massachusetts debtor turned the tables. He owed nearly £100 in specie to a Rhode Island creditor, so he took goods valued at about $70 (roughly one-fifth of his debt's actual value) to Rhode Island, auctioned them off for paper money, and then "had the wickedness and effrontery" to tender the paper money to his creditor to extinguish his debt.[90] Rhode Island changed its law as a result of these sorts of practices, but only to prevent nonresidents from using the debt-lodging procedure against Rhode Islanders, not vice versa.

Rhode Island also appears to have been unique in systematically using its heavily depreciated paper money forcibly to pay off virtually its entire state debt during peacetime. As discussed in chapter 2, the legislature passed "forced payment" legislation that compulsorily retired all outstanding state debt at a large discount. It required holders of state debt to tender their debt securities to the state and receive depreciated state paper money in return, or forfeit the securities. It did this each year for part of the total debt. Rather than accommodating public creditors, one historian writes, Rhode Island had "swatted" them with "brutal directness."[91] From the creditors' perspective, the state had, at a minimum, deprived them of profits they reasonably expected on their investments and, at worst, caused them to take a significant loss. In 1788, Hugh Williamson wrote of the state's actions, "the whole State debt is soon to be expunged by a kind of legerdemain, for little or no money has issued, during the process, out of the Treasury."[92] That, of course, was precisely what Rhode Island taxpayers wanted: to eliminate the state debt without having to pay taxes to do it.

Rhode Island's paper money and debt laws were highly unusual in yet another respect: they touched off interstate legislative warfare. By August 1786, Massachusetts and Connecticut both had passed laws severely limiting the rights of creditors from paper-money states, including Rhode Island, to collect debts due from their residents. The new laws provided that their residents could pay debts to such out-of-state creditors in the same manner in which debtors in paper-money states could pay their debts. That nullified Rhode Island's effort to prevent out-of-state debtors from paying Rhode Island creditors with its paper money. Connecticut also prepared a protest to Congress claiming that Rhode Island's laws violated the Articles of Confederation. However, even had that been true, the Confederation would have had no power to do anything to remedy the violation. After describing various states' issuance of paper money to Thomas Jefferson, James Madison wrote that "among the numerous ills with which this practice is pregnant, one I find is that it is producing the same warfare and retaliation among the states as is produced by the State regulations of commerce."[93]

Whether Rhode Island's fiscal policies were defensible, as some historians claim, or not, by the end of 1786 many Americans fervently condemned them. In a letter reprinted by newspapers in eight states, a southern resident wrote to his Rhode Island correspondent that "matters have come to such an alarming crisis, that the confederation must take notice of you" for "your Legislature . . . are dangerous to the community at large." Many of his state's citizens believed, he wrote, that "when the convention meets in Philadelphia . . . measures will be taken to reduce you to order and good government, or strike your State out of the union and annex you to others."[94] As remarkable as those sentiments were, the writer had company.

Americans around the country and even sympathetic foreign observers exploded in outrage over Rhode Island's policies. Massachusetts Supreme Court justice Francis Dana wrote to Elbridge Gerry expressing the hope that "a bold politician wou'd seize upon" Rhode Island's "abominations and anti federal conduct" to annihilate it as a state. Philadelphia Convention delegate Richard Dobbs Spaight wrote to North Carolina leader James Iredell that "the General Assembly of Connecticut have reprobated . . . the conduct of . . . Rhode Island. . . . I should not be surprised if they were to compel them by force to do justice to their citizens." A Massachusetts resident wrote, "The other states will justly consider [Rhode Island] as *cheats,*—traitors to the nation . . . and armed plunderers of their neighbours." A Connecticut resident wrote that the law was "the most extraordinary that ever disgraced the annals of democratical tyranny," an act of "human depravity." Secretary of War Henry Knox wrote to the marquis de Lafayette that "no little State of Greece ever exhibited greater turpitude . . . plundering the Orphan and Widow by virtue of laws." Leading English liberal and longtime American supporter Richard Price described Rhode Island's "knavery" as a "triumph" for America's opponents in a letter excerpted in at least thirty-five newspapers.[95]

Even before the Rhode Island's law's effects were known, William Grayson of Virginia thought that paper money caused interstate damage. He wrote to James Madison about pending discussions in Congress concerning Confederation reform that the "Eastern people . . . would not agree if it rested with them that Congress should have the power of preventing the states from cheating one another as well as their own citizens by means of paper money."[96] Grayson's comments are important because they reflect his view that paper money was a form of fraud that harmed Congress's ability to raise revenue and interfered with interstate commerce as well. In short, by 1786 paper money had become an interstate as well as an intrastate problem. Rhode Island's policies, including their blatant discrimination in favor of its residents and against nonresidents, strongly reinforced many Americans' concerns that paper money could cause interstate harm. But the Confederation was powerless to do anything about it. And as Grayson saw, that would never change as long as Congress had to agree to reforms.

Economic Relief and the Confederation

American creditors as a class, who were nearly all middling or wealthy individuals, were no friends of 1780s economic-relief laws except when they could profit from them. They were deeply disgusted by their frequent inability to protect their assets' value and to collect debts as a result of those laws. And there is little question that many hoped that they could prevent such laws from being adopted by states in the future. That remained true despite their periodic willingness to join expedient coalitions supporting paper money or debt relief. The question here, though, is how their views affected the Confederation's fate.

Many political leaders—both strong nationalists like Nathaniel Gorham and strong federalists like Richard Henry Lee—also disliked paper-money and debt-relief laws. But the Confederation had no power to block them. Nor did anyone seek such powers before the 1787 Philadelphia Convention. No effort in Congress seems to have been made after the war to prohibit such laws.[97] Instead, the available sources include rumors that some members of Congress, such as William Grayson, may have wanted Congress to propose a bar on issuance of state paper money. But such proposals were either never made or were abandoned behind the scenes.[98]

Most notably perhaps, when Congress's Grand Committee (composed of representatives of all thirteen states) made its extensive Confederation reform proposals in August 1786, no change in state powers over paper money or debt relief was proposed. That strongly suggests that insufficient support existed in Congress for limits on such state powers. The Confederation's inability to prevent passage of state economic-relief laws did not delegitimize it further in the eyes of reformers, however. They already wanted other fundamental structural changes. At most, its inability to prevent interstate harms added an item to their already lengthy indictment of the Confederation's flaws.

Nor is there any substantial evidence that Confederation reform supporters saw the need for reform as more urgent because of what they viewed as a popular paper-money "mania" in 1785–86. There is little doubt that in several states a fairly large amount of popular collusion to prevent debt and tax collection by obstructing law enforcement occurred during this period.[99] And rebels who appeared in arms or threatened violence in various states undoubtedly often had substantial (though unquantifiable) tacit support in the broader populations, sometimes including members of local militias. But popular economic-relief movements in nearly all of the states were adequately politically addressed by relief laws, almost always without use of significant government force to suppress them.

As chapter 8 shows, in states other than Massachusetts, the number of people who were willing to use violence against government to obtain relief appears to have been fairly small. To give just one example here, in New Hampshire, the number of armed men who demanded economic relief in 1786 was a few hundred. Their resistance melted away when they were confronted by an armed force organized by the governor, without any actual battle.[100] Many Americans whose economic circumstances suggest that they might have been willing to support popular insurgencies chose instead to move west. Westward expansion provided an important "safety valve" against popular discontent (much as it did throughout the nineteenth century). In states other than Massachusetts, economic unrest appears to have been largely contained without significant organized violence, by states' willingness to provide relief.

Moreover, popular movements remained predominantly peaceful in the 1780s despite the fact that state legislatures were willing to provide only limited relief. In New York, South Carolina, and Pennsylvania, emissions of paper money were adopted only after proposals for much larger emissions were first defeated. In nearly every state, demands for debtor-friendly property-tender laws were either defeated or, if enacted, quickly repealed.

Conclusion

Taken as a whole, the states' relief policies had limited economic effects. Paper-money issues were too small to combat deflation. Instead, they depreciated in several states; and in a number of them, depreciation was substantial. Debt relief provided a welcome temporary respite from creditors' claims, but typically did not significantly decrease, and sometimes increased, actual debt levels. In short, state legislatures almost always responded to popular pressure for economic relief by balancing it against conflicting creditor and wealth-holder interests. That usually meant choosing to provide moderate relief, enough to mollify discontent and not more.

While economic-relief policies dampened popular discontent, they had other important political effects as well. They created significant concerns about what many leaders, both nationalist and federalist, saw as state majority abuses of minority rights. Pennsylvania's paper money and bank debate in particular led to much broader concerns about majority power that reinforced opposition to paper money across the country and resulted in a severe political backlash. Rhode Island's actions then created a widely shared perception that one state's paper-money and debt-relief policies could unfairly damage other states' residents, not just its own. For James Madison, state economic-relief laws were yet another example of states' unchecked "aggressions" against each other under the Confederation that justified a more powerful central government. But it is important to appreciate that for Madison, those laws were only one more instance of states' licentious behavior that he thought justified their subordination to a national government. And Madison was not alone.

The tumultuous events of the mid-1780s forced Americans to confront anew a fundamental problem inherent in republican government: whether majority power should sometimes be limited to protect minorities. From the perspective of someone committed to the idea that the majority will should always be supreme, concern over majority tyranny could be described as counterrevolutionary. But judging from the debate on economic-relief issues in the 1780s, it is difficult to believe that Americans uniformly thought that they had fought the revolution for the purpose of ensuring that the majority will would always prevail. Preventing all forms of tyranny—the oppressive use of power—while still creating an effective national government would be an abiding concern of the 1787 Philadelphia Convention. Delegates there would examine states' economic-relief powers in that context, but as only one of many potential ways in which government power might be abused.

8

Shays's Rebellion

THE FINAL BATTLE OF THE AMERICAN REVOLUTION?

By mid-1786, the Confederation's future seemed dim. Economic conditions in much of the country remained severely depressed. Many leaders thought that the Confederation was about to collapse, and that a political crisis was imminent. Some feared that republican popular government itself was proving to be a failure.

In late August 1786, a popular insurgency (or "Regulation"), commonly called Shays's Rebellion, broke out in Massachusetts. The insurgents demanded large-scale political and economic reforms, including paper money and tax and debt relief. Thousands of insurgents blocked the sittings of Massachusetts courts to press their demands. The insurgency was an order of magnitude larger than any other organized postwar economic-relief movement. The sources suggest that Massachusetts's distinctively harsh pro-creditor policies affecting both taxes and debt were to blame for Shays's Rebellion.

The Regulators saw their actions as continuing a tradition of popular resistance to tyranny that included the American Revolution. Most Massachusetts leaders, on the other hand, believed that their actions violated fundamental republican principles. The legislature provided some relief, but rejected rebels' major demands. In late January 1787, government troops easily defeated insurgents attacking the Confederation's Springfield arsenal and by early February effectively ended the insurgency.

Shays's Rebellion caused many Massachusetts federalists to conclude that the Confederation needed to be strengthened. Some historians claim that the rebellion also set off a wave of backcountry resistance to debt and taxes in vari-

ous states. That unrest supposedly frightened wealthy elites across the country into drafting the 1787 Constitution, primarily to repress popular economic relief measures. There was sporadic disorganized violence from Vermont to Virginia in 1786–87, but its scale was minor, and it was easily suppressed.

George Washington did not reenter politics because of Shays's Rebellion. He thought that the rebellion clearly demonstrated the weakness of both state and Confederation governments. It provided a powerful new argument for a stronger central government that nationalists had long advocated for other reasons.

***

> We were told, during the continuance of the late war, that if we could support our independency, our lands would rise in value, and that a free trade would enhance the price of our produce. . . . But what are the present state of facts as they respect the yeomanry of this Commonwealth? Our real estates, since the peace, have fallen in value two-thirds. Our taxes are so high, together with calls of a private nature [i.e., debts], that our stock, in cattle, are greatly diminished. . . . The greater part then of those who gloriously supported our independence now find their moveables vanishing like empty shades, their lands sinking under their feet.

A Massachusetts farmer writing during Shays's Rebellion, 1786[1]

> That part of your Letter, where in you say, that you had hoped to have seen only Peace in future, after surmounting the Horrors of one war . . . was too powerful for me, and the Tears involuntary flowed . . . have we been contending against the tyranny of Britain, to become the sacrifice of a lawless Banditti?

Abigail Adams writing to her sister Mary Smith Cranch on Shays's Rebellion in early 1787[2]

In early February 1786, retired Massachusetts general Benjamin Lincoln wrote to Congressman Rufus King advocating that northern states form their own separate confederation. He claimed that it was pointless to give Congress additional powers, because the states would not obey its decisions. They could not be forced to do so because

Congress lacked effective coercive powers. Lincoln told King that the "United States . . . seem to be little more than a name." Because sectional interests were so sharply conflicting, "they [i.e., the different sections] are not really embarked in the same bottom." Lincoln contended that southern slave states would never agree to Congress's use of commerce powers to protect New England's vital shipping. It would be better to divide the Confederation to ally the common interests of northern states, Lincoln told King.[3]

Almost exactly one year later, Lincoln led Massachusetts state troops through a blinding winter snowstorm on a thirty-mile overnight march to make a surprise attack at Petersham that finally crushed the armed insurgency today commonly called Shays's Rebellion.[4] (The rebellion was named after Revolutionary War veteran Daniel Shays, who became one of its main leaders.) Lincoln's expedition had been paid for with money loaned by wealthy Massachusetts merchants. Neither the Confederation nor Massachusetts had money to pay for it. Like most Massachusetts leaders, Benjamin Lincoln had not seen Shays's Rebellion coming—and like many of them, instead of supporting a breakup of the Confederation, he became a nationalist (and, in 1787, a Federalist, that is, a supporter of the new Constitution) as a result.

This chapter discusses the insurgency and its causes, as well as responses to it by the state and Confederation governments. It also examines its influence on state and national public opinion about the Confederation. Shays's Rebellion strengthened the movement for Confederation reform primarily because it starkly illuminated the Confederation's and Massachusetts's impotence in the face of a divisive armed rebellion. It is useful to begin by considering the state of the Confederation and conditions in Massachusetts shortly before the insurgency started.[5]

Confederation Conditions before the Rebellion

Benjamin Lincoln was not alone in taking a pessimistic view of the Confederation's future by mid-1786, just before Shays's Rebellion began. In June 1786, Congressman Theodore Sedgwick of Massachusetts wrote to his wife Pamela that the Confederation's inaction on his state's needs meant that "Massachusetts has lost every advantage, she as a state expected in consequence of independence."[6] By early August, Sedgwick was advocating the breakup of the Confederation in frustration over what he saw as southern resistance to New England's urgent needs for commerce powers and to the Spanish treaty. Confederation officials and other American leaders had equally gloomy views. Rufus King wrote to Elbridge Gerry that the Confederation would certainly dissolve unless something was done to supply it with revenues.[7] The Board of Treasury concluded that the Confederation was insolvent and might collapse. In the summer of 1786, before the rebellion broke out, John Jay and George Washington agreed that a political crisis was imminent.

Jay wrote to Washington in June that "our affairs seem to lead to some crisis—some Revolution." It was "too true" that various states had violated the Treaty of Peace on British debts. The country's conduct was "wrong" and would result in "Evils and Calamities." He was especially concerned that "the better kind of People" will be led by the "Insecurity of Property, the Loss of Confidence in their Rulers, & the Want of public Faith & Rectitude, to consider the Charms of Liberty as imaginary and delusive." "Such Men" would be disgusted by public policies, he feared, and have their minds prepared "for almost any change that may promise them Quiet & Security."[8] Though Jay did not spell his thoughts out, he seems to have been hinting that wealthy individuals might countenance a military takeover to form a monarchy.

Responding to Jay in mid-August, Washington agreed that "our affairs are rapidly drawing to a crisis." He wrote that "we have probably had too good an opinion of human nature in forming our confederation. Experience has taught us, that men will not adopt & carry into execution, measures the best calculated for their own good without the intervention of a coercive power. I do not conceive we can exist long as a nation, without having lodged somewhere a power which will pervade the whole Union in as energetic a manner, as the authority of the different state governments extends over the several states."[9] For Washington, a nation could not survive without a government able to enforce its laws throughout its territory, in other words, to exercise sovereignty over it. By "coercive power," he meant that the government must be able to use force to enforce its laws. To pay the costs of law enforcement, a national government must have the ability to collect taxes.

Washington's letter makes clear that national government's ability to tax effectively was his primary concern. He focused on the fact that Congress could not get states to obey requisitions, which "are actually little better than a jest and a bye word through out the Land." The same problem existed, he thought, where the country's ability to require treaty compliance was concerned. He told Jay, "If you tell the Legislatures they have violated the treaty of peace . . . they will laugh in your face." Washington agreed that there was a danger that "the better kind of people . . . will have their minds prepared for any revolution whatever. We are apt to run from one extreme into another." He expressed concern that there might even be support for an American monarchy. But, Washington concluded, as a private citizen "it is not my business to embark again on a sea of troubles." With some bitterness, he reminded Jay that his views on the need for stronger central government expressed in his circular to the states in 1783 "have been neglected, tho' given as a last legacy in the most solemn manner." Despite his conviction that the Confederation would eventually collapse if fundamental reforms were not made, in the summer of 1786 Washington was content to remain in private life.[10]

Thus, although Benjamin Lincoln and George Washington had precisely the same view of the underlying problem facing the Confederation in the summer of 1786, they had sharply conflicting ideas about how to solve it. Lincoln wanted the Confederation divided because it was unable to enforce its laws and could not protect his section's interests. Washington wanted a nation powerful enough to enforce its laws in a way that could surmount sectional conflicts. But in mid-1786, there was little or no common ground between their views. The Spanish-treaty impasse soon made matters even worse by greatly increasing sectional discord.

Massachusetts Conditions and the Rebellion's Causes

The dismal prospects for the Confederation were matched by sorely blighted conditions in New England. Economic conditions there were still severely depressed, and it seems likely that in western Massachusetts they were as bad as or worse than they were anywhere else in the country. Wages and prices for agricultural commodities and land were very low; exports were severely depressed. Interest rates were far higher than normal. Creditors seeking to collect debts had headed to the courts in large numbers.[11] Massachusetts taxes had increased to a level four to five times as high as they had been before the war.[12] One Boston observer wrote in the spring of 1786, "Bankruptcies are daily taking place; taxes cannot be collected in sufficient quantities to support the credit of government."[13] Severe political controversy had already erupted in neighboring Rhode Island. In hindsight, it seems clear that by 1786, the stage was set for a showdown in Massachusetts as well.

During 1786, various Massachusetts towns petitioned its legislature (the General Court) for economic relief. The town of Athol pointed to a scarcity of specie as the reason why people could not pay their debts. However, the town argued, if property instead of cash could be "received in payment," debts could be paid.[14] Other petitions complained about oppressive taxes, and opposed paying state taxes to meet Confederation requisitions.[15] Still others objected to taxes imposed to pay the state's domestic debt.[16] They claimed that "the many" were being taxed to support "the few," which was unfair, especially during a severe recession. The Worcester County town of Lunenburg submitted a petition asking that in order to pay both taxes and private debts, paper money be issued. It said that "the People are disabled from paying their debts both Public and private and many have been, and more still are liable to be forced to Gaol."[17] The Worcester County petition said that "the people in general are extremely embarrassed with public and private debts."[18]

By 1786, many western farmers and farm laborers were experiencing enormous economic insecurity, and felt that they were about to lose everything that they had fought the revolution for. The attitudes of yeoman farmers were well summed up by a writer in Boston's *Massachusetts Gazette*. He said that "our taxes are so high, together with calls of a private nature [i.e., debts], that our stock and cattle are greatly diminished. . . . [T]he greater part then of those who gloriously supported our independence now find their moveables vanishing like empty shades, their lands sinking under their feet."[19]

While western Massachusetts residents, in particular, were complaining about debt and taxes, there were complaints from other parts of Massachusetts as well, but they were rather different. From Braintree (just south of Boston), Mary Smith Cranch wrote to her sister Abigail Adams in London after the insurgency began:

> The People will not pay their Tax, nor their debts of any kind, and who shall make them? These things affect us most severely. Mr. Cranch has been labouring for the Publick for three or four years without receiving Scarcely any pay. The Treasury has been So empty that he could not get it, and now my Sister there is not a penny in it. The Publick owe us three Hundred pound and we cannot get a Shilling of it, and if the People will not pay their Tax how Shall we ever get it. An attendance upon the court of common pleas was the only thing that has produc'd any cash for above two year. . . . If we had not liv'd with great caution we must have been in debt, a thing I dread more than the most extream Poverty.[20]

The Massachusetts treasury was empty when Shays's Rebellion began because Massachusetts tax delinquencies were very high. The defaults were concentrated especially in the impoverished areas of western Massachusetts.[21] There the system was also widely regarded as unfair. In part that was because after the war, it depended increasingly on regressive poll (i.e., head) taxes. The legislature had increased the total amount of state taxes paid by polls from 30 percent to 40 percent between 1778 and 1786. In 1784, Worcester in central Massachusetts paid 32.3 percent of its taxes in polls, while Suffolk County, where wealthy Boston was located, paid only 22.8 percent.[22] Western Massachusetts farmers deeply resented such policies. There were tax protests in the state's western areas even before the war ended; some were violent.[23]

The Massachusetts court system was also regarded as oppressive by much of the state's population. In part, that was because it executed the ever-growing demands of private creditors and state tax officials. But it was also extremely costly for debtors. A careful study concludes that "Massachusetts's court fees were extremely high, comprising a substantial portion of the median debt even when a creditor simply obtained a[n uncontested] default judgment."[24] In debt cases, losers had to pay the winners attorneys' fees as well. Small wonder that by 1786 there were numerous popular proposals for eliminating entire levels of courts and some for outlawing attorneys.[25]

However, the 1786 legislature turned a deaf ear to all of these popular complaints. It rejected the Lunenburg petition for paper money by a large margin, and declined to permit property to be used to pay debts. It approved new taxes, including those needed to pay the unpopular 1785 requisition requested by Congress.[26] Adding to that burden, the legislature was engaged in a tax program designed to pay off the entire Massachusetts state debt in five years. That meant that taxes that many regarded as unfairly high would continue for a long time.[27]

Subsequent events showed that there was strong popular sympathy in Massachusetts for the insurgents' economic-relief proposals. Historians have sought to understand why by examining the rebellion's causes. Most of the controversy about causation has centered on whether, as many contemporaries believed, the insurgents were primarily discontented debtors or whether the insurgency was a tax rebellion. A majority of Regulators whose occupations are known were either western yeoman farmers or agricultural laborers. Some historians conclude that a central role in creating the insurgency was played by a growing chain of indebtedness due to postwar foreign imports made on credit that added to preexisting debts. That chain stretched from England to the Massachusetts backcountry and tightened greatly during the recession, until it threatened to crush many western residents, especially farmers.[28]

According to one study, in three Massachusetts counties 66 percent of the known insurgents had been taken to court for unpaid debts.[29] A more recent historian denies, however, that there was any correlation between indebtedness and participation in the insurgency. He contends that in five western insurgent counties where there was extensive indebtedness, in 72 out of 187 towns no one joined it.[30] Some historians who think that the insurgency was principally a tax rebellion argue that Massachusetts tried to retire state and Confederation debts too quickly, imposing taxes that were too high as a result. Others argue that the public was unhappy either about specific taxes, for example those intended to pay Confederation debts such as commutation, or about the perceived unfairness of the tax system itself. Some citizens claimed that the tax system benefited the wealthy at the expense of the poor.[31]

However, the sources suggest that both substantial specie debts and heavy taxes played a role in fueling the insurgency.[32] The 1786 town petitions and county convention grievances show that both private debts and public taxes (also a kind of debt) were subjects of popular complaints for which remedies were sought. There is no indication that the insurgents offered to pay one category of debt but refused to pay the other. The strategy that the insurgents chose for their Regulation, blocking the courts, had the benefit that it would prevent the collection of both debts and taxes. Creditors had been considerably more aggressive about collecting debts than Massachusetts typically had been about collecting its taxes. Some contemporaries viewed the insurgents' claims about oppressive taxes as pretexts.[33] But as we have seen, Massachusetts' hard-line pro-creditor policies and oppressive courts had created public sympathy of varying degrees for insurgents' complaints about both debts and taxes.

The Course of the Insurgency

In western Massachusetts, popular conventions were held concerning the legislature's actions in Hampshire, Worcester, and Middlesex counties. Regulators at those conventions listed as grievances high taxes, including Massachusetts's payment of Confederation requisitions; private debts; and high government and court expenses. They asked that government and legal expenses and fees be reduced. They also requested that taxes be cut or made easier to pay through paper money, and sought debt relief. Some petitions also sought major political reforms, including moving the General Court westward, eliminating the Court of Common Pleas, and abolishing the Massachusetts state senate (one of the legislature's two houses, and a bastion of wealthy conservatives).[34] Regulators decided that they would block the sitting of the Massachusetts courts until their grievances were redressed by the legislature.

Beginning on August 29, 1786, crowds of Regulators obstructed the sittings of various Massachusetts courts.[35] These protests were peaceful, though the threat to use violence if the courts attempted to hold sessions was always present. By the end of 1786, rebels had blocked roughly ten separate court sessions, all except for one (Concord) located in western Massachusetts. The sitting of the court at Concord was blocked after twenty-four towns asked the governor not to call out the militia to enforce the law against those seeking to obstruct it, because they feared local resistance and bloodshed.[36] Many citizens seem to have opposed the use of force against the Regulators even if they did not agree with their demands. The practical effect of their position was to enable the Regulators to close the courts as leverage to force the legislature to accede to those demands. In response to the Regulation, the governor called the legislature into a special session beginning on September 28. Its decision to try to address some insurgent complaints did not reflect sympathy for the idea that Regulation was an acceptable form of republican political action.

The Regulators themselves believed that their popular conventions were part of a hallowed American revolutionary tradition of resistance to tyrannical government. There is little question that Massachusetts revolutionaries had engaged in very similar extralegal political action against the British during the revolution.[37] The 1776 Declaration of Independence itself could be read as sanctioning "permanent revolution," since it contended that "whenever any form of Government becomes destructive of" the "unalienable rights" of "all men," "it is the Right of the People to alter or abolish it." So it is understandable that the Regulators, many of whom were war veterans, saw themselves as part of an unfinished American Revolution.

Most Massachusetts postwar elected leaders, on the other hand, regarded Regulation backed by the threat of armed violence as a wholly illegitimate form of political action. It was a repudiation of republican government, not its fulfillment. That was not, as might be thought, a pretext concealing their opposition to the insurgents' economic demands. Leading revolutionaries such as Samuel Adams and John Adams believed strongly that politics had changed fundamentally after independence and the popular adoption of new state constitutions. John Adams had been a critic of popular conventions and what he saw as their misguided claims to political authority since at least 1783. He, Benjamin Franklin, and John Jay had publicly attacked conventions' actions regarding the Treaty of Peace in a joint letter to Congress.[38] In 1784, Samuel Adams had sharply criticized conventions held in Connecticut challenging Congress's grant of commutation pay to army officers as useless at best, and dangerous at worst. Their actions, he wrote, threatened to make them "Enemies to our happy Revolution & the Common Liberty."[39] Also in 1784, he had attacked the retired military officers' association, the Society of the Cincinnati. An important basis for his criticism of it was that like conventions, it could become an independent political authority subversive of elected governments.[40]

In Samuel Adams's view, popular conventions were a direct threat to the concept of republican government. It was founded on the bedrock principle that political decisions should be made exclusively by officials elected under a popularly established constitution. Rufus King explained the implications of that idea to state legislator Daniel Kilham. King wrote that "grievances can not be suffered in a Government constituted as our Government is. The laws are the acts of a majority of the people . . . every citizen is bound to submit to this majority—such laws cannot be considered as Grievous."[41] Under a republican constitution, it was inherently impossible to have grievances that would justify Regulation. Thomas Jefferson described the rebels' acts as "absolutely unjustifiable," probably for similar reasons.[42] For ad hoc popular movements to wield military power was nothing more than mob rule, and a form of treason.

Popular conventions had strong defenders as well. In the course of an extended argument in favor of their frequent use, one Massachusetts farmer wrote: "History can produce no instance of a people's losing their freedom by Conventions of their private citizens, or even by mobs; but many melancholy instances can be produced of empires being enslaved by the artifices of usurping rulers. . . . Will the virtuous yeomanry of Massachusetts, who disdained to stoop to foreign tyrants, now bow their necks to internal despots? Let such men remember the fate of their predecessors and tremble."[43]

Despite disagreements over Regulation, there was considerable public sympathy for some of the insurgents' complaints. "Men who have respectable Standings and Characters and possessed of decent Shares of Property are said to countenance the general Insurgency tho' they avowedly claim less Reform (as they call it) than the others," a Pennsylvania congressman reported.[44] There was also a potent fear that a military response to the insurgency might lead to enormous bloodshed. As one attentive contemporary observed, "It is thought, by those best acquainted with the State of things there, that not a drop of blood can be Spilt, nor Captive taken, without the immediate consequence of a civil War."[45] Rufus King told Congress that "scarce a man was without a father, a brother, a friend in the mass of the people [insurgents]."[46] Therefore, the Massachusetts government sought to offer insurgents first an olive branch and then, as a last resort, a sword. The legislature passed resolutions supporting Massachusetts governor Bowdoin and reproving the insurgents. But it initially split over suspension of the writ of habeas corpus, and the proposed adoption of a property-tender act. However, after the insurgents attempted to co-opt the Hampshire County government to create an insurgent militia, the legislature agreed to suspend the writ of habeas corpus.

The legislative special session also passed some reform legislation. It adopted a limited property-tender act, and a law allowing many kinds of produce to be received in payment of older specie taxes. It broadened the jurisdiction of local courts in order to limit the power and costs of the Court of Common Pleas. It offered a general indemnity to insurgents, despite warnings that this would encourage the Regulation. But the insurgents' major demands, for paper money and large-scale debt relief, had been rejected. No one accepted the indemnity.[47] One historian, however, concludes that the legislature's actions provided relief that weakened the Regulation in western areas.[48]

While the legislature was meeting in special session, a secret debate was occurring about protection of the Confederation arsenal at Springfield, Massachusetts. The arsenal was an exceptionally valuable military target, because it contained at least 450 tons of military supplies, including 1,300 barrels of powder, a brass foundry, cannon, and 7,000 small arms with bayonets. That was enough materiel to support a substantial insurgency.[49] Surprisingly, the insurgents had not immediately attempted to capture it. Ominously, however, they had kept their option to do so open by coercing local militia into agreeing not to reinforce it.

In late October, Secretary of War Knox convinced Congress to authorize additional Confederation troops to protect the Springfield arsenal and combat the insurgency.[50] There was only one problem: the Confederation was insolvent, so Congress had no money to pay its new troops. It therefore authorized officials to seek a loan to obtain the funds and an accompanying requisition to repay it. Since everyone knew that the states would not pay the requisition, Congress pledged the revenues from western land sales to secure the loan. Only one state, Virginia, paid any of the requisition, and no one was willing to loan the Confederation money.[51]

In Middlesex and other eastern Massachusetts counties, the insurgency had ended by December 1.[52] It had eastern sympathizers, but it lacked sufficient support in those areas to successfully block courts there. The state government decided to round up insurgents from the Groton area (northwest of Boston), and succeeded in capturing and jailing several major leaders. They took the oath of allegiance to the state in mid-December. By then, however, Massachusetts leader Nathaniel Gorham reported to Henry Knox that "the great Body of the People are more convinced that the [mob] must be suppressed by arms."[53]

By late December 1786, it was clear to everyone that courts would be permitted to sit in western Massachusetts only if the government backed them with force.[54] But the state government had no money to pay troops. The legislature authorized it to borrow money to fund military operations. It took time to raise the loan funds from wealthy Boston and seacoast merchants, who were understandably skeptical that they would ever get their money back. Eventually, more than £5,000 was raised to support troops.[55] They were assembled and began to prepare for battle.

The military confrontations that ensued in late January and early February 1787 were a pathetic debacle for the rebels. When the first and only actual "battle" of the insurgency came, the rebel forces were defeated with ease. While some historians have claimed that more than five thousand men took some part in the Massachusetts Regulation, only about two thousand of them were in the field by then. As one historian noted, despite months of organizing, that was a very small fraction of the number that had turned out during an earlier popular militia action that preceded the Revolutionary War in 1774.[56]

On January 25, 1787, rebel forces led by Daniel Shays moved toward the Confederation arsenal in Springfield and were met by Massachusetts general William Shepard and his troops. Shepard was an experienced commander who had fought in twenty-two engagements across much of the north during the Revolutionary War. Shepard's forces had artillery, and the poorly armed insurgents did not. Shepard warned Shays that he would use his cannon if the insurgents did not cease their advance, but they continued to march toward the state's lines. After firing a warning round with no result, Shepard used his artillery again, killing four of Shays's men and wounding roughly twenty others. Daniel Shays and his fellow commander Luke Days and their forces then fled Springfield, utterly routed.

Park Holland, a Revolutionary War veteran who served with Massachusetts forces against the insurgents, wrote an account of the battle.[57] It shows that participants felt that they were fighting a civil war. Holland wrote that "Gen. Shepherd remarked to me that at no time in his life was he ever called upon to perform so painful a duty, as when he ordered good aim to be taken at Shays and his men, many of whom had fought at his side, & stood firm through the most trying scenes of the late war." Holland continued, "I had served in the company of Shays [during the Revolutionary War]. I knew him to be a brave and good soldier, or officer."[58] He was happy that he had not had to watch Shays being fired on. General Shepard did not exaggerate when he reported that "had I been disposed to destroy them [Shays's forces], I might have charged upon their rear and flanks with my Infantry and the two field pieces, and could have killed the greater part of his whole army within twenty-five minutes. There was not a single musket fired on either side."[59]

In early February 1787, after General Lincoln sought unsuccessfully to negotiate a peaceful surrender with Shays, Shays's forces again fled. Lincoln's troops then marched all night through a snowstorm to hunt them down at Petersham and captured nearly all of them. Shays again fled. From that time on, there were only sporadic guerilla raids. The raids caused some personal hardship to their victims, but ultimately had little broader effect. Scattered groups of insurgents seem to have received some support from sympathetic citizens as they hid in neighboring states. But in New York, Governor George Clinton personally led state troops to its northern border to make certain that they were not given sanctuary there.

Thus, by early February 1787, the insurgency had been suppressed with remarkable ease. But the Massachusetts treasury was still empty, and its citizens were still discontented. The legislature authorized criminal prosecutions against insurgents, and about two dozen were tried and convicted of treason or lesser offenses. All but two of those convicted were eventually either pardoned or received commuted sentences (two insurgents were later hung, but for robbery). Hundreds of other rebels received legislative indemnity, were pardoned, or received commutations. So the rebellion caused astonishingly little loss of life.[60] What political effects did it have?

Reaction in Massachusetts

In early 1787, Abigail Adams expressed the views of many Massachusetts citizens and leaders when she wrote that the Shays rebels were "lawless banditti" who were seeking to "destroy a Government." She wrote passionately to her sister Mary Smith Cranch that their lawless conduct was endangering the revolution:

> When I came to that part of your Letter, where in you say, that you had hoped to have seen only Peace in future, after surmounting the Horrors of one war the Idea was too powerful for me, and the Tears involuntary flowed. . . . The thoughts which naturally occurred to me, were for what have we been contending against the tyranny of Britain, to become the sacrifice of a lawless Banditti? Must our glory be thus shorn and our Laurels thus blasted? Is it a trifling matter to destroy a Government, will my countrymen justify the Maxim of tyrants, that Mankind are not made for freedom. I will however still hope that the Majority of our fellow citizens are too wise virtuous and enlightened to permit these outrages to gain group and triumph.[61]

Nevertheless, the Shays insurgency roiled Massachusetts politics. In 1787, a new legislature, with many more western towns represented and many new members, effectively conceded some insurgent demands. It declared what amounted to a tax holiday and adopted property-tender legislation. However, efforts to obtain paper money again failed. Governor James Bowdoin was handily defeated for reelection because his opponent John Hancock received overwhelming support in areas sympathetic to the rebellion. Some historians argue that these political reverses were the most important factor in causing Massachusetts elite federalists to be willing to accept a stronger central government as a way of protecting their property and interests.[62] But it seems clear that federalist sentiment began to change well before February 1787 when the rebellion was crushed. Just after that, the legislature agreed to send delegates to the Philadelphia Convention in May, a clear sign of changed sentiment.

Massachusetts conservatives were an elite coalition whose members, some federalists and some nationalists, held a range of views on the rebellion. Some, such as Abigail Adams, thought that the insurgency was a temporary phenomenon brought on by excessive debt. Other archconservatives such as Stephen Higginson saw popular reforms and extreme democracy as inevitably leading to leveling and economic redistribution. All were deeply disturbed, however, by the Massachusetts government's unwillingness or inability to act forcefully against the rebellion.

Many Massachusetts leaders believed initially that the Shays rebels were primarily discontented debtors who had only themselves to blame for their troubles. The legislature issued a report claiming that the insurgents had brought their problems on themselves, by buying imported goods they could not afford to pay for. After learning of the popular conventions, Abigail Adams wrote to her uncle Cotton Tufts in October and blamed "that rage for Luxury which has produced many of the evils for which our people are now groaning." She said that it could be cured by encouraging agriculture and manufactures to end the "idleness" that "is the parent of contention and disobedience." In private at least, she thought that the Revolutionary War was to blame for introducing "Luxury and extravagance of every description" to the "lower class of people who can least bear wealth" and who "grew indolent and overbearing" and "in reality . . . felt little of the publick burden." Now they are "obliged to labour more Gain less and pay more," and "foolishly think the fault lies with their rulers."[63] (She deleted these draft remarks about the lower class and the war from her final letter to Tufts.) But other federalist leaders, such as Rufus King, thought that both imprudently high taxes and creditor pressures on debtors might be responsible for the insurgency.[64]

Some Massachusetts archconservatives, on the other hand, saw the problem as stemming from the Regulators' support for leveling and extreme democracy. Theodore Sedgwick, for example, wrote that "every man of observation is convinced that the end of Government Security cannot be obtained by the exercise of principles founded on democratic equality." After the rebellion ended, he described economic policies supported by Regulators as "a war" "levied on the virtue, property and distinctions in the Community" that would never end, but "will again and again break out."[65] Stephen Higginson agreed that unless government was made stronger, "the people of the interior parts" of the New England states have "by far too much political knowledge and too strong a relish for unrestrained freedom." They would "not rest easy till they possess the reins of Government, and have divided property with their betters, or they shall be compelled by force to their proper stations and mode of living."[66] Massachusetts archconservatives saw social life in a Hobbesian vein as a permanent war of classes using government as a lever for power.

As the insurgency continued, conservative confidence in the Massachusetts state government and its underlying principles began to decline sharply. As Stephen Higginson wrote in late November, referring to the effects of the insurgency on public opinion, "I never saw so great change in the public mind, on any occasion, as has lately appeared in this State as to the expediency of increasing the powers of Congress, not merely as to commercial Objects, but generally."[67] Higginson himself had long supported a stronger central government. He understood this change in others' opinions as a reaction against the legislature's misguided behavior in dealing with the insurgency. Many conservatives such as Theodore Sedgwick thought that the legislature was mistakenly willing to compromise important economic principles to accommodate the rebels' demands. More importantly, it had proved unwilling or unable for a considerable time to use force to suppress it as it should have.

As Abigail Adams wrote, "We shall wait with impatience for the result of General Lincolns expedition. . . . Government seem afraid to use the power they have, and recommend and intreat where they ought to *Command*, which makes one apprehend that the evil lies deeper than the Heads or Hands of Shays or Shattucks."[68] Others, however, saw the insurgency as a powerful challenge to their views on human nature and its relationship to republican government.

Massachusetts congressman Rufus King saw the rebellion as posing a potentially deadly threat to the viability of the American Revolution itself. He believed that the Massachusetts government should "seize, try and punish" the Shays ringleaders. If it did not, "all must be given up to lawless influence," and the result would be that "our Revolution will be our misfortune." Failure to put down the rebellion would prove that "cause of America" was not the cause of "Freedom and Humanity," but instead meant that the country would become "the Scorn of nations."[69] Those were views Abigail Adams would have endorsed. King addressed the Massachusetts legislature in mid-October during the insurgency. Remarkably, he opposed the Annapolis Convention's call to the states for the 1787 Philadelphia Convention, arguing that Congress was the only proper forum for Confederation reform. He did so even though none of the 1786 congressional Grand Committee's reform proposals had been adopted by Congress, showing how greatly he feared Congress's loss of power over the reform process.[70]

But only a few days later, King wrote to Theodore Sedgwick that "I myself have been an Advocate for a Government free as air; my Opinions have been established upon the belief that my country men were virtuous, enlightened, and governed by a sense of Right & Wrong." King said he had seen commerce and luxury as the enemies of republicanism. Now, however, he was beginning to think that "there is but too much reason to fear, that the Framers of our constitutions, & Laws, have proceeded on principles that do not exist."[71] Shortly after that, he wrote to his friend, state legislator Daniel Kilham, criticizing the state government for failing to act aggressively against the rebels. If vigorous action was not taken, "there is good reason to despair of the Commonwealth and to give all up to wild Anarchy & confusion."[72] Like King and Elbridge Gerry, most Massachusetts conservatives had been strong federalist supporters of the Confederation's existing structure and had opposed holding a national reform convention. They now reluctantly joined other Massachusetts leaders such as Nathaniel Gorham, Caleb Davis, and Stephen Higginson who had long supported a stronger central government. By February 1787, King was writing to Gerry that he was inclined to accept that Massachusetts should send delegates to the Philadelphia Convention, and that Gerry should agree as well.[73]

Nathaniel Bishop of Richmond in western Massachusetts experienced a similar change of heart about Massachusetts government. He wrote to Massachusetts leader Caleb Davis in the spring of 1787 that "events which have taken place during the late insurrection are such as have painted upon my mind a new picture of human nature. I could never have believed that so enlightened a people as the citizens of this Commonwealth are, could have been so mad as to have struck directly at the life of every social enjoyment." Government needed to be stronger. He predicted that if Massachusetts "falls by the power of faction, every state in the Union must inevitably fall after it."[74]

When Massachusetts federalists found the insurgency shaking their convictions about human nature, they were reaching a conclusion that leaders elsewhere had also arrived at. As Congressman Edward Carrington of Virginia wrote to Governor Edmund Randolph in a December letter about the insurgency, "Man is impatient of restraint; nor will he conform to what is necessary to the good order of society, unless, he is perfect in discernment and Virtue, or, the Government under which he lives, is efficient. The Fathers of the American Fabric seem to have supposed the first of these principles, peculiarly, our lot, and have chosen it for a foundation: in the progress of experiment, the fallacy is discovered, and the whole pile must fall, if the latter cannot be supplied."[75] Carrington's view that "efficient" government—government that had coercive power to restrain people—was needed was not just a conclusion that he thought was important because of Shays's Rebellion. It was at the heart of his—and nationalists'—disagreement with federalists about the proper foundations of the Confederation as well.

Massachusetts federalists had been forced by events to accept a painful new political reality, the need for government coercive power at the national level to maintain order. While there is little doubt that most of them were economic conservatives, their primary concern was that the divided Massachusetts government had proved unwilling or unable to use force when needed to maintain the rule of law against an armed rebellion because it was unpopular to do so.

Reaction outside Massachusetts

One central fact about the rebellion was not lost on most leaders across the country: the Confederation's weakness had forced Massachusetts to fend for itself. Although Congress had authorized new troops that could be used there, it requisitioned nearly half of them from Massachusetts itself, and it could not pay for any of them. Historian Frederick Marks III was quite right to conclude that the insurgency graphically demonstrated the Confederation's impotence.[76] Stephen Higginson wrote to Secretary of War Henry Knox immediately after the insurgency was defeated, attempting to use state and Confederation weakness as an argument for strengthening the Confederation. He contended that because "all the States are at least equally exposed to such commotions," and "none of them are capable of the exertions we [Massachusetts] have made," the Confederation must be empowered to defend the states. If it was not strengthened, the "Insurgents will soon rise up and take the reins from them."[77]

Some supporters of stronger central government such as Higginson realized, however, that the insurgency might well have limited political effects after its defeat. He urged Confederation officials such as Congressman Nathan Dane and Henry Knox to push for reform "while the fire burns," because, he conceded, its effects "will not be durable, perhaps."[78] But by then, others were questioning whether Shays's Rebellion was really typical of conditions around the country. As Henry Knox wrote to Higginson, by the spring of 1787, people with whom he spoke were questioning whether the insurgency might not be due to "local causes." That meant that they thought it reflected a failure of Massachusetts government, not a problem to which the Confederation needed to respond.[79]

There are persuasive reasons for thinking that Shays's Rebellion was largely the product of distinctive local circumstances. First, economic conditions in western Massachusetts were somewhat, perhaps even considerably, worse than they were in most of the country. That meant that debtors and taxpayers there carried heavier burdens in meeting their obligations. Second, the number of people involved in the insurgency and its geographic extent dwarfed the violent unrest or "regulation" anywhere else in the country. The course of the insurgency demonstrated that there were underlying systemic grievances felt not just by the active rebels but by a significant fraction of the entire Massachusetts population. Finally, no other state government resisted granting meaningful economic relief as strenuously as did Massachusetts. Taken together, these factors created the preconditions for a perfect political storm, and the Shays insurgency was that storm. It was the high-water mark of violent social unrest during the postwar Confederation period. Its easy defeat in Massachusetts made the spread of such insurgencies much less likely.[80]

Some historians believe, however, that the Massachusetts insurgency was contagious, and set off a wave of backcountry rebellion across the country.[81] There were indeed instances of sporadic violence against courts, government officials such as sheriffs, and buildings in various states during 1786 and 1787. As was true of all efforts to obstruct courts and tax collectors throughout the postwar period, they certainly evidenced some individuals' and groups' discontent with the status quo. But the violent incidents and other protests to which historians point to support their claim that Shays's Rebellion was contagious were minor in scale compared to it, and were all suppressed without great difficulty. By the time most of them occurred, the movement for the Philadelphia Convention was under way; others noted by historians took place during 1787, some while the convention was meeting.

In the remainder of New England, reaction to Shays's Rebellion involved small numbers of men scattered across several states. James Madison noted that there did not appear to be any Shays-like rebellion brewing in Connecticut. The state had acted quickly to break up a small planned court blockage by arresting rebel leaders, and no further unrest occurred.[82] Madison attributed that to the fact that Connecticut was declining to pay Confederation requisitions, so taxes there did not increase.[83] Some Connecticut leaders, such as Oliver Wolcott, seem to have concluded that Shays's Rebellion meant that Congress was impotent and a stronger government was needed.[84] In New Hampshire, a 1786 revolt involving at most a few hundred men was quickly suppressed by the governor with militia support. New Hampshire towns then decisively voted down its main demand, for paper money.[85] Vermont suppressed a rebellion involving thirty men and passed strict laws to prevent further outbreaks.[86] Rhode Island's majority had enthusiastically adopted paper money and debt relief. Most discontent there was in merchant communities.

There appears to have been little organized discontent in the Mid-Atlantic states, again probably because significant popular economic-relief demands had been at least partly met. Benjamin Franklin regarded Shays's Rebellion as being of minor importance.[87] There were isolated incidents in York, Pennsylvania, in late 1786 and early 1787 in which farmers sought to block forced sales of cattle and other property, as well as other incidents of collusion and resistance to debt and tax collection.[88] But, as one historian points out, the state's decision to issue paper money had satisfied many farmers.[89] While there were sporadic violence and some temporary courthouse closings in New Jersey and Maryland involving relatively small numbers of men, nothing resembling an organized or geographically extensive insurgency seems to have occurred in either state.[90] In the South, we have already seen how the South Carolina legislature successfully defused popular protests in

1785 by granting economic relief. The most interesting case there is that of Virginia.

Virginia's economy was still depressed in 1787. As in other states, there had been popular resistance to debt and tax collections during the postwar period. The legislature had issued its call to the states for the Philadelphia Convention in late 1786. In 1787, several violent incidents occurred. Shortly after the Philadelphia Convention began, the King William County clerk's office was burned. The New Kent County jail and clerk's office were burned in an attack by John Posey and three associates on July 12, during the Philadelphia Convention. Posey was later captured and hanged.[91] In August 1787, when the Philadelphia Convention had been under way for several months, a debtor named Adonijah Mathews attempted to organize a tax-resistance movement in Greenbrier County. The county jail there was burned, and about 150 people formed an association to resist payment of a particular state certificate tax and all "private debts." A recent historian claims that that movement forced the legislature to repeal the challenged state tax.[92]

Contemporary news reports suggest, however, that the small Mathews revolt fizzled out. By September 20, 1787, it was reported that Mathews had been captured (or possibly recaptured), acknowledged his offense, and jailed. The association was not adopted in other counties, and "all are quiet" in Greenbrier County.[93] The Virginia state government did not think that it was necessary to mobilize troops in response to events in Greenbrier. Instead, it directed the attorney general to prosecute those responsible, with militia assistance if needed.[94] More importantly, the sum total of the 1787 Virginia arsons and protests described above involved a few government buildings scattered around the state in counties that contained about 4 percent of the state's population, not an organized rebellion. They collectively involved perhaps 500 to 1,000 individuals in a state with a free population of about 350,000 people, so their scale was quite small compared to Shays's Rebellion.[95] When much of the violence occurred, the Philadelphia Convention was already under way. In light of Virginia's limited history of violent insurgency, it is particularly illuminating to consider the reactions of major Virginia leaders to the earlier, far larger, and much better organized Shays's Rebellion.

Shays's insurgency was not regarded as a significant threat by either Patrick Henry or Thomas Jefferson.[96] Jefferson famously responded to Abigail Adams's stern condemnation of it by writing that a little rebellion now and then was a good thing, like a "storm in the Atmosphere."[97] As his metaphor suggests, Jefferson thought that rebellions cleared the political air by crystallizing grievances. They forced governments to respond to public concerns in ways that they otherwise might not have. Jefferson wrote to James Madison that while he regarded Shays's Rebellion with "no uneasiness," he felt very differently about the "possibility that the navigation of the Mississippi may be abandoned to Spain" as a result of the Spanish treaty. Jefferson told Madison that he regarded the Spanish treaty as an "act of separation" between the "Eastern & Western country."[98] Patrick Henry did not soften his opposition to the 1787 Constitution in the least as a result of the rebellion, or concede that it showed any need for Confederation reforms. Other Virginians were concerned by the rebellion, including Henry Lee, Jr., James Madison, and George Washington. It is important to understand both the reasons for their concerns and the effects they had on their decisions about Confederation reform.

Of course, Lee, Madison, and Washington already strongly favored a far stronger Confederation with full tax and military powers before Shays's Rebellion ever occurred. The rebellion had little effect on their desire to see the Confederation fundamentally reformed. The Annapolis Convention had already recommended that the Philadelphia Convention be held before news of the rebellion reached Annapolis, so it played no role in that recommendation. Virginia nationalist leaders were, however, alarmed by the rebellion for several reasons.

First, they seem to have at least initially credited exaggerated and apparently baseless opinions of the size and extreme political views of the rebellion. Secretary of War Knox, one of the few Confederation officials with firsthand knowledge, wrote Washington that in New England "people of similar sentiments" to those in Massachusetts amounted to "twelve or fifteen thousand desperate, and unprincipled men."[99] Congressman Henry Lee, Jr., sent Washington a string of letters beginning in September that contained a series of dire predictions about the insurgency and its spread to other states. In mid-October, Lee went Knox one better and wrote Madison that there might be 40,000 seditious men in Massachusetts alone.[100] Quite remarkably, Lee did so even after Knox had informed Congress in early October that he thought that there were roughly 1,200 Massachusetts insurgents, 300 of whom had no firearms.[101] As the insurgency progressed, it became clear that there was a very large gap between the number of its sympathizers and the number of people actually willing to join its forces. The actual insurgency in the field was relatively small. The insurgency's military weakness and ineptitude were amply confirmed by the actual "battles" that occurred in early 1787.

Washington's reaction to the news of Shays's Rebellion is particularly revealing. Historian Merrill Jensen claimed that the rebellion alarmed him to the point where he agreed to reenter politics and attend the Philadelphia Convention.[102] Jensen's claim is mistaken. Washington had been following newspaper reports on the insurgency, and had received some correspondence suggesting that similar sentiments were widespread in New England, by late October 1786. He then wrote to his former aide David Humphreys in Connecticut, asking him to "for Gods sake tell me, what is the cause of all these commotions? Do they proceed from licenciousness, British influence disseminated by the Tories, or real grievances which admit of redress? If the latter, why has the remedy been delayed. . . . If the former, why are not the powers of government tried at once? It is as well to be without them, as not to live under their exercise." He added that he was "really mortified beyond belief" at the possibility that British predictions that Americans could not govern themselves might be true.[103] Washington's letter to Humphreys is noteworthy because despite his profound disagreement with what he understood were the insurgents' demands, he had kept an open mind, and wanted to know whether they had real grievances that deserved redress. He wanted the government to respond effectively and to use force only if it was clearly warranted.

Not long afterward, Washington received a letter from Henry Knox claiming (with no clear foundation in fact) that the rebels were "agrarians" who wanted all property equally divided. Knox said that a stronger government must be created because "this dreadful situation has alarmed every man of principle and property in New England."[104] Henry Lee, Jr., repeated Knox's inflammatory and probably baseless claim.[105] Lee then wrote Washington that Congress might invite him to visit it and perhaps to use his influence to seek reconciliation with the rebels. Washington responded to Lee that "influence is no government." He admonished him as well that if the rebels had real grievances, they should be addressed.[106] The same day, Washington announced to the Society of the Cincinnati that he would resign its presidency when his term ended in 1787.[107] Soon after that, he declined to serve as a delegate at the Philadelphia Convention despite the urgings of James Madison, Edmund Randolph, and others.[108] In short, Washington may have been alarmed by Shays's insurgency, but he was equally if not more concerned by what he saw as Massachusetts's dysfunctional response to it. And he was not alarmed enough by either to agree to leave Mount Vernon to do anything about it.

Lee, Madison, and Washington were concerned about the possibility that armed rebellions might occur in other states. As Washington put it, "there are combustibles in every State." But in the same letter in which he made that statement, Washington wrote that in Virginia, "a perfect calm prevails at present, and a prompt disposition to support, and give energy to the foederal system is discovered."[109] It is apparent from Washington's letter that by the end of 1786, he saw no evidence that discontent from Shays's Rebellion had spread to Virginia. To the contrary, by then Virginia had already agreed to send delegates to Philadelphia to strengthen the Confederation.

For Washington, what was most important about the rebellion was that it was proof that he had been right all along in arguing for a stronger central government. It showed vividly how weak the states and the Confederation were. He wrote to James Madison, "What stronger evidence can be given of the want of energy in our governments than these disorders? If there exists not a power to check them, what security has a man of life, liberty or property? . . . Thirteen sovereignties pulling against each other, and all tugging at the foederal head will soon bring ruin on the whole."[110] Washington's primary concern was not with the insurgents' economic agenda, though he strongly disliked it. Instead, it was with the states' and Confederation's inability to respond to the insurgents' willingness to use armed force to advance it. As we saw earlier, he had expressed much the same concerns about the need to create effective national sovereignty to John Jay before Shays's Rebellion ever began.

By late February 1787, if not before, Washington knew that there was no reason to regard Shays's Rebellion as a continuing threat. It had been crushed without difficulty. Accounts of the insurgents' collapse that he received plainly showed that the movement had been far weaker than Washington originally had been informed it was. By then, there was little indication that similar insurgencies would spread. On February 25, Washington wrote to Henry Knox congratulating him "on the happy termination of this insurrection." Still, based on that and other events such as a bitter paper-money fight in Maryland, he believed that "our Affairs, generally, seem really to be approaching to some awful crisis." Yet he was still unwilling to leave his "tranquil retirement."[111]

From the end of the war onward, Washington had been advocating major reforms of Confederation government to achieve national unity and power. Shays's insurgency had strengthened his position. In late March, he described his overall view of Shays's significance to the Marquis de Lafayette. He wrote Lafayette that "these disorders are evident marks of a defective government, indeed the thinking part of the people of this Country are now so well satisfied of this fact that most of the Legislatures have appointed, & the rest it is said will appoint, delegates to meet at Philadelphia . . . in general Convention . . . to revise, and correct the defects of the federal System."[112] In late March 1787, he reversed course and agreed to attend the Philadelphia Convention (his reasons are discussed in detail in chapter 9).

Conclusion

The principal lasting effect of Shays's Rebellion was that it persuaded a sufficient number of staunch Massachusetts federalists that the Confederation needed reform to enable it to protect their state against a future popular insurgency. Their reactions to Shays's insurgency show that many Massachusetts federalists believed they needed protection against what they now realized was the distinct possibility that a popular mob would be able to dominate forcibly a state that had a weak or seriously divided government. Shays's Rebellion had permanently altered many federalists' perception of the ideal balance between liberty and order in a republic. They were now prepared to consider Confederation reforms at a national convention. And the rebellion had added support for the view already held for other reasons by nationalist leaders such as Washington that the country needed a more powerful central government.

PART 4

Confederation Collapse and Its Consequences

9

"The Truth Is, We Have Not a Government"

CONFEDERATION STALEMATE AND THE ROAD TO THE PHILADELPHIA CONVENTION

During 1786, many American leaders believed that the Confederation was about to collapse. It could not pay its debts. Congress's 1783 tax proposals were effectively dead. There was no prospect that Congress would receive effective commerce powers. Britain refused to turn over its western forts. Congress reached impasse on the Spanish treaty. It could not pay troops to combat Shays's Rebellion or increasing Indian attacks. And it was unable to act on proposed new reforms. Yet during 1786, several Virginia and Massachusetts congressmen opposed holding a national reform convention.

The battle over the Confederation's future began in November when, in a surprising change, Virginia's legislature agreed to call for the 1787 Philadelphia Convention. Virginia's action stemmed from an important shift in public opinion about the need for a stronger national government. Yet opponents of key reforms were still very powerful in Virginia. Several states promptly chose convention delegates. But in Massachusetts and New York there were strong efforts to kill the convention outright or to prevent it from proposing major reforms. Those states were dragged to the table kicking and screaming, in today's phrase. Congress itself then grudgingly agreed to support holding the convention in early 1787. Its support was understood as a "no confidence" vote on both the Confederation and on Congress's ability to reform it. Its decision signaled the Confederation's collapse.

George Washington saw the Philadelphia Convention as a double-edged sword. He hoped to create a sovereign national government capable of becoming a continental empire. He foresaw major state resistance to that goal. Consequently, the convention could succeed only if enough Americans supported such reforms. But if it failed to reach agreement on them, that would finally destroy the Confederation. He was determined to participate at Philadelphia only if he concluded that the states' convention arrangements showed that it would be possible to reach agreement on thorough reforms. He was prepared to reach an intersectional grand bargain if necessary to achieve major reforms.

James Madison's preconvention proposals radically reconceived the national republic. He blamed the states for most of the Confederation's failings. He sought far broader national powers. The Confederation had to be able to prevent states from failing to obey it, or from interfering with its powers. Madison also wanted to prevent states from harming each other. Finally, he hoped to prohibit popular majorities from harming minorities. But Madison's draconian "solution" to perceived abuses of state and popular authority—giving Congress a complete veto over all state laws—would have destroyed the states.

***

The General Assembly of this Commonwealth, taking into view the actual situation of the Confederacy, as well as reflecting on the Alarming representations made from time to time by the United States in Congress, particularly in their act of the fifteenth day of February last, can no longer doubt that the crisis is arrived at which the good people of America are to decide the solemn question, whether they will by wise and magnanimous efforts reap the just fruits of that independence, which they have so gloriously acquired, and of that union which they have cemented with so much of their common blood.

Excerpt from the Virginia legislature's December 1786 resolution calling for the 1787 Philadelphia Convention[1]

In late 1785, the Virginia legislature rejected James Madison's proposal to give the Confederation greater commerce powers. From its ashes came the legislature's alternative, the Annapolis Convention, to be held in September 1786. For the majority, the Annapolis Convention's primary purpose was to consider how states' commerce powers might be harmonized to meet Confederation goals, not to create new powers for Congress. Yet only one year later, at Madison's request, the Virginia legislature unanimously issued a call to all of the states for the 1787 Philadelphia Convention. It was well understood that the convention might propose broad new Confederation powers, including commerce and tax powers. Yet the legislature proposed no limits on the convention's agenda.

Madison rightly saw Virginia's call as a remarkable turn of events. He wrote to Jefferson that there had been a "revolution of sentiment which the experience of one year has effected in this Country." In his view, the resolution's approval showed that the "evidence of the dangerous defects in the Confederation has at length proselyted the most obstinate adversaries to a reform."[2] The decisions about the convention made by Virginia and other states over the next few months were actually the first major battles over the Confederation's collapse.

This chapter examines how and why the convention actually took place, and how various leaders viewed America's situation just before it began. It discusses why public opinion on the Confederation in major states such as Virginia had changed in a year, and the main reasons that led key states to agree to the Philadelphia Convention. It shows that federalist leaders in critically important states tried either to block the convention completely or to tie delegates' hands to prevent fundamental Confederation reforms. It also examines Virginia nationalist leaders' concerns about the convention and their preparations for it, because their efforts were representative of the Philadelphia Convention movement.

The Confederation Heads toward a Crisis

As we have seen, in George Washington's view the Confederation was not a sovereign government. The disruptive events of 1786 made clear how just how important it was that the Confederation lacked sovereignty. As political and socioeconomic conditions deteriorated, it could do little to control events except to plead and cajole. Its chronic weakness became far harder to ignore when it faced growing difficulties on every front. By the end of 1786, the Confederation had reached stalemate on every major issue that had confronted it since 1783.

In February 1786, a congressional committee chaired by Rufus King had reported that the Confederation was insolvent. It concluded that "the crisis has arrived" when "the people of these United States . . . must decide whether they will support their rank as a nation, by maintaining the public faith at home and abroad."[3] The committee found that the Confederation requisition system needed to be replaced by the Confederation taxes proposed in 1783—the 5 percent impost (i.e., import) tax and supplemental taxes. Otherwise, the Confederation would be unable to preserve the country's public faith. Congress approved its recommendations.[4] By then, even many strongly federalist leaders had reached the conclusion that the requisition system was fundamentally flawed. Board of Treasury member Arthur Lee wrote to Samuel Adams in February, gravely concerned about the Confederation's survival. He told Adams that over a two-month period, "not one dollar has come in to the Receivers throughout the Union," even though the Confederation needed nearly $70,000 every two months to operate. By 1787, he wrote, the Confederation's expenses were expected to jump to more than $260,000 every two months. But, Lee said, there was "not the smallest prospect" that New York would agree to Congress's 1783 impost proposal. Instead, its legislature was "wholly occupied about emitting paper money."[5]

The fiscal news during the rest of the year justified Congress's fears. In June 1786, the Board of Treasury issued a report confirming that Confederation insolvency was about to lead to default on its foreign loans. The board's accompanying letter to Congress said that to avoid "Bankruptcy," and "preserve the Union of the several States from Dissolution," the states needed to immediately adopt Congress's 1783 tax proposals. Two of the three signatories, Samuel Osgood and Arthur Lee, were among the country's staunchest federalists.[6] Yet in fall 1786, the New York legislature rejected the impost.[7] Despite Congress's urgent pleas, it rejected the impost again in 1787.[8] Even if it had agreed, it would have made no difference, because in the fall of 1786 Pennsylvania had effectively withdrawn its support for the impost. James Monroe reported that "both parties" in Pennsylvania supported that decision. Pennsylvania leaders believed that the legislature's action would "endanger" the Confederation, compelling reforms.[9] There was no realistic prospect that Congress's 1783 tax proposals would ever be adopted under the Confederation.

By early 1787, James Madison reported to Virginia leader Edmund Pendleton that "not a single state complies with the requisitions, several pass them over in silence, and some positively reject them."[10] The Confederation could not pay either its foreign or its domestic creditors. Not surprisingly, Rufus King wrote to Elbridge Gerry and predicted that unless the Confederation received added revenue, it would collapse.[11] Soon after that, he told Gerry that "the People generally through the confederacy remark that we are at a crisis."[12] But insurmountable fiscal problems were only the beginning of the bad news that rained down on the Confederation in a torrent in 1786.

In the spring of 1786, the British government rejected John Adams's demand that it surrender its western military posts. Of Britain's views at the time Abigail Adams wrote from London, "there is not a less Hostile Spirit here against America than there was during the administration of Lord North. They Hate us and the French equally, and every effort to crush us, to breed ill will amongst us, to ruin our commerce, to destroy our navigation will be, and is studiously practised."[13] By May 1786, Congress had received word of Britain's refusal.[14] If the United States attacked the forts, that would abrogate the peace treaty and ignite a new war. The Confederation lacked the funds to raise an army in any event. Britain would be able to retain the forts indefinitely under the Confederation.

Britain's refusal to abandon its forts greatly strengthened the hand of western Indian tribes opposed to US expansion. As discussed earlier, during 1786, several tribes attacked Kentucky settlements and threatened death to Americans who sought to settle west of the Ohio River. In mid-1786, Congress rejected Virginia governor Patrick Henry's urgent pleas for assistance to Kentucky. Shortly afterward, Congress became embroiled in the Spanish-treaty debate, which ended sectional cooperation on most issues. In the fall of 1786, Congress had received credible reports of possible broad-ranging western Indian uprisings, and learned that its surveyors had been blocked by Indians.[15] Congress agreed to authorize added troops for the army to combat Shays's Rebellion and hostile Indians, but had no money to pay them. It lacked even the money needed to "buy off" the Barbary coast pirates, whose attacks continued. Thus, by the end of 1786, it was clear that the Confederation lacked both the necessary powers and the revenues to deal with pressing challenges from foreign governments, Indian tribes, and domestic rebels alike. It was wholly incapable of successfully confronting either external or internal military threats.

In the face of these difficulties, in mid-1786, Congressman Charles Pinckney of South Carolina proposed that Congress authorize a national convention to consider Confederation reforms. Virginia congressman James Monroe immediately opposed Pinckney's proposal.[16] Surprisingly, James Madison agreed with Monroe. Madison thought that it would be better for the Annapolis Convention to meet before attempting any broader reform.[17] He also told Monroe, however, that the Virginia legislature would not in any event have given its delegates authority broader than the narrow authority they had granted for the Annapolis Convention.[18] In August 1786, he told Jefferson that although he favored a national convention, "I despair so much of its accomplishment at the present crisis that I do not extend my views beyond a Commercial Reform." Madison blamed his despair on the Spanish-treaty proposal pending in Congress. He predicted to Jefferson that it would create vociferous opposition to expansion of Confederation powers.[19]

From his vantage point in London, American ambassador to Britain John Adams was deeply dismayed by the fact that the Confederation was insolvent, and unable to pay its debts. He thought that the Confederation was losing other nations' support and confidence by financial dishonesty. He expressed his thoughts on America's troubled situation on July 4, 1786, writing to Massachusetts official Cotton Tufts:

> As to Politicks, all that can be said is summarily comprehended in a few words. Our Country is grown, or at least has been dishonest. She has broke her Faith with Nations, & with her own Citizens. And Parties are all about for continuing this dishonourable Course. She must become Strictly honest and punctual to all the world before she can recover the Confidence of any body at home or abroad. The Duty of all good Men is to join, in making this Doctrine popular, and in discountenancing every Attempt against it. This Censure is too harsh I suppose for common Ears, but the essence of these Sentiments must be adopted throughout America, before we can prosper. Have our People forgotten every Principle of Public and Private Credit?[20]

Despite the Confederation's dire straits, reform efforts in Congress were stillborn.[21] In August 1786, after months of debate a Grand Committee of Congress (whose twelve members represented nearly every state) proposed a series of Confederation reforms.[22] But political gridlock prevented any action on them. Instead, they were published in newspapers. Congress itself became moribund. More than 45 percent of Congress's members were new in both 1786 and 1787. Between November 1786 and August 1787, on only three days were as many as ten states represented in Congress. Congress was often incapable of acting except when it was unanimous. After November 1786, Congress normally acted only in emergencies.[23]

Through mid-1786, even in the face of complete Confederation stalemate many Virginia leaders were just as reluctant to consider broad-ranging Confederation reforms as were Massachusetts leaders. They were unwilling to find a way to end the stalemate through a national convention outside Congress. What was the road—or more precisely, what were the different roads—that led critical states to Philadelphia a year later? We consider the struggle over authorizing the convention in three politically closely divided major states, Virginia, New York, and

Massachusetts, which together had about 35 percent of the country's free population. Because of their size and strategic locations, their willingness to adopt reforms was essential to creating any replacement for the Confederation. (Delegates from other states, particularly Pennsylvania and South Carolina, also played important roles at the Philadelphia Convention itself. But there was little controversy in those states about appointing delegates to the convention or over the convention's scope, so they are not discussed here.)[24]

Virginia

In November 1786, the Virginia legislature unanimously approved Madison's Philadelphia Convention proposal. The resolution justified the convention by referring to the "Alarming representations" about the Confederation's insolvency made by Congress, "particularly in their Act of the fifteenth day of February last." In the February 15 King committee report (discussed earlier), Congress had concluded that the requisition system had failed. That made it an "utter impossibility" to preserve the "faith of the federal government" by paying its just debts. Virginia's legislature gave the Confederation's inability to pay the nation's debts as the primary reason why reform was needed. The Confederation's failures, it found, meant that "the crisis is arrived at which the good people of America are to decide the solemn question, whether they will by wise and magnanimous efforts reap the just fruits of that Independence which they have so gloriously acquired."[25] The resolution confirms what we have seen since 1783: Virginia's highest reform priority was giving the Confederation effective tax powers. But in a sharp departure from past practice, the legislature imposed no limits on the reforms the convention could consider. That unmistakably signaled to other states Virginia's acceptance that they would propose consideration of additional reforms such as Confederation commerce powers. It evinced the state's willingness to consider entering into a "grand bargain" with them that included such reforms in order to obtain its own goals.

Madison interpreted the legislature's unanimity as meaning that everyone in Virginia now agreed that there were "dangerous defects" in the Confederation that required reform. There are good reasons to think that he was wrong. As readers will recall, the Spanish-treaty impasse had actually sharply decreased support in Virginia for strengthening the Confederation among prominent leaders such as Patrick Henry. Nor had Virginia opposition to strong Confederation commerce powers decreased after the Annapolis Convention. To the contrary, Madison received a letter from prominent Virginian Edmund Pendleton in December, after Virginia called for the Philadelphia Convention. Pendleton expressed grave concern that the Confederation might obtain stronger commerce powers.[26] In the circumstances, we might have expected a contest in Virginia's legislature over authorizing the convention. Yet that did not happen. That suggests that public opinion had recently changed in important ways.

The most important cause of changed opinion was that during 1786, it became clear to Virginians that the Confederation and the state were unwilling or unable to protect western settlers against Indian attacks. Western settlers were extremely unhappy about that. As one of their leaders, George Muter, wrote from Kentucky to Madison in early 1787:

> The situation of the people of this district, from the war with the Indians, is really distressing. The [Virginia state] expeditions of last fall [led by General Clark], tho' carried on at a vast expense, seem not to have been attended, with one single good consequence: on the contrary, there is reason to believe, the Indians have gained a greater degree of confidence than they before possessed, & have been more irritated against us than they were. They seem now to be pushing us on every side; mischief has been done lately, on the frontiers of almost every County in the district, and parties have even ventured to commit their depredations, within about 15 miles of Danville. . . . A great many poor people have already been forced to remove from their habitations, & it is not to be doubted, but that many more will be forced to follow their example. There seems to be no security at present, but in the very thickest settled parts of the Country.[27]

Muter told Madison that settlers believed that Congress should assist them, but "have little hopes of any good arising to them" from Congress's newly authorized troops or "from any other exertion by Congress in their favour whatever." Kentucky settlers had little confidence that either Virginia or the Confederation would protect them. The Spanish-treaty controversy had also significantly weakened Confederation support in the Kentucky district. Muter told Madison that people there were "greatly alarmed at the prospect of the navigation of the Mississippi being given up."[28] Support for making Kentucky a state separate from Virginia (and perhaps outside the Union as well) was growing.

In contrast to Kentucky, in parts of western Virginia farther east (i.e., closer to the Virginia Piedmont), which were unable to separate from Virginia, state and Confederation weakness in responding to Indian threats and Britain's retention of its forts had had the opposite effect. The year's events increased support for strengthening the Confederation. That significant change in political sentiment can be inferred from the dramatic change in the legislature's voting patterns on laws preventing payment of British debts. In 1784, Patrick Henry had successfully opposed changes in Virginia laws to meet the peace-treaty requirement on British debts. Virginia's mountain, Shenandoah Valley, and western counties had provided the entire margin of victory for Henry's position.[29]

After Britain refused to relinquish its forts in 1786, a renewed fight on repayment of British debts broke out in the Virginia legislature. But this time, many legislators from western Virginia supported changing the law to permit British creditors to recover debts. In November 1787, Henry lost an important vote on the British debts issue, due entirely to his loss of western support.[30] Historians think that westerners' primary motivation in changing their position was to remove any justification for Britain's retention of its forts. Most of them were primarily concerned about the continuing ill effects of Native American warfare, which the forts supported and encouraged.[31] They were increasingly inclined to favor a central government powerful enough to force Britain to change its policies. Their changed views made them critically important new allies of eastern Virginians such as George Washington.

Shays's Rebellion probably also played a role in changing Virginia attitudes about the Confederation, but it was fairly limited. As discussed in chapter 8, it strengthened the hand of those nationalists who thought that the Confederation needed to be able to tax effectively and fund an army. Kentuckian George Muter expressed concern to Madison that Shays's Rebellion might spread, but how far was "impossible to foresee." Muter hoped that it would "produce an inclination in the minds of all men, to use every endeavour, to bring about such an amendment in the federal union as has, now, become absolutely necessary."[32] In other words, he hoped that the insurgency would strengthen the case for Confederation reforms that he already believed were sorely needed to protect western settlers.

Virginia's decision to call for the Philadelphia Convention was based primarily on overarching concerns for preserving public faith and providing effective military defense against both foreign and domestic threats, particularly Indian warfare. The legislature overwhelmingly defeated both paper-money and various debt-relief proposals during the month in which it approved the Philadelphia Convention. From that, it seems fair to conclude that concerns about state economic-relief laws played a relatively minor role in Virginia's decision to call for the Philadelphia Convention. (They played a somewhat larger part in James Madison's reform proposals, as we will shortly see.)

Madison soon came to understand, however, that the legislature's apparent unanimity about the convention was deeply misleading. Reformers had actually "pushed through an open door," because Patrick Henry had chosen not to oppose Madison's convention resolution. That did not mean that Henry supported the convention's goals. Madison realized, after Henry and several others opposed to Confederation reforms declined to serve as delegates, that Henry was "keeping his powder dry." He would be free to oppose Confederation reforms proposed in Philadelphia. As Madison sarcastically described Henry's action, "I fear that this step has proceeded from a wish to leave his conduct unfettered on another theatre [Virginia politics] where the result of the Convention will receive its destiny from his omnipotence."[33] Madison's remark shows us not only his visceral dislike for Henry but, more importantly, just how strongly he feared Henry as an opponent.

Massachusetts

In fall 1786, Massachusetts congressmen Rufus King and Nathan Dane successfully opposed having Congress support the Annapolis Convention's recommendation to hold the Philadelphia Convention.[34] They argued that under the Articles, only Congress was authorized to propose amendments to the Confederation for consideration by the states. It would "derogate from the dignity and Weight of that body" to have a convention assume that responsibility, they contended. Virginia congressman Edward Carrington wrote that their position "is an elevated idea, and, in an efficient Sovereignty, would be a wise one." But, Carrington said, "the truth is, we have not a government to Wield and Correct." Instead, he wrote, we "must pursue the most certain means for obtaining one" through a convention.[35] Carrington's response showed the enormous gap that still existed at the end of 1786 between the Massachusetts delegation's perspective and the views that had now come to the fore in Virginia. Carrington and many other Virginians looked at the events of 1786, and concluded that "we have not a government," or, in other words, that the Confederation had already collapsed.

The Massachusetts congressional delegation, on the other hand, still held out hope for reform and improvement under the existing Confederation. More than four months elapsed from the time in October 1786 when the Annapolis recommendation was presented to the Massachusetts legislature until it acted on the issue of the state's attendance at the Philadelphia Convention. The delay was not due to Shays's Rebellion alone. Congressmen King and Dane separately addressed the legislature in fall, 1786 during the rebellion. They both vociferously opposed the Annapolis recommendation because it called for action on reform outside Congress.[36] The legislature ultimately considered Virginia's

Philadelphia Convention resolution immediately after Shays's insurgency was defeated. A bitter fight ensued, but opinions had changed.

There is good reason to think that many members of the influential Massachusetts business community decided in the wake of Shays's insurgency that they could no longer afford to have the Confederation be wholly ineffectual. They were very disturbed by the temporizing reaction of what they believed were a pro-business governor and legislature to the insurgency. Because public opinion was divided, the forcible measures that they desired to suppress the rebellion were not taken immediately. When the state decided to use force, it had to borrow money from merchants to fund an army. In such a divided political climate, Massachusetts might not be able to collect taxes to pay even its preexisting debts, and much of that money was also owed to businessmen. Finally, some of their legislative representatives appeared to be willing to "sell out" to the insurgents on major economic issues such as paper money and debt relief.[37]

After Shays's insurgency, leading businessmen such as Nathaniel Gorham wanted the Confederation to be able to protect them militarily. Gorham, who had been heavily involved in coordinating Massachusetts's suppression of the insurgency, wrote to Secretary of War Henry Knox that "sensible and bold men shall be chosen for the [Philadelphia] convention if I can have any influence in the business." He then recommended that Knox move Confederation troops to Springfield.[38] Even ardent federalists such as Elbridge Gerry now agreed that protection was needed. Writing to James Monroe, Gerry said that he thought the Philadelphia Convention was very important, because "unless a system of Government is adopted by *Compact, Force* I expect will plant the Standard: for such an anarchy as now exists cannot last long. Gentlemen seem to be impressed with the necessity of establishing some efficient system, & I hope it will secure us against domestic as well as Foreign Invasion."[39] Leading merchant Stephen Higginson wrote to Secretary Knox that the Union must "have the power also of compelling obedience" to its decisions, or "our federal Constitution will be a mere dead letter."[40]

In mid-February 1787, Rufus King wrote to Elbridge Gerry that he and Gerry should not oppose the convention. He said that "events are hurrying us to a Crisis, prudent and sagacious men should be ready to seize the most favorable Circumstances to establish a more perfect & vigourous Government." He recommended that Gerry serve as a delegate.[41] By then, King perceived that events were moving in favor of holding the convention and creating a new government, and he did not want either himself or his allies to be left out of the process.

However, Massachusetts senator Samuel Adams wanted to prevent Massachusetts from sending delegates to the convention at all or, failing that, to sharply restrict their authority. Nathaniel Gorham wrote to Secretary Knox, an ardent nationalist, that Adams "is full of doubts & difficulties and finding that he cannot obstruct the report generally wishes to limit the Commission in such manner as I think will exceedingly injure the business."[42] In mid-February, Massachusetts received word that Virginia and North Carolina had appointed delegates for the convention with unrestricted authority. But despite that, even many Massachusetts legislators who accepted holding the convention wanted to limit its agenda and delegates' authority.

The Massachusetts Senate, apparently at Adams's instigation, proposed that the primary purpose of the meeting be "the trade and commerce of the United States." Other changes could be considered only if they were "consistent with the true republican spirit & genius of the present articles of Confederation." That vague limitation would permit Massachusetts's delegates to oppose the convention's consideration of almost any reform other than trade and commerce if they chose to do so. Moreover, the senate's proposal instructed the delegates "by no means to interfere with" Article 5 of the Articles of Confederation. That article included requirements for equal state voting in Congress, annual election of congressional delegates, the right of states to recall and replace them, and term limits, among other provisions. The legislature wanted to preserve its very tight control over the state's congressmen. It may well also have intended to prevent any change in equal state voting in Congress by the Philadelphia Convention.[43]

The legislature on February 22 agreed to the senate's proposals. If the Massachusetts convention delegates chose to interpret the restrictions on their authority broadly, as many legislators clearly hoped they would, they would have completely tied their own hands on critical issues facing the convention. Among other things, requiring continued equal state voting would have made restructuring Congress to redistribute power among the states utterly impossible. Had large states been unable to increase their influence in Congress by ending equal state voting, they would unquestionably have balked at providing new Confederation tax or commerce powers. The convention would have failed to remedy what many saw as the Confederation's major defects.

But remarkably, several weeks later, the legislature reversed its position and removed the senate restrictions. Our sources do not directly explain why. But the decision's timing strongly suggests that at least some legislators changed their minds after learning of Congress's February 21 resolution approving the convention (discussed below). We know that Massachusetts's convention delegates were finally chosen on March 3, just after the legislature learned of Congress's action. On March 5, a Massachusetts newspaper reported that the states' delegates had been chosen "agreeably to a resolution of Congress of the 21st of February 1787."[44]

That news report was mistaken, and may have been politically motivated.[45] It was inaccurate for two reasons. The legislature had authorized choosing delegates before it learned of Congress's action, and its restrictions on delegates' authority were inconsistent with Congress's resolution. Yet several other Massachusetts newspapers soon repeated the same misleading claim.[46] These newspaper accounts expediently justified the legislature's decision to send delegates to Philadelphia as simply a matter of following Congress's wishes. But that same justification also added to pressure on the legislature not to impose restrictions on delegate authority.

We also know that the Massachusetts Senate insisted on the restrictions on delegate authority until four days after the states' delegates had been chosen, so it is clear that there was strong support for them. On March 7, the Massachusetts House of Representatives seems to have forced the removal of the restrictions (probably over Samuel Adams's vigorous objections).[47] Surprisingly, the legislature also specifically ordered that its original action restricting delegates' authority should not be published. That was a sure sign of the sensitivity and potential divisiveness of that issue, especially in the wake of Shays's Rebellion.[48] Whatever its motivation was, the legislature's removal of its restrictions on its delegates sharply increased their bargaining flexibility and power at the convention.

Yet looking forward, Massachusetts leaders had reason to be fearful about whether their state would gain or lose from the convention. They could reasonably anticipate that the convention would propose increased national tax powers. But they also knew that there would be powerful sectional opposition to broad commerce powers and particularly to the Spanish treaty. And the convention would almost certainly depart from an equal one-vote-per-state rule for Congress. That strengthened fears that creating a new government risked lessening Massachusetts's power (by diluting New England's influence) and enabling national rule by an "aristocracy." But after Shays's Rebellion, Massachusetts leaders were grudgingly willing to run these considerable risks. Their removal of restrictions on their delegates meant that they were now willing to consider entering into a "grand bargain" at the convention if needed to achieve Massachusetts's goals.

New York

On February 15, 1787, New York's legislature again refused by a wide margin to agree to Congress's 1783 impost tax proposal. Since that meant that New York would keep its lucrative state impost, Governor Clinton and his allies could keep direct taxes low. They had also issued paper money for economic relief, which had been successful in dampening political unrest. Neither the state's Clintonian legislative majority nor their constituents saw any reason to change the Confederation status quo on those issues. Not surprisingly, therefore, when

Alexander Hamilton and his allies moved in support of the Philadelphia Convention just days after losing the Confederation impost vote, Clinton's forces strenuously opposed them. But Hamilton had adopted a creative though fairly risky strategy. He essentially sought a congressional referendum on the Confederation. Both Congress and the New York legislature were meeting in New York City at the time, so events moved quickly.

At Hamilton's request, on February 17 the New York Assembly (the legislature's lower house) effectively proposed that if Congress agreed to support the convention, New York would appoint delegates. In the New York Senate, Clinton's legislative manager Abraham Yates, Jr., led the opposition to the assembly's proposal. Hamilton's father-in-law and longtime political ally, retired general Philip Schuyler, was his primary opponent. According to Schuyler's account of Yates's speech against Hamilton's proposal, "Aristocracy, king, despot, unlimited powers, sword and purse fell from him in all the confusion of unintelligible jargon. In short, he was outrageous."[49] The senate agreed to the assembly proposal by a one-vote margin on February 20.[50]

Some historians think that Hamilton's proposal squeaked through only because of fears caused by Shays's Rebellion, but such fears probably played a minor role in the outcome.[51] New York did not face a significant local insurgency, and had had little difficulty in coping with the minor remnants of the Shays's insurgency that fled to northern New York. The state assembly passed the convention proposal without even a recorded vote, suggesting that disagreement about it there was limited. The senate's sharply split vote on the convention followed familiar lines of geographic cleavage that suggest that economic factors were considerably more important. Nearly every single senator from New York City and its surrounding areas, where most of the state's interstate and international trade occurred, supported the convention, while nearly all of the opposition came from senators representing hinterland rural areas.[52] The senate's voting pattern strongly resembled those found in the state's earlier splits over paper money and the impost. These considerations suggest that economic divisions played the dominant role in the state's convention politics. And divided state politics created another very important hurdle: Congress still had to agree to support the convention before New York would act at all.

In Congress, there was considerable opposition to the New York delegates' proposed convention authorization resolution, which some congressmen understandably thought was intended to torpedo the Philadelphia Convention.[53] New York's proposal was offered as a substitute for a convention resolution proposed by a congressional committee. The committee's resolution had accepted Virginia's proposed meeting place and dates and "strongly recommended" that states send delegates to the convention. It effectively ratified Virginia's action in calling for it. The New York proposal, on the other hand, omitted either a fixed meeting place or a fixed date for a meeting. That omission was likely to cause extensive delay in holding any convention and perhaps would even enable opponents to pressure legislatures that had already authorized delegates to reverse themselves. It also tellingly omitted the word "strongly" from its recommendation to the states. But a divided Congress rejected it.

Ultimately, on February 21 Congress agreed to a tepid compromise resolution proposed by Massachusetts, which acceded to Virginia's proposed date and place but then described the Philadelphia Convention merely as "expedient." James Madison wrote that even that compromise was regarded as a "deadly blow to the existing Confederation" by both reformers and those opposed to reform alike.[54] That reaction reflected the importance of what had happened. A majority of Congress had voted in support of permitting a body wholly separate from and not chosen by Congress to consider Confederation reform with an unlimited agenda. That vote was effectively a momentous "no confidence" vote both on the Confederation and on Congress's ability to make urgently needed reforms. It was a strong sign that the Confederation had collapsed. Congress's approval of the convention might be thought of as the death knell of the Confederation.

Sectional tensions threatened even Congress's approval of the compromise convention resolution. Retired general William Irvine wrote to Pennsylvania leader James Wilson that it was "with some difficulty" that Congress approved the resolution authorizing the convention. He said that "the Eastern Delegates [i.e., Massachusetts and the rest of New England] were all much against the measure—indeed I think they would never have come into it—but that they saw it would be carried without them. Then they joined—which made it a piece of patched work—but this was thought better than to keep up the smallest appearance of opposition to public view."[55] In short, both convention supporters and opponents wanted to keep up a deceptive facade of unity as it moved forward. But New York opponents were not done trying to stop it.

When the Philadelphia Convention issue came back to the New York legislature on February 28, Governor Clinton's forces sought to hobble it fatally. Senator Yates offered an amendment to require that any convention proposals be "not repugnant to or inconsistent with" the New York state constitution.[56] That would limit delegates' powers in a way that Senator Philip Schuyler believed "if carried, would have rendered their mission absolutely useless."[57] Schuyler was plainly correct. The purpose of Yates's amendment was to prohibit the convention from proposing that the Confederation be given any tax powers.[58] It would have completely tied the convention's hands on the central issue that everyone understood would face it.

Even more fundamentally, denying the Confederation tax powers would have prevented any agreement by the convention at all. If the convention had been unable to grant such powers, no "grand bargain" that resolved all the issues dividing the country could have been made. Other proposed reforms such as Confederation commerce powers would then also either have failed to be adopted due to sectional and state jealousies or have been rendered wholly ineffectual by the lack of Confederation tax powers. Thus, the convention would have failed—and that, of course, was Yates's and Clinton's goal. The senate deadlocked on Yates's amendment, and it was defeated only by the casting vote of the senate president, Lieutenant Governor Pierre van Cortlandt. Well before the convention, Schuyler predicted, quite correctly as things turned out, that Clinton and his supporters would oppose any constitution it proposed because it would be inconsistent with the "political system which prevails with a certain [Clinton] junto."[59]

Schuyler wrote to a trusted correspondent that a strong new government was needed, with enough power "not only to oppose an enemy but to prevent internal commotions" such as Shays's Rebellion. If not, he predicted that the Confederation "must sooner or later give way to perhaps a chance government which may be a despotism, arbitrary monarchy, aristocracy, or, what is still worse, an oligarchy." He continued, "I dread a dissolution of all union. Immediate quarrels between the states will ensue. These quarrels will beget armies, armies a conqueror, and this conqueror may give us such a government as prevails at Constantinople. Certainly, in such a case, we cannot hope for a better than that France groans under." In an apparent reflection on the need to prevent a future rebellion like Shays's insurgency, and perhaps actions by individual states that harmed other states as well, Schuyler concluded, "Let us therefore, seriously strive to obtain such a government as will secure to us that degree of liberty which is consistent with the social state, not that degree which empowers part of the community, uncontrolled, to injure the whole. That is licentiousness."[60] Since Schuyler had supported holding a national reform convention since 1782, he would have supported holding the convention even if he had not been concerned about the need for effective defense against internal rebellions. But those concerns undoubtedly reinforced his view that reforms were needed. Schuyler's opinions about what the future inevitably held if the Confederation was not sufficiently strengthened were shared by many nationalists.

The Philadelphia Convention's Prospects

Events preceding the Philadelphia Convention in key states show us just how bitterly Confederation reform was opposed even before it took shape there. Influential federalist leaders in several states had tried unsuccessfully to block the convention or to prevent it from reaching agreement. In Virginia, Patrick Henry instead shrewdly planned to use his powerful control of the legislature to defeat its proposals during ratification if he objected to them.

Ultimately, only Rhode Island chose to boycott the Philadelphia Convention. State majority legislators professed that they refused to send delegates to it due to their high regard for the existing Confederation. The honesty of their claim was quickly put to the test. After the legislature voted by a large majority to refuse to send delegates, convention supporters proposed that the legislature agree to assess a state tax to pay the pending Confederation requisition. (Since the end of 1783, Rhode Island had paid only $7,800 in requisitions, and had an outstanding requisition balance of about $207,000 by mid-1787.) The proposed tax was not agreed to; the issue was instead "deferred" to a future legislature (i.e., the tax was effectively killed; through mid-1788 nothing further was paid).[61] The legislature then refused a request from the state of Massachusetts that Rhode Island issue a proclamation to apprehend Shays's rebels who came to Rhode Island. And it expanded Rhode Island's program forcibly to retire state debts using depreciated state paper money (discussed in chapter 7). Not surprisingly, in late March 1787 a Massachusetts newspaper described these proceedings in a large-type headline as "Quintessence of Villany! *Or Proceedings of the Legislature of the State of Rhode-Island, at their Late Session*."[62] (Eventually, Rhode Island would agree to join the Union only after extensive coercion from the new federal government. Historians agree that its desire to continue its fiscal program was the principal reason for its unwillingness to join voluntarily.)[63]

As the convention approached, though nationalists had narrowly avoided defeat or obstruction in major states, there were still dark clouds looming on the horizon. Some of them they saw clearly, while some of the darkest and most threatening were hidden from view. The next section looks at the perspectives of two major nationalist leaders, George Washington and James Madison, on the convention just before it was held. Their views were representative of nationalists' concerns.

Washington's Road to Philadelphia

For George Washington, the Philadelphia Convention was both a major political dilemma and a source of considerable personal anxiety. As readers will recall, in November 1786, he initially declined to serve as a Philadelphia Convention delegate despite the repeated urgings of nationalists such as James Madison. In late March 1787, Washington changed his mind and agreed to serve. As we will see, he had concerns far larger than Shays's insurgency to weigh in making his decision. He was trying to determine whether the country was at last ready for real Confederation reforms. If not, he thought that it would break up into pieces and that a civil war or European aggression would follow. He wanted to preserve his ability to lead no matter what turn events took.

Washington was acutely aware long before the convention that many states would oppose the transfer of sovereignty to the national government. He wrote to John Jay that "a thirst for power, and the bantling—I had liked to have said monster—sovereignty, which have taken such fast hold of the States individually," when joined to state leaders' ambitions "will . . . form a strong phalanx against it."[64] He was also well aware that there would be strong opposition to giving the Confederation substantial military powers, especially from New England. In light of the northern and southern sections' sharply divided views on the desirability of Washington's preferred reforms, it was quite foreseeable that it would be possible to achieve them only by making a grand bargain. It would necessarily include changes sought primarily by northern states, such as Confederation commerce powers. In theory, a national convention would provide a forum in which it might be possible to make such a grand bargain. But Washington was uncertain whether in light of political conditions the Philadelphia Convention could succeed either in reaching such a bargain or, if it did, in having it approved by the states. As had been his custom during the Revolutionary War, he sought advice before making a decision.

Washington consulted several of his closest Revolutionary War comrades, including Secretary of War Knox and retired colonel David

Humphreys. He was especially concerned about the northern-state boycott of the Annapolis Convention, and wanted to understand why it had happened.[65] He specifically asked them to tell him what the "States to the Eastward" who had boycotted that convention thought about the idea of "*the [Philadelphia] Convention* & the measures they are pursuing to contravene, or give efficacy to it."[66] Both men originally opposed Washington's convention attendance. Knox was concerned about possible damage to Washington's reputation, because opinions were split about the convention's legality and desirability.[67] Humphreys thought that the convention's recommendations might fail to be adopted by the states. He also thought that "we may have what [constitutional forms] we please, but without coercion, they are as irrelevant as the wind."[68]

In early March 1787, Virginia governor Edmund Randolph wrote to Washington and pleaded with him to reconsider convention attendance. He told him that "every day brings forth some new crisis, and the confederation is, I fear, the last anchor of our hope." He pointed out that Congress had approved the convention. Randolph made the dire prediction that "I doubt, whether the existence of [Congress] even thro' this year may not be questionable under our present circumstances."[69] But Washington did not accept Randolph's plea. He still had to resolve his deepest fears about the convention's prospects.

The sources suggest that Washington was unwilling to participate in the Philadelphia Convention unless and until he could be certain that it had a reasonable prospect of success. He viewed the failure of the Annapolis Convention as strong evidence that the states were not prepared for thorough Confederation reform. As he explained to David Humphreys, if the Philadelphia Convention likewise failed, "it may be considered as an unequivocal proof that the States are not likely to agree in any general measure which is to pervade the Union, & consequently, that there is an end put to Foederal Government."[70] In other words, Washington was convinced that if the convention was unsuccessful, the Confederation would dissolve. There would not be another chance for reform. Washington was concerned about his own stature and effectiveness as a leader if dissolution occurred. He believed his credibility would be compromised by being part of a failed effort.[71] Though he has been criticized for taking that cautious view, it was entirely consistent with his belief that the dissolution of the Union would be followed by civil discord or foreign invasion.

There were certain fundamental conditions that Washington thought were necessary for the Philadelphia Convention's success, though they might not guarantee it. At a minimum, broad participation was essential. States must not boycott it. In addition, delegates chosen for it must be capable men who were unfettered by restrictive state instructions intended to block the "radical cures" that he thought were needed.[72] In view of the distinct possibility that Patrick Henry would seek to defeat the convention's proposals, and the bitter contests that occurred over it in both New York and Massachusetts, Washington's caution about attending a convention destined to fail was well-advised. That most states ultimately made distinguished appointments, and gave their delegates a free hand, was important evidence to him that they strongly desired a successful convention and would strive to reach agreement on needed changes by mutual concessions.[73]

In mid-March 1787, Secretary Knox reversed his position on Washington's attendance. He informed Washington that eleven states had chosen delegates, and that "great reliance may be placed on the wisdom and vigor of their [the delegates'] Councils and judgements."[74] Knox's assurances and his own observations probably helped assuage Washington's concerns, and in late March 1787 he agreed to attend. But he still needed to settle on his own approach to the convention. Here as elsewhere, he did not intend to follow anyone else's lead blindly.

Washington decided that he was not interested in participating in a convention that made only piecemeal reforms. He wanted to use this rare opportunity to get to the heart of the Confederation's problems and to solve them. He told James Madison that he wanted the convention delegates to be able to consider and if necessary make "radical" proposals to cure the Confederation's problems "whether they are agreed to [by the states] or not." He wanted to "probe the defects of the

Constitution to the bottom" and to address them without equivocation or "temporising expedient."[75] It is uncertain whether Washington knew exactly how literally Madison would interpret his instructions, but they led Madison to make some radical proposals, discussed shortly.

Washington's overarching goal was to create a government that was a sovereign power capable of governing America as it expanded westward—a continental empire. To achieve that, first and foremost, it needed the power to tax, which would enable it to pay its just debts and to support an army. Some of the Confederation's difficulties might also be the result of poor governance in some states. But unless an underlying problem could be solved, other reforms would not matter. He told Madison that he thought it was essential to provide "the means of coercion in the Sovereign [that] will enforce obedience to the Ordinances of a General Government; without which, everything else fails."[76]

It was readily foreseeable that to create a sovereign national government would require making a grand bargain at the convention that accommodated sharply conflicting sectional interests on matters such as commerce, military power, and western expansion. As we have seen in earlier chapters, Washington's views on various Confederation problems, such as commerce issues, were usually "continental" and not based on sectional bias, unlike those of many other leaders. That made him well-placed to participate in making such a grand bargain. Washington also frankly admitted that he did not know how the convention ought to solve what he thought was the ultimate problem facing the national government—its ability to become an actual sovereign able to enforce its decisions throughout its territory.[77]

At the same time, however, Washington did not commit himself to support any particular proposals. Shortly before the convention began, he prepared a summary of constitutional reform proposals he had received from John Jay of New York, Henry Knox of Massachusetts, and James Madison (all fervent nationalists). It contains no evaluative comments, though he had already expressed skepticism to each of them about some aspects of their proposals. Nor does it contain any indication that he supported any specific proposal.[78] Not being tied to specific proposals would give him maximum flexibility in negotiating a grand bargain.

In short, Washington was a firm nationalist—and one who supported republican principles—but he was also a pragmatist, not an ideologue. That made him the ideal leader of forces seeking to negotiate a new constitution that transferred sovereignty from the states to the national government. He kept an open mind about how far reform could go and still be politically acceptable to the states and different sections. Throughout his career, Washington frequently approached political problems as if he were an independent judge dispassionately deciding a lawsuit between other contesting parties. That distinctive habit of mind enabled him patiently and persistently to search for common ground without becoming entangled in local, sectional, or ideological disputes. It amply justified Benjamin Franklin's letter to Washington telling him that his participation in Philadelphia would "be of the greatest Importance to the Success of the" convention.[79]

Madison Reconceives the National Republic

By April 1787, James Madison was convinced that the Confederation had "*mortal* diseases." He hoped that "the general chaos or at least partition of the Union which offers itself as the alternative" would produce a "[s]pirit of concession on all sides" at the convention.[80] He told Virginia governor Edmund Randolph that unless it devised a better republican government, "it is pretty certain" that either a monarchy or separate confederations "will take place."[81] In preparation for the Philadelphia meeting, Madison wrote letters sketching out his proposals for Confederation reform. He also created a summary of the Confederation's defects. Historians refer to it as his "Observations on the Vices of the Political System of the United States."[82] Madison's work provides a comprehensive catalog of the Confederation's defects as he and most other nationalists saw them in early 1787. But it went far beyond that.

Madison's efforts taken together constituted a radical reconception of republican national government. His criticisms centered not just on fundamental problems that the Confederation had failed to address since 1783, but also on what he saw as state governments' abuses. He thought that the states were heavily if not wholly responsible for the Confederation's failures as well as their own. Madison's critique also concentrated on a central unresolved problem of postwar republicanism, majority tyranny. His reform proposals involved both new national government powers and restrictions on state powers.

Madison told Washington that the Confederation should be given broad new substantive powers: "complete authority in all cases which require uniformity; such as the regulation of trade, including the right of taxing both exports and imports."[83] As expected given Madison's strong support for national tax powers, his "Vices" analysis listed "failure of the states to comply with Constitutional requisitions" as the first major defect of the Confederation. But Madison's proposals for reform of the "political system"—by which he essentially meant the Confederation and its relation to the states as well as the state governments themselves—went far beyond advocating new powers.

Madison's most far-reaching positive reform proposal was to abandon the Articles' equal-state-voting rule to give the large states more power in Congress. He wanted to base representation instead on "populousness," that is, relative state populations. His proposal addressed the Confederation government's maldistribution of political power compared to the country's distribution of population and wealth. Remarkably, Madison told Washington that "I am ready to believe such a change will not be attended with much difficulty."[84] He apparently did not grasp that his proposal was Rufus King's worst nightmare about Confederation reform. As the Massachusetts Senate's strenuous efforts to prevent that state's Philadelphia delegates from having authority to agree to change key parts of the Articles of Confederation made clear, many leaders there probably agreed with King.

Madison told Washington that northern states would accept the change in congressional voting power because they were populous now, while southern states would benefit because they would be populous later. Madison seems not to have appreciated that New England states, including Massachusetts, were also concerned about regional power loss. And unlike Washington, but like many northern and southern leaders during the Spanish-treaty and commerce-power controversies, Madison apparently saw control of the national government as potentially a sectional zero-sum contest. That meant that one section's gains through control of the national government, such as agreeing to the Spanish treaty, could be another section's loss, with no offsetting national benefits. Many of Madison's remaining proposals restricted the states' external and internal powers.

Madison emphasized that it was essential to protect the United States from state encroachments on its powers. He thought that states should be prevented from engaging in activities implicating powers reserved to the national government. Madison gave as examples "the wars and Treaties of Georgia with the Indians," and "the troops raised and to be kept up by Massachusetts."[85] He also thought that certain federal powers needed to be exclusive to be effective. An example was that state paper money would interfere with a federal coinage power.[86]

Madison also believed that it was essential that the Confederation be able to enforce its laws. But he lacked any clear idea of how to achieve that goal. By 1787, few leaders thought that using force against states to compel their obedience was a practical solution in a divided political climate, and most understood that in any event using it would risk civil war. Madison's correspondence contains only vague suggestions, which indicate that he still thought that it would be necessary to rely on national military or economic power to enforce state compliance.

Madison thought that the Confederation needed to prevent the states from harming each other. He gave examples of states' causing harm to other states through trade laws. New York and Maryland had laws discriminating in favor of vessels belonging to their own citizens and against those of citizens of other states (and foreign countries). He also cited state paper-money and debt-relief laws as "aggressions on the rights of other states."[87] Some historians have suggested that such interstate harms were not really an important problem facing the

Confederation. But both the vitriolic reactions and states' changed laws in response to Rhode Island's fiscal policies, and New Jersey's outright refusal to pay clearly lawful Confederation requisitions due to New York's import taxes, strongly suggest the contrary.

In the aftermath of Shays's Rebellion, Madison thought that the Confederation needed explicit authority to protect the states against internal violence. In theory, republics were governed by majorities.[88] However, Madison recognized that it was possible for minorities to take over states by force, particularly if they were joined by "those whose poverty excludes them from a right of suffrage" or even more dangerously, by slaves.[89] He envisioned several different ways in which minority revolts could succeed—scenarios that went far beyond Shays's insurgency. A successful armed revolt could be led by disaffected members of an elite, not just by impoverished farmers. The prospect of future armed insurgencies against states, no matter their source, justified adding such protection to the Confederation's powers.

Finally, Madison thought that political minorities, including in his view the wealthy, needed protection against majority tyranny. Madison had tried to protect minority rights before. He had actively supported religious freedom in Virginia to protect religious minorities against compulsory taxation and repression by Virginia's established state church. But the Spanish-treaty controversy had led him to conceive of such oppression more generically. Madison now saw the northern states' treaty actions as an example. He wrote to Virginia congressman James Monroe that even if all thirteen states supported Jay's position on the treaty and closed the Mississippi, "I shall never be convinced it is expedient, because I cannot conceive it to be just."[90] In Madison's view, every possible form of majority tyranny needed to be prevented, because all were violations of minority rights.

By fall 1786, concern about majority tyranny had become a prominent facet of Madison's thought. Both national and state republican governments could be guilty of it.[91] During the Spanish-treaty dispute, he attacked the contemporary political maxim "that the interest of the majority is the political standard of right and wrong." Madison thought that it would instead actually be in the majority's interest to "despoil & enslave the minority of individuals." He extended this idea to the Confederation: "in a federal community" a majority would have an interest in making "a similar sacrifice of the minority of the component states."[92] He saw states' issuance of paper money as an example of majority tyranny, but he conceived of majority abuses as a much broader problem. He would have agreed with Thomas Paine that Pennsylvania had engaged in majority tyranny when it revoked the charter of the Bank of North America. To permit republican majorities to govern without limits that protected minorities was licentiousness. Madison's concerns about state-government failures and abuses went far beyond their economic-relief laws. He and others saw such majority tyranny as an inherent problem of republics, stemming from human nature, that needed to be prevented at all levels of government. But Madison's "solution" to that problem was itself deeply problematic.

Madison's proposed solution to the broad range of difficulties that he thought were created by states' abuses of external and internal powers was to give Congress the power to veto state laws it deemed inconsistent with its authority or national harmony "*in all cases whatsoever* . . . as heretofore exercised by the Kingly prerogative."[93] Such a congressional sledgehammer could be used to block nearly every action any state took. Madison wanted to shackle the states' political and economic powers in the interests of protecting both the Confederation and their own citizen minorities against them. But had it not been the assertion of just such a power by Great Britain that had helped fuel the revolution? Of all of Madison's politically tone-deaf proposals during this period, this one belongs at the top of the list. It would have been all that was necessary to convince New York federalists that Congress really did want to be "King." It would have justified their claims about oppressive central power during the New York impost tax debate, and would have confirmed Massachusetts federalists' deepest fears about "aristocratic" government.

Ironically, Madison claimed that giving Congress veto power was necessary because consolidating the states into one government was politically out of the question. He argued that there was no other way to prevent the state abuses he perceived.[94] Yet Madison's proposal actually amounted to just that—consolidation—in the eyes of many contemporaries. (Madison was by no means alone—John Jay's reform proposals, for example, would have had much the same result.) They would have been unshakably convinced that Madison's proposal would destroy the states.

Conclusion

The road to the Philadelphia Convention was a long and winding one because powerful opposition in key states in different sections of the country had to be overcome before it could take place. The Confederation was visibly failing on every important dimension of governance by late 1786. Thoughtful leaders knew that it was stalemated on every major issue it had confronted since 1783. There was no longer any prospect whatsoever that piecemeal tax and commerce reforms could succeed. Remarkably, knowledge of those realities alone did not persuade leaders in critical states such as Massachusetts to agree to a national reform convention with an open, unlimited agenda. Instead, at the end of 1786, leaders in several major states still thought that their states had more to lose from major Confederation reforms than they stood to gain from them. What caused these states to change their positions?

Some historians think that Shays's Rebellion played a major or even a decisive role in changing opinions among elite conservatives across the country about the need for a stronger national government. But that is an overly broad generalization, because its effects depended almost entirely on the differing political and economic situations in various parts of the country. The sources suggest that in much of the country, other factors were predominant in spurring the convention movement, and that Shays's insurgency had a distinctly subordinate place.

In Massachusetts, the necessary change in opinion almost certainly did occur as a result of Shays's Rebellion. It is commonly claimed that the alarmed Massachusetts elite sought added federal powers merely to suppress popular economic-relief demands such as paper money. But the insurgency had far broader and more powerful effects on elite opinion than that. It showed Massachusetts federalists that when public opinion was divided, their state government might be unable or unwilling to suppress even an armed rebellion. It also showed them that the state might not be able to collect taxes to pay even its internal creditors, let alone the Confederation. Some Massachusetts archconservatives such as Stephen Higginson did hope that a stronger central government would be a bulwark against popular economic demands. But before the insurgency they had been in the minority in seeking stronger central government. Shays's Rebellion made a stronger Confederation far more attractive to Massachusetts federalists such as Rufus King because it caused them to doubt their state's ability to govern effectively.

In Virginia, on the other hand, western settlement led to chronic postwar conflict with Native Americans. By 1786, expanding frontier warfare had exposed both the state's and the Confederation's weakness. Many western Virginians decided that they needed a stronger national government. Leaders were also alarmed by the Confederation's impending bankruptcy. The primary reform goals of Virginia nationalists were thus effective national tax and military powers. Shays's Rebellion reinforced the argument for strengthening the Confederation, but played a relatively small role in Virginians' decisions. Some nationalist leaders such as Madison also hoped that the national government would be empowered to prevent paper-money and similar relief laws. But many leading Virginia federalists agreed with those particular views, and that did not alter their opposition to the convention (and especially to its results).[95]

In New York, nationalists who had long supported Confederation tax and commerce powers provided the main support in the legislature for the convention. They may have been marginally aided by fears about a future insurgency there. But by and large, such concerns merely reinforced preexisting views that the Confederation needed major reform. Particularly in view of the absence of serious unrest in New York, it does not seem likely that fear of future rebellions played much of a role in either the legislature's willingness to support the convention or in weakening opposition to it there. Enormous resistance still remained to fundamental Confederation change in New York, at least on the issue of tax powers.

The common thread running through shifts in public opinion in these states is that they occurred because enough influential citizens with lives and property to protect concluded (for very different reasons) that neither their states nor the Confederation was capable of protecting their interests. Meanwhile, the Confederation's looming financial collapse meant that Americans also had to confront the distinct possibility that foreign aggression, civil war, or some far less desirable form of government—whether monarchy, dictatorship, or separate confederations—would take its place. Under pressure from these growing fears, key states reluctantly agreed to run the risk of a national reform convention. They did so even though it was readily foreseeable that it would quite probably propose fundamental changes in the country's government.

The successful fight to hold the Philadelphia Convention is strong evidence that the battle for American hearts and minds over national government sovereignty had been at least partly won. Based on the Confederation's failures and the differing reform priorities of key states, the principal questions before the convention would be whether the states and sections would be willing to confer effective tax, military, and commerce powers on the national government, and what they would receive in return. It was also unavoidable that the convention would consider issues posed by western expansion. It would necessarily address claims of interstate harm and possible interference with national policies stemming from state trade and economic-relief policies, such as import taxation and paper money. Finally, it would have to decide whether and how to respond to Madison's critique of state powers and majority tyranny. In agreeing to hold the convention with an unlimited agenda, the states had tacitly agreed that they would be willing to consider entering into a grand bargain that would comprehend most, if not all, of these issues. The Confederation's political collapse together with their fears for the future brought them to Philadelphia, not an enlightened effort to find common ground.

But because the convention would quite foreseeably propose to transfer sovereignty to the national government, it would ultimately be compelled to face an entirely separate problem. How could a central government obtain the support of its people to become an effective continental republic? On the eve of the convention, experienced leaders still could not grasp how a national government could obtain obedience to its decisions by states (and their citizens) without using military force, the antithesis of republican government. The convention would have no choice but to confront that perplexing problem.

The American Revolution had created the Confederation. But without the deliberative work of the convention, the Confederation's collapse would have failed to create a new nation.

Conclusion

THE BIRTH OF THE AMERICAN EMPIRE

In our endeavours to establish a new general government, the contest, nationally considered, seems not to have been so much for glory, as existence. It was for a long time doubtful whether we were to survive as an independent Republic, or decline from our fœderal dignity into insignificant & wretched fragments of Empire.

George Washington to Henry Lee, Jr., shortly after the Constitution was ratified[1]

On the eve of the Philadelphia Convention in May 1787, the fate of the Confederation hung in the balance. Every state except Rhode Island ultimately agreed to send delegates because they were unwilling to risk the consequences of the Confederation's imminent dissolution.[2] Nearly all delegations felt, however reluctantly, that they had no choice but to consider strengthening it. But the delegates still needed to decide whether to try to revive it, or to abandon it for a fundamentally different government. They were acutely aware that there was still strong public support for what many citizens saw as the Confederation's foundational idea—that republican liberty depended on decentralized national government. There would inevitably be strenuous resistance to any large departure from the existing Confederation. In arranging the convention, however, the stage had been set for a "grand bargain"—a broad agreement that resolved a series of major political issues—if the delegates chose to make one.

The convention made just such an intersectional-elite grand bargain. Acting nearly unanimously, it boldly jettisoned the Confederation structure and proposed the creation of a radically different central government. The new government would be an effective national sovereign that would have full authority and the necessary resources to enforce its decisions over the objections of any individual state or section.[3] The convention's proposal sharply redistributed political power among the states. The new government would possess independent powers over taxation, national defense, and commerce. The proposal also imposed major—some said devastating—new limits on state powers. They included a ban on state paper money and many forms of debt relief. Compared to the Confederation, the convention called for a national government that was almost staggeringly powerful.

The convention's grand bargain may have seemed farsighted to some Americans, but as we will see, its radical nature shocked at least some, perhaps even many, leaders. It may well have been a product of political necessity rather than of choice. Except as part of a grand bargain, it is very likely that none of the major reforms sought by the country's different sections would have been adopted. After all, the convention was held because piecemeal reforms had failed. For four years, groups with various interests had proposed such reforms, particularly to the Confederation's tax and commerce powers. As we have seen, none of them had been adopted. As Virginia congressman William Grayson recognized, that was because supporters of particular reforms such as Confederation commerce powers hoped that they could achieve only the reforms they wanted without having to agree to reforms they did not want, for example, changes in equal state voting in Congress.

By 1787, however, the hope that piecemeal Confederation reform could succeed was dead. But what we have seen of the country's sectional divisions strongly suggests that that would have been equally true at the convention itself. If Massachusetts, for example, had insisted that the convention approve a broad commerce power, but then had refused to agree to a key reform sought by the southern states, such as broad tax powers, it is extraordinarily unlikely that the convention would have reached agreement. And quite strikingly, the convention's grand bargain adopted what can fairly be described as the most radical version of each major new substantive power it conferred on the central government. The word "radical" here includes both the breadth of the powers and the extent to which they disturbed the political status quo. The convention's commerce power was more radical politically even than James Monroe's "radical" proposal, because it could be exercised by majority vote. Its proposed tax power was essentially unlimited, and exercisable by majority vote—far broader than Congress's 1783 proposal. The radicalism of these proposals meant that it was readily foreseeable that they would encounter very great political opposition. This suggests that unless they had been agreed to together in a grand bargain, they would not have been agreed to at all.

One conclusion can quickly be drawn about the convention's proposal. It would have been politically far less risky to propose a less powerful government. That the convention chose not to do that could be viewed as arrogant class warfare or foolish overreaching by the elite delegates, many of whom were wealthy men. Or it could be seen as the convention's collective judgment that the risk needed to be taken. This book's analysis supports the view that the delegates took very large political risks not out of selfish class interest, and not just from perceived necessity, but from objective necessity.

This conclusion shows that the Confederation's failures led to the critical features of the convention's proposed new government. It also shows how the proposed Constitution ended stalemate government. Because of the circumstances of its creation, however, the Constitution was necessarily a pragmatic political compromise. This had important long-term consequences for the country.

The Convention

SHAPING THE CONVENTION'S AGENDA

The list of Confederation postwar failures is an impressively long one. It had ended the war heavily in debt, but lacked the power to tax. The states failed to pay Congress's requisitions, so the Confederation's debt problem worsened during the mid-1780s. Congress was unable to enforce its treaty commitments. Many states openly violated the 1783 Treaty of Peace requirement to permit British prewar-debt repayment. The Confederation's response was empty exhortations. When Britain retaliated by refusing to give up its western forts, the Confederation was unable to respond. When Britain and France restricted American trade, the Confederation was powerless to retaliate. When American settlers violated Confederation restrictions on frontier settlement and the treaty rights of Native Americans, the Confederation was unable to enforce its laws and treaty commitments. Instead, Virginia brazenly raised troops to attack Indians outside its borders. When Spain closed the Mississippi River to Americans, Congress permanently deadlocked over Spain's decision. When states adopted paper money, debt relief, or trade laws that harmed other states' citizens, the Confederation was powerless to prevent such harms. When armed rebellion broke out in Massachusetts, the state's merchants financed the military response, because the Confederation was unable to pay the troops it authorized to combat it. It was not even clear that the Confederation had the authority to raise troops to aid Massachusetts.

By late 1786, the Confederation was permanently insolvent and unable to pay its foreign and domestic debts. Despite years of debate, it had stalemated over proposed reforms to increase its powers in areas such as taxation and commerce. It had become deadlocked on other pressing national issues as well, especially those related to western expansion. Many leaders believed its dissolution was inevitable. And the political environment in which the Confederation had operated was changing in other important ways as well.

We have seen that during the mid-1780s, a strenuous contest was occurring across America about the proper boundaries of republican government and liberty. Did republican government mean unlimited majority rule, or should it include protections for minorities against the majority will, at least in some cases? That issue arose in various contexts throughout the 1780s, most notoriously in the revocation of the Bank of North America charter by Pennsylvania, but also with respect to paper money, debt contracts, and other issues such as religious freedom. Over time, unhappiness grew about claims that the majority will should always prevail. Thomas Paine's highly visible defection from the Pennsylvania Constitutionalists, the critical political backlash against their actions, and southern states' dismay over the Spanish treaty are among the most salient examples.[4]

In the mid-1780s, Americans also began to wonder if republican liberty included a state's untrammeled ability to inflict harm on citizens of other states. Rhode Island's harsh treatment of noncitizen debtors and creditors, and various states' trade laws favoring their citizens over noncitizens, suggest that some states thought that they could harm noncitizens with impunity. But there were increasing numbers of people around the country who disagreed, as Connecticut's and Massachusetts's strong protests against Rhode Island's actions indicated. Similarly, New Jersey's outright refusal to pay Confederation requisitions in protest against New York's import taxes showed that its citizens strongly felt that they needed central-government protection from New York's overreaching. Thus, Americans were forced by events to reevaluate the limits of republican government and liberty in the mid-1780s. That reassessment inevitably became part of the convention's agenda as well. The Confederation's and the states' actions were to be judged in this new political context. But why had the Confederation failed repeatedly to resolve pressing national problems?

As this book has shown, critically important Confederation decisions had chronically been frustrated by the self-interest of the states and their political leaders. The states were often "free riders," taking advantage of Confederation actions without paying their costs. The states' unwillingness to pay nearly 70 percent of the money Congress requested from them to honor the country's war debts incurred on their behalf offers a good example. There were strong political incentives for states to engage in such free riding. The road to popularity was to keep state taxes as low as possible. Free riding avoided the need to raise taxes or to increase tax collections (and foreclosures, etc.) in order to pay them. In another example, Massachusetts was unable to persuade other states to support its trade-retaliation efforts against Britain; instead, some states took advantage of its restrictions to benefit their own trade. There was no realistic prospect that state free riding would ever end under the Confederation.

The states' strong desire to keep their taxes low also led them to block proposed Confederation tax reforms. By 1786, a majority of states had declined to provide supplemental taxes to the Confederation as Congress had requested in 1783. New York's refusal to agree to Congress's 1783 impost proposal reflected the same desire to keep direct taxes low. As long as states could veto Confederation reforms at little cost (or even with benefits) to themselves, it was highly unlikely that reforms that increased Confederation powers would ever occur.

Other major Confederation failures stemmed from sectional "jealousies" that were frequently based on significant conflicts of economic or political interest. Proposals for Confederation commerce powers broad enough to enable Congress to substantially influence British policy, such as those advocated by Virginia congressman James Monroe, failed primarily due to sectional conflicts. Many southern-state leaders feared that such powers would be used by northern states to take economic advantage of their section. The Spanish-treaty impasse stemmed from sectional conflicts that arose from the differing effects of western development and foreign trade on various regions. In 1786, northern states had almost nothing to gain, and a good deal to lose, from western development. But southern states saw western development as integral to their economic future. Sectional divides and states' self-interested decisions materially weakened the Confederation. But it proved utterly incapable of overcoming them, and instead became permanently stalemated on all major issues during this period.

In short, the Confederation could not have avoided its failures through better leadership, less "partisanship" between federalists and nationalists, or by altering specific policies. State "free riding" was common and virtually uncontrollable, and sectional divides were often irresolvable. Moreover, under the Articles of Confederation, the use of single-state and sectional vetoes was explicitly authorized and often virtually cost-free politically. All of these problems were worsened by the country's severe mid-1780s recession, but all of them would have existed even had economic conditions been far better.

But the Confederation had an even deeper problem that underlay many of its failures. Congress could not enforce its decisions against states that disobeyed them. It completely lacked the practical ability to enforce its laws and treaties throughout its territory. Since a government's ability to enforce its laws is one of the essential attributes of sovereignty, the Confederation was not an actual sovereign. After several years of postwar experience with the Confederation, George Washington saw its inability to compel obedience to its laws as its fundamental flaw. Before the Convention, however, major leaders such as Washington and Madison did not know of any workable means to enable a national government to enforce its laws peacefully (as opposed to using military force).

Washington and other nationalists were convinced that the Confederation's lack of sovereignty would lead to its eventual collapse if not cured. The country was experiencing enormous centrifugal political stresses at the time. They included state "free riding"; western expansion; European empires' efforts to impede and divide Americans on trade, territory, and other matters; strong sectional jealousies flowing from severe economic or political conflicts; and increasingly bitter interstate conflicts over core economic issues such as trade, taxes, paper money, and debt. These mounting strains on unity persuasively supported their belief.

Curing the Confederation's flaws by creating a sovereign national government became the convention's principal goal. Unfortunately, that goal also presented by far the greatest political obstacle facing its work. It was precisely the change that the states would resist most strongly. Historical experience strongly suggests that such sovereignty disputes are rarely if ever decided peacefully (as opposed to by force), except when such a transfer of sovereignty is widely enough perceived as necessary.[5] Both individual states and America's various regions saw central government sovereignty as a serious, indeed perhaps fatal, threat to their autonomy. As the events of the mid-1780s showed, they were not prepared to agree to yield their sovereignty to a central government unless persuaded that it was essential. In this book, we have traced how that perception of necessity arose and why disparate groups of Americans came to believe for different reasons that the country faced a political crisis. And we have shown that for them the Confederation's transformation into a national sovereign became an unavoidable, objective necessity.

THE CONVENTION'S SOLUTION

Once it decided to create a sovereign, the convention needed to develop a proposal that could end stalemate government. Its solution was to provide for broad intersectional power sharing in the new government. The convention shared control of the government's powers by limiting equal state voting to the Senate, and redistributing both House of Representatives and presidential voting power among the states according to population. That reallocation of voting strength made the new distribution of national political power a considerably more accurate reflection of the relative population and hence the wealth of the states. That had the important effect of increasing the influence of what today we would think of as the national-majority will in the new government's affairs. And that in turn increased its legitimacy from the perspective of many contemporary Americans.

Power sharing had several fundamentally important effects. It made it politically possible to confer major new powers on the national government: independent tax, military, and commerce powers. These new substantive powers accommodated both northern and southern sections' top reform priorities. Power sharing allowed the elimination of sectional vetoes over the use of the new powers.[6] In other words, power sharing was a necessary precondition of the convention's grand bargain. It also generally increased states' and sections' incentives to comply with national policies.

The new power-sharing arrangements, together with the states' and sections' willingness to confer fundamental new powers on the new government and to permit them to be exercised by majority vote, were at the heart of ending stalemate government. Moreover, power sharing also politically enabled the convention to create a new, workable path for the enforcement of national laws. Law enforcement would occur directly against citizens in most cases, which meant that the new government would not have to undertake the futile effort to compel obedience from states. That sharply reduced states' ability to engage in "free riding."

A final critical step in ending stalemate government was to limit states' powers. It is very important to appreciate the discerning manner in which the convention achieved that goal. Though it placed significant limits on state powers, the convention rejected Madison's proposal for a congressional veto over state laws, instead restricting specific state powers. That permitted each state (during the Constitution's drafting and again during constitutional ratification) to decide whether it benefited enough from other parts of the convention's proposal to be willing to yield the specified powers. States did not need to fear an unlimited federal veto over their laws. Had Madison's veto proposal instead been adopted, it seems highly likely that the Constitution would not have been ratified. State majorities would quite probably not have been willing to accept virtually unlimited national authority to block their laws.

The effects of the convention's approach to state sovereignty can be seen clearly in its tax proposals. As we have seen, all of Congress's original 1783 tax-reform proposals ultimately foundered. In retrospect, neither aspect of the 1783 proposals had any realistic prospect of adoption because both violated fundamental economic and political interests of various states. Under the Confederation, there was good reason to think that the states were never going to yield their tax powers voluntarily. That meant that the Confederation was never going to be able to pay its bills.

As discussed in chapters 2 and 3, some historians claim that the Confederation's failure to pay its debts (at least its domestic debts) was unimportant, and could not have justified major Confederation reforms. As we have seen, Congress rejected that position, maintaining that the Confederation should pay both its foreign and domestic debts in full. The convention rejected it as well by proposing that the new government have virtually unlimited tax powers, and restricting specific kinds of state taxation, but not others. That was a bold, risky proposal that the convention majority undoubtedly knew would encounter strong resistance in states such as New York.[7]

It is helpful to recall what was at stake on the debt issue from the convention majority's perspective. If America did not pay its bills, experienced leaders such as John Adams were convinced that it would have no future ability to borrow. In that event, it could finance a future war only by taxation. But American leaders of every political persuasion uniformly agreed that the Revolutionary War itself could never have been financed by taxation. America not only depended heavily on credit to run much of the war; it had no alternative but to do so. It could not raise and collect enough taxes to pay for the war while it was being fought (at least without becoming a military dictatorship). If America voluntarily destroyed its credit—whether with foreign or domestic creditors, or both—by refusing to pay its bills, it would lose its ability to fight future wars. In other words, failing to preserve America's public faith would mean that its government was forfeiting an essential attribute of sovereignty—the ability to control its territory militarily. The country's breakup would be only a matter of time.

Notably, the convention wanted to ensure that the new government's tax powers would be large enough to permit it to pay all of the Confederation's foreign and domestic debts, and to provide for future military contingencies as well. Hence, rather than proposing central government tax powers limited to a 5 percent import tax or impost, as some might have expected, the convention sought virtually unlimited taxation powers.[8] In light of the enormous controversy that existed over taxation, seeking unlimited central-government tax powers was the single greatest political risk taken by the convention. It emphasized the great importance that its delegates placed on maintaining public faith and strengthening military power to provide both external and internal defense. The new tax and military powers when combined with the changed path of law enforcement made the proposed government an effective national sovereign.

In order to reach agreement and to make ratification possible, however, the convention had no political alternative but to make concessions to persistent sectional jealousies and states' sovereignty claims. First, the convention agreed that neither treaties nor constitutional amendments could be adopted except by supermajority consent. Treaties required the consent of two-thirds of the Senate; amendments required consent of three-fourths of the states. The minority vetoes thus created were, initially at least, in reality primarily sectional vetoes. The southern states received enough Senate voting power to block any proposed treaty such as the Spanish treaty.[9] And every major section of the country possessed enough votes to block *any* constitutional amendment. Second, the so-called three-fifths clause counted three-fifths of slave populations as part of each state's voting population for purposes of congressional representation and presidential elections. From this sectionally biased provision, the southern slave states received a significant long-term voting premium in the House of Representatives and in the Electoral College (which elects the president). Because of the amendment provisions' requirements, the three-fifths clause could not be changed without southern states' consent, which would never be forthcoming, so it was effectively permanent. Finally, as a compromise after a lengthy, bitter convention fight, all states received equal voting power in the Senate without regard to their population or wealth. And each state was given independent power to veto any change to that provision, which meant that it also became a permanent part of the Constitution.

Thus, although the Constitution ended stalemate government in ordinary circumstances during the early Republic, it did so only by creating significant costs that the nation would be forced to pay in the future. Space will not permit full discussion of those costs, but a few examples will be helpful. One such cost was the sectional distortions of politics before the Civil War caused by the three-fifths clause. Another was that it made certain kinds of peaceful political change by democratic means—such as the abolition of slavery—virtually impossible. The main elements of the convention's grand bargain were important steps in the direction of creating an enduring national government that could avoid stalemates. But because of the need to garner sufficient state and sectional support to gain constitutional ratification with the consent of at least nine states, it also necessarily included some features protecting states and sections against majority decisions. Some of them, such as the three-fifths clause, within a fairly short time came to be criticized as anti-republican or as weakening the national government, primarily because they distorted the influence of the majority will.

Conflicting Visions of Nationhood

The convention's proposals to create a sovereign national government forced Americans to reconsider what made them one country. The Revolutionary War had bound Americans together from necessity. In peacetime, it quickly became clear that they were often divided and unwilling to seek common ground. During the mid-1780s, nationalists and federalists had fundamentally conflicting ideas about the nature of government and its relation to liberty. The nationalist-dominated convention's proposals were a direct challenge to federalist thought. For federalists, the Confederation was the "perfect republican plan." States were sovereign and independent republican governments. In the Confederation, they were associated as equals in a national council, its Congress. The central government was merely an instrument of the states' collective will, not a separate government. A national republic was a confederation of state republics for limited purposes such as collectively deciding on war and peace, nothing more.

As Samuel Adams expressed it, in the federalist conception, Congress's decisions were to be followed because they were the "cement of the union." Government need not be concerned about enforcing the will of Congress—it would inevitably be followed. In the federalist view, giving the central government tax resources and law enforcement powers would actually be dangerous in any event. Stronger central government would lead to tyranny exercised by a small coterie of aristocratic officials and enforced by a standing army. A stronger central government would inevitably become an American version of the corrupt British or French governments. It followed that republicanism and continental empire were inherently incompatible. Because that view of government was axiomatic for many federalists such as Richard Henry Lee, the Confederation's failures did not materially alter their views. But the unavoidable reality remained that the Confederation's laws and treaties were not being obeyed; the states and their citizens repeatedly violated them.

In some instances as early as the end of the war, however, and certainly by the eve of the convention, nationalist leaders had a conflicting idea of nationhood. They envisioned a national government not as a mere agent, but instead with sovereign powers independent from those of the individual states. Nationalists believed that republicanism and continental empire could be reconciled. I focus on the views of Washington and Madison in the following because they were among the most important nationalist leaders, and were active in the reform movement throughout the period. While it is not possible to present full expositions of their thought here, this discussion will show that they emphasize different core features of national government.

Washington thought that states and citizens in an expanding nation were bound together principally by economic and political interest, not solely by patriotism, virtue, or republican principles. Creating a nation therefore necessarily meant finding a way to bind people together by interest. First and foremost, that meant that a national government needed to be a sufficiently powerful and flexible framework for sharing common interests and resolving common concerns.

Washington thought that to endure, the national government must be sovereign. Washington's perspective implied, among other things, that he did not see either states or sections as normally entitled either to prevent, or to demand protection against, national decisions made by majority will. Writing to his political confidant Dr. David Stuart, Washington strongly defended the Constitution's majority-vote commerce power against an attack by Virginian George Mason. "There must be reciprocity or no Union," Washington said, making his deep unhappiness with Mason clear when he continued, "which is preferable will not become a question in the mind of any true patriot."[10] For Washington, denying southern states a sectional veto over commerce powers' use was a price well worth paying for union.

Washington believed that republican liberty and continental empire could be reconciled. Power would be used responsibly if exercised under the right circumstances; its mere existence would not lead to its abuse. Power should not be limited more than was essential merely because it might sometimes be corruptly used. In his view, leaders would not become tyrants because when they left office they would be equally subject to the laws that they had made.

Madison, on the other hand, focused particularly on ensuring justice as a major purpose of national government. His concept of justice included as a central feature the protection of what he saw as minority rights against majority popular will. In his view, that included suppressing state (and federal) power to redistribute wealth in certain popular ways, such as paper-money and property-tender laws. In that specific sense, Madison's thought was "antidemocratic" and protected the class interest of the wealthy by shielding wealth against unlimited democratic power. Madison thought that states could be overwhelmed by unrestrained popular will and could damage the national government as well as unjustly impairing the rights of minorities and of other states. He believed that what he saw as the potential for selfish sectional aggression also needed to be eliminated. The proposed constitution's sectional veto over its treaty power (i.e., requiring a two-thirds vote for treaties) was justified on that basis, with the proposed Spanish treaty as an example.[11]

Washington's majoritarian nationalism prevailed at the convention and formed the basis of its grand bargain. But as we have seen, it made significant concessions in the face of state and sectional jealousies, and it did not prevail unequivocally. Many of the convention's proposed limits on state powers, such as state taxation of imports, could be justified on the basis that they were necessary to make new federal powers effective. But the convention also adopted provisions to implement some of the protections against states' actions affecting minorities, particularly the wealthy, that Madison had advocated. This book has shown that curing the Confederation's defects was the convention's principal purpose, not protection of existing wealth against popular forms of redistribution such as paper money or debt relief. But wealth protection was certainly one goal of many delegates. As might have been expected from an elite intersectional agreement that combined the interests of various parts of the country, the convention chose to protect wealth constitutionally not just in the forms of "hard" money and creditors' claims, but in the form of slaves.

Washington and Madison also had differing views about what the convention had achieved. In the summer of 1788, Washington wrote to Thomas Jefferson. He described the largely completed constitutional ratification contest, particularly the amendments proposed by constitutional opponents (by then called Anti-Federalists). Surprisingly, he indicated that he would have been willing to accept some, perhaps even many, of them if needed in order to guarantee ratification. He told Jefferson, "For myself, I was ready to have embraced any tolerable compromise that was competent to save us from impending ruin."[12] The only exception, he told Jefferson, was that he thought that any amendment that prevented direct taxation would have made it impossible for the new federal government "to do justice to the public creditors and retrieve the National character." In that event, "we may as well recur to the old Confederation."[13] For Washington, of course, the power to impose direct taxes also meant that the country would have the resources needed to raise an army in the event of future conflicts. Military power could also protect Americans as they moved westward. Washington's new government had the potential to become a continental empire.

Writing to Henry Lee, Jr., Washington offered an equally surprising perspective on the new Constitution. He told Lee that in his view the contest over the Constitution had been a contest not for "glory" but for "existence." He believed that it had been "for a long time doubtful" whether the United States would survive as an "independent Republic," or "decline" into "insignificant & wretched fragments of empire." For Washington, the constitution was principally a political framework for national survival, avoiding a dissolution of the Confederation into separate smaller governments. The inescapable reality was that the United States existed in an imperial world. It could either maintain its "foederal dignity" by strengthening its national government or it would inevitably face dissolution followed by eventual European imperial takeover or civil war.[14]

But Washington understood that there were fundamentally important political limits to the apparently large paper powers conferred by the Constitution. As he wrote to Jefferson, "If the system [the new government] can be put in operation without touching much the Pockets of the People, perhaps, it may be done; but, in my judgment, infinite circumspection & prudence are yet necessary in the experiment."[15] Washington was acutely aware that citizens would jealously watch the new government and especially its taxes. He knew that the people would steadfastly resist anything that remotely resembled an effort to build the new government into a massive British-style empire at the expense of their pocketbooks. Unless the process of developing the new government was managed carefully, it might be destroyed by popular resistance.[16]

Madison, on the other hand, saw the convention as a failure because it had not agreed to his proposal for a congressional veto over state laws. When he wrote to Thomas Jefferson shortly after the convention to report on it, he spent several pages of his letter ardently defending that proposal, which Jefferson had sharply criticized.[17] He explained that without a national veto, the states would eventually frustrate the use of national powers. Washington, on the other hand, understood that the national government had been given the powers it needed. The real question was whether it would be permitted to exercise them by the people.

In 1788, Anti-Federalists had a very different view of what the Constitution was really intended to do. In the Virginia ratifying convention,

Patrick Henry had attacked it by arguing that its supporters wanted a "great" and "splendid" government. They had imperial ambitions. "Some way or other we must be a great and mighty empire; we must have an army, and a navy, and a number of things." Americans, Henry argued, had traditionally believed that the main object of government was to protect liberty. But now, "the American spirit, assisted by the ropes and chains of consolidation, is about to convert this country [in]to a powerful and mighty empire." That was "incompatible with the genius of republicanism."[18] In effect, Henry was charging that Constitution supporters (now usually called Federalists) had overreached, creating a government so powerful that it would destroy liberty. He denied that there was a crisis that required large new federal powers, and argued that the government would inevitably become corrupt.

Although Henry's views had strong support across the country, the political climate had changed sufficiently since 1783 that they narrowly lost. The Constitution was ratified by eleven states initially (Rhode Island and North Carolina were holdouts).[19] It should not surprise readers of this book to learn, however, that it was approved by very small margins in states essential to its ratification, such as Virginia, New York, and Massachusetts. As contemporaries knew, rejection in any one of those states would in all probability have destroyed the essence of the Constitution, its creation of a national sovereign. It would have required a second convention that would almost certainly have weakened the new government dramatically. In those three states, the Constitution received on average 53 percent of the ratification delegates' votes.

Ratification came as a deep shock to some leading Anti-Federalists. Richard Henry Lee wrote to northern Anti-Federalist leader John Lamb, just after Virginia narrowly ratified the constitution in the summer of 1788, "It will be considered, I believe, a most extraordinary epoch in the history of mankind, that in a few years there should be so essential a change in the minds of men. 'Tis really astonishing, that the same people, who have just emerged from a long and cruel war in defence of liberty, should now agree to fix an elective despotism upon themselves and their posterity."[20]

It was only when the 1787 Constitution replaced the collapsing Confederation and ended stalemate government that Americans were able to create a nation that had sufficient power to become a continental empire. The Constitution's principal purpose was to provide the sinews of war that made the country's expansion and defense possible. It protected existing wealth against popular reforms, but simultaneously held open the promise of great new wealth as Americans surged westward. As Washington recognized, whether America created an empire and what form it took would ultimately be up to its people to decide.

America's western expansion had dramatic, often unforeseeable consequences, many of which seem very unfortunate, indeed deeply tragic, to us today. But by 1860, the West had grown sufficiently to become the fulcrum of a relentless challenge to the growth of slavery, one of the largest forms of wealth that had received constitutional protection in 1787. Thanks to Abraham Lincoln's invincible courage and peerless statesmanship, and the massive financial resources and military might made available to the federal government by the Constitution, the nation survived the Civil War and ended government-sanctioned slavery. The deeply flawed Confederation could never have won that great victory for human freedom.

EPILOGUE

While researching this book and writing it over several years, I was often asked by people I met to tell them what it was about. When I described the Confederation's troubles as it became a stalemate government, people often responded by saying in substance "Oh, that sounds like America today." Their responses surprised me at first, because I had started work on this book for reasons that had nothing to do with America's current political quagmire.

I began working on the book because I was intrigued by my discovery that Alexander Hamilton had wanted to hold a national Confederation reform convention as early as 1783, and that James Madison, of all people, had opposed him on that issue. Madison claimed that it was unnecessary; he was certain that Congress and the states would agree to give the Confederation tax powers. How wrong Madison had turned out to be, I realized. And then I began to think about how the Confederation had fallen apart very quickly after the Revolutionary War, even though most people had agreed with Madison in 1783 that they did not see a need for much change in their national government. What had happened in only four years to cause the Confederation to lose public confidence to the point where it was replaced by a dramatically different government? This book is my answer to that question.

Having answered it in what you've already read, I can now say that although their views did not change my purpose in writing the book or my approach to it in any significant way, I think that people who see a resemblance between the collapse of the stalemated Confederation and America's current problems are on to something. I cannot possibly do the resemblances I see between them even rough justice here. But perhaps some readers will be interested if I close with a few personal observations about America's situation today based on what I have learned in writing this book.

The Constitution was a brilliant solution to the Confederation stalemate, as I hope the book's conclusion shows. But as it also shows, the Constitution was necessarily a pragmatic political compromise, and that meant that even from its drafters' point of view, it had some flaws. They began to become more generally apparent by the late eighteenth century as politics became more democratic.[1] Some of them stemmed from the Philadelphia Convention's decisions to prevent the majority popular will from operating in certain circumstances, usually because it felt compelled to protect sectional or state interests.

Several of the Constitution's original provisions that limit the effects of the popular will still exist today. And because the relative populations and wealth of the states have changed dramatically since 1787, these same provisions now play an important role in the chronic inability (or unwillingness) of America's federal government today to make badly needed political reforms that have strong popular support. In short, they are among the significant causes of today's stalemate—not, I would emphasize, the whole explanation for it by any means—but they play an important part. Space limits will permit me to give only one example here.

As noted in the conclusion, the Constitution provides that states have an equal vote in the US Senate. At the time the Constitution was adopted, the total population of the largest state, Virginia, was about twelve times as large as the population of the smallest state, Delaware. Today, the population of the largest state, California, is roughly sixty-five times as large as the population of the smallest state, Wyoming. Yet all states still have equal Senate voting strength. And under Article 5 of the Constitution, each state, no matter how small, has the ability by itself to prevent any change in that arrangement. Further, despite today's enormous disparities in state population and wealth, all states still have equal power to block constitutional amendments.

Those who have read the conclusion will understand that the Philadelphia Convention's decision to redistribute voting power in the national government among the states by limiting equal state voting was the foundation that made it possible for our national government to function effectively. Among other things, it made it possible for that government to gain tax, military, and commerce powers that Americans today uniformly agree are essential to our national welfare. At the convention, leading nationalists such as Pennsylvanian James Wilson, Virginian James Madison, and others strongly favored redistributing states' voting power. From their viewpoint, the national government would not be sufficiently responsive to the country's popular will as a whole—that is, truly representative and hence truly republican—until states' populations and influence were closely correlated. It follows that they would be deeply concerned by the far larger disparity between state populations and political influence that exists in states' equal Senate voting strengths today.

The Constitution's provisions permitting equal state Senate voting were part of a hard-fought compromise at the convention to begin with. The Senate voting provisions suited their time well enough to be part of a workable compromise, and they certainly helped make it politically possible for the Constitution to be adopted. But that is a far cry from saying that they work well enough today to govern a country of 320 million people.

Stalemate government, we have seen, is a result of political choices. It is time we took a hard look at how well the Founders' choices about states' Senate voting power and similar provisions limiting the popular will are standing up in modern times. I am convinced that they would favor doing so, just as they were willing to reexamine the Confederation from the ground up in order to cure its flaws. If we conclude that these provisions are contributing to our current stalemate, I am equally convinced that they would expect us to change them, because they did not think that stalemate governments could survive.

ACKNOWLEDGMENTS

My wife Mary's unstinting love, support, and encouragement for my work made this book possible. She also provided helpful comments on it throughout its long gestation.

I have also been quite moved by the remarkable generosity of the scholars who have helped me at various stages of the work. I am happy to have this opportunity to express my deep gratitude to them.

I thank the following people for particularly extensive help: Peter Onuf, for his constant support and mentorship, for thoughtful comments throughout the book's evolution, and especially for his continual encouragement to "think beyond" the existing historiography in order to conceive the project as broadly as possible; and Max Edling, for offering perceptive criticisms and suggestions on the work throughout its writing, which materially improved it in numerous respects, though we may disagree on various points. I also offer my very warm thanks to Daniel Walker Howe for his enlightening suggestions on the manuscript, which aided me greatly in sharpening it. Words cannot fully express the debt I owe to my gifted editor, John Tryneski, for his patience, unflinching candor, and insights as he strove to foster and improve my work over the years.

I'd also like to acknowledge my vast debt to the late Rick Beeman for his friendship, support, and encouragement not just of this project but throughout my career. I am grateful for his exemplary contributions to American history and its teaching, which have repeatedly assisted me in my work on this and other projects. And I am especially grateful to him because despite being in considerable pain and knowing that he was fatally ill, he agreed to read the entire manuscript and provided detailed comments on it that improved it significantly. Rick was a lovely and good man, and I will miss him greatly.

My thanks to others who provided considerable help also: David Waldstreicher, for his remarkably patient, painstaking, and constructive editing of an article that became an important part of chapter 7; my former colleague John Storella, for his thoughtful comments on early drafts of chapters 1 and 2, which helped me make the book more accessible to readers; Alan Taylor, for his perceptive and candid comments on the book proposal; Michael Klarman, for offering helpful comments on an article on paper money and in a dialogue on Rhode Island's actions; Justin du Rivage, for sharing his manuscript of his thought-provoking book, *Revolution against Empire*, and perceptive comments on two chapters; Allan Kulikoff, for providing page proofs of his very informative article on the economic effects of the American Revolution and its aftermath, whose influence will be seen throughout the book; and Peter H. Lindert and Jeffrey G. Williamson, for providing a draft chapter of their important book on the late-eighteenth-century American economy, *Unequal Gains: American Growth and Inequality since 1700* (Princeton: Princeton University Press, 2016). Mary Sarah Bilder generously shared her remarkable knowledge of James Madison, particularly his notes of congressional debates. She also deserves belated thanks for graciously assisting my research for an earlier work on slavery and the Constitution. My former colleague Luis Acosta, now at the Library of Congress, provided helpful guidance and assistance on several research issues.

Many other scholars and informed individuals also responded to queries with helpful information and materials, including John J. McCusker; Bruce Mann; Stephen Conway; Jenny Bourne Wahl; Lorena Walsh; Winifred B. Rothenberg; Jon Kukla; Chris Kingston; Robert E. Wright; Edward Lengel; Bill Ferraro; Benjamin Huggins; Alvin Rabushka; John Ragosta; David A. Skeel, Jr.; Robert McDonald; Joseph Dooley; Doug Bradburn; Stephen McLeod; Charles Calomiris; Mike Caires; and Karen Rowlett.

I thank Charles (Chuck) McCurdy for his scholarship and his masterful teaching, both of which have contributed greatly to my continuing education, as well as for his continued support of my work.

I am happy to offer thanks to William Pettigrew and Kenneth Finchem of the University of Kent (Canterbury, UK), for their gracious hospitality and support. My visit to Canterbury included a helpful opportunity to present an early account of the 1780s paper-money controversy to the Kent History Research Seminar. I also thank Joshua Getzler for the opportunity to present my account of that controversy to the Oxford Legal History Seminar, and to Michael R. T. Macnair, Perry Gauci, and others for their perceptive comments on it.

I would like to thank Joann Hoy for her superb copyediting of the final manuscript. I also thank Tim Mennel and Erin DeWitt of the University of Chicago Press for their painstaking care in shepherding the work through various aspects of its development there.

Many thanks also to the helpful staff at various research libraries, especially Barbie Selby, University of Virginia (UVA); Heather M. Riser, Small Special Collections Library, UVA; Kent Olson, UVA Law Library; Minor Weisiger, Library of Virginia (LVA); Brett Tarter (formerly at LVA); Francis Pollard, Virginia Historical Society; Julie Miller and Jeff Flannery, Library of Congress; Cornelia King, Library Company of Philadelphia; Tal Nadan, Tom Lannon, and Brandon Westerheim, New York Public Library; Tammy Kiter, New-York Historical Society; Betsy Boyle and Sabina Beauchard, Massachusetts Historical Society; and the University of Washington. A special thanks goes to the staff of the Seattle University School of Law Library, particularly Susan Kezele and A. Robert Menanteaux, for their extensive assistance over several years.

A gift from my mother, Patricia Van Cleve, made possible an important part of the research. Her continued enthusiasm for the book helped make it a labor of love.

Finally, I am grateful for the continued support provided by Seattle

University School of Law and its dean, Annette Clark, for my research, including student assistants. I thank Michael Withy, Amy Whiting Riedel, Stephen Papik, and Emily Fox for their helpful research. I also thank former associate dean Paul Holland for his consistent interest in my work, and for providing me with support for it. He also provided me with an opportunity to teach subjects that have, most serendipitously, contributed considerably to my ability to understand some of the central issues in the book.

Though this book is far better than it would otherwise have been because of the considerable help I've received both from those mentioned above and from others throughout my life, not named here, to whom I am also very grateful, the opinions expressed in it and any errors it contains are my sole responsibility.

ABBREVIATIONS

AA Abigail Adams

AFC L. H. Butterfield and Marc Friedlaender, eds., *Adams Family Correspondence*, vol. 4 (Cambridge, MA: Belknap Press of Harvard University Press, 1973); and Margaret A. Hogan, C. James Taylor, Celeste Walker, Anne Decker Cecere, Gregg L. Lint, and Hobson Woodward, eds., *Adams Family Correspondence*, vol. 7 (Cambridge, MA: Harvard University Press, 2005).

DHRC Merrill Jensen, John P. Kaminski, Gaspare J. Saladino, Richard Leffler, Charles H. Schoenleber, and Margaret A. Hogan, eds., *The Documentary History of the Ratification of the Constitution*, 27 vols. to date (Madison: State Historical Society of Wisconsin, 1976–2015).

FO National Archives and Records Administration, Founders Online, http://founders.archives.gov/

GBC George Bancroft Collection, Manuscripts and Archives Division, New York Public Library

GW George Washington

GW Writings John C. Fitzpatrick and David M. Matteson, eds., *The Writings of George Washington from the Original Manuscript Sources, 1745–1799 . . .* , 39 vols. (Washington, DC: Government Printing Office, 1931–44).

HFC George Bancroft, *History of the Formation of the Constitution of the United States of America*, 2 vols. (New York: D. Appleton and Co., 1882).

HSP Historical Society of Pennsylvania, Philadelphia

JA John Adams

JCC Worthington Chauncey Ford, ed., *Journals of the Continental Congress, 1774–1789*, 34 vols. (Washington, DC: Government Printing Office, 1904–36).

JM James Madison

LCRK Charles King, *The Life and Correspondence of Rufus King*, 6 vols. (New York: G. P. Putnam's Sons, 1894–1900).

LDC Paul H. Smith and Ronald M. Gephart, eds., *Letters of Delegates to Congress, 1774–1789*, 26 vols. (Washington, DC: Library of Congress, 1976–2000).

LOC Library of Congress, Manuscript Division

LVA Library of Virginia, Richmond

MHS Massachusetts Historical Society, Boston

NYHS New-York Historical Society

NYPL New York Public Library, Manuscript Division

PGW W. W. Abbot, Dorothy Twohig, Philander D. Chase, Beverly H. Runge, Mark A. Mastromarino, Frank E. Grizzard, Jr., Beverly S. Kirsch et al., eds., *Papers of George Washington: Confederation Series*, 6 vols. (Charlottesville: University of Virginia Press, 1992–97).

PHK Henry Knox Papers, Gilder Lehrman Collection, New-York Historical Society (originals at NYHS; consulted only microfilm and online versions)

PJA Gregg L. Lint, C. James Taylor, Robert F. Karachuk, Hobson Woodward, Margaret A. Hogan, Sara B. Sikes, Mary T. Claffey, and Karen N. Barzilay, eds., *The Papers of John Adams*, vol. 15 (Cambridge, MA: Harvard University Press, 2010); Gregg L. Lint, C. James Taylor, Robert Karachuk, Hobson Woodward, Margaret A. Hogan, Sara B. Sikes, Sara Martin et al., eds., *Papers of John Adams*, vol. 16 (Cambridge, MA: Harvard University Press, 2012); and Gregg L. Lint, C. James Taylor, Sara Georgini, Hobson Woodward, Sara B. Sikes, Amanda A. Mathews, and Sara

Martin, eds., *Papers of John Adams*, vol. 17 (Cambridge, MA: Harvard University Press, 2014).

PJM William T. Hutchinson, William M. E. Rachal, Robert Rutland, Charles F. Hobson, Frederika J. Teute, Thomas Mason, J. C. A. Stagg et al., eds., *Papers of James Madison: Congressional Series*, vols. 1–10 (Chicago: University of Chicago Press, 1962–77); vols. 11–17 (Charlottesville: University of Virginia Press, 1977–91).

RK Rufus King

SSC Small Special Collections Library, University of Virginia, Charlottesville

TJ Thomas Jefferson

VHS Virginia Historical Society, Richmond

NOTES

The spelling of words in eighteenth-century quotations in this book has sometimes been altered for one or more of the following reasons: to make them easier for modern readers to understand; to conform spelling of a frequently used word for which widely different spellings were found (e.g., "Mississippi"); and, on a few occasions, to correct obvious misspelling to improve readability. Such alterations are generally indicated in notes as "spelling modernized," but in minor instances may be silent. On rare occasions, punctuation has been altered to fit smoothly into this book's text. None of the spelling or punctuation changes alters the substantive meaning of any quotation.

Some of the citations in these notes provide uniform resource locators (URLs) that can be used to find documents in public online databases such as Founders Online. While these URLS are believed to be accurate, readers should be aware that such databases sometimes change URLs, and that other problems may occur in using them. Therefore, such document citations also provide sufficient information to permit the document to be searched for on the relevant website.

Introduction

1. Cabinet of Versailles to Louis-Guillaume Otto, August 30, 1787, trans. George Bancroft, excerpted in George Bancroft, *History of the Formation of the Constitution of the United States of America* (*HFC*), 2:438.

2. Of course, "republicanism" was a slippery term that meant many different things to different people during the 1780s. There seems to have been fairly wide

agreement that republics were representative governments chosen by some form of popular consent, but almost every other aspect of republicanism's meaning in practice was contested. In this book, the term is used in a context linking it to a specific part of that ongoing debate, such as the debate over whether republican legislatures should be composed of one house or two. This book focuses particularly on the contemporary controversies over the limits of majority power in republics and what form of national republican government could coexist with state republics without hampering or destroying them.

3. For a history of the political philosophies and social forces that underlay the creation of the Articles of Confederation, see Merrill Jensen, *The Articles of Confederation: An Interpretation of the Social-Constitutional History of the American Revolution, 1774–1781* (1940; repr., Madison: University of Wisconsin Press, 1970). For the division of authority between the Confederation and the states, see Max M. Edling, "Consolidating a Revolutionary Republic," in *The World of the Revolutionary American Republic: Land, Labor, and the Conflict for a Continent*, ed. Andrew Shankman (London: Routledge, 2014), 170.

4. Throughout this book, the terms "Native American" and "Indian" are used interchangeably, as are the terms "tribe" and "nation" when referring to their groups. Anglicized versions of tribal names are used. "Indian country" refers to unceded lands. Quotations are not altered to conform to these usages, however.

5. Edling, *Revolution*, 155–57; Merrill Jensen, *The New Nation: A History of the United States during the Confederation, 1781–1789* (New York: Vintage Books, 1950), 313–26.

6. John Fiske, *The Critical Period of American History, 1783–1789* (Boston: Houghton Mifflin, 1889); John Bach McMaster, *A History of the People of the United States from the Revolution to the Civil War* (New York: D. Appleton and Co., 1911); Andrew C. McLaughlin, *The Confederation and the Constitution, 1783–1789* (New York: Harper and Bros., 1905; repr., New York: Collier Books, 1971). McLaughlin did not think economic conditions were as bad as Fiske did, but largely agreed with him that the period was one of crisis. George Bancroft seems to have believed that the creation of the Constitution was inevitable. George Bancroft, *History of the Formation of the Constitution of the United States of America* (New York: D. Appleton and Co., 1882), 1:117–19. For a thoughtful recent overview of the historiography, see Edling, "Consolidating a Revolutionary Republic," 165–68. For excellent analyses of additional earlier works that discuss the connection between arguments about Confederation collapse and constitutional formation in 1787, see Richard B. Morris, "The Confederation Period and the American Historian," *William and Mary Quarterly*, 3rd ser., 13, no. 2 (1956):

139–56; James H. Hutson, "The Creation of the Constitution: Scholarship at a Standstill," *Reviews in American History* 12, no. 4 (1984): 463–77.

7. The leading modern surveys of the period's events are Jensen, *New Nation*, and Richard B. Morris, *The Forging of the Union, 1781–1789* (New York: Harper and Row, 1987). Other significant works include Jack Rakove, *The Beginnings of National Politics: An Interpretive History of the Continental Congress* (New York: Knopf, 1979); Gordon S. Wood, *The Creation of the American Republic, 1776–1787* (1969; repr., Chapel Hill: University of North Carolina Press, 1998), 391–467; Forrest McDonald, *E Pluribus Unum: The Formation of the American Republic, 1776–1790*, 2nd ed. (Indianapolis, IN: Liberty Press, 1979); Frederick W. Marks III, *Independence on Trial: Foreign Affairs and the Making of the Constitution* (Baton Rouge: Louisiana State University Press, 1973); and Jackson T. Main, *The Antifederalists: Critics of the Constitution, 1781–1788* (Chapel Hill: University of North Carolina Press, 1961). Earlier works of note include Charles Warren, *The Making of the Constitution* (Boston: Little, Brown, 1928); Allan Nevins, *The American States during and after the Revolution, 1775–1789* (New York: Macmillan, 1924); Edward Channing, *History of the United States: American Revolution, 1761–1789*, vol. 3 (New York: Macmillan, 1912); and particularly the seminal work of Charles A. Beard, *An Economic Interpretation of the Constitution of the United States* (1935 edition; repr., New York: Macmillan, 1941). There are also various works that claim that the Articles of Confederation did not create a national government, but most contemporaries plainly thought that it was one (despite occasional disagreements about its character), so they are not considered further. See David C. Hendrickson, *Peace Pact: The Lost World of the American Founding* (Lawrence: University Press of Kansas, 2003), 136; Alfred H. Kelly, Winfred A. Harbison, and Herman Belz, *The American Constitution: Its Origins and Development*, 7th ed. (New York: Norton, 1991), 1:76.

8. Beard, *Economic Interpretation*, 48.

9. Jensen, *New Nation*, xiii.

10. Ibid., 423–28; E. James Ferguson, *The Power of the Purse: A History of American Public Finance, 1776–1790* (Chapel Hill: University of North Carolina Press, 1961), 238–50.

11. Jensen, *Articles of Confederation*, 245; Beard, *Economic Interpretation*, 52–63. More recent histories by Woody Holton, *Unruly Americans and the Origins of the Constitution* (New York: Hill and Wang, 2007), and Terry Bouton, *Taming Democracy: "The People," the Founders, and the Troubled Ending of the American Revolution* (Oxford: Oxford University Press, 2007), substitute a claimed struggle over economic democracy, redistributive taxation, and popular government for

Beard's version of class struggle. They argue that strong popular movements during the period would have led to more democratic and economically egalitarian government, which was suppressed by the Constitution. As the historian Gordon Wood concludes, Holton's and Bouton's claims are in large part variants of the Beard thesis. Gordon S. Wood, *Empire of Liberty: A History of the Early Republic, 1789–1815* (Oxford: Oxford University Press, 2009), 30 n. 69.

Michael Klarman's recent work, *The Framers' Coup: The Making of the United States Constitution* (Oxford: Oxford University Press, 2016), advocates an interpretation similar to Holton's and Bouton's. Klarman writes that he is "especially drawn to the view, long advanced by others, that the Constitution was a conservative counterrevolution" (x). He agrees that the Confederation had various defects that needed to be remedied (11–72). But he contends that the Constitution was "even more a reaction to the economic relief measures enacted by most states in the mid-1780s" (74). Klarman's study was received after this manuscript's completion, but its main arguments concerning events prior to the Philadelphia Convention are fully addressed in this book.

The arguments that the Constitution had an economic-class or property-class basis (particularly Charles Beard's version), or any economic-interest basis, have been criticized. For critiques, see Forrest McDonald, *We the People: The Economic Origins of the Constitution* (Chicago: University of Chicago, 1958); and Robert Eldon Brown, *Reinterpretation of the Formation of the Constitution* (Boston: University of Massachusetts Press, 1963). However, recent writers have provided new empirical evidence that economic interests did play an important role in support for and opposition to the Constitution. Robert A. McGuire, *To Form a More Perfect Union: A New Economic Interpretation of the Constitution* (Oxford: Oxford University Press, 2003). McDonald himself (in *E Pluribus Unum*) later concluded that greedy and self-interested actions by politicians and various economic-interest groups, at the state level in particular, played a leading role in enabling the formation of the Constitution by straining the bonds of union to the breaking point.

12. Wood, *Creation*, 393–94. There were prominent Confederation defenders, including Patrick Henry and George Clinton, who denied that any crisis requiring major changes existed. For examples of leaders who thought there was a crisis and some who did not, see Morris, "Confederation Period," 139–44.

13. Rufus King (RK) to Elbridge Gerry, May 5, 1786, in *Letters of Delegates to Congress, 1774–1789* (*LDC*), 23:269.

14. People then used the word "crisis" in several different ways. For example, a "crisis" could mean a conjunction, or coming together, of independent events that created a favorable opportunity for action that would not otherwise have

existed. See, for example, James Madison to Ambrose Madison, August 7, 1786, in *Papers of James Madison* (*PJM*), 9:89.

15. *Oxford English Dictionary*, compact ed. (Oxford: Oxford University Press, 1971 [repr. of first ed.]), s.v. "crisis."

16. On the other hand, contemporaries did not typically use "crisis" to mean that "the house is on fire."

17. Recent economic historians conclude that there was an exceptionally severe, long-lasting economic downturn after the war. It may well have lasted through the end of the 1780s in a sizable part of the country. See the important work of Peter H. Lindert and Jeffrey G. Williamson, "American Incomes before and after the Revolution," *Journal of Economic History* 73, no. 3 (2013): 725–65; and Peter H. Lindert and Jeffrey G. Williamson, *Unequal Gains: American Growth and Inequality since 1700* (Princeton, NJ: Princeton University Press, 2016); the excellent essay by Allan Kulikoff, "'Such Things Ought Not to Be': The American Revolution and the First Great Depression," in *The World of the Revolutionary American Republic: Land, Labor, and the Conflict for a Continent*, ed. Andrew Shankman (New York: Routledge, 2014), 134–64; and James F. Shepherd and Gary M. Walton, "Economic Change after the American Revolution: Pre- and Post-war Comparisons of Maritime Shipping and Trade," *Explorations in Economic History* 13 (1976): 397–422. For the view that the 1780s were probably the worst decade in American economic history other than the 1930s, see Thomas K. McCraw, *The Founders and Finance: How Hamilton, Gallatin and Other Immigrants Forged a New Economy* (Cambridge, MA: Harvard University Press, 2012), 47, 375 n. 4. John J. McCusker and Russell Menard, *The Economy of British North America, 1607–1789* (Chapel Hill: University of North Carolina Press, 1985), portray this period as one of severe recession. But I am inclined to agree that some contemporaries saw indications of renewed growth in some parts of the country by 1787–88, as Merrill Jensen argues (*New Nation*, 248–52). The recovery was uneven, however; both the South and New England appear to have had worse conditions than the Mid-Atlantic states as of the early 1790s.

18. Some supporters of stronger central government, such as the archconservative Massachusetts merchant Stephen Higginson, did seek federal powers as a means of protecting property holders against what they saw as inevitable continuing popular demands for wealth redistribution. But the existence of one supporter of "agrarian law" wealth redistribution among the Massachusetts Shays insurgents would not demonstrate that such beliefs were the basis for that rebellion. Similarly here, the relevant question is to what extent views like Higginson's motivated the reform movement as a whole. This book contends that reform had far broader motivations, and that protecting wealth played a limited role overall.

19. As Richard Morris observed, this was ultimately what John Fiske meant by his use of the term "critical period." Morris said, "Fiske used the term 'critical' first to settle the question whether there was to be a national government or a group of small city-states. Secondly, he used the term to describe what he regarded to be the utter incompetence of the states and the federal government to deal with the problem of postwar reconstruction." Morris, "Confederation Period," 145.

20. Ferguson, *Power of the Purse*, 220–50; Wood, *Creation*, 394–95.

21. See chapters 1 and 9.

22. Douglass G. Adair, "'Experience Must Be Our Only Guide': History, Democratic Theory, and the United States Constitution," in *Fame and the Founding Fathers: Essays by Douglass Adair*, ed. Trevor Colbourn (New York: Norton, 1974), 107–23.

23. Beard, *Economic Interpretation*, xvii.

24. Morris, "Confederation Period," 139. As will become clear later, the "Federalists" during the ratification contest referred to here are often nearly the polar ideological opposites of the "federalists" in the late Confederation period discussed in this book.

25. RK to Theodore Sedgwick, May 21, 1786, *LDC*, 23:305–6.

Chapter One

1. Abner Nash to James Iredell, January 8, 1783, *LDC*, 19:565.

2. Morris had numerous detractors who accused him of self-dealing to gain from his official positions during and after the war. Contemporaries (and later historians) also condemned what they saw as Morris's leadership of efforts during the 1780s to increase central-government power by granting it tax and commerce powers, claiming it was motivated by his antidemocratic views and desire to create an "aristocratic junto" that would control the country. See Jensen, *New Nation*, 366–70; Ferguson, *Power of the Purse*, 120–22; Bouton, *Taming Democracy*, 70–80. For a recent biography, see Charles Rappleye, *Robert Morris* (New York: Simon and Schuster, 2010).

3. James Madison (JM), Notes of debates, January 9–10, 13, 1783, *LDC*, 19:570, 580. See also E. James Ferguson, ed., *The Papers of Robert Morris, 1781–1784*, digital ed., vol. 7 (Pittsburgh, PA: University of Pittsburgh Press, 2011), http://digital.library.pitt.edu/cgi-bin/t/text/text-idx?idno=31735060482050;view=toc;c=pittpress, 265–67, 287–88, 310. Morris stated the overdrafts as 3.5 million French livres; I have converted that amount at 5.4 livres/$1 following Ferguson, *Power of the Purse* (e.g., 41, 235). Technically, Morris had issued "bills of exchange." Such bills were written orders by one person instructing a second per-

son to pay a third, and were precursors of modern checks. Bruce Mann, *Republic of Debtors: Bankruptcy in the Age of Independence* (Cambridge, MA: Harvard University Press, 2002), 11–12. Financial amounts in this book are presented in the currency and amounts found in the sources, unless otherwise stated.

4. JM, Notes of debates, January 13, 1783, *LDC*, 19:579–81.

5. Stephen Conway, *The War of American Independence, 1775–1783* (London: Edward Arnold, 1995), 247.

6. Kulikoff, "Such Things Ought Not to Be," 144; John Ferling, *A Leap in the Dark: The Struggle to Create the American Republic* (New York: Oxford University Press, 2003), 260. For general histories of the revolution and the war, see Robert Middlekauff, *The Glorious Cause: The American Revolution, 1763–1789*, rev. ed. (Oxford: Oxford University Press, 2005); Patrick Griffin, *America's Revolution* (Oxford: Oxford University Press, 2013); Conway, *War of American Independence*; Charles Royster, *A Revolutionary People at War: The Continental Army and American Character, 1775–1783* (Chapel Hill: University of North Carolina Press, 1979).

7. Stephen Conway, *A Short History of the American Revolutionary War* (London: Tauris, 2013), 125.

8. Kulikoff, "Such Things Ought Not to Be," 136, 138, 147.

9. Adam and Mary Jones to "Dear Brother," Library of Virginia (LVA), MS 24826; William Heath to George Washington, August 11, 1782, Founders Online (FO), http://founders.archives.gov/documents/Washington/99-01-02-09097.

10. Griffin, *America's Revolution*, 174–80 (quotation at 178).

11. Ibid., 183–90.

12. Henry Knox to George Washington, September 22, 1782, FO, http://founders.archives.gov/documents/Washington/99-01-02-09553.

13. Hugh Williamson to Thomas Ruston, June 21, 1783, *LDC*, 20:353; John Jay to Robert R. Livingston, July 19, 1783, transcribed by George Bancroft, George Bancroft Collection, Manuscripts and Archives Division, New York Public Library (GBC), vol. 277; Alexander Hamilton to R. R. Livingston, August 13, 1783, Bancroft transcription, GBC, 277:473; Henry Van Schaack to Theodore Sedgwick, September 8, 1783, Sedgwick Family Papers, Massachusetts Historical Society (MHS), box 4.

14. Conway, *War of American Independence*, 160.

15. Printer's note to Arthur Lee to the Public, July? 1783, *LDC*, 19:509 n. 2; Lewis-Oliver partnership agreement, box 9, Briscoe-Stuart Papers, Small Special Collections Library, University of Virginia (SSC).

16. Nevins, *American States*, 394; Mary Beth Norton, *Liberty's Daughters: The Revolutionary Experience of American Women, 1750–1800* (Ithaca, NY: Cor-

nell University Press, 1980), 274; Cassandra Pybus, "Jefferson's Faulty Math: The Question of Slave Defections in the American Revolution," *William and Mary Quarterly* 62, no. 2 (2005): 243–64.

17. Kulikoff, "Such Things Ought Not to Be," 136–37; Lindert and Williamson, *Unequal Gains*, 90.

18. Robert A. McGuire, "The Founding Era, 1774–1791" in Price Fishback et al., *Government and the American Economy: A New History* (Chicago: University of Chicago Press, 2007), 61.

19. Conway, *American Revolutionary War*, 129.

20. William G. Anderson, *The Price of Liberty: The Public Debt of the American Revolution* (Charlottesville: University Press of Virginia, 1983), 24.

21. McGuire, "Founding Era," 61; Ben Baack, "Forging a Nation State: The Continental Congress and the Financing of the War of American Independence," *Economic History Review* 54, no. 4 (2001): 654; Kulikoff, "Such Things Ought Not to Be," 139–40.

22. Stephen Collins to Mary Hayley, June 16, 1783; and Stephen Collins to Executors of William Neale, March 31, 1783; both in Stephen Collins Letterbook (microfilm, Library of Congress, Manuscript Division [LOC]).

23. Ferguson, *Power of the Purse*, 134.

24. George Washington (GW) to Nathanael Greene, February 6, 1783, in *The Writings of George Washington from the Original Manuscript Sources, 1745–1799 . . .* (*GW Writings*), 26:104.

25. Nathanael Greene to Richard Henry Lee, August 22, 1785, Edward Carrington Papers, Virginia Historical Society (VHS); North Carolina delegates to Alexander Martin, October 22, 1782, *LDC*, 19:289.

26. Kulikoff, "Such Things Ought Not to Be," 139–40; Augusta County Petition to Virginia House of Delegates, June 8, 1784, LVA, http://www.virginiamemory.com/collections/petitions; GW to Elias Boudinot, February 26, 1783, FO, http://founders.archives.gov/documents/Washington/99-01-02-10720.

27. Wood, *Empire of Liberty*, 27–30; Robert Abraham East, *Business Enterprise in the American Revolutionary Era* (1938; repr., New York: AMS Press, 1979).

28. John Jenks to Stephen Collins, March 26, 1783, Papers of Stephen Collins, LOC.

29. John Joyce to Robert Dickson, March 24, 1785, VHS, reprinted in *Virginia Magazine of History and Biography* 23 (1915): 407 (printed version varies slightly from original). I thank Jon Kukla for this reference. Hugh Blair Grigsby, *The History of the Federal Convention of 1788* (Richmond: Virginia Historical Society, 1890), 14.

30. See, e.g., Woody Holton, "Abigail Adams: Bond Speculator," *William and Mary Quarterly* 64 (October 2007): 821–38.

31. Norton, *Liberty's Daughters*, 189.

32. Abigail Adams (AA) to John Adams (JA), June 17, 1782, in *Adams Family Papers: An Electronic Archive*, MHS, https://www.masshist.org/digitaladams/archive/doc?id=L17820617aa&bc.

33. For an overview, see Norton, *Liberty's Daughters*, 188–91.

34. Peter S. Du Ponceau to R. R. Livingston, October 15, 1783, Bancroft transcription, GBC, 277:491–93.

35. Jackson T. Main, "Government by the People: The American Revolution and the Democratization of the Legislatures," *William and Mary Quarterly* 23, no. 3 (1966): 391–407.

36. A classic discussion of these constitutions is J. R. Pole, *Political Representation in England and the Origins of the American Republic* (Berkeley: University of California Press, 1971), 190–204, 270–77 passim.

37. George Lux to Theodorick Bland, November 17, 1782, *LDC*, 20:163 n. 3–165 (quotation at 164; emphasis original).

38. Benjamin Rush to Charles Lee, October 24, 1779, in L. H. Butterfield, ed., *Letters of Benjamin Rush* (Philadelphia: American Philosophical Society, 1951), 1:244.

39. The "federalist" terminology is employed by Merrill Jensen, *New Nation*, xvii–xviii. Its use here does not, however, imply agreement with Jensen's views on various issues unless explicitly stated. Some federalists supported strengthening the Confederation in significant ways after the war even though that would have reduced state powers, so the terminology is at best an approximation.

40. See Elbridge Gerry to JA, November 23, 1783, *LDC*, 21:158–59.

41. Richard Henry Lee to William Whipple, July 1, 1783, in *Letters of Richard Henry Lee*, ed. James Curtis Ballagh (1911–14; repr., New York: Da Capo Press, 1970), 2:284.

42. Tristram Dalton to Elbridge Gerry, December 1, 1783, Elbridge Gerry Letters, box 2, MHS.

43. See Main, *Antifederalists*, 8–10; Bernard Bailyn, *The Ideological Origins of the American Revolution* (Cambridge, MA: Harvard University Press, 1967), 96.

44. James Burgh, *Political Disquisitions; or an Enquiry into public Errors, Defects, and Abuses . . .* (Philadelphia: Robert Bell and William Woodhouse, 1775), quoted in Main, *Antifederalists*, 9.

45. David Howell to William Greene, January 12, 1785, *LDC*, 22:108.

46. "Nationalist" is the term used for this group by both Jensen and E. James Ferguson. It too is potentially misleading: many supporters of strong national

government wanted to preserve states, though some did not. And nationalists often disagreed about what added powers the Confederation should be given.

47. GW to Alexander Hamilton, March 31, 1783, *GW Writings*, 26:277.

48. Oliver Ellsworth to Governor Trumbull, July 10, 1783, GBC, 178:25; Major Samuel Shaw to John Eliot, February 23, 1783, GBC, 37:555.

49. GW to Benjamin Harrison, March 4, 1783, *GW Writings*, 26:184.

50. Ibid., 184–85 (emphasis original).

51. GW to William Gordon, July 8, 1783, *GW Writings*, 26:49, 51–52.

52. Adair, "Experience Must Be Our Only Guide."

53. JM, Notes of debates, February 13, 1783, *LDC*, 19:692; Hugh Williamson to James Iredell, February 17, 1783, *LDC*, 19:699.

54. Middlekauff, *Glorious Cause*, 595. The French alliance completely altered the war's dimensions and military balance, markedly weakening the British position. Griffin, *America's Revolution*, 162–64, 169. Some American generals believed that the United States would not have won the war without French aid. Commenting on the 1781 military campaigns, including Yorktown, General Nathanael Greene wrote to Benjamin Rush (February 1, 1782, GBC, 198:159), "The events of the last year have been important; and I wish for the honor of America, they had been more the work of our own hands. I cannot help feeling a kind of humility when I consider we are not to be free by our own exertions."

55. Those intending to retire included Richard Henry Lee, Theodorick Bland, George Washington, nearly all the army's generals and most officers, including Alexander Hamilton, and many more.

56. AA to Mercy Otis Warren, September 5, 1784, FO, http://founders.archives.gov/documents/Adams/04-05-02-0232.

57. Preliminary Articles of Peace between Great Britain and the United States, November 30, 1782, in *Journals of the Continental Congress, 1774–1789* (*JCC*), 24:244–50 (April 15, 1783).

58. Bethel Saler, *The Settlers' Empire: Colonialism and State Formation in America's Old Northwest* (Philadelphia: University of Pennsylvania Press, 2015), 17. For some of Congress's reactions to the preliminary articles of peace, see, e.g., Gunning Bedford, Jr., to Governor Nicholas Van Dyke, March 12, 1783, *LDC*, 20:3; Samuel Holten to John Hancock, March 12, 1783, *LDC*, 20:11.

59. The Definitive Treaty of Peace between the United States and His Britannic Majesty, *JCC*, 26:23–28 (also known as the Paris Peace Treaty of September 3, 1783).

60. McMaster, *History of the People of the United States*, 130; Charles R. Ritcheson, *Aftermath of Revolution: British Policy toward the United States, 1783–1795* (Dallas, TX: Southern Methodist University Press, 1969), 62.

61. Ezra Stiles, "The United States Elevated to Glory and Honour" (Worcester, MA: Isaiah Thomas, 1785), 44, 60.

62. Samuel Flagg Bemis, *The Diplomacy of the American Revolution* (1935; repr., Bloomington: Indiana University Press, 1965), 218–20, 241–42.

63. Ibid., 221–22.

64. Middlekauff, *Glorious Cause*, 613.

65. Lindert and Williamson, *Unequal Gains*, 49, 94.

66. In New England, roughly half by value of commodity exports during 1768–72 came from fishing and whaling. The middle colonies' exports were quite different, as they were mostly farm products. More than 70 percent by value were grain and grain products. More than 70 percent of the upper South's exports were of tobacco. About 75 percent of the lower South's exports were of rice or indigo. All data in this paragraph are derived from tables in the excellent overview of the colonial economy in McCusker and Menard, *Economy of British North America*, 108, table 5.2; 130, table 6.1; 174, table 8.2; 199, table 9.3.

67. Ibid.

68. McCusker and Menard, *Economy of British North America*, 12, 81–83.

69. Historians disagree somewhat about the overall importance of exports to the American economy just before the war. Some think that they represented on average about 15–18 percent of total income, while others think that they were less significant. In any event, exports had a multiplier effect. They generated considerable numbers of jobs both on many farms and in cities. Exports were disproportionately important to the economies of the major coastal cities. Ibid., 85–86. Lindert and Williamson ("American Incomes," 754) estimate 6–7 percent. These estimates are not directly comparable, however. If Lindert and Williamson's data are adjusted to account for their differing estimate of 1774 national income, and if one adds in estimates for invisible earnings and coastal trade, as McCusker and Menard do, the two estimates would be closer, perhaps considerably so.

70. Lindert and Williamson, "American Incomes," 753.

71. Prices for farm products in Massachusetts fell much further. Winifred B. Rothenberg, "A Price Index for Rural Massachusetts, 1750–1855," *Journal of Economic History* 39, no. 4 (1979): 979, figure 1.

72. Richard Hildreth, quoted in Lindert and Williamson, "American Incomes," 754.

73. In the first camp, taking the more optimistic view, are Jensen, *New Nation*, 177–257; Gordon C. Bjork, "The Weaning of the American Economy: Independence, Market Changes, and Economic Development," *Journal of Economic History* 24, no. 4 (1964): 541–60; McGuire, "Founding Era," 56–88; Middlekauff, *Glorious Cause*, 611–13; East, *Business Enterprise*, 239–57.

74. For this view, see particularly Lindert and Williamson, "American Incomes," 741–55; Kulikoff, "Such Things Ought Not to Be," 134–64. For export trade data consistent with the idea of a severe economic downturn in the 1780s, see James F. Shepherd and Gary M. Walton, "Economic Change after the American Revolution: Pre- and Post-war Comparisons of Maritime Shipping and Trade," *Explorations in Economic History* 13 (1976): 397–422. Shepherd and Walton (401–3, 420) conclude that their data contradict Jensen's views on exports. See also Curtis P. Nettels, *The Emergence of a National Economy, 1775–1815* (New York: Holt, Rinehart and Winston, 1962), 45–64.

75. Kulikoff, "Such Things Ought Not to Be," 148–49. The analysis in Lindert and Williamson, "American Incomes," 741–55, would support an even deeper income decline, one the authors say "could have been America's greatest income slump ever, in percentage terms" (741), constituting "a true economic disaster" (752).

76. Joseph Reed to Dennis de Berdt, October 2, 1784, Joseph Reed Papers, New-York Historical Society (NYHS), microfilm reel 3.

77. Caroline County petition to Virginia legislature, November 16, 1784, LVA, http://www.virginiamemory.com/collections/petitions.

78. Richard Henry Lee to JM, November 20, 1784, *LDC*, 22:25.

79. Mann, *Republic of Debtors*, 177–78.

80. William Grayson to the governor of Virginia, January 22, 1785, LVA, Misc. microfilm reel 4918.

81. Hannah North to Caleb Davis, September 19, 1785, Caleb Davis Papers, MHS.

82. Richard Cranch to John Adams, October 13, 1785, in *The Papers of John Adams* (*PJA*), 17:508.

83. Morris, *Forging of the Union*, 260.

84. (Richmond) *Virginia Gazette and Weekly Advertiser*, May 24, 1787.

85. James Duncanson to James Maury, July 3, 1787, Papers of James Maury, SSC.

86. Quoted in Mann, *Republic of Debtors*, 31.

87. Nettels, *Emergence of a National Economy*, 48.

88. Stephen Collins to Harrison and Ansley, June 17, 1783; and Stephen Collins to Pearsall and Glover, July 22, 1783, Stephen Collins Letterbook, microfilm, LOC. See also Nalbro Frazier to Frederick William Geyer, September 25, 1783; Nalbro Frazier to W. North Ingraham, September 22, 1783; and Nalbro Frazier to Wm. Price and Company, July 3, 1784, Nalbro Frazier Letterbook, New York Public Library, Manuscript Division (NYPL).

89. Thomas Willing to John Dickinson, January 15, 1785 (notes on envelope), Papers of John Dickinson, Library Company of Philadelphia.

90. John M. Nesbitt to Nicholas Low, November 26, 1784, Nicholas Low Papers, NYHS.

91. Nettels, *Emergence of a National Economy*, 50–51.

92. Joshua Johnson to Wallace and Muir, December 29, 1785; and January 13, 1786, Joshua Johnson Papers, LOC (microfilm).

93. Susan B. Carter et al., eds., *Historical Statistics of the United States* (Cambridge: Cambridge University Press, 2006), 5:653, table Eg275–284.

94. (Alexandria) *Virginia Journal and Alexandria Advertiser*, April 29, 1784; Ralph Wormeley, Jr., to Wakelin Welch and Co., September 21, 1785; and July 21, 1788, Papers of Ralph Wormeley, SSC.

95. William Hamilton to Jasper Yeates, April 10, 1784; April 24, 1784; May 26, 1784; and August 30, 1784, Jasper Yeates Papers, HSP.

96. Wallace and Gholson agreement, August 25, 1784, Papers of William Fleming, LVA.

97. *Richmond Virginia Gazette*, November 6 and 20, 1784; *Baltimore Maryland Gazette or Baltimore General Advertiser*, October 22, 1784.

98. John Joyce to Robert Dickson, March 24, 1785, VHS (quotation from manuscript), repr., *Virginia Magazine of History and Biography* 23 (1915): 412 (printed version varies slightly from original).

99. Ralph Wormeley, Jr., to Wakelin Welch and Co., September 21, 1785, Papers of Ralph Wormeley, SSC.

100. William Hamilton to Jasper Yeates, February 22, 1787, Jasper Yeates Papers, HSP.

101. Fairfax Bryan to Dr. Denny Fairfax, June 22, 1787, MS 13056-a, SSC.

102. Ralph Wormeley, Jr., to Welch and Co., July 26, 1788, Papers of Ralph Wormeley, SSC.

103. Winifred B. Rothenberg, "The Emergence of a Capital Market in Rural Massachusetts, 1730–1838" *The Journal of Economic History* 45, no. 4 (1985): 790 (cited in Lindert and Williamson, "American Incomes," 738 n. 19).

104. AA to JA, January 3, 1784, FO, http://founders.archives.gov/documents/Adams/04-05-02-0158.

105. Sidney Homer and Richard Sylla, *A History of Interest Rates*, 4th ed. (Hoboken, NJ: John Wiley and Sons, 2005), 274. Short-term loan rates also appear to have been far higher than long-term rates. South Carolinian David Ramsay wrote to Pennsylvanian Benjamin Rush in July 1785 that he wanted to borrow money for speculation in "Carolina indents." Ramsay said was willing to pay 7.5 percent per month for the loan. Later in 1785, John Adams inveighed against Massachusetts "shylockism," which he understood involved charging interest rates of 5 percent per month. David Ramsay to Benjamin Rush, July 21,

1785, *LDC*, 22:524; JA to Elbridge Gerry, December 13, 1785, FO, http://founders.archives.gov/documents/Adams/99-01-02-0428.

106. Joshua Johnson to Wallace and Muir, July 5, 1786, Joshua Johnson Papers, LOC (microfilm).

107. Collin McGregor to John McKenzie, March 6, 1787, Collin McGregor Letterbook, NYPL.

108. Thomas Jefferson (TJ) to Archibald Stuart, January 25, 1786, Papers of Archibald Stuart, VHS.

109. An insightful history of debt's evolving economic and cultural role is Mann, *Republic of Debtors.*

Chapter Two

1. JA to RK, June 14, 1786, in *The Life and Correspondence of Rufus King* (*LCRK*), 1:185.

2. Charles Thomson to John Dickinson, January 20, 1785, *LDC*, 22:124.

3. For general treatments of the issues in this chapter, see *Ferguson, Power of the Purse*; Jensen, *New Nation*; Morris, *Forging the Union*; Ritcheson, *Aftermath of Revolution.*

4. Harry Alonzo Cushing, ed., *Writings of Samuel Adams* (New York: G. P. Putnam's Sons, 1908), 4:304.

5. *JCC*, 24:282.

6. GW to Elisha Boudinot, May 10, 1783, FO, http://founders.archives.gov/documents/Washington/99-01-02-11240 (emphasis original).

7. *JCC*, 24:283.

8. Ibid.

9. Max M. Edling, "'So Immense a Power in the Affairs of War': Alexander Hamilton and the Restoration of Public Credit," *William and Mary Quarterly* 64, no. 2 (2007): 295.

10. GW to Joseph Reed, May 28, 1780, FO, http://founders.archives.gov/documents/Washington/99-01-02-01910.

11. Richard Henry Lee to the States, January 21, 1785, *LDC*, 22:125.

12. GW to TJ, May 2, 1788, quoted in Marks, *Independence on Trial*, 45.

13. Ferguson, "State Assumption of the Federal Debt," 404.

14. Roger Brown's data extending through March 1788 suggest that the states paid 37 percent of $13.7 million in requisitions, including indents. That would imply an estimated average annual deficit of $1.42 million. Roger H. Brown, *Redeeming the Republic: Federalists, Taxation, and the Origins of the Constitution* (Baltimore: Johns Hopkins University Press, 1993), 14, table I. Brown's data overstate state support for the Confederation during most of the postwar period, because

more than $1.3 million in indents appear to have been contributed by four states (Massachusetts, New York, Pennsylvania, and Virginia) between June 30, 1787, and March 1788 (i.e., 69.8 percent of the total indent amounts contributed, and more than 25 percent of total state contributions, during 1781–88). Those contributions all were made after the Philadelphia Convention began. These four states had paid only about 33 percent of the total amounts requisitioned from them as of June 30, 1787. Because of indents' small market value, these late contributions represented only a small fraction of their face value in actual monetary support. The result was that these states' payment records looked much better on paper than they would have otherwise, at a small cost to them. These late contributions do not change the fact that overall the states contributed about 31 percent of their requisition quotas between 1781 and mid-1787.

15. Board of Treasury Report, September 28, 1787, Henry Knox Papers (PHK), Gilder Lehrman Collection (GLC), NYHS, microfilm reel 21. This assumes total payments of $3.7 million in specie and "indents" (certificates of interest) by 450,000 free households. Compare Edwin J. Perkins, *American Public Finance and Financial Services, 1700–1815* (Columbus: Ohio State University Press, 1994), 189, table 9.1. Estimates of total payments are modified by removing contributions of $1.3 million in indents; see explanation in note 14 above.

16. Chapter 3 discusses the states' ability to raise tax revenues.

17. William Grayson to William Short, April 16, 1787, *LDC*, 24:266 (spelling modernized).

18. Robert R. Livingston to GW, April 9, 1783, FO, http://founders.archives.gov/documents/Washington/99-01-02-11029.

19. Charles Pinckney's speech to the New Jersey Assembly, March 13, 1786, *LDC*, 23:192.

20. Some historians claim that there was no agreement about whether the involuntary debts were Confederation, as opposed to state, debts. Ferguson, *Power of the Purse*, 179. That view is mistaken. Confederation officials who incurred them thought they had been incurred on its behalf, and expected it to repay them, not states. Those who loaned money to the Confederation—voluntarily or involuntarily—understood that it was indebted to them, and expected it to make repayment. Throughout the mid-1780s, Congress ratified these decisions and planned its finances accordingly.

War's necessities introduced some complications. The states assumed additional debts that might have been regarded as (or were) Confederation debts, in one case in 1780 because Congress requested that they do so, and in several others voluntarily. Such actions do not alter the basic fact that Congress had decided that the outstanding Confederation debt as of 1783 was its debt. Ferguson (ibid.,

125–76) views Congress's actions in maintaining and expanding the debt as part of a "counterrevolution in finance" engineered by power-hungry, aristocratic nationalists led by Robert Morris, the superintendent of finance, in 1782 and 1783. But after Morris resigned and his office was eliminated, Congress made no effort to change the debt's status.

21. For these claims, see Ferguson, *Power of the Purse*, 220, 236–37; Jensen, *New Nation*, 382–88. The Confederation's limited income other than that from loans or requisitions came from one-time asset sales of western lands.

22. February 15, 1786, *JCC*, 30:72, 73–75.

23. RK to Elbridge Gerry, June 18, 1786, *LCRK*, 1:137.

24. Arthur Lee to Elbridge Gerry, June 16, 1786, Elbridge Gerry Letters, MHS.

25. JM, "Vices of the Political System of the United States," April 1787, *PJM*, 9:345–58 (quotation at 348).

26. GW to Alexander Hamilton, March 4, 1783, *GW Writings*, 26:185–88; Jensen, *New Nation*, 67, 71; JM, Notes of debates, January 13, 1783, *JCC*, 25:851–53; *JCC*, 24:206–10, 286.

27. Washington had written to Congress that the 1780 ordinance's adoption was desperately needed to retain officers, who were threatening to leave in large numbers. It was generally thought that the army would collapse if that happened. GW to Samuel Huntington, President, Continental Congress, October 11, 1780, FO, http://founders.archives.gov/documents/Washington/99-01-02-03536; *JCC*, 18:958–62; Ferguson, *Power of the Purse*, 156.

28. Historians have been intrigued by attempts to influence the tax debate by manipulating the army's demands to strengthen the hand of other public creditors. That chain of events culminated in the so-called Newburgh conspiracy. Accounts include Morris, *Forging of the Union*, 43–50; Jensen, *New Nation*, 67–73; Ferguson, *Power of the Purse*, 155–71. Ferguson points particularly to signs of maneuvering surrounding the conspiracy as evidence that Congress was overwhelmed by combined army–public-creditor pressure. Public-creditor interests may have sought to take advantage of army pressure. JM, Notes of debates, March 17, 1783, *JCC*, 25:926. But the sources suggest that it is mistaken to think that in agreeing to commutation, Congress was overwhelmed by creditor or army pressure. The tax-powers question went to the heart of the Confederation's ability to pay its debts, and Congress had sought very similar powers as early as 1781. Washington resisted efforts by public-creditor interests to force the army into an alliance, warning that such efforts could easily backfire. GW to Alexander Hamilton, April 16, 1783, *GW Writings*, 26:323–25. Moreover, Charles Royster's analysis (*Revolutionary People at War*, 333–51) of commutation suggests that

Congress probably had little reason to be concerned about the army's threats, as officers and common soldiers were not united.

29. Samuel Holten to Benjamin Wadsworth, August 14, 1783, *LDC*, 19: 551–53.

30. Samuel Adams to Noah Webster, April 30, 1784, in Cushing, *Writings of Samuel Adams*, 4:304.

31. JM to Edmund Randolph, September 8, 1783, *LDC*, 20:629; Ferguson, *Papers of Robert Morris*, 7:412–13.

32. Conway, *War of American Independence*, 174–75.

33. Ibid., 175.

34. *JCC*, 24:146–48, 206–10.

35. *JCC*, 25:607–11.

36. See Main, *Antifederalists*, 74, 106–9 (quotations at 108–9; punctuation modified).

37. John K. Alexander, *Samuel Adams: The Life of an American Revolutionary* (Lanham, MD: Rowman and Littlefield, 2011), 270.

38. As one result, by mid-1784 Confederation commutation notes were selling for about 15 percent of their face value. Joseph Barrell to Samuel Blachley Webb, June 29, 1784, in *Correspondence and Journals of Samuel Blachley Webb*, ed. Worthington Chauncey Ford (New York [Lancaster, PA]: Wickersham Press, 1893), 3:39.

39. Oliver Ellsworth to Jonathan Trumbull, Sr., July 10, 1783, GBC, 178: 23–25.

40. *HFC*, 1:23; Baack, "Forging a Nation," 648–50.

41. Holton, *Unruly Americans*, 72.

42. Baack, "Forging a Nation," 639–40, 654.

43. Ferguson, *Power of the Purse*, 183.

44. Ephraim Paine to Robert R. Livingston, May 24, 1784, *LDC*, 21:640.

45. Ferguson, *Power of the Purse*, 223.

46. Board of Treasury Report, September 28, 1787, 2–3, PHK, microfilm reel 21.

47. Elbridge Gerry to JA, February 14, 1785, Elbridge Gerry Papers, MHS.

48. Jensen, *New Nation*, 400.

49. Charles Thomson to John Dickinson, January 20, 1785, *LDC*, 22:123.

50. Ferguson, *Papers of Robert Morris*, 6:55.

51. Ferguson, *Power of the Purse*, 234, 240–41. There is no factual basis for Ferguson's claim that Congress recommended this. See note 60 below.

52. For details on Pennsylvania paper money and other similar bargains, see chapter 7.

53. Ferguson, *Power of the Purse*, 243–44.

54. Ibid., 244.

55. For reactions to Rhode Island's policies, see chapter 7.

56. Main, *Antifederalists*, 84.

57. Henry Knox to James Swan, November 4, 1786, PHK, GLC02437.03326.

58. Ferguson, *Power of the Purse*, 223, 241.

59. It would also have created enormous potential for fraud and speculation.

60. Ferguson (*Power of the Purse*, 241) claims that Congress eventually agreed that the best solution to the Confederation's financial problems would be to divide up its debt among the states. He points to an August 16, 1786, report from a three-member committee advocating this approach, and says it was a "supremely practical" idea. Congress did not agree. It took no action on that report, and its actions were inconsistent with it. Even the August 1786 Grand Committee report that proposed various major amendments to the Articles, though never formally approved by Congress, fails to support Ferguson's claim. *JCC*, 31:494–98.

61. David Ramsay to Ralph Izard, December 1, 1785, *LDC*, 23:44 n. 2.

62. Ibid., 43. For Congress's hopes that western lands would pay Confederation debts, see William Ellery to Francis Dana, December 3, 1783, *LDC*, 21:177; Roger Sherman to William Williams, May 4, 1784, *LDC*, 21:581–82; and Elbridge Gerry to JA, July 14, 1785, Elbridge Gerry Papers, MHS.

63. Frederick Merk, *History of the Westward Movement* (New York: Knopf, 1978), 102–16; Ferguson, *Power of the Purse*, 238–39.

64. Jacob M. Price, *Capital and Credit in British Overseas Trade: The View from the Chesapeake, 1700–1776* (Cambridge, MA: Harvard University Press, 1980), 6.

65. Ibid., 7, 9, tables 1 and 2.

66. Secretary Jay to Congress, October 13, 1786, *JCC*, 31:797–99.

67. Price, *Capital and Credit*, 7, 9, tables 1 and 2.

68. For a description of various laws and British treaty charges, see *JCC*, 31:784–830.

69. Ibid.

70. George Mason to Patrick Henry, May 6, 1783, in William Wirt Henry, *Patrick Henry: Life, Correspondence and Speeches* (New York: Charles Scribner's Sons, 1891), 2:187.

71. Secretary Jay to Congress, October 13, 1786, *JCC*, 31:825–27.

72. Ritcheson, *Aftermath of Revolution*, 65–69.

73. Emory G. Evans, "Private Indebtedness and the Revolution in Virginia, 1776 to 1796," *William and Mary Quarterly* 28, no. 3 (1971): 349–74.

74. Morris, *Forging of the Union*, 143, 203–4. For the interconnected prob-

lems of Native American relations and the forts, see Samuel Flagg Bemis, *Jay's Treaty: A Study in Commerce and Diplomacy* (New York: Macmillan, 1923), 4–11.

75. Morris, *Forging of the Union*, 143, 203–4; *JCC*, 31:784–830.

Chapter Three

1. Oliver Ellsworth to Governor Trumbull, July 10, 1783, *HFC*, 1:324.

2. David Howell to Jabez Bowen, April 12, 1784, *LDC*, 21:514.

3. Conway, *War of American Independence*, 4–5.

4. Alvin Rabushka, *Taxation in Colonial America* (Princeton, NJ: Princeton University Press, 2008), 15, 796, 825, 863.

5. Conway, *War of American Independence*, 17.

6. Kulikoff, "Such Things Ought Not to Be," 149.

7. Griffin, *America's Revolution*, 209.

8. Roger H. Brown, *Redeeming the Republic*, 3–4, 53–138.

9. Ibid., 53–68 (quotation at 63). For another account of Pennsylvania tax resistance, see Bouton, *Taming Democracy*, 145–63.

10. Roger H. Brown, *Redeeming the Republic*, 34; Kulikoff, "Such Things Ought Not to Be," 149.

11. Roger H. Brown, *Redeeming the Republic*, 33–36.

12. The analysis in this paragraph assumes for conservatism that in 1783, there were about 451,000 free households, or 2.7 million free people, in the United States, and that population did not grow during these years. Requisition data are in chapter 2. The estimated free population is based on backcasting 1790 census data assuming a growth rate of 2 percent per year, while the number of free households estimated is consistent with Roger Brown's household sizes for different regions.

Lindert and Williamson's data suggest that a somewhat larger number of free households probably existed in 1783. See http://gpih.ucdavis.edu (subfile referred to as "American incomes 1774, full-time assumptions").

13. The diaries of Colonel Francis Taylor of Orange County, Virginia, contain various examples of cash transactions during the mid-1780s in which Taylor, a banker and money broker, loaned cash, or converted items such as military certificates to cash, to others for the purpose of paying taxes. Francis Taylor, Diary of Colonel Francis Taylor, microfilm M-665, SSC. The papers of international merchants such as Henry Drinker and Stephen Collins of Philadelphia, and John de Neufville and Sons, show that there were frequent complaints—usually made by debtors as an excuse for nonpayment—about the scarcity of money, particularly from debtors in certain parts of the country such as Virginia. But despite what those major merchants saw as unusually depressed conditions and high exchange

rates, their records show that cash was available and that bills of exchange could be purchased for a sufficiently high premium. See, for example, letter from Henry Drinker and a fellow trustee to Frederick Pigou (London), November 12, 1785, describing thousands of pounds of payments in bills of exchange expected to be made to Pigou by various debtors over the following months (Henry Drinker letterbook, vol. 18A, Henry Drinker Papers, HSP); letter documenting exchange of gold coins for £90 in New York currency and its conversion to Pennsylvania currency, from Pearsall and Glover, New York, to Stephen Collins, Philadelphia, December 10, 1783 (Stephen Collins Papers, LOC); letters documenting physical shipments together amounting to thousands of dollars in specie from the United States to England for conversion into hundreds of pounds worth of British sterling credits in London, (1) from Harrison [and] Ansley, London to Stephen Collins, January 4, 1786, and February 4, 1786; and (2) from Birkbeck & Blakes, London, to Stephen Collins, February 1, 1786 (Stephen Collins Papers, LOC); and letter documenting purchase of an £90 sterling bill of exchange, Gervais & Owen to John de Neufville, September 15, 1786, Papers of John de Neufville and Sons, LOC.

14. For recent data, see Lindert and Williamson, "American Incomes," 756.

15. Calculations shown are based on Virginia's estimated total population as of 1783, Virginia debts of £2 million to British creditors (converted to dollars at £1 = $4.40), and an estimated household size of 9.5 (following Roger H. Brown, *Redeeming the Republic*, 35, table 3 note). They are intended only as an approximation.

16. Lindert and Williamson, "American Incomes," 756.

17. Roger H. Brown, *Redeeming the Republic*, 128–31.

18. "Solicitor's Report of Delinquent Sheriffs," April 23, 1789, Virginia Executive Communications, Misc. microfilm reel 4918, LVA.

19. Kulikoff, "Such Things Ought Not to Be," 149–50.

20. Holton, *Unruly Americans*, 55–82, 85–95 passim.

21. Ibid., 66–71; Kulikoff, "Such Things Ought Not to Be," 150.

22. For a similar point regarding debt politics in New York, see Jackson T. Main, *Political Parties before the Constitution* (Chapel Hill: University of North Carolina Press, 1973), 134.

23. B. U. Ratchford, *American State Debts* (Durham, NC: Duke University Press, 1941), 45–46 (quotation at 46).

24. John P. Kaminski, *Paper Politics: The Northern State Loan-Offices during the Confederation, 1783–1790* (New York: Garland, 1989), 148.

25. Roger H. Brown, *Redeeming the Republic*, 258.

26. Tristram Dalton to JA, October 18, 1785, *PJA*, 17:520 (emphasis original).

27. JM, Notes of debates, January 27, 1783, *LDC*, 19:618.

28. James Sullivan to JA, October 10, 1785, *PJA*, 17:501.

29. Arthur Lee to Samuel Adams, January 29, 1783, *LDC*, 19:638–39.

30. Arthur Lee to Elbridge Gerry, June 16, 1786, Elbridge Gerry Letters, MHS.

31. If, as some federalists contended, Congress was properly regarded merely as an executive for the states, rather than as an independent legislative body, then the political issue was much the same as it had been in Britain's transformative struggle between Crown and Parliament. For a helpful discussion, see Jerrilyn Greene Marston, *King and Congress: The Transfer of Political Legitimacy, 1774–1776* (Princeton, NJ: Princeton University Press, 1987). Thanks to Peter Onuf for this reference.

32. David Howell to William Greene, February 5, 1784, *LDC*, 21:340.

33. Jonathan Arnold to Daniel Cahoon, December 7, 1782, *LDC* 19:463–64; David Howell to Theodore Foster, October 12, 1782, *LDC*, 19:253.

34. "Grotius," *Boston Gazette and Country Journal*, February 10, 1783.

35. "A.C.," *Salem Gazette*, February 13, 1783.

36. Samuel Osgood to JA, January 14, 1784, *LDC*, 21:277.

37. Samuel Osgood to Stephen Higginson, February 2, 1784, *LDC*, 21:326.

38. Jensen, *New Nation*, 409.

39. "A Farmer," *Boston Independent Chronicle and Universal Advertiser*, July 15, 1782.

40. "A Friend to Rhode Island and the Union," *Boston Independent Chronicle and Universal Advertiser*, January 16, 1783.

41. Charles Pinckney, speech to the New Jersey Assembly, March 13, 1786, *LDC*, 23:192.

42. Rhode Island delegates to William Greene, October 15, 1782, *LDC*, 19:265.

43. David Howell to Jabez Bowen, April 12, 1784, *LDC*, 21:515.

44. Samuel Wharton to John Cook, January 6, 1783, *LDC*, 19:551 (emphasis original).

45. JM, Notes of debates, December 24, 1782, *LDC*, 19:502.

46. GW to Benjamin Harrison, March 4, 1783, *GW Writings*, 26:184.

47. JM, Notes of debates, February 21, 1783, *LDC*, 19:720–22 (quotations at 721).

48. Samuel Wharton to John Cook, January 6, 1783, *LDC*, 19:550 (spelling modernized).

49. JM, Notes of debates, December 24, 1782, *LDC*, 19:502.

50. For sources regarding the so-called Newburgh conspiracy, which some

historians think demonstrates that the army and/or public creditors "strong-armed" Congress into adopting the 1783 tax proposals, see chapter 2, note 28, and Holton, *Unruly Americans*, 67–71. Carefully read, the Newburgh evidence does not show that Congress reached a different substantive decision than it would have otherwise due to pressure, though members certainly took the army's and creditors' views into account, as they had throughout the revolution.

51. Nathaniel Gorham to Caleb Davis, February 26, 1783, *LDC*, 19:736–37 (spelling modernized).

52. Robert Morris to Nicholas Van Dyke, February 22, 1783, Nicholas Van Dyke Papers, LOC.

53. For the text of the tax proposal, see *JCC*, 24:257–61.

54. Roger H. Brown, *Redeeming the Republic*, 143–44; Jensen, *New Nation*, 400; Ferguson, *Power of the Purse*, 223, 241–44.

55. Nevins, *American States*, 636.

56. JM, Notes of debates, January 28, 1783, *LDC*, 19:626.

57. Ibid., 627.

58. JM, Notes of debates, February 26, 1783, *LDC*, 19:738–43.

59. E.g., Tristram Dalton to Elbridge Gerry, April 13, 1784, Elbridge Gerry Papers, MHS.

60. JM, Notes of debates, February 26, 1783, *LDC*, 19:738–43.

61. JM, Notes of debates, January 28, 1783, *LDC*, 19:624.

62. JM, Notes of debates, January 27, 1783, *LDC*, 19:618–19.

63. Jensen, *New Nation*, 409.

64. JM, Notes of debates, January 28, 1783, *LDC*, 19:627–28.

65. *JCC*, 24:257–61.

66. For background, see Ferguson, *Power of the Purse*, 146, 166; Brown, *Redeeming the Republic*, 23–24.

67. *JCC*, 24:258–59.

68. *JCC*, 24:259. In an important concession to state concerns, both taxes were to be collected by individuals appointed by the states, but amenable to and removable by Congress. *JCC*, 24:258.

69. Nathan Dane to Caleb Davis, February 19, 1786, *LDC*, 23:155.

70. Stephen Higginson to Samuel Adams, June 10, 1783, Samuel Adams Papers, LOC (original at NYPL).

71. By 1786, eleven states had approved the new allocation formula, even though most rejected the supplemental tax itself.

72. JM, Notes of debates, February 26, 1783, *LDC*, 19:741 (abbreviation modified).

73. JM, Notes of debates, February 21, 1783, *LDC*, 19:723.

74. GW to Bushrod Washington, November 9, 1787, in *Papers of George Washington: Confederation Series* (*PGW*), 5:421–26.

75. Nathan Dane to Edward Pulling, January 8, 1786, *LDC*, 23:85.

76. GW to Reverend William Gordon, July 8, 1783, *GW Writings*, 26:49–52 (quotations at 52, 49).

77. GW to the States, June 8, 1783, *GW Writings*, 26:489.

78. David Howell to Thomas G. Hazard, August 26, 1783, *LDC*, 20:595; Stephen Higginson to Arthur Lee, January 27, 1784, in *Proceedings of the Massachusetts Historical Society*, 2nd ser. (Boston: Massachusetts Historical Society, 1894), 8:177–81.

79. David Howell to Thomas G. Hazard, August 26, 1783, *LDC*, 20:594.

80. Ibid. For Gerry's views, see Elbridge Gerry to John Adams, November 23, 1783, FO, http://founders.archives.gov/documents/Adams/06-15-02-0185.

81. David Howell to Jabez Bowen, April 12, 1784, *LDC*, 21:514.

82. Samuel Osgood to Stephen Higginson, February 2, 1784, *LDC*, 21:328.

83. Jensen, *New Nation*, 410.

84. Tristram Dalton to JA, June 16, 1784, *PJA*, 16:234.

85. Stephen Higginson to Elbridge Gerry, October 6, 1783, *LDC*, 21:25; Stephen Higginson to Theodorick Bland, October 6, 1783, *LDC*, 21:26 n. 1; James Warren to JA, January 28, 1785, *PJA*, 16:498–500.

86. Joseph L. Davis, *Sectionalism in American Politics, 1774–1787* (Madison: University of Wisconsin Press, 1977), 54.

87. See, e.g., Connecticut delegates to Jonathan Trumbull, Sr., September 2, 1783, *LDC*, 20:615–16.

88. Thomas C. Cochran, *New York in the Confederation: An Economic Study* (1932; repr., Port Washington, NY: Kennikat Press, 1970), 168–69.

89. Ferguson, *Power of the Purse*, 239–40.

90. Alexander Hamilton, "Remarks on an Act Granting to Congress Certain Imposts and Duties [15 February 1787]," FO, http://founders.archives.gov/documents/Hamilton/01-04-02-0030.

91. Cochran, *New York in the Confederation*, 187–88. Cochran calculates (167 n. 17) that over the four-year period, 51 percent of state revenues (exclusive of paper money) came from import taxes.

92. E. Wilder Spaulding, *New York in the Critical Period, 1783–1789* (New York: Columbia University Press, 1932), 153, 156–57, 173.

93. Cochran, *New York in the Confederation*, 170.

94. This account of the reception of Hamilton's speech relies on Nevins, *American States*, 289.

95. GW to the States, June 8, 1783, *GW Writings*, 26:489.

96. Oliver Ellsworth to Governor Trumbull, July 10, 1783, *HFC*, 1:324.

97. Richard Henry Lee to George Mason, May 15, 1787, in Ballagh, *Letters of Richard Henry Lee*, 2:421.

Chapter Four

1. *JCC*, April 30, 1784, 26:318–19.

2. Stephen Higginson to JA, August 8, 1785, FO, http://founders.archives.gov/documents/Adams/99-01-02-0168.

3. Kulikoff, "Such Things Ought Not to Be," 136–37; Lindert and Williamson, *Unequal Gains*, 77–95. Historians disagree somewhat about the overall importance of exports to the American prewar economy. Some think that they represented on average about 15–18 percent of total income; others think that they were less significant. See discussion in chapter 1, note 69.

4. Lindert and Williamson, "American Incomes," 753.

5. For the view that Americans agreed on the need for Confederation trade powers, see Morris, *Forging of the Union*, 151. For the view that state commerce regulations were effective, see Jensen, *New Nation*, 400. For other treatments of commercial issues during this period, see Cathy D. Matson and Peter S. Onuf, *A Union of Interests: Political and Economic Thought in Revolutionary America* (Lawrence: University Press of Kansas 1990), 67–81; Marks, *Independence on Trial*; Ritcheson, *Aftermath of Revolution*; and Joseph L. Davis, *Sectionalism in American Politics*.

6. On Confederation weakness and America's ability to make treaties, see Eliga Gould, *Among the Powers of the Earth: The American Revolution and the Making of a New World Empire* (Cambridge, MA: Harvard University Press, 2012), 126.

7. Adam Smith, *An Inquiry into the Nature and Causes of the Wealth of Nations*, ed. Edwin Cannan (1904; repr., Chicago: University of Chicago Press, 1976); Bemis, *Jay's Treaty*, 26–33.

8. Morris, *Forging of the Union*, 138–39.

9. Marks, *Independence on Trial*, 110.

10. Morris, *Forging of the Union*, 206–8; Marks, *Independence on Trial*, 89; *JCC*, February 28, 1786, 30:87–88.

11. John Quincy Adams, quoted in Marks, *Independence on Trial*, 115 n. 32.

12. Some historians have argued that the United States was able to replace its lost trade with Britain and other European powers by developing new markets. There is little direct evidence to support this claim, and depressed prices for major exports such as rice and tobacco strongly support the opposite conclusion.

13. Marks, *Independence on Trial*, 56. Some goods were still admitted, but excluded were major exports such as dairy products, fish, and cured meats.

14. John Francis Mercer to Henry Tazewell, September 13, 1783, *LDC*, 20:671; Morris, *Forging of the Union*, 137–39.

15. John Baker Holroyd (Earl of Sheffield), "Observations on the Commerce of the American States" (Philadelphia, 1783).

16. JM to Edmund Randolph, August 30, 1783, *LDC*, 20:607. Sheffield's analysis on credit turned out to be correct. Ritcheson, *Aftermath of Revolution*, 21.

17. JA to Robert R. Livingston, July 14, 1783, *PJA*, 15:111–14 (quotation at 111–12).

18. North Carolina Delegates to Alexander Martin, October 19, 1783, *LDC*, 21:75–76.

19. Stephen Conway, "Britain and the Revolutionary Crisis, 1763–1791," in *The Oxford History of the British Empire: The Eighteenth Century*, ed. P. J. Marshall (Oxford: Oxford University Press, 1998), 344.

20. JA to Jonathan Jackson, October 1, 1785, *PJA*, 17:485.

21. For information on the progress of domestic manufacturing, see Jensen, *New Nation*, 219–33, 282–301, and East, *Business Enterprise*. Increased manufacturing during this period changed neither British policy nor the massive trade deficits America ran with Britain (for the latter, see Morris, *Forging of the Union*, 132).

22. McDonald, *We the People*, 381–82; McCusker and Menard, *Economy of British North America*, 82–88, 108–11.

23. Jensen, *New Nation*, 198–99. Americans were permitted to export most goods to England itself on much the same terms as if they were still a colony. American goods had to be carried in British ships, but Jensen argues that they faced mostly nondiscriminatory duties and drawbacks (163). Another historian argues that despite that, important exports faced heavy, sometimes even prohibitive, duties, with damaging results. Marks, *Independence on Trial*, 58–63.

24. Marks, *Independence on Trial*, 56–58. For a view that substantial smuggling occurred, see Bjork, "Weaning of the American Economy," 551–53.

25. Stephen Higginson to JA, August 8, 1785, FO, http://founders.archives.gov/documents/Adams/06-17-02-0174.

26. Morris, *Forging of the Union*, 141.

27. Nettels, *Emergence of a National Economy*, 52.

28. Morris, *Forging of the Union*, 140, table.

29. West Indian exports to the United States also fell sharply. Selwyn H. H. Carrington, "The American Revolution and the British West Indies' Economy" in

British Capitalism and Caribbean Slavery: The Legacy of Eric Williams, ed. Stanley L. Engerman and Barbara L. Solow (1987; repr., Cambridge: Cambridge University Press, 2004), 156, tables 8 and 11.

30. Ralph Wormeley, Jr., to John Grymes, July 12, 1785, Ralph Wormeley Papers, SSC.

31. *Richmond Virginia Gazette and Weekly Advertiser*, August 13, 1785.

32. Henry Drinker to Frederick Pigou, November 12, 1785, Henry Drinker Letterbook, Henry Drinker Papers, HSP; Richard G. Miller, "The Federal City, 1783–1800," in *Philadelphia: A 300-Year History*, ed. Russell Frank Weigley, Nicholas B. Wainwright, and Edwin Wolf II (New York: Norton, 1982), 157.

33. Tristram Dalton to Elbridge Gerry, December 30 [20?], 1783, Elbridge Gerry Letters, MHS.

34. Joseph L. Davis, *Sectionalism in American Politics*, 85.

35. Richard Henry Lee to John Jay, September 11, 1785, in Ballagh, *Letters of Richard Henry Lee*, 2:389; James McHenry to GW, August 1, 1785, *PGW*, 3: 166–67.

36. Jensen, *New Nation*, 213, 282–85; Main, *Antifederalists*, 4–8, 271–74.

37. "Committee of Congress Report," September 25?, 1783, *LDC*, 20:701–2 (spelling modernized).

38. *JCC*, April 30, 1784, 26:321–22.

39. Ibid., 318–19.

40. McMaster, *History of the People of the United States*, 1:206–7.

41. Joseph L. Davis, *Sectionalism in American Politics*, 90.

42. Tristram Dalton to JA, December 21, 1784, *PJA*, 16:475.

43. Stephen Higginson to JA, August 8, 1785, FO, http://founders.archives.gov/documents/Adams/06-17-02-0174.

44. Nevins, *American States*, 642–44.

45. On discriminatory and protective duties, see Jensen, *New Nation*, 298–300; Marks, *Independence on Trial*, 80–83.

46. Nevins, *American States*, 558–63.

47. Morris, *Forging of the Union*, 233–34; Jensen, *New Nation*, 170–74.

48. Marks, *Independence on Trial*, 110–11 (quotation from Gerry letter to RK, March 1785, at 111); Morris, *Forging of the Union*, 146–48, 210–11.

49. Benjamin Franklin to Robert R. Livingston, July 22[–26], 1783, in *Papers of Benjamin Franklin*, ed. Ellen R. Cohn et al. (New Haven: Yale University Press, 2011), 40:369 (emphasis original).

50. Thomas Rodney's Diary, May 2, 1786, *LDC*, 23:256; Morris, *Forging of the Union*, 217–19; Jensen, *New Nation*, 211–13.

51. Committee report, March, 28, 1785, *JCC*, 28:201.

52. James Monroe to TJ, April 12, 1785, *LDC*, 22:326; James Monroe to TJ, June 16, 1785, *LDC*, 22:461.

53. *JCC*, 28:201–5.

54. James Monroe to JM, July 26, 1785, *HFC*, 1:446.

55. James Monroe to TJ, August 15, 1785, *LDC*, 22:562.

56. Samuel Bryan to George Bryan, May[?] 1785, George Bryan Papers, HSP.

57. Ibid.

58. Cochran, *New York in the Confederation*, 164–65.

59. General Assembly of New Jersey, "An Act to authorize the United States in Congress assembled to regulate foreign Trade," in *Acts of the Tenth General Assembly of the State of New Jersey . . .* (Trenton: Isaac Collins, 1785), 223–24 (chap. 109, November 26, 1785).

60. Jensen, *New Nation*, 290–92.

61. JA to John Jay, June 26, 1785, FO, http://founders.archives.gov/documents/Adams/06-17-02-0115.

62. Joseph L. Davis, *Sectionalism in American Politics*, 99–102; Ritcheson, *Aftermath of Revolution*, 23; Jensen, *New Nation*, 292–93.

63. James Bowdoin to Nicholas Van Dyke, July 10, 1786, Nicholas Van Dyke Papers, LOC.

64. Joseph L. Davis, *Sectionalism in American Politics*, 99.

65. Massachusetts Delegates to James Bowdoin, September 3, 1785, *LDC*, 22:610–11.

66. Ibid., 612, 613.

67. Samuel Adams wrote to Elbridge Gerry (September 19, 1785, *HFC*, 1:457) that a "general revision of the confederation appears to me to be a dangerous measure," but also expressed a desire for Confederation commerce powers.

68. RK to Nathan Dane, September 17, 1785, *LDC*, 22:635–37.

69. RK to Caleb Davis, November 3, 1785, *LDC*, 22:720.

70. See, for example, *Richmond Virginia Gazette and Weekly Advertiser*, August 13, 1785 (dateline New York, July 21).

71. RK to Daniel Kilham, July 25, 1785, *LDC*, 22:531.

72. RK to JA, November 2, 1785, *LDC*, 22:715 (emphasis original).

73. GW to James McHenry, August 22, 1785, *PGW*, 3:198–99.

74. McMaster, *History of the People of the United States*, 1:274–77.

75. George D. Harmon, "The Proposed Amendments to the Articles of Confederation," *South Atlantic Quarterly* 24 (October 1925): 430–32.

76. Ibid., 432.

77. JM to GW, December 9, 1785, *PGW*, 3:439–42 (quotation at 439).

78. Ibid., 439–40.

79. *Richmond Virginia Gazette and Weekly Advertiser*, August 13, 1785.

80. JM to James Monroe, March 19, 1786, FO, http://founders.archives.gov/documents/Madison/01-08-02-0269.

81. The convention ended September 14. The earliest Baltimore report of a court blockage by Massachusetts rebels occurred on September 15.

82. See, e.g., Matson and Onuf, *Union of Interests*, 80.

83. Ralph Ketcham, *James Madison: A Biography* (Charlottesville: University Press of Virginia, 1990), 185.

84. Louis-Guillaume Otto to Comte de Vergennes, October 10, 1786, *HFC*, 2:401.

85. Ketcham, *James Madison*, 185.

86. In August 1786, a committee of Congress had included a broad commerce-powers proposal similar to Monroe's as one of several proposed Articles amendments. However, supporters lacked the votes needed to actually propose these amendments to the states; Congress never acted on them.

87. Stephen Higginson to JA, July 1786, FO, http://founders.archives.gov/documents/Adams/99-01-02-0708.

88. RK to Jonathan Jackson, June 11, 1786, *LDC*, 23:352–53.

89. Theodore Sedgwick to Caleb Strong, August 6, 1786, *LDC*, 23:436.

90. Nathaniel Gorham to Caleb Davis, February 23, 1786, *LDC*, 23:161.

91. William Grayson to JM, May 28, 1786, *LDC*, 23:320.

92. JM to TJ, August 12, 1786, *PJM*, 9:96; see also JM to TJ, March 18, 1786, FO, http://founders.archives.gov/documents/Madison/01-08-02-0268.

93. Louis-Guillaume Otto to Comte de Vergennes, October 10, 1786, *HFC*, 2:400.

94. Ibid., 401.

95. *HFC*, 1:269–70.

Chapter Five

1. Arthur Lee to JA, March 6, 1785, *PJA*, 16:546.

2. RK to Elbridge Gerry, June 8, 1786, *LDC*, 23:340.

3. Louis-Guillaume Otto to Comte de Vergennes, in Paul G. Sifton, "Otto's *Memoire* to Vergennes, 1785," *William and Mary Quarterly*, 3rd ser., 22, no. 4 (1965): 641.

4. *Richmond Virginia Gazette or American Advertiser*, April 12, 1786 (same article, *Philadelphia Pennsylvania Packet*, March 28, 1786).

5. Saler, *Settlers' Empire*, 17.

6. Jensen, *New Nation*, 357.

7. Ferling, *Leap in the Dark*, 257.

8. Rosanna Wallace to Anne Fleming, October 23, 1784, Papers of William Fleming, LVA; Jensen, *New Nation*, 357; Ira Berlin, *Many Thousands Gone: The First Two Centuries of Slavery in North America* (Cambridge, MA: Harvard University Press, 1998), 369, table 1.

9. Richard Henry Lee to JM, November 20, 1784, *LDC*, 22:25; Annette Kolodny, ed., "The Travel Diary of Elizabeth House Trist: Philadelphia to Natchez, 1783–84," in *Journeys in New Worlds: Early American Women's Narratives*, ed. William L. Andrews (Madison: University of Wisconsin Press, 1990), 226; Merk, *History of the Westward Movement*, 118–25.

10. Thomas Pickering to RK, June 4, 1785, *LCRK*, 1:107.

11. "Extract of a letter from General Irvine to the Secy. at War," in JM to Benjamin Harrison, November 15, 1782, *LDC*, 19:391.

12. Josiah Harmar to John Dickinson, February 8, 1785, in Samuel Hazard, ed., *Pennsylvania Archives* (Philadelphia: Joseph Severns and Co., 1854), 10:406.

13. Ray Allen Billington, *Westward Expansion: A History of the American Frontier*, 3rd ed. (New York: Macmillan, 1967), 210.

14. Leonard J. Sadosky, *Revolutionary Negotiations: Indians, Empires and Diplomats in the Founding of America* (Charlottesville: University of Virginia Press, 2009), 129.

15. Merk, *History of the Westward Movement*, 92; Griffin, *America's Revolution*, 186–90.

16. Recent accounts of the postwar conflict between Native Americans and white settlers include Kathleen DuVal, *Independence Lost: Lives on the Edge of the American Revolution* (New York: Random House, 2015); Sadosky, *Revolutionary Negotiations*; William H. Bergmann, *The American National State and the Early West* (Cambridge: Cambridge University Press, 2012); and Saler, *Settler's Empire*.

17. *JCC*, September 22, 1783, 25:602.

18. Virginia Delegates to Benjamin Harrison, September 8, 1783, *LDC*, 20:643.

19. Ibid., 644.

20. Ibid.

21. GW quoted in Samuel Holten to Aaron Wood, September 11, 1783, *LDC*, 20:650.

22. DuVal, *Independence Lost*, 250–53 (quotation at 252).

23. Billington, *Westward Expansion*, 200.

24. For an incisive account of the Virginia cession, see Peter S. Onuf, *The Origins of the Federal Republic* (Philadelphia: University of Pennsylvania Press, 1983), 87–102.

25. New York Delegates to George Clinton, September 19, 1783, *LDC*, 20:691.

26. John Francis Mercer to Henry Tazewell, September 13, 1783, *LDC*, 20:671.

27. Jensen, *New Nation*, 352–54.

28. *JCC*, July 27, 1787, 33:427–30.

29. The text of the ordinance is in *JCC*, April 23, 1784, 26:275–79.

30. For seminal works on the creation of the national domain, state formation, and Confederation western-development policy and their influence on American constitutional history, see Onuf, *Federal Republic*, and his *Statehood and Union: A History of the Northwest Ordinance* (Bloomington: Indiana University Press, 1987).

31. Onuf, *Statehood and Union*, 46–49.

32. Ibid., 49–52; Jensen, *New Nation*, 354; Billington, *Westward Expansion*, 216.

33. Edward Bancroft to William Frazer, May 28, 1784, *HFC*, 1:368.

34. Caroline County petition, November 16, 1784, LVA, Legislative Petitions Digital Collection, http://www.virginiamemory.com/collections/petitions.

35. Arthur Lee to John Adams, March 6, 1785, *PJA*, 16:546.

36. Ibid.

37. For an account of Washington's tour, see John Ferling, *The Ascent of George Washington: The Hidden Political Genius of an American Icon* (New York: Bloomsbury Press, 2009), 248–51; GW to Thomas Smith, December 7, 1785, *PGW*, 3:438–39.

38. Ferling, *Ascent of Washington*, 250–55 (quotation at 250).

39. GW to Benjamin Harrison, October 10, 1784, *PGW*, 2:86–98 (quotation at 92).

40. Ibid., 93.

41. GW to Richard Henry Lee, August 22, 1785, *PGW*, 3:196; GW to Samuel Purviance, Jr., March 10, 1786, *PGW*, 3:594.

42. For discussion of these conflicts, see Morris, *Forging of the Union*, 224–26; Jensen, *New Nation*, 331–37; Onuf, *Federal Republic*, 8–10, 58–71.

43. Morris, *Forging of the Union*, 187–89.

44. Sadosky, *Revolutionary Negotiations*, 137.

45. Billington, *Westward Expansion*, 211; Morris, *Forging of the Union*, 188.

46. Papers of William Fleming, LVA (spelling modernized). Fleming was a convention delegate.

47. Joseph Martin to Patrick Henry, March 26, 1785, in Henry, *Patrick Henry*, 3:282–84.

48. Jensen, *New Nation*, 357.

49. Bergmann, *American National State*, 27–29.

50. William Grayson to GW, April 15, 1785, *PGW*, 2:500–501.

51. GW to William Grayson, April 25, 1785, *PGW*, 2:520.

52. Billington, *Westward Expansion*, 209.

53. Jensen, *New Nation*, 354–57.

54. Robert Ernst, *Rufus King: American Federalist* (Chapel Hill: University of North Carolina Press, 1968), 55.

55. The leading history of the 1787 Northwest Ordinance passed by Congress in July, 1787, which established territorial government for that area, is Onuf, *Statehood and Union*.

56. William Irvine to John Dickinson, May 25, 1785, John Dickinson Papers, Library Company of Philadelphia.

57. James Wilkinson to John Dickinson, August 11, 1785, John Dickinson Papers, Library Company of Philadelphia.

58. Billington, *Westward Expansion*, 212.

59. Merk, *History of the Westward Movement*, 102–16.

60. Arthur St. Clair's speech, August 18, 1786, *LDC*, 23:493.

61. Arthur St. Clair, Notes of debates [August 18, 1786], *LDC*, 23:490.

62. Samuel Meredith to Thomas Fitzsimons, November 26, 1786, *LDC*, 24:34.

63. DuVal, *Independence Lost*, 256.

64. Ibid., 24–25, 28–29, 33, 82–90, 257. McGillivray himself became a slave-plantation owner after the war. Ibid., 248–49.

65. Ibid., 258.

66. Ibid., 258–59.

67. Ibid., 311.

68. Ibid., 312.

69. Griffin, *America's Revolution*, 184. Like McGillivray, Brant owned household slaves and farmed using slaves as well. See Benjamin J. Drew, *A north-side view of slavery. The refugee: or, The narratives of fugitive slaves in Canada. Related by themselves, with an account of the history and condition of the colored population of Upper Canada* (Boston: J. P. Jewett and Co., 1856), 192–95.

70. Daniel K. Richter, "Native Peoples of North America and the Eighteenth-Century British Empire," in *The Oxford History of the British Empire: The Eighteenth Century*, ed. P. J. Marshall (Oxford: Oxford University Press, 1998), 368.

71. Merk, *History of the Westward Movement*, 143.

72. See Lawrence B. A. Hatter, "Channeling the Spirit of Enterprise: Commercial Interests and State Formation in the Early American West, 1763–1825" (Ph.D. diss., University of Virginia, 2011), 42–43.

73. Alan Taylor, "Divided Ground: Upper Canada, New York, and the Iroquois Six Nations, 1783–1815," *Journal of the Early Republic* 22, no. 1 (2002): 61.

74. Ibid., 58–59; Billington, *Westward Expansion*, 221. For a general account of British policy toward Native Americans and forts, see Ritcheson, *Aftermath of Revolution*, 165–71.

75. Josiah Harmar to Henry Knox, May 7, 1786 (spelling modernized), Alfred T. Goodman Papers, Western Reserve Historical Society History Library (original), http://wardepartmentpapers.org/document.php?id=1471 (image).

76. Harmar had held that view for some time. As early as 1785, he had written Secretary of War Knox that the Indians would not take treaties seriously as long as Britain kept its posts. Alan S. Brown, "The Role of the Army in Western Settlement: Josiah Harmar's Command, 1785–1790," *Pennsylvania Magazine of History and Biography* 93, no. 2 (1969): 166 n. 19.

77. Patrick Henry to the Virginia Delegates in Congress, April 16, 1785, in Henry, *Patrick Henry*, 3:293.

78. Patrick Henry to Colonel Joseph Martin, in ibid., 295.

79. "Colonel William Christian," in Charles M. Meacham, *A History of Christian County Kentucky*, http://www.westernkyhistory.org/christian/meacham/p1chap1.html; "Colonel William Christian," http://www.kentuckygenealogy.org/christian/colonel_william_christian.htm.

80. Diary of Colonel Francis Taylor, May 9, 1786, SSC.

81. DuVal, *Independence Lost*, 298–304.

82. Henry, *Patrick Henry*, 2:286.

83. Patrick Henry to the Virginia Delegates in Congress, May 16, 1786, in ibid., 3:350–52.

84. Patrick Henry to the President of Congress, May 16, 1786, in ibid., 353.

85. Ibid., 353–54.

86. William Grayson to JM, May 28, 1786, *LDC*, 23:321; *JCC*, 30:373.

87. James Manning to Jabez Bowen, June 9, 1786, *LDC*, 23:344.

88. RK to Elbridge Gerry, June 8, 1786, *LDC*, 23:340.

89. *JCC*, 30:374–75.

90. *JCC*, 30:376–77.

91. *JCC*, 30:381.

92. Charles Pettit to James Wilson, July 2, 1786, *LDC*, 23:381.

93. Patrick Henry to the Virginia Delegates in Congress, July 5, 1786, in Henry, *Patrick Henry*, 3:363–64.

94. Ibid.

95. Ibid., 365–66.

96. Virginia Delegates to Patrick Henry, July 17, 1786, *LDC*, 23:407.

97. Josiah Harmar to Henry Knox, August 10, 1786, Western Reserve Historical Society History Library, Alfred T. Goodman Papers (original), http://wardepartmentpapers.org/document.php?id=1769 (image).

98. *JCC*, 31:656–58, 662.

99. Merk, *History of the Westward Movement*, 102–5.

100. *Richmond Virginia Independent Chronicle*, October 11, 1786 (dateline Philadelphia September 28).

101. Josiah Harmar to Henry Knox, October 10, 1786, http://wardepartmentpapers.org/document.php?id=1936.

102. RK to James Bowdoin, October 19 [i.e., 20], 1786, *LDC*, 23:606.

103. RK to Elbridge Gerry, October 19, 1786, *LCRK*, 1:191.

104. RK to James Bowdoin, October 19 [i.e., 20], 1786, *LDC*, 23:606 (spelling modernized).

105. RK to Elbridge Gerry, October 19, 1786, *LCRK*, 1:191.

106. Lee signed his name Henry Lee, Jr., but is sometimes referred to as Henry Lee III. Known popularly as "Light-Horse Harry Lee," he was a first cousin once removed of Richard Henry Lee, with whom he is sometimes confused.

107. *JCC*, October 30, 1786, 31:917.

108. Ibid.; Alan S. Brown, "Role of the Army in Western Settlement," 166 n. 19.

109. Virginia Delegates to Edmund Randolph, December 24, 1786, *LDC*, 24:56.

110. Josiah Harmar to Henry Knox, May 14, 1787, Western Reserve Historical Society History Library, Alfred T. Goodman Papers (original), http://wardepartmentpapers.org/document.php?id=2401 (image).

111. Billington, *Westward Expansion*, 211.

Chapter Six

1. JM to TJ, August 12, 1786, FO, http://founders.archives.gov/documents/Madison/01-09-02-0026.

2. Charles Thomson's Notes of Debates, August 18, 1786, *LDC*, 23:495–98 (quotation at 496).

3. Theodore Sedgwick to Caleb Strong, August 6, 1786, *LDC*, 23:436.

4. Arthur P. Whitaker, *The Spanish-American Frontier, 1783–1795: The Westward Movement and the Spanish Retreat in the Mississippi Valley* (Boston: Houghton Mifflin, 1927), 63–67 (quotation at 67); Marks, *Independence on Trial*, 24–35. Other accounts of the Spanish-treaty issue include Morris, *Forging of the Union*, 232–44; Jensen, *New Nation*, 170–73; Joseph L. Davis, *Sectionalism in American Politics*, chaps. 7 and 8, esp. 118–26; Calvin Jillson and Rick K. Wilson, *Congres-*

sional Dynamics: Structure, Coordination and Choice in the First American Congress, 1774–1789 (Stanford, CA: Stanford University Press, 1994), 267–73; Samuel Flagg Bemis, *Pinckney's Treaty: America's Advantage from Europe's Distress, 1783–1800* (New Haven, CT: Yale University Press, 1960), 37–108. The spelling of "Mississippi" has been conformed throughout.

5. Kathleen DuVal, "Independent for Whom? Expansion and Conflict in the South and Southwest," in *The World of the Revolutionary American Republic: Land, Labor, and the Conflict for a Continent*, ed. Andrew Shankman (New York: Routledge, 2014), 100.

6. Whitaker, *Spanish-American Frontier*, 64–74; Bemis, *Pinckney's Treaty*, 12.

7. JM to TJ, August 20, 1784, FO, http://founders.archives.gov/documents/Madison/01-08-02-0058.

8. Richard Henry Lee thought optimistically that Spain's position was a bargaining stance that concealed its true diplomatic objectives. Richard Henry Lee to Patrick Henry, February, 14, 1785, in Ballagh, *Letters of Richard Henry Lee*, 2:332.

9. Merrill Jensen et al., eds., *The Documentary History of the Ratification of the Constitution*, 27 vols. to date (Madison: State Historical Society of Wisconsin, 1976–2015; *DHRC*), 13:149.

10. *JCC*, August 25, 1785, 29:658.

11. Bemis, *Pinckney's Treaty*, 24.

12. Jensen, *New Nation*, 170.

13. Bemis, *Pinckney's Treaty*, 24.

14. Ibid., 24, 62.

15. Ibid., 62; Marks, *Independence on Trial*, 26–27; Charles Pinckney's Speech, August 10, 1786, *LDC*, 23:449–52.

16. Bemis, *Pinckney's Treaty*, 62; Marks, *Independence on Trial*, 27–28.

17. Monroe to JM, May 31, 1786, FO, http://founders.archives.gov/documents/Madison/01-09-02-0014.

18. Morris, *Forging of the Union*, 239–40.

19. RK to Elbridge Gerry, June 4, 1786, *LDC*, 23:331–34 (quotations at 331–32).

20. Ibid., 332–33.

21. James Monroe to JM, May 31, 1786, FO, http://founders.archives.gov/documents/Madison/01-09-02-0014.

22. JM to Monroe, June 21, 1786, *PJM*, 9:82.

23. Ibid., 83.

24. Henry Lee, Jr., to GW, April 21, 1786, *PGW*, 4:25–26.

25. GW to Henry Lee, Jr., June 18, 1786, *PGW*, 4:117–18 (emphasis original; angle brackets in source).

26. Henry Lee, Jr., to GW, July 2, 1786, *LDC*, 23:382. It is uncertain how much Lee's views were influenced by the fact that Gardoqui lent him $5,000. Marks, *Independence on Trial*, 27. Lee later told Washington (August 7, 1786, *LDC*, 23:438) that he thought the treaty would cause more political trouble for the Confederation than it was worth.

27. "Fabius," *Charleston Columbian Herald*, April 6, 1786.

28. Nevins, *American States*, 346.

29. Marks, *Independence on Trial*, 24. By early 1787, Spanish vessels trading with Vincennes had been intercepted by settlers who announced that they would block Spanish trade if Spain blocked their trade.

30. *JCC*, August 3, 1786, 31:467–84.

31. Louis-Guillaume Otto to Comte de Vergennes, September 10, 1786, *HFC*, 2:391.

32. *JCC*, August 3, 1786, 31:481.

33. Ibid., 467–484.

34. Ibid., 481.

35. Marks, *Independence on Trial*, 25, quoting Samuel Hardy to Patrick Henry, December 5, 1784, *LDC*, 22:50.

36. James Monroe to JM, May 31, 1786, FO, http://founders.archives.gov/documents/Madison/01-09-02-0014.

37. TJ to Archibald Stuart, January 25, 1786, Archibald Stuart Papers, VHS.

38. Henry Lee, Jr., to GW, August 7, 1786, *LDC*, 23:438.

39. Bemis, *Pinckney's Treaty*, 87–88; Charles Pinckney's Speech, [August 10, 1786], *LDC*, 23:446–58.

40. Charles Thomson's Notes of Debates, August 16, 1786, *LDC*, 23:486 (first quotation); August 18, 1786, *LDC*, 23:495–98 (quotation at 496).

41. Charles Thomson, Notes of debates, August 16, 1786, *LDC*, 23:486.

42. Charles Thomson, Notes of debates, August 18, 1786, *LDC*, 23:495–98 (quotation at 496); Arthur St. Clair, Notes of debates, [August 18, 1786], *LDC*, 23:490.

43. Charles Thomson, Notes of debates, August 18, 1786, *LDC*, 23:495–98.

44. Arthur St. Clair, Notes of debates, August 18, 1786, *LDC*, 23:490.

45. Henry Lee, Jr., to GW, October 11, 1786, *LDC*, 23:591.

46. RK to Jonathan Jackson, September 3, 1786, *LDC*, 23:542.

47. James Monroe to TJ, August 19, 1786, *LDC*, 23:498; October 12, 1786, *LDC*, 23:596.

48. Louis-Guillaume Otto to Comte de Vergennes, August 23, 1786, *HFC*, 2:384–86.

49. Jillson and Wilson, *First American Congress*, 270–73.

50. James Monroe to Patrick Henry, August 12, 1786, *LDC*, 23:462–66 (quotation at 465).

51. Louis-Guillaume Otto to Comte de Vergennes, September 10, 1786, *HFC*, 2:392.

52. Robert Abraham East, "The Massachusetts Conservatives in the Critical Period" in *The Era of the American Revolution*, ed. Richard B. Morris (New York: Columbia University Press, 1939), 372–74.

53. Theodore Sedgwick to Caleb Strong, August 6, 1786, *LDC*, 23:436.

54. James Monroe to JM, September 3, 1786, FO, http://founders.archives.gov/documents/Madison/01-09-02-0036 (abbreviation spelled out).

55. For contemporary thought on separate confederations, see Matson and Onuf, *Union of Interests*, 83–86, 89.

56. Timothy Bloodworth to Richard Caswell, September 29, 1786, *LDC*, 23:573.

57. Nevins, *American States*, 346.

58. *JCC*, 32:197–99.

59. Ibid.

60. Josiah Harmar to Henry Knox, May 14, 1787, Alfred T. Goodman Papers, Western Reserve Historical Society Library (original), http://wardepartmentpapers.org/document.php?id=2401 (image).

61. "Extract of a letter from Davidson County . . . ," *Alexandria Virginia Journal and Alexandria Advertiser*, February 15, 1787.

62. Nevins, *American States*, 567.

63. Thomas Fitzsimons to General Samuel Meredith, March 10, 1787, Clymer-Meredith-Read Family papers, NYPL. Nevins (*American States*, 568) thinks that Pennsylvania adopted instructions against the treaty, but as Fitzsimons's letter shows, that is mistaken. Madison's correspondence also indicates that the legislature did not take a position. See also *DHRC*, 13:150–51.

64. Timothy Bloodworth to Richard Caswell, September 29, 1786, *LDC*, 23:573; JM to Monroe, October 5, 1786, *PJM*, 9:140.

65. JM to GW, December 7, 1786, *PGW*, 4:448.

66. Thomas A. Bailey, *A Diplomatic History of the American People*, 8th ed. (New York: Meredith Corp., Appleton Century Crofts, 1969), 62.

67. Nevins, *American States*, 346–47.

68. Ibid., 347.

69. JM to TJ, March 19, 1787, *LDC*, 24:151–55.

70. JM to GW, December 7, 1786, *PGW*, 4:448 (abbreviation spelled out).

71. William Grayson to JM, November 22, 1786, *LDC*, 24:31.

72. Samuel Meredith to Thomas Fitzsimons, November 26, 1786, *LDC*, 24:36 (reporting conversation with RK).

73. JM, Notes of debates, March 29, 1787, *LDC*, 24:181.

74. Cabinet of Versailles to Louis-Guillaume Otto, August 30, 1787, *HFC*, 2:438–39.

75. *JCC*, April 13, 1787, 32:184–204.

76. JM, Notes of debates, April 18, 1787, *LDC*, 24:237–38; April 23, 1787, *LDC*, 24:248.

77. JM, Notes of debates, April 26, 1787, *LDC*, 24:260.

78. *JCC*, July 4, 1787, 32:299–300.

79. Nathan Dane to RK, July 5, 1787, *LDC*, 24:347–48.

80. John Brown to James Breckenridge, January 28, 1788, *LDC*, 24:630 (spelling modernized; punctuation added to printed text based on review of original in Papers of James Breckenridge, SSC).

81. As discussed in an earlier work, the Philadelphia Convention finessed the sectional impasse on the treaty by making a "western bargain" embodied in Congress's adoption of the Northwest Ordinance of 1787 while the Convention was meeting. George William Van Cleve, *A Slaveholders' Union: Slavery, Politics, and the Constitution in the Early Republic* (Chicago: University of Chicago Press, 2010), 158–66. In his leading history of the constitutional convention, Richard Beeman agrees with that conclusion. See Richard Beeman, *Plain, Honest Men: The Making of the American Constitution* (New York: Random House, 2009), 217. For further detail, see the conclusion to this book.

Chapter Seven

1. Robert A. Becker, "Salus Populi Suprema Lex: Public Peace and South Carolina Debtor Relief Laws, 1783–1788," *South Carolina Historical Magazine* 80, no. 1 (1979): 74.

2. JM to TJ, August 12, 1786, *PJM*, 9:95.

3. American colonies in the eighteenth century issued several forms of paper money, a process then commonly called emitting bills of credit. There were two major types of emission. The first involved bills of credit that today might be called "tax anticipation notes," a form of government borrowing referred to by some later historians as "currency finance." Such bills circulated as a form of money. The second type was a "loan office" (or "land-banking") program. In such programs, bills of credit issued by a colony were appropriated for use by its government loan office, which used them to fund loans to borrowers. The bills were

then useable as currency. For details see George William Van Cleve, "The Anti-Federalists' Toughest Challenge: Paper Money, Debt Relief, and the Ratification of the Constitution," *Journal of the Early Republic* 34, no. 4 (2014): 534.

Despite their name, bills of credit actually were government-debt instruments, just as US Treasury notes and bills today are. They were promises that the government would give a specified amount of credit to the holder of the bill against debts, such as taxes, owed to it. But they were transferable, so they could be used as currency. Merchants also issued private payment notes, usually called bills of exchange, and these circulated as an important form of currency.

4. Economic relief accounts include Jensen, *New Nation*, 316–26; Morris, *Forging of the Union*, 154–59; Perkins, *American Public Finance*, 143–86; Holton, *Unruly Americans*, 96–123 passim. For Virginia debtor protection, see Evans, "Private Indebtedness and the Revolution in Virginia," 349–74. For Massachusetts, see also Roger H. Brown, *Redeeming the Republic*, 113–19. The symbol "£" in this chapter means pound, but refers only to whichever state's currency is being discussed; i.e., £1,000 in a discussion of South Carolina means 1,000 South Carolina pounds, not 1,000 British pounds sterling, unless otherwise stated.

5. Morris, *Forging of the Union*, 260.

6. McGuire, "Founding Era," 61; Kulikoff, "Such Things Ought Not to Be," 139–40.

7. Charles W. Calomiris, "Institutional Failure, Monetary Scarcity, and the Depreciation of the Continental," *Journal of Economic History* 48 (March 1988): 64. Others attribute it to the rise of private banking: Robert E. Wright, *The Origins of Commercial Banking in America, 1750–1800* (Lanham, MD: Rowman and Littlefield, 2001), 85–86.

8. This is a very rough order-of-magnitude estimate, since issues that were made in state currencies of differing values are being combined here without first being separately converted to equivalents such as dollars. However, the order-of-magnitude estimate is conservative because it assumes that each state's emission (in state pounds) was instead an issue of the same number of British pounds sterling and then it employs a widely used conversion rate (£1 = $4.44; see Lindert and Williamson, "American Incomes," 742) to estimate a dollar value for all of them in total.

9. Kulikoff, "Such Things Ought Not to Be," 139–40, 149. Total 1785–86 emissions, if on the order of £1 million British pounds sterling equivalent, would have been less than 10 percent of state emissions in 1779 alone. Ibid. On the size of the economy, see Lindert and Williamson, "American Incomes," 743–45.

10. GW to Thomas Stone, February 16, 1787, *PGW*, 5:38; JM to TJ, August 12, 1786, *PJM*, 9:95.

11. JM to TJ, March 18, 1786, *PJM*, 8:502.

12. Holton, *Unruly Americans*, 110–12.

13. GW to Thomas Stone, February 16, 1787, *PGW*, 5:38.

14. Holton, *Unruly Americans*, 58.

15. William Grayson to JM, March 22, 1786, *LDC*, 23:204.

16. Calomiris, "Institutional Failure," 50–51.

17. Ibid., 63.

18. Richard P. McCormick, *Experiment in Independence: New Jersey in the Critical Period, 1781–1789* (New Brunswick, NJ: Rutgers University Press, 1950), 71.

19. Holton, *Unruly Americans*, 59.

20. Ibid., 59. Henry Laurens to Henry Blundell, July 4, 1785, in *The Papers of Henry Laurens*, ed. David R. Chesnutt and C. James Taylor (Columbia: University of South Carolina Press, 2003), 16:574. In the 1780s, "legal tender" usually meant that paper money could be used to pay at the money's face value (as opposed to its market value) either a public or private debt, without a creditor's consent (usually instead of payment in specie, i.e., gold or silver). When paper money was not made "legal tender," it could usually be used to pay public debts such as taxes, but private creditors could not be forced to accept it at face value, at least where a contract called for payment in specie.

21. Campbell County, Virginia petition, October 30, 1786, LVA, http://www.virginiamemory.com/collections/petitions.

22. "Willing to Learn," *Elizabeth Town Political Intelligencer and New-Jersey Advertiser*, December 21, 1785.

23. Holton, *Unruly Americans*, 60–64.

24. On Massachusetts, see Roger H. Brown, *Redeeming the Republic*, 113–19; Perkins, *American Public Finance*, chap. 8.

25. Main, *Political Parties*, table 12.6, votes 4–6, 336–38 (surveying four to six states' votes).

26. In the mid-1780s, four states—New Jersey, Georgia, Rhode Island, and North Carolina—granted full legal-tender status to their paper money. In other issuing states, state money could be tendered only for public debts; in New York, though, paper money could also be tendered if suit was brought to force payment of a private debt. Jensen, *New Nation*, 316–26.

27. For debtor-creditor conflicts, see Main, *Political Parties*, 60–66.

28. Becker, "Salus Populi," 68–69.

29. Ibid., 70; Jensen, *New Nation*, 318. Economic historians draw a distinction between the use of money as a medium of exchange and its use as a unit of account during this period, but for this chapter's purposes that distinction may

be disregarded. See Ronald W. Michener and Robert E. Wright, "State 'Currencies' and the Transition to the U.S. Dollar: Clarifying Some Confusions," *American Economic Review* 95, no. 3 (2005): 685–86.

30. Perkins, *American Public Finance*, 163.

31. *Charleston Columbian Herald*, September 28, 1785.

32. *Newport Mercury*, February 26, 1785.

33. *Charleston State Gazette of South-Carolina*, April 3, May 1, May 4, June 26, June 29, August 10, August 14, September 11, and December 14, 1786; *Charleston Columbian Herald*, February 2, 1786.

34. Holton, *Unruly Americans*, 113; McDonald, *We the People*, 388; Edward Carrington to James Mercer, September 1, 1786, *LDC*, 23:538; South Carolina Delegates to William Moultrie, September 15, 1786, *LDC*, 23:560; Gervais & Owen to John de Neufville, August 8, 1786, and September 15, 1786, Papers of John de Neufville and Sons, LOC; John Owen to Henry Laurens, September 1, 1786, in Chesnutt and Taylor, *Papers of Henry Laurens*, 16:671. There are conflicting reports, for example, JM to TJ, August 12, 1786, *PJM*, 9:94, but reports of actual transactions such as those cited here are more reliable.

35. Nevins, *American States*, 525; Becker, "Salus Populi," 67–72.

36. Becker, "Salus Populi," 70; Perkins, *American Public Finance*, 162; Nevins, *American States*, 526. Originally, the law allowed a creditor to accept state paper money instead. In 1786, creditors lost that right and were compelled to accept appraised property. Nevins, *American States*, 526.

37. Henry Laurens to Bourdieu, Chollet & Bourdieu, October 20, 1785, in Chesnutt and Taylor, *Papers of Henry Laurens*, 16:601 (capitalization modernized).

38. Becker, "Salus Populi," 71.

39. Louis-Guillaume Otto to Comte de Vergennes, March 17, 1786, *HFC*, 1:488.

40. Gervais & Owen to John de Neufville, August 8, 1786, Papers of John de Neufville and Sons, LOC.

41. Henry Laurens to Bridgen & Waller, January 4, 1787, in Chesnutt and Taylor, *Papers of Henry Laurens*, 16:678 (spelling modernized).

42. Becker, "Salus Populi," 74; Walter B. Edgar, *South Carolina: A History* (Columbia: University of South Carolina Press, 1998), 247.

43. "Curtius," *Elizabeth Town Political Intelligencer and New-Jersey Advertiser*, January 4, 1786.

44. Georgia's legislature was sharply divided over the paper-money emission. The money was theoretically secured by projected sales of lands still held by Indians; that security was worthless unless the state captured those lands. Many Savannah merchants and mechanics agreed among themselves not to

accept the paper money despite its legal-tender status. Kenneth Coleman, *The American Revolution in Georgia, 1763–1789* (Athens: University of Georgia Press, 1958), 214; George R. Lamplugh, *Politics on the Periphery: Factions and Parties in Georgia, 1783–1806* (Newark: University of Delaware, 1986), 54; Jensen, *New Nation*, 323.

45. Jensen, *New Nation*, 319–20. North Carolina merchants refused to take the paper money; some even developed their own currency. Merchant resistance was so strong that sometimes use of paper money by those regarded as "evil-minded" persons led to "broken heads." James R. Morrill, *The Practice and Problems of Fiat Finance: North Carolina in the Confederation, 1783–1789* (Chapel Hill: University of North Carolina Press, 1969), 68–69; JM to TJ, August 12, 1786, *PJM*, 9:94.

46. For a detailed history of paper-money controversies in these states, see Kaminski, *Paper Politics*. For this coalition analysis, I am indebted to Perkins, *American Public Finance*, 144.

47. Bouton, *Taming Democracy*, 91–92; Robert L. Brunhouse, *The Counter-Revolution in Pennsylvania, 1776–1790* (1942; repr., Harrisburg: Pennsylvania Historical Commission, 1971), 131–32, 151.

48. Perkins, *American Public Finance*, 144; Arthur Pendleton Hall II, "State-Issued Bills of Credit and the United States Constitution: The Political Economy of Paper Money in Maryland, New York, Pennsylvania, and South Carolina, 1780–1789" (Ph.D. diss., University of Georgia, 1991), 75–76.

49. *Philadelphia Evening Herald*, March 5, 1785.

50. Ferguson, *Power of the Purse*, 229.

51. Holton, *Unruly Americans*, 71.

52. Brunhouse, *Counter-Revolution in Pennsylvania*, 170–71 (quotation at 170). Brunhouse argues that various legislators were also financially interested in the legislation, as does Forrest McDonald, *E Pluribus Unum*, 95–99. But McDonald's account suggests that other motives played an important role as well.

53. Holton, *Unruly Americans*, 88–91 passim.

54. See McDonald, *E Pluribus Unum*, 95–99; Perkins, *American Public Finance*, 146–47.

55. Roland M. Baumann, "'Heads I Win, Tails You Lose': The Public Creditors and the Assumption Issue in Pennsylvania, 1790–1802," *Pennsylvania History* 44 (July 1977): 198. Merchants prominently opposed the bill. *Philadelphia Pennsylvania Packet and Daily Advertiser*, February 24, 1785; March 1, 1785.

56. Pennsylvania General Assembly, *Minutes of the Second Session of the Ninth General Assembly* (Philadelphia, 1785), 195–206, 213.

57. Ibid.; Bouton, *Taming Democracy*, 135–36.

58. RK to Elbridge Gerry, June 8, 1786, *LDC*, 23:341; Michener and Wright, "State 'Currencies,'" 688–89; Nevins, *American States*, 522.

59. McDonald, *E Pluribus Unum*, 77.

60. Morris, *Forging of the Union*, 155; Perkins, *American Public Finance*, 120.

61. Main, *Antifederalists*, 44–45 (quotations at 45).

62. For the debate and William Findley's role in it in the context of evolving ideas about interestedness and civic virtue, see Gordon S. Wood, "Interests and Disinterestedness in the Making of the Constitution," in *Beyond Confederation: Origins of the Constitution and American National Identity*, ed. Richard Beeman, Stephen Botein, and Edward C. Carter II (Chapel Hill: University of North Carolina Press), 69–109.

63. Pennsylvania General Assembly, *Debates and Proceedings . . . on the . . . Charter of the Bank* (Philadelphia, 1786), 22, 66. Some Pennsylvanians apparently wanted private banks banned. Main, *Antifederalists*, 46.

64. Pennsylvania General Assembly, *Minutes of the Second Session*, 204, 212, 367.

65. Thomas Paine to Thomas Fitzsimons, April 19, 1785, repr., *Philadelphia Pennsylvania Packet*, December 17, 1785.

66. Thomas Paine, *Dissertations on Government, the Affairs of the Bank, and Paper-Money* (Philadelphia: Charles Cist, 1786), 7–9, 45, 46–48 (quotations at 8, 46). Background: Eric Foner, *Tom Paine and Revolutionary America* (1976; updated ed., Oxford: Oxford University Press, 2005), 197–203.

67. Paine's paper-money attack: e.g., New York Packet, March 6, 1786; Boston Massachusetts Centinel, March 15, 1786; and May 24, 1786; Charleston State Gazette of South-Carolina, April 3, 1786; New Haven Connecticut Journal, April 20, 1786; Providence (RI) United States Chronicle, May 18, 1786; Portsmouth New Hampshire Gazette and General Advertiser, June 8, 1786.

68. Response to Paine: *Elizabethtown Political Intelligencer and New-Jersey Advertiser*, May 3, 1786. Paine was charged with having been paid for his attack, an allegation he vigorously denied and for which no substantial evidence has ever been offered. See Paine's letter to the *Philadelphia Pennsylvania Packet*, April 4, 1786.

69. *Philadelphia Independent Gazetteer*, November 27, 1786, quoted in M. L. Bradbury, "Legal Privilege and the Bank of North America," *Pennsylvania Magazine of History and Biography* 96 (April 1972): 164; Janet Wilson, "The Bank of North America and Pennsylvania Politics, 1781–1787," *Pennsylvania Magazine of History and Biography* 66 (January 1942): 26.

70. Spaulding, *New York in the Critical Period*, 145.

71. Ibid., 144–48; Arthur Pendleton Hall II, "State-Issued Bills," 192.

72. Kaminski, *Paper Politics*, 149; Spaulding, *New York in the Critical Period*, 148; *Journal of the Assembly of the State of New-York . . . Eighth Session* (New York, 1785), 145.

73. "Memorial and Petition of the Corporation of the Chamber of Commerce," *New York Packet*, March 6, 1786; *Journal of the Assembly of the State of New-York . . . Ninth Session* (New York, 1786), 53–54, 57–58, 68; Arthur Pendleton Hall II, "State-Issued Bills," 196–97.

74. McDonald, *E Pluribus Unum*, 112; Kaminski, *Paper Politics*, 148.

75. Kaminski, *Paper Politics*, 148.

76. Holton, *Unruly Americans*, 113.

77. Paterson and the anonymous writer are quoted in McCormick, *Experiment in Independence*, 71, 73, respectively (quotation emphasis original).

78. Ruth Bogin, "New Jersey's True Policy: The Radical Republican Vision of Abraham Clark," *William and Mary Quarterly* 35 (January 1978): 100–109 (quotation at 106).

79. "Willing to Learn," December 21, 1785, *Elizabethtown Political Intelligencer and New-Jersey Advertiser*; "Curtius," ibid., January 4, 1786; Jensen, *New Nation*, 322.

80. William Grayson to JM, March 22, 1786, *PJM*, 8:509; New Jersey General Assembly, *Votes and Proceedings of the Tenth General Assembly of the State of New-Jersey . . . Second Sitting* (Trenton, 1786), 80, 82, 83; McCormick, *Experiment in Independence*, 200–202.

81. Nevins, *American States*, 522–23.

82. McCormick, *Experiment in Independence*, 212; Perkins, *American Public Finance*, 153; Ferguson, "State Assumption of the Federal Debt," 403–24.

83. Nevins, *American States*, 570 (capitalization modernized).

84. Kaminski, *Paper Politics*, 125; Michener and Wright, "State 'Currencies,'" 689 n. 13.

85. Irwin H. Polishook, *Rhode Island and the Union, 1774–1795* (Evanston, IL: Northwestern University Press, 1969), 124–26.

86. Jonathan M. Chu, *Stumbling toward the Constitution: The Economic Consequences of Freedom in the Atlantic World* (New York: Palgrave Macmillan, 2012), 119.

87. Pauline Maier, *Ratification: The People Debate the Constitution, 1787–1788* (New York: Simon and Schuster, 2010), 224; Mary M. Schweitzer, "State-Issued Currency and the Ratification of the U.S. Constitution," *Journal of Economic History* 49 (June 1989): 318; Ferguson, *Power of the Purse*, 243; *Boston Independent Chronicle and the Universal Advertiser*, July 27, 1786; Jensen, *New Nation*, 324; Polishook, *Rhode Island and the Union*, 127, 132–33, 145–47, 154–61.

88. *Philadelphia Pennsylvania Packet*, July 20, 1786 (dateline Providence, July 6).

89. Chu, *Stumbling toward the Constitution*, 120 (emphasis original).

90. *Alexandria (VA) Journal*, September 7, 1786.

91. Jensen, *New Nation*, 324.

92. Hugh Williamson to James Iredell, July 7, 1788, in Griffith J. McRee, *Life and Correspondence of James Iredell* (New York: D. Appleton and Co., 1858), 2:227.

93. JM to TJ, August 12, 1786, *PJM*, 9:95.

94. *Newport Herald*, April 12, 1787, *DHRC*, 13:80.

95. *DHRC*, 13:80 n. 1 (Dana letter); Richard Dobbs Spaight to James Iredell, July 2, 1787, in McRee, *Iredell*, 162; *Boston Massachusetts Gazette*, May 29, 1786; *New-Haven Gazette and Connecticut Magazine*, June 1, 1786, 122; Henry Knox to Marquis de Lafayette, April 26, 1788, PHK, microfilm reel 22 (original GLC02437.03860); Richard Price to Benjamin Rush, January 26, 1787, *DHRC*, 13:101.

96. William Grayson to JM, May 28, 1786, *LDC*, 23:320.

97. The Confederation refused to accept state paper money as payment under Confederation requisitions, but that had little practical impact since states could simply ignore them.

98. See Louis-Guillaume Otto to Comte de Vergennes, June 17, 1786, *HFC*, 1:511.

99. Holton, *Unruly Americans*, 145–61.

100. Ibid., 149–50.

Chapter Eight

1. "A Freeman," *Worcester Magazine* 2, no. 28 (1786): 337 (punctuation modernized).

2. AA to Mary Smith Cranch, February 25, 1787, *Adams Family Correspondence* (*AFC*), 7:470 (spelling modernized).

3. Benjamin Lincoln to RK, February 11, 1786, *LCRK*, 1:156–60 (quotation at 157).

4. Some historians call the popular actions "the Regulation," the rebels' preferred term. I use as its equivalents either "rebels" or "insurgents," terms commonly used by contemporaries.

5. General accounts of Shays's Rebellion include David P. Szatmary, *Shays' Rebellion: The Making of an Agrarian Insurrection* (Amherst: University of Massachusetts Press, 1980); Richards, *Shays's Rebellion*; Richard B. Morris, "Insurrection in Massachusetts," in *America in Crisis*, ed. Daniel Aaron (New York: Knopf, 1952), 21–49; Robert A. Feer, *Shays's Rebellion* (New York: Garland, 1988);

Robert A. Gross, "A Yankee Rebellion? The Regulators, New England, and the New Nation," *New England Quarterly* 82, no. 1 (2009); Joseph Parker Warren, "The Shays Rebellion: A Study in the History of Massachusetts" (Ph.D. diss., Harvard University, 1900); Roger H. Brown, *Redeeming the Republic*, 97–121. A recent narrative account is Sean Condon, *Shays's Rebellion: Authority and Distress in Post-revolutionary America* (Baltimore: Johns Hopkins University Press, 2015). Michael Klarman (*Framers' Coup*, 74) claims that "Shays's Rebellion, together with the tax and debt relief measures enacted in most states during the 1780s, played a critical role in both the calling of the Constitutional Convention and the drafting of the Constitution itself."

6. Theodore Sedgwick to Pamela Dwight Sedgwick, June 24, 1786, *LDC*, 23:372.

7. RK to Elbridge Gerry, April 30, 1786, *LCRK*, 1:134.

8. John Jay to GW, June 27, 1786, *PGW*, 4:130–32.

9. GW to John Jay, August 15, 1786, *PGW*, 4:212–13.

10. Ibid.

11. Nevins, *American States*, 534.

12. Holton, *Unruly Americans*, 29.

13. John Lathrop to Richard Price, March 1786, in Richard Price, *Letters to and from Richard Price, D.D., F.R.S., 1767–1790* (Cambridge, MA: John Wilson and Son, University Press, 1903), 78.

14. Main, *Antifederalists*, 57.

15. Ibid., 58.

16. Ibid.

17. Feer, *Shays's Rebellion*, 46.

18. Reprinted in *Worcester Magazine*, September 1786.

19. Szatmary, *Shays' Rebellion*, 36.

20. Mary Smith Cranch to AA, September 24, 1786, *AFC*, 7:342 (spelling modernized).

21. Kulikoff, "Such Things Ought Not to Be," 149–50.

22. Morris, *Forging of the Union*, 259.

23. Roger H. Brown, *Redeeming the Republic*, 103–4.

24. Claire Priest, "Colonial Courts and Secured Credit: Early American Commercial Litigation and Shays' Rebellion," *Yale Law Journal* 108, no. 8 (1999): 2417.

25. Main, *Antifederalists*, 59.

26. Acts of Massachusetts 1785, chap. 74 (March 23, 1786), in *Acts and Laws of the Commonwealth of Massachusetts* (Boston: Wright and Potter, 1890–98), 3:580.

27. Perkins, *American Public Finance*, 179–86.

28. Szatmary, *Shays' Rebellion*, 66.

29. Ibid.

30. Richards, *Shays's Rebellion*, 58–63.

31. Ibid., 58–80; Perkins, *American Public Finance*, 179–86; Holton, *Unruly Americans*, 74–77; Winifred B. Rothenberg, "The Invention of American Capitalism: The Economy of New England in the Federal Period," in *Engines of Enterprise: An Economic History of New England*, ed. Peter Temin (Cambridge, MA: Harvard University Press, 2000), 72–73. Thanks to Professor Rothenberg for this reference.

32. Ferguson, *Power of the Purse*, 247.

33. That was Henry Knox's view, for example. As chapter 2 shows, many Massachusetts citizens should have been capable of paying taxes. However, in depressed conditions, many western farmers there might not have been able to do so without severe hardship, particularly if they had private debts as well.

34. Main, *Antifederalists*, 59. State senate seats were allocated geographically based on property taxes paid, biasing representation in favor of wealthy eastern areas of the state. Senators also needed to own significant amounts of property to be eligible to serve. East, "Massachusetts Conservatives," 362.

35. August 29 is the date most often used as the insurgency's beginning. See, e.g., Szatmary, *Shays' Rebellion*, 58–59.

36. Joseph Parker Warren, "Shays Rebellion," 108–18. Note to readers on page references to Warren dissertation: Warren's handwritten dissertation (referred to here and in subsequent notes as Joseph Parker Warren, "Shays Rebellion,") contains 242 sequentially numbered pages, followed by two separately paginated chapters (4 and 5) and several appendices. Citations to Warren dissertation page numbers in notes not accompanied by a chapter number are citations to the first sequence of pages; citations that include a chapter number and page number refer to one of the separately paginated chapters; and citations to appendix I (Park Holland narrative), which is unpaginated, give no page numbers.

37. Morris, "Insurrection in Massachusetts," 28–30.

38. The American Peace Commissioners to Elias Boudinot, September 10, 1783, FO, http://founders.archives.gov/documents/Franklin/01-40-02-0380.

39. Samuel Adams to Noah Webster, April 30, 1784, in Cushing, *Writings of Samuel Adams*, 4:305.

40. Samuel Adams to JA, April 6, 1784, *PJA*, 16:164.

41. RK to Daniel Kilham, November 19 1786, *LDC*, 24:30 (spelling modernized).

42. TJ to JM, January 30, 1787, *PJM*, 9:247.

43. "A Freeman," *Worcester Magazine* 2, no. 28 (1786): 338 (punctuation and spelling modernized).

44. Charles Pettit to the President of Pennsylvania, October 18, 1786, *LDC*, 23:604.

45. Edward Carrington to Edmund Randolph, December 8, 1786, *LDC*, 24:43.

46. JM, Notes of debates, February 19, 1787, *PJM*, 9:276.

47. Joseph Parker Warren, "Shays Rebellion," 166–67.

48. Van Beck Hall, *Politics without Parties: Massachusetts, 1780–1791* (Pittsburgh, PA: University of Pittsburgh Press, 1972), 218–19.

49. Joseph Parker Warren, "The Confederation and the Shays Rebellion," *American Historical Review* 11, no. 1 (1905): 44.

50. Massachusetts leaders did not want it publicly known that its congressional delegates had sought Confederation military protection. Knox had also received reports of hostilities being planned by western Indian tribes. Congress's authorization of the added troops was designated publicly as being for that purpose.

51. Joseph Parker Warren, "Shays Rebellion," chap. 5, 73.

52. Feer, *Shays's Rebellion*, 321; Joseph Parker Warren, "Shays Rebellion," 183.

53. Nathaniel Gorham to Henry Knox, December 13, 1786, PHK, microfilm reel 19, GLC02437.03377.

54. Joseph Parker Warren, "Shays Rebellion," 190.

55. Nevins, *American States*, 536.

56. Richard D. Brown, "Shays's Rebellion and the Ratification of the Federal Constitution in Massachusetts," in *Beyond Confederation: Origins of the Constitution and American National Identity*, ed. Richard Beeman, Stephen Botein, and Edward C. Carter II (Chapel Hill: University of North Carolina Press, 1987), 115.

57. Holland was one of General Lincoln's troops who arrived at the arsenal shortly after Shays' forces fled.

58. Joseph Parker Warren, "Shays Rebellion," appendix I (unpaginated).

59. Ibid., 210–11. Historian Richard Morris ("Insurrection in Massachusetts," 44) agreed with Shepard's views.

60. Feer, *Shays's Rebellion*, 412–14, 420, 425–26.

61. AA to Mary Smith Cranch, February 25, 1787, *AFC*, 7:470 (spelling modernized).

62. Van Beck Hall, *Politics without Parties*, 257.

63. AA to Cotton Tufts (letter and draft), October 10, 1786, *AFC*, 7:360, 364 (spelling modernized).

64. RK to JA, October 3, 1786, *LDC*, 23:580. There were rumors that the insurgents had or sought some connection with Britain, but historians doubt such claims. Neither Congress nor Massachusetts formally investigated them to my knowledge.

65. Theodore Sedgwick to RK, June 18, 1787, *LCRK*, 1:224.

66. Stephen Higginson to Nathan Dane, March 3, 1787, in American Historical Association, *Annual Report for the Year 1896* (Washington, DC: Government Printing Office, 1897), 1:754.

67. Stephen Higginson to Henry Knox, November 25, 1786, ibid., 743.

68. AA to Mary Smith Cranch, February 25, 1787, *AFC*, 7:472 (emphasis original; spelling modernized).

69. RK to Elbridge Gerry, September 17, 1786, *LDC*, 23:563 (emphasis original).

70. Rufus King's Address [to Massachusetts legislature], October 11, 1786, *LDC*, 23:587–90.

71. RK to Theodore Sedgwick, October 22, 1786, *LDC*, 23:612.

72. RK to Daniel Kilham, October 29, 1786, *LDC*, 23:620.

73. RK to Elbridge Gerry, February 18, 1787, *LCRK*, 1:215.

74. Nathaniel Bishop to Caleb Davis, May 24, 1787, Caleb Davis Papers, box 12, MHS.

75. Edward Carrington to Edmund Randolph, December 8, 1786, *LDC*, 24:42.

76. Marks, *Independence on Trial*, 139.

77. Stephen Higginson to Henry Knox, February 13, 1787, PHK, microfilm reel 19, GLC02437.03452.

78. Stephen Higginson to Henry Knox, January 20, 1787, PHK, microfilm reel 19, GLC02437.03418.

79. Henry Knox to Stephen Higginson, February 25, 1787, PHK, microfilm reel 19, GLC02437.03468.

80. Gross, "Yankee Rebellion?," makes the contrary case.

81. See, e.g., Morris, *Forging of the Union*, 264–66. Michael Klarman (*Framers' Coup*, 88) claims that "altogether, during the 1780s, scores of western counties across half a dozen states endured taxpayer and debtor revolts that temporarily closed courts." That claim implicitly acknowledges that in a majority of states, courts were continuously open after the war. Moreover, in most other states to which Klarman refers, courts were actually open during most of that period as well, because temporary court closings in parts of those states were just that—temporary.

82. Szatmary, *Shays' Rebellion*, 77.

83. JM to James Madison, Sr., February 25, 1787, *LDC*, 24:118–19.

84. Szatmary, *Shays' Rebellion*, 127.

85. Ibid., 78–79.

86. Ibid., 78.

87. Jensen, *New Nation*, 249.

88. Terry Bouton (*Taming Democracy*, 160–63) reports that the main York incident involved roughly two hundred men. Perhaps later incidents there involved additional people. What seems clear is that armed violence was very limited in Pennsylvania, though there were various incidents of intimidation and popular "no bid" pacts, etc., regarding taxes. Ibid., 145–63.

89. Szatmary, *Shays' Rebellion*, 126.

90. Ibid., 124–25.

91. Edmund Pendleton to JM, August 12, 1787, *PJM*, 17:518; Holton, *Unruly Americans*, 146. Though Pendleton's letter reports that the King William courthouse was burned as well, that seems to have been a mistake on his part. See John Dawson to James Madison, June 12, 1787, FO, http://founders.archives.gov/documents/Madison/01-10-02-0028, n. 5.

92. Holton, *Unruly Americans*, 12.

93. *Richmond Virginia Gazette and Weekly Advertiser*, September 20, 1787.

94. Council of Virginia, August 20, 1787, Misc. microfilm reel 5375, LVA.

95. Holton, *Unruly Americans*, 11–13, 145–52.

96. For Henry's reaction, see Richard R. Beeman, *Patrick Henry: A Biography* (New York: McGraw-Hill, 1974), 137.

97. TJ to AA, February 22, 1787, in *The Adams-Jefferson Letters*, ed. Lester J. Cappon (Chapel Hill: University of North Carolina Press, 1959), 173.

98. TJ to JM, January 30, 1787, FO, http://founders.archives.gov/documents/Madison/01-09-02-0126.

99. GW to JM, November 5, 1786, quoting Henry Knox, *PGW*, 4:332.

100. Henry Lee, Jr., to JM, October 19, 1786, *PJM*, 9:144.

101. Ibid., 9:144–45 n. 3.

102. Jensen, *New Nation*, 250.

103. GW to David Humphreys, October 22, 1786, *PGW*, 4:297.

104. Henry Knox to GW, October 23, 1786, *PGW*, 4:300.

105. Henry Lee, Jr., to JM, October 19, 1786, *PJM*, 9:144.

106. GW to Henry Lee, Jr., October 31, 1786, *PGW*, 4:319.

107. GW to Society of the Cincinnati, October 31, 1786, *PGW*, 4:316.

108. GW to JM, November 18, 1786, *PGW*, 4:382.

109. GW to Henry Knox, December 26, 1786, *PGW*, 4:332.

110. GW to JM, November 5, 1786, *PGW*, 4:482.

111. GW to Henry Knox, February 25, 1787, *PGW*, 5:52.

112. GW to Marquis de Lafayette, March 25, 1787, *PGW*, 5:106.

Chapter Nine

1. *The Statutes at Large: Being a Collection of All the Laws of Virginia, from the First Session of the Legislature in the Year 1619*, ed. William Waller Hening (Richmond: George Cochran, 1823), 12:256.

2. JM to TJ, December 4, 1786, *PJM*, 9:189. Printed versions say that Madison wrote "affected," not "effected"; review of the manuscript image online supports the reading here.

3. *JCC*, February 15, 1786, 30:75.

4. *JCC*, February 15, 1786, 30:72, 75; Henry Lee, Jr., to JM, February 16, 1786, *LDC*, 23:152.

5. Arthur Lee to Samuel Adams, February 14, 1786, Samuel Adams Papers, LOC (original at NYPL).

6. *JCC*, June 27, 1786, 30:366 (letter of June 22, 1786).

7. Ferguson, *Power of the Purse*, 239–40.

8. Ibid.

9. James Monroe to JM, September 12, 1786, *PJM*, 9:122–23.

10. JM to Edmund Pendleton, February 24, 1787, *PJM*, 9:295.

11. RK to Elbridge Gerry, April 30, 1786, *LCRK*, 1:134.

12. RK to Elbridge Gerry, May 5, 1786, *LDC*, 23:269.

13. AA to Charles Storer, May 22, 1786, *AFC*, 7:187–90 (spelling modernized).

14. James Manning to John Collins, May 26, 1786, *LDC*, 23:311.

15. RK to James Bowdoin, October 19 [i.e., 20], 1786, *LDC*, 23:606; RK to Elbridge Gerry, October 19, 1786, *LCRK*, 1:191.

16. Thomas Rodney's Diary, May 3, 1786, *LDC*, 23:262–63.

17. JM to James Monroe, May 13, 1786, *PJM*, 9:55.

18. JM to James Monroe, March 19, 1786, *PJM*, 8:504–6.

19. JM to TJ, August 12, 1786, *PJM*, 9:96–97 (italics indicating words in code omitted).

20. JA to Cotton Tufts, July 4, 1786, *AFC*, 7:241–42.

21. JM to James Monroe, October 5, 1786, *PJM*, 9:141.

22. *JCC*, August 7, 1786, 31:494–98.

23. Marks, *Independence on Trial*, 129; Jillson and Wilson, *First American Congress*, 156, table 5.2.

24. For the authoritative account of the Philadelphia Convention of 1787, see Beeman, *Plain Honest Men*. However, for issues concerning Madison's in-

volvement and its possible influence on the historical record, see also Mary Sarah Bilder, *Madison's Hand: Revising the Constitutional Convention* (Cambridge, MA: Harvard University Press, 2016).

25. "Bill Providing for Delegates to the Convention of 1787," *PJM*, 9:163–64 (JM draft of resolution text showing amendments).

26. Edmund Pendleton to JM, December 9, 1786, *PJM*, 9:201–4.

27. George Muter to JM, February 20, 1787, *PJM*, 9:281 (spelling modernized).

28. Ibid., 280–81.

29. This account relies heavily on the excellent treatment of the British debts issue in Jackson T. Main, "Sections and Politics in Virginia, 1781–1787," *William and Mary Quarterly*, 3rd ser., 12, no. 1 (1955): 103–4 passim.

30. *Journal of the Virginia House of Delegates*, November 1787, http://hdl.handle.net/2027/hvd.32044015536139, 51–52.

31. Main, *Antifederalists*, 32–33. Henry later managed to gain approval of a compromise that permitted British debt repayment, but only if Britain cured its treaty violations by giving up the forts, etc. The earlier vote was nevertheless strong evidence of sharply shifting western sentiment.

32. George Muter to JM, February 20, 1787, *PJM*, 9:281–82.

33. JM to GW, March 18, 1787, *LDC*, 24:150.

34. Edward Carrington to JM, December 18, 1786, *LDC*, 24:53–54.

35. Ibid. (spelling modernized).

36. See Dane remarks to Massachusetts legislature, November 9, 1786, *LDC*, 24:20.

37. East, "Massachusetts Conservatives," 349–91. The conservatives were a coalition whose members had more diverse opinions on key issues than East claims.

38. Nathaniel Gorham to Henry Knox, February 18, 1787, PHK, 19:172 (microfilm ed.), original at GLC02437.03460.

39. Elbridge Gerry to James Monroe, June 11, 1787 (emphasis original), Elbridge Gerry Letters, MHS (original at James Monroe Papers, LOC).

40. Stephen Higginson to Henry Knox, February 8, 1787, American Historical Association, *Annual Report for the Year 1896*, 1:745.

41. RK to Elbridge Gerry, February 11, 1787, *LDC*, 24:91 (spelling modernized).

42. Nathaniel Gorham to Henry Knox, February 18, 1787, PHK, 19:172 (microfilm ed.); original at GLC02437.03460.

43. Massachusetts General Court, "Resolution Authorizing the Appointment of Delegates and Providing Instructions for Them, 22 February," *DHRC*,

1:205; Papers of Samuel Adams, LOC (original at NYPL). The language of the third paragraph of the February 22 resolution is ambiguous. Its explicit requirement that Massachusetts's "commissioners" should "by no means" "interfere with the fifth of the articles of the Confederation" could have been intended to prohibit the Massachusetts Philadelphia Convention delegates only from agreeing to alter certain parts of Article 5 concerning the annual election, recall, term limits, and plural office-holding of delegates to Congress. Even if interpreted in that narrower manner, however, that paragraph's provision alone would have created major obstacles to reaching an agreement at the Philadelphia Convention. Among other things, it would have prevented the creation of a senate with six-year terms, or even a house of representatives with two-year terms.

44. *Boston American Herald*, March 5, 1787.

45. Ibid.

46. *Boston Massachusetts Centinel*, March 7, 1787; *Charlestown (MA) American Recorder and Charlestown Advertiser*, March 9, 1787.

47. Massachusetts House of Representatives, "House Resolution of 7 March Repealing the Resolution of 22 February," *DHRC*, 1:207–8.

48. Ibid., 205.

49. Philip Schuyler to Henry Van Schaack, March 13, 1787, in Henry C. Van Schaack, *Memoirs of the Life of Henry Van Shaack* . . . (Chicago: A. C. McClurg and Co., 1892), 150–51.

50. *Journal of the Senate of the State of New York*, 10th session (New York: Samuel and John Loudon, 1789), 35.

51. Cochran, *New York in the Confederation*, 179. Some historians think that Clinton's forces overreached by defeating the impost, but that seems unlikely. Nevins, *American States*, 289.

52. *Journal of the Senate of the State of New York*, 10th session, 35.

53. JM, Notes on Debates, February 21, 1787, *PJM*, 9:291; *JCC*, 32:72–74.

54. JM, Notes of debates, February 21, 1787, *PJM*, 9:291.

55. William Irvine to James Wilson, March 6, 1787, *LDC*, 24:129.

56. *HFC*, 1:274; *Journal of the Senate of the State of New York*, 10th session, 45.

57. Philip Schuyler to Henry Van Schaack, March 13, 1787, in Van Schaack, *Memoirs*, 151.

58. Alexander Hamilton had attacked at length the view held by many New York legislators that the New York constitution barred the grant of impost tax (or any other tax) powers to the Confederation during debate just days earlier. The assembly rejected his position, ultimately voting 36–21 against granting such powers. Alexander Hamilton, "Remarks on an Act Granting to Congress Cer-

tain Imposts and Duties," [15 February 1787], FO, http://founders.archives.gov/documents/Hamilton/01-04-02-0030.

59. Philip Schuyler to Henry Van Schaack, March 13, 1787, in Van Schaack, *Memoirs*, 151.

60. Ibid., 154.

61. Treasury of the United States, Register's Office, "Schedule of Requisitions on the several States by the United States in Congress assembled . . . shewing . . . the Amount paid thereon, and the Balances due 30th June 1787," September 25, 1787, PHK, reel 21 (microfilm ed.); Roger H. Brown, *Redeeming the Republic*, 14.

62. *Boston Massachusetts Centinel*, March 28, 1787.

63. Maier, *Ratification*, 224; Jürgen Heideking, *The Constitution before the Judgment Seat: The Prehistory and Ratification of the Constitution*, ed. John P. Kaminski and Richard Leffler (Charlottesville: University of Virginia Press, 2012), 242.

64. GW to John Jay, March 10, 1787, *PGW*, 5:79.

65. GW to Henry Knox, December 26, 1786, *PGW*, 4:482.

66. GW to David Humphreys, December 26, 1786, *PGW*, 4:479 (emphasis original).

67. Henry Knox to GW, January 14, 1787, *PGW*, 4:520–21.

68. David Humphreys to GW, January 20, 1787, *PGW*, 4:526–30 (quotation at 527; spelling modernized).

69. Edmund Randolph to GW, March 11, 1787, *PGW*, 5:83–84.

70. GW to David Humphreys, December 26, 1786, *PGW*, 4:480.

71. Ibid.

72. GW to Henry Knox, April 2, 1787, *PGW*, 5:199.

73. Edward Carrington to TJ, June 9, 1787, *HFC*, 2:426.

74. Henry Knox to GW, March 19, 1787, *PGW*, 5:97.

75. GW to JM, March 31, 1787, *PGW*, 5:116.

76. Ibid., 115 (spelling modernized). At the beginning of his letter, Washington makes an extremely rare joke comparing his own opinions to depreciated paper money.

77. Ibid.

78. "Notes on the Sentiments on the Government of John Jay, Henry Knox, and James Madison," ca. April 1787, *PGW*, 5:163–66.

79. Benjamin Franklin to GW, April 3, 1787, *PGW*, 5:122.

80. JM to James Madison, Sr., April 1, 1787, *PJM*, 9:359 (emphasis original).

81. JM to Edmund Randolph, February 25, 1787, *PJM*, 9:299.

82. JM, "Vices of the Political System of the United States," April 1787, *PJM*, 9:345–58. Some historians think that Madison may have added at least some of the commentary contained in his "Vices" at a later time, but if so, that would not affect the present analysis. See Bilder, *Madison's Hand*, 44–46, 94–95, 243–44.

83. JM to GW, April 16, 1787, *PGW*, 5:145 (spelling modernized).

84. Ibid.

85. JM, "Vices," *PJM*, 9:348–49. Massachusetts would, of course, not have agreed that its troops were an unconstitutional encroachment on federal authority.

86. Ibid., 9:349–50.

87. JM, "Vices," *PJM*, 9:349.

88. Ibid., 350 (spelling modernized).

89. Ibid., 351.

90. JM to James Monroe, October 5, 1786, *PJM*, 9:141.

91. Ibid.

92. Ibid.

93. JM to GW, April 16, 1787, *PJM*, 9:383.

94. Ibid.

95. Historian Eli Merritt claims that the "Mississippi River question" (that is, the Spanish treaty and western expansion) was as significant as Shays's Rebellion in leading to the convention. Merritt, "Sectional Conflict and Secret Compromise: The Mississippi River Question and the United States Constitution," *American Journal of Legal History* 35, no. 2 (1991): 121. Merritt's work indicates the powerful political ramifications of western settlement issues. But in Virginia, and perhaps in some other southern states as well, the sources support the conclusion that western expansion strains and the treaty impasse played a considerably more important role than Shays's Rebellion in shaping public opinion on the Confederation.

Conclusion

1. GW to Henry Lee, Jr., September 22, 1788, *PGW*, 6:529. I thank Peter Onuf for this reference.

2. As discussed in chapter 9, Rhode Island's legislative majority chose to boycott the convention primarily out of concern that Rhode Island's fiscal program would be outlawed by the convention.

3. The convention made an essential "side bargain" by having Congress simultaneously adopt the Northwest Ordinance of 1787. See note 6 below.

4. For more on conflicting conceptions of republicanism and liberty, see Wood, *Creation*, 403–13.

5. A principal lesson that can be drawn from the history of British seventeenth-century politics is that sovereignty disputes are rarely resolved peacefully except where there is unusually widespread recognition of the need for systemic change. In Britain, a century-long contest between Parliament and the Crown over the control of sovereign power included a lengthy civil war between the two sides, followed by the restoration of the monarchy in 1660. But the monarchy then irreversibly and peacefully lost power to Parliament in 1688, when it suffered an unusually broad loss of public support. An admirable synthesis of the period's history is Mark Kishlansky, *A Monarchy Transformed: Britain, 1603–1714* (London: Penguin Books, 1997).

6. The convention successfully finessed the sectional divide over western expansion by having Congress adopt the Northwest Ordinance of 1787 during the convention. I have previously analyzed the relationship between the Constitution and Congress's simultaneous adoption of the Northwest Ordinance during the convention. Van Cleve, *Slaveholders' Union*, 158–66. Briefly, the Northwest Ordinance enabled northern land syndicates to take a major stake in the development of the northwest through land sales discussed in chapter 5. In return, northern states abandoned their efforts to obtain the Spanish treaty. As Congressman John Brown of Virginia's Kentucky district wrote, the passage of the ordinance had led to a "total change in Sentiment" on the treaty because "many Inhabitants of the Eastern States of great Influence & powerful Connections have become Adventurers." John Brown to James Breckenridge, January 28, 1788, *LDC*, 24:630.

7. The tax powers proposals were the greatest risk taken by the Philadelphia Convention despite the fact that historian Woody Holton (*Unruly Americans*, 239–43) is right to conclude that federal import-tax powers were politically quite appealing to some states such as New Jersey.

8. To protect states and regions against unfair taxation, the proposed direct-taxation powers were limited by a weighted proportionality requirement that included an agreed-on formula for including part of southern slave populations.

9. The ability to prevent similar future sectionally biased treaties such as the Spanish treaty was cited at the Philadelphia Convention as an important justification for requiring a two-thirds vote for treaty approvals. Hugh Williamson to JM, June 2, 1788, *LDC*, 25:136.

10. GW to Dr. David Stuart, October 17, 1785, *PGW*, 5:379–80.

11. Hugh Williamson to JM, June 2, 1788, *LDC*, 25:135–36.

12. GW to TJ, August 31, 1788, *PGW*, 6:493.

13. Ibid. (spelling modernized).

14. GW to Henry Lee, Jr., September 22, 1788, *PGW*, 6:528–31 (quotations at 529).

15. GW to TJ, August 31, 1788, *PGW*, 6:493.

16. See the excellent treatment of this core problem facing the new federal government in Edling, *Revolution*.

17. JM to TJ, October 24, 1787, FO, http://founders.archives.gov/documents/Madison/01-10-02-0151.

18. Patrick Henry, quoted in Maier, *Ratification*, 265.

19. Rhode Island and North Carolina initially refused to ratify the Constitution. In both states, the primary opposition probably came from supporters of state paper money. Van Cleve, "Anti-Federalists' Toughest Challenge," 547–48.

20. Richard Henry Lee to General John Lamb, June 27, 1788, in Ballagh, *Letters of Richard Henry Lee*, 2:475.

Epilogue

1. On these changes see Sean Wilentz, *The Rise of American Democracy: Jefferson to Lincoln* (New York: Norton, 2005).

BIBLIOGRAPHY

This bibliography provides information for all sources cited, except those listed in the abbreviations and those noted in the next sentence. Historical periodicals, state statutes, government documents, and materials from public online databases are not included. To assist research, it also includes some sources that were consulted but not cited. The bibliography begins by presenting information about primary sources: first, printed primary sources, including Confederation documents; next, manuscript sources. Documentation for secondary works follows, divided into books, book sections, periodicals, and dissertations and theses.

Printed Primary Sources (Including Modern Editions)

BOOKS, PAMPHLETS, SPEECHES, CORRESPONDENCE, AND ESSAYS

American Historical Association. *Annual Report for the Year 1896*. Vol. 1. Washington, DC: Government Printing Office, 1897.

Ballagh, James Curtis, ed. *Letters of Richard Henry Lee*. New York: Macmillan, 1911–14. Reprint, New York: Da Capo Press, 1970.

Bowdoin, James, Thomas L. Winthrop, and Sir John Temple. *Bowdoin-Temple Papers*. Vol. 2. Reprint, Collections of the Massachusetts Historical Society, ser. 7, vol. 6. Boston: Massachusetts Historical Society, 1907.

Butterfield, L. H., ed. *Letters of Benjamin Rush*. 2 vols. Philadelphia: American Philosophical Society, 1951.

Cappon, Lester J., ed. *The Adams-Jefferson Letters*. Chapel Hill: University of North Carolina Press, 1959.

Chesnutt, David R., and C. James Taylor, eds. *The Papers of Henry Laurens*. Vol. 16. Columbia: University of South Carolina Press, 2002.

Cohn, Ellen R., Jonathan R. Dull, Karen Duval, and Kate M. Ohno, eds. *Papers of Benjamin Franklin*. Vol. 40. New Haven: Yale University Press, 2011.

Cornell, Saul. "Notes and Documents: Reflections on 'the Late Remarkable Revolution in Government': Aedanus Burke and Samuel Bryan's Unpublished History of the Ratification of the Federal Constitution." *Pennsylvania Magazine of History and Biography* 112, no. 1 (1988): 103–30.

Cumings, Henry. "A Sermon Preached at Billerica, December 11, 1783." Boston: T. and J. Fleet, 1784.

Cushing, Harry Alonzo, ed. *Writings of Samuel Adams*. New York: G. P. Putnam's Sons, 1908.

Drew, Benjamin J. *A North-Side View of Slavery. The Refugee: Or, the Narratives of Fugitive Slaves in Canada. Related by Themselves, with an Account of the History and Condition of the Colored Population of Upper Canada*. Boston: J. P. Jewett and Co., 1856.

Ferguson, E. James, ed. *The Papers of Robert Morris, 1781–1784*. Vol. 6. Digital ed. Pittsburgh: University of Pittsburgh Press, 2011. http://digital.library.pitt.edu/cgi-bin/t/text/text-idx?idno=31735060482019;view=toc;c=pittpress.

———, ed. *The Papers of Robert Morris, 1781–1784*. Vol. 7. Digital ed. Pittsburgh: University of Pittsburgh Press, 2011. http://digital.library.pitt.edu/cgi-bin/t/text/text-idx?idno=31735060482050;view=toc;c=pittpress.

Ford, Worthington Chauncey, ed. *Correspondence and Journals of Samuel Blachley Webb*. 3 vols. New York [Lancaster, PA]: Wickersham Press, 1893.

———, ed. *Letters of Joseph Jones of Virginia, 1777–1787*. Washington, DC: Department of State, 1889.

Hazard, Samuel, ed. *Pennsylvania Archives*, vol. 10. Philadelphia: Joseph Severns and Co., 1854.

Henry, William Wirt. *Patrick Henry: Life, Correspondence and Speeches*. 3 vols. New York: Charles Scribner's Sons, 1891.

Holroyd (Earl of Sheffield), John Baker. "Observations on the Commerce of the American States." Philadelphia, 1783.

Kolodny, Annette, ed. "The Travel Diary of Elizabeth House Trist: Philadelphia to Natchez, 1783–84." In *Journeys in New Worlds: Early American Women's Narratives*, ed. William L. Andrews, 181–232. Madison: University of Wisconsin Press, 1990.

Lynd, Staughton. "Abraham Yates's History of the Movement for the United

States Constitution." *William and Mary Quarterly*, 3rd ser., 20, no. 2 (1963): 223–45.

Massachusetts Historical Society. *Proceedings of the Massachusetts Historical Society*. 2nd ser., vol. 8. Boston: Massachusetts Historical Society, 1894.

McRee, Griffith J. *Life and Correspondence of James Iredell*. 2 vols. New York: D. Appleton and Co., 1858.

Paine, Thomas. *Dissertations on Government, the Affairs of the Bank, and Paper-Money*. Philadelphia: Charles Cist, 1786.

Pennsylvania General Assembly, *Minutes of the Second Session of the Ninth General Assembly*. Philadelphia, 1785.

Pynchon, William. *The Diary of William Pynchon of Salem: A Picture of Salem Life, Social and Political, and Century Ago*. Ed. Fitch Edward Oliver. Boston: Houghton Mifflin, 1890.

Price, Richard. *Letters to and from Richard Price, D.D., F.R.S., 1767–1790*. Cambridge, MA: John Wilson and Son, University Press, 1903.

Ramsay, David. *The History of the American Revolution*. 2 vols. Philadelphia, 1789.

Rutland, Robert A. *The Papers of George Mason, 1725–1792*. 3 vols. Chapel Hill: University of North Carolina Press, 1970.

Sifton, Paul G. "Otto's *Memoire* to Vergennes, 1785." *William and Mary Quarterly*, 3rd ser., 22, no. 4 (1965): 626–45.

Smith, Adam. *An Inquiry into the Nature and Causes of the Wealth of Nations*. Ed. Edwin Cannan. 1904. Reprint, Chicago: University of Chicago Press, 1976.

Stiles, Ezra. "The United States Elevated to Glory and Honour." Worcester, MA: Isaiah Thomas, 1785.

Syrett, Harold C., ed. *Papers of Alexander Hamilton*. Vol. 1 (1768–78). New York: Columbia University Press, 1961.

———, ed. *The Papers of Alexander Hamilton*. Vol. 3 (1782–86). New York: Columbia University Press, 1962.

United States. Secretary of the Treasury. "Report on the Public Credit," January 1790. In Congress of the United States, *American State Papers: Documents, Legislative and Executive, of the Congress of the United States*. Washington, DC: Gales and Seaton, 1832, vol. 5 (vol. 1, *Finance Series*).

Van Schaack, Henry C. *Memoirs of the Life of Henry Van Shaack . . .* Chicago: A. C. McClurg and Co., 1892.

Virginia Historical Society. "Reluctant Ratifiers: Virginia Considers the Federal Constitution: An Exhibition, Virginia Historical Society, Richmond, 2 June–15 December 1988." Ed. E. Lee Shepard. Richmond: Virginia Historical Society, 1988.

CONFEDERATION STATUTES AND TREATIES

Confederation. *Articles of Confederation*. http://avalon.law.yale.edu/18th_century/artconf.asp.

Confederation. *The Definitive Treaty of Peace between the United States of America and His Brittanic Majesty*. In *Journals of the Continental Congress, 1774–1789*, ed. Worthington Chauncey Ford, 26:23–28. Washington, DC: Government Printing Office, 1904–36. (Also known as the Treaty of Paris of September 3, 1783.)

Manuscript Sources

Adams Family Papers. Virginia Historical Society, Richmond.

Adams, Samuel. Papers. Manuscript Division, Library of Congress. Photostats; originals at New York Public Library.

Allason Papers. Library of Virginia, Richmond.

Bancroft, George, Collection. New York Public Library.

Benson Papers. New York Public Library.

Biddle, Clement, Letters. New York Public Library.

Bingham, William, Papers. Manuscript Division, Library of Congress.

Bleecker, A. L., Letterbook. New-York Historical Society.

Breckenridge and Gilmer Families Papers. Small Special Collections Library, University of Virginia, Charlottesville.

Breckenridge, James, Papers. Small Special Collections Library, University of Virginia, Charlottesville.

Briscoe-Stuart Papers. Small Special Collections Library, University of Virginia, Charlottesville.

Bryan, Fairfax, to Dr. Denny Fairfax. Letter. Small Special Collections Library, University of Virginia, Charlottesville.

Bryan, George, Papers. Historical Society of Pennsylvania, Philadelphia.

Campbell, Duncan, Letters to Duncan Campbell. Small Special Collections Library, University of Virginia, Charlottesville.

Caroline County petition to legislature, November 16, 1784. Virginia Historical Society, Richmond.

Carrington, Edward, Papers. Virginia Historical Society, Richmond.

Carter, Robert, Papers. Small Special Collections Library, University of Virginia, Charlottesville.

Clinton, DeWitt, Papers. New-York Historical Society.

Clymer-Meredith-Read Family Papers. New York Public Library.

Coles, John, Ledgers. Small Special Collections Library, University of Virginia, Charlottesville.

Collins, Stephen, Letterbook. Microfilm. Manuscript Division, Library of Congress.

Collins, Stephen, Papers. Manuscript Division, Library of Congress.

Cox, James, Jr., Business papers. Small Special Collections Library, University of Virginia, Charlottesville.

Dana Family Papers. Massachusetts Historical Society, Boston.

Dana, Francis, Correspondence. Massachusetts Historical Society, Boston.

Dane, Nathan, Papers and miscellaneous letters. Massachusetts Historical Society, Boston.

Davis, Caleb, Papers. Massachusetts Historical Society, Boston.

Dickinson, John, Papers. R. R. Logan Collection. Historical Society of Pennsylvania, Philadelphia.

Dickinson, John, Papers. Library Company of Philadelphia.

Drinker Family, Papers. Historical Society of Pennsylvania, Philadelphia.

Drinker, Henry, Papers. Vol. 18A, Henry Drinker letterbook, 1762–86. Historical Society of Pennsylvania, Philadelphia.

Fitzgerald, John, Letters, 1783–1784. Library of Virginia, Richmond.

Fleming, William, Papers. Library of Virginia, Richmond.

Force, Peter, Collection. Manuscript Division, Library of Congress.

Frazier, Nalbro, Letterbook. New York Public Library.

Gerry, Elbridge, Letters. Photocopies. Massachusetts Historical Society, Boston.

Gerry, Elbridge, Papers. Microfilm. Massachusetts Historical Society, Boston.

Goodman, Alfred T., Papers. Western Reserve Historical Society, Cleveland, OH. (Consulted online only.)

Gorham, Nathaniel, Miscellaneous letters. Massachusetts Historical Society, Boston.

Grayson, William, to Nathan Dane. Letters. Small Special Collections Library, University of Virginia, Charlottesville.

Henry, Patrick, Executive papers, 1784–86. Microfilm. Library of Virginia, Richmond.

Heth, William, Diary. Manuscript Division, Library of Congress.

Higginson Family Papers. Massachusetts Historical Society, Boston.

Hooe and Harrison to De Neufville and Co., Amsterdam. Letters. Small Special Collections Library, University of Virginia, Charlottesville.

Inhabitants of the western country, Petition to legislature, November 17, 1786. Library of Virginia, Richmond.

Jervis, Leonard, Papers. Manuscript Division, Library of Congress.
John de Neufville and Sons. Papers. Manuscript Division, Library of Congress.
John de Neufville and Sons. Records. Microfilm. New-York Historical Society.
Johnson, Joshua (London). Papers, 1785–1788. Microfilm. Peter Force Collection, Manuscript Division, Library of Congress.
Johnston, Zachariah, Papers. Library of Virginia, Richmond.
Jones, Adam. Letter, September 10, 1785. Library of Virginia, Richmond.
Joyce, John, to Robert Dickson. Letter. Virginia Historical Society, Richmond.
King, Rufus, Papers. New-York Historical Society.
Lee Family Papers. Microfilm. Small Special Collections Library, University of Virginia, Charlottesville.
Lee, Charles Carter, and the Lee Family. Papers. Small Special Collections Library, University of Virginia, Charlottesville.
Lee, Henry, Jr., to Henry Lee, April 19, 1786. Virginia Historical Society, Richmond.
Livingston, Gilbert, Papers. New York Public Library.
Low, Nicholas, Papers. New-York Historical Society.
Mason Family Papers. Library of Virginia, Richmond.
Maury Family Papers. Small Special Collections Library, University of Virginia, Charlottesville.
Maury, James, Papers. Small Special Collections Library, University of Virginia, Charlottesville.
McGregor, Collin, Letterbook. New York Public Library.
Morris Family Papers. Small Special Collections Library, University of Virginia, Charlottesville.
Payne Family Papers. Library of Virginia, Richmond.
Putnam-Jackson-Lowell Papers. Massachusetts Historical Society, Boston.
Reed, Joseph, Papers. Microfilm. New-York Historical Society.
Rumsey Family papers. Manuscript Division, Library of Congress.
Scott Family Papers. Library of Virginia, Richmond.
Sedgwick Family Papers. Massachusetts Historical Society, Boston.
Smith, Huie and Alexander. Records. Manuscript Division, Library of Congress.
Stephen Collins and Son. Papers. Manuscript Division, Library of Congress.
Stuart Family Papers. Virginia Historical Society, Richmond.
Stuart, Archibald, Papers. Virginia Historical Society, Richmond.
Tayler-Cooper Family Papers. New York Public Library.
Taylor, Francis, Diary. Small Special Collections Library, University of Virginia, Charlottesville.
Tilghman, William, Papers. Historical Society of Pennsylvania, Philadelphia.
Tucker-Ewell Papers. Library of Virginia, Richmond.

Van Dyke, Nicholas, Papers. Manuscript Division, Library of Congress.

Virginia Auditor of Public Accounts. Lists of delinquent taxes, 1782–90. Library of Virginia, Richmond.

Virginia Auditor of Public Accounts. Auditors Papers (letters received). Library of Virginia, Richmond.

Virginia. Executive Communications. "Solicitor's Report of Delinquent Sheriffs," April 23, 1789, miscellaneous microfilm reel 4918, Library of Virginia, Richmond.

Virginia. Executive communications and letterbooks, 1783–87. Library of Virginia, Richmond.

Virginia. Miscellaneous microfilm reel 5375 (official correspondence, 1786–87). Library of Virginia, Richmond.

Virginia. Miscellaneous papers. Library of Virginia, Richmond.

Virginia. Miscellany. Small Special Collections Library, University of Virginia, Charlottesville.

Walker, Joseph, Notebooks. Library of Virginia, Richmond.

Waln Family Papers. Historical Society of Pennsylvania, Philadelphia.

Webb, James, Papers. Library of Virginia, Richmond.

Wormeley, Ralph, Papers. Small Special Collections Library, University of Virginia, Charlottesville.

Yeates, Jasper, Papers. Historical Society of Pennsylvania, Philadelphia.

Secondary Works

BOOKS

Alexander, John K. *Samuel Adams: The Life of an American Revolutionary*. Lanham, MD: Rowman and Littlefield, 2011.

Anderson, William G. *The Price of Liberty: The Public Debt of the American Revolution*. Charlottesville: University Press of Virginia, 1983.

Bailey, Thomas A. *A Diplomatic History of the American People*. 8th ed. New York: Meredith Corp., Appleton Century Crofts, 1969.

Bailyn, Bernard. *The Ideological Origins of the American Revolution*. Cambridge, MA: Harvard University Press, 1967.

Beard, Charles A. *An Economic Interpretation of the Constitution of the United States*. 1935 edition. Reprint, New York: Macmillan, 1941.

Becker, Robert A. *Revolution, Reform, and the Politics of American Taxation, 1763–83*. Baton Rouge: Louisiana University Press, 1980.

Beeman, Richard R. *Patrick Henry: A Biography*. New York: McGraw-Hill, 1974.

———. *Plain, Honest Men: The Making of the American Constitution*. New York: Random House, 2009.

Bemis, Samuel Flagg. *The Diplomacy of the American Revolution*. 1935. Reprint, Bloomington: Indiana University Press, 1965.

———. *Jay's Treaty: A Study in Commerce and Diplomacy*. New York: Macmillan, 1923.

———. *Pinckney's Treaty: America's Advantage from Europe's Distress, 1783–1800*. New Haven, CT: Yale University Press, 1960.

Bergmann, William H. *The American National State and the Early West*. Cambridge: Cambridge University Press, 2012.

Berlin, Ira. *Many Thousands Gone: The First Two Centuries of Slavery in North America*. Cambridge, MA: Harvard University Press, 1998.

Bilder, Mary Sarah. *Madison's Hand: Revising the Constitutional Convention*. Cambridge, MA: Harvard University Press, 2016.

Billington, Ray Allen. *Westward Expansion: A History of the American Frontier*. 3rd ed. New York: Macmillan, 1967.

Bouton, Terry. *Taming Democracy: "The People," the Founders, and the Troubled Ending of the American Revolution*. Oxford: Oxford University Press, 2007.

Briceland, Alan V. *1788: The Year of Decision: Virginia's Ratification of the United States Constitution*. Richmond: Virginia Department of Education, 1989.

Brock, Leslie V. *The Currency of the American Colonies, 1700–1764: A Study in Colonial Finance and Imperial Relations*. New York: Arno Press, 1975.

Brown, Robert Eldon. *Reinterpretation of the Formation of the Constitution*. Boston: University of Massachusetts Press, 1963.

Brown, Roger H. *Redeeming the Republic: Federalists, Taxation, and the Origins of the Constitution*. Baltimore: Johns Hopkins University Press, 1993.

Brunhouse, Robert L. *The Counter-Revolution in Pennsylvania, 1776–1790*. 1942. Reprint, Harrisburg: Pennsylvania Historical Commission, 1971.

Bullock, Charles J. *The Finances of the United States from 1775 to 1789, with Special Reference to the Budget*. Madison: University of Wisconsin, 1895.

Channing, Edward. *History of the United States: American Revolution, 1761–1789*. Vol. 3. New York: Macmillan, 1912.

Chu, Jonathan M. *Stumbling toward the Constitution: The Economic Consequences of Freedom in the Atlantic World*. New York: Palgrave Macmillan, 2012.

Cochran, Thomas C. *New York in the Confederation: An Economic Study*. 1932. Reprint, Port Washington, NY: Kennikat Press, 1970.

Coleman, Kenneth. *The American Revolution in Georgia, 1763–1789*. Athens: University of Georgia Press, 1958.

Condon, Sean. *Shays's Rebellion: Authority and Distress in Post-revolutionary America*. Baltimore: Johns Hopkins University Press, 2015.

Conway, Stephen. *A Short History of the American Revolutionary War*. London: Tauris, 2013.

———. *The War of American Independence, 1775–1783*. London: Edward Arnold, 1995.

Davis, Joseph L. *Sectionalism in American Politics, 1774–1787*. Madison: University of Wisconsin Press, 1977.

DuVal, Kathleen. *Independence Lost: Lives on the Edge of the American Revolution*. New York: Random House, 2015.

East, Robert Abraham. *Business Enterprise in the American Revolutionary Era*. 1938. Reprint, New York: AMS Press, 1979.

Edgar, Walter B. *South Carolina: A History*. Columbia: University of South Carolina Press, 1998.

Edling, Max M. *A Revolution in Favor of Government: Origins of the U.S. Constitution and the Making of the American State*. Oxford: Oxford University Press, 2003.

Ellis, Joseph J. *His Excellency: George Washington*. New York: Knopf, 2004.

Ernst, Joseph Albert. *Money and Politics in America, 1755–1775*. Chapel Hill: University of North Carolina Press, 1973.

Ernst, Robert. *Rufus King: American Federalist*. Chapel Hill: University of North Carolina Press, 1968.

Feer, Robert A. *Shays's Rebellion*. New York: Garland, 1988.

Ferguson, E. James. *The Power of the Purse: A History of American Public Finance, 1776–1790*. Chapel Hill: University of North Carolina Press, 1961.

Ferling, John. *The Ascent of George Washington: The Hidden Political Genius of an American Icon*. New York: Bloomsbury Press, 2009.

———. *A Leap in the Dark: The Struggle to Create the American Republic*. New York: Oxford University Press, 2003.

Fiske, John. *The Critical Period of American History, 1783–1789*. Boston: Houghton Mifflin, 1889.

Flexner, James T. *Washington: The Indispensable Man*. 1974. Reprint, New York: New American Library, 1984.

Foner, Eric. *Tom Paine and Revolutionary America*. 1976. Updated ed., Oxford: Oxford University Press, 2005.

Freeman, Douglas Southall. *George Washington: A Biography*. Vol. 6. New York: Charles Scribner's Sons, 1954.

Gould, Eliga. *Among the Powers of the Earth: The American Revolution and the Making of a New World Empire*. Cambridge, MA: Harvard University Press, 2012.

Griffin, Patrick. *America's Revolution*. Oxford: Oxford University Press, 2013.

Grigsby, Hugh Blair. *The History of the Federal Convention of 1788*. Richmond: Virginia Historical Society, 1890.

Gross, Robert A., ed. *In Debt to Shays*. Charlottesville: University Press of Virginia, 1993.

Hall, Van Beck. *Politics without Parties: Massachusetts, 1780–1791*. Pittsburgh, PA: University of Pittsburgh Press, 1972.

Heideking, Jürgen. *The Constitution before the Judgment Seat: The Prehistory and Ratification of the Constitution*. Ed. John P. Kaminski and Richard Leffler. Charlottesville: University of Virginia Press, 2012.

Hendrickson, David C. *Peace Pact: The Lost World of the American Founding*. Lawrence: University Press of Kansas, 2003.

Hildreth, Richard. *History of the United States of America*. 6 vols. New York: Harper and Sons, 1877–80.

Holton, Woody. *Unruly Americans and the Origins of the Constitution*. New York: Hill and Wang, 2007.

Homer, Sidney, and Richard Sylla. *A History of Interest Rates*. 4th ed. Hoboken, NJ: John Wiley and Sons, 2005.

Hurst, J. Willard. *A Legal History of Money in the United States*. Lincoln: University of Nebraska Press, 1971.

Jensen, Merrill. *The Articles of Confederation: An Interpretation of the Social-Constitutional History of the American Revolution 1774–1781*. 1940. Reprint, Madison: University of Wisconsin Press, 1970.

———. *The New Nation: A History of the United States during the Confederation, 1781–1789*. New York: Vintage Books, 1950.

Jillson, Calvin, and Rick K. Wilson. *Congressional Dynamics: Structure, Coordination and Choice in the First American Congress, 1774–1789*. Stanford, CA: Stanford University Press, 1994.

Johnson, Andrew J. *The Life and Constitutional Thought of Nathan Dane*. New York: Garland, 1987.

Johnson, Calvin. *Righteous Anger at the Wicked States: The Meaning of the Founders' Constitution*. Cambridge: Cambridge University Press, 2005.

Kaminski, John P. *Paper Politics: The Northern State Loan-Offices during the Confederation, 1783–1790*. New York: Garland, 1989.

Kelly, Alfred H., Winfred A. Harbison, and Herman Belz. *The American Constitution: Its Origins and Development*. 7th ed. Vol. 1. New York: Norton, 1991.

Ketcham, Ralph. *James Madison: A Biography*. Charlottesville: University Press of Virginia, 1990.

Kishlansky, Mark. *A Monarchy Transformed: Britain, 1603–1714*. London: Penguin Books, 1997.

Klarman, Michael J. *The Framers' Coup: The Making of the United States Constitution*. Oxford: Oxford University Press, 2016.

Lamplugh, George R. *Politics on the Periphery: Factions and Parties in Georgia, 1783–1806*. Newark: University of Delaware Press, 1986.

Libby, Orin Grant. *The Geographical Distribution of the Vote of the Thirteen States on the Federal Constitution, 1787–88*. 1894. Reprint, New York: Burt Franklin, 1969.

Lindert, Peter H., and Jeffrey G. Williamson. *Unequal Gains: American Growth and Inequality since 1700*. Princeton, NJ: Princeton University Press, 2016.

Maier, Pauline. *Ratification: The People Debate the Constitution, 1787–1788*. New York: Simon and Schuster, 2010.

Main, Jackson T. *The Antifederalists: Critics of the Constitution, 1781–1788*. Chapel Hill: University of North Carolina Press, 1961.

———. *Political Parties before the Constitution*. Chapel Hill: University of North Carolina Press, 1973.

Mann, Bruce. *Republic of Debtors: Bankruptcy in the Age of Independence*. Cambridge, MA: Harvard University Press, 2002.

Marks, Frederick W., III. *Independence on Trial: Foreign Affairs and the Making of the Constitution*. Baton Rouge: Louisiana State University Press, 1973.

Marston, Jerrilyn Greene. *King and Congress: The Transfer of Political Legitimacy, 1774–1776*. Princeton, NJ: Princeton University Press, 1987.

Matson, Cathy D., and Peter S. Onuf. *A Union of Interests: Political and Economic Thought in Revolutionary America*. Lawrence: University Press of Kansas, 1990.

McCormick, Richard P. *Experiment in Independence: New Jersey in the Critical Period, 1781–1789*. New Brunswick, NJ: Rutgers University Press, 1950.

McCraw, Thomas K. *The Founders and Finance: How Hamilton, Gallatin and Other Immigrants Forged a New Economy*. Cambridge, MA: Harvard University Press, 2012.

McCusker, John J. *How Much Is That in Real Money? A Historical Commodity Price Index for Use as a Deflator of Money Values in the Economy of the United States*. 2nd ed. Worcester, MA: American Antiquarian Society, 2001.

McCusker, John J., and Russell Menard. *The Economy of British North America, 1607–1789*. Chapel Hill: University of North Carolina Press, 1985.

McDonald, Forrest. *E Pluribus Unum: The Formation of the American Republic, 1776–1790*. 2nd ed. Indianapolis, IN: Liberty Press, 1979.

———. *We the People: The Economic Origins of the Constitution*. Chicago: University of Chicago Press, 1958.

McGuire, Robert A. *To Form a More Perfect Union: A New Economic Interpretation of the Constitution*. Oxford: Oxford University Press, 2003.

McLaughlin, Andrew C. *The Confederation and the Constitution, 1783–1789*. New York: Harper and Bros., 1905; reprint, New York: Collier Books, 1971.

McMaster, John Bach. *A History of the People of the United States from the Revolution to the Civil War*. New York: D. Appleton and Co., 1911.

Merk, Frederick. *History of the Westward Movement*. New York: Knopf, 1978.

Middlekauff, Robert. *The Glorious Cause: The American Revolution, 1763–1789*. Rev. ed. Oxford: Oxford University Press, 2005.

Millett, Allan R., Peter Maslowski, and William B. Feis. *For the Common Defense: A Military History of the United States from 1607 to 2012*. 3rd ed. New York: Free Press, 2012.

Morgan, Edmund S. *The Birth of the Republic, 1763–89*. 3rd ed. Chicago: University of Chicago Press, 1992.

Morrill, James R. *The Practice and Problems of Fiat Finance: North Carolina in the Confederation, 1783–1789*. Chapel Hill: University of North Carolina Press, 1969.

Morris, Richard B. *The Forging of the Union, 1781–1789*. New York: Harper and Row, 1987.

———. *The Peacemakers: The Great Powers and American Independence*. New York: Harper and Row, 1965.

Nettels, Curtis P. *The Emergence of a National Economy, 1775–1815*. New York: Holt, Rinehart and Winston, 1962.

Nevins, Allan. *The American States during and after the Revolution, 1775–1789*. New York: Macmillan, 1924.

Norton, Mary Beth. *Liberty's Daughters: The Revolutionary Experience of American Women, 1750–1800*. Ithaca, NY: Cornell University Press, 1980.

Onuf, Peter S. *The Origins of the Federal Republic*. Philadelphia: University of Pennsylvania Press, 1983.

———. *Statehood and Union: A History of the Northwest Ordinance*. Bloomington: Indiana University Press, 1987.

Perkins, Edwin J. *American Public Finance and Financial Services, 1700–1815*. Columbus: Ohio State University Press, 1994.

Pole, J. R. *Political Representation in England and the Origins of the American Republic*. Berkeley: University of California Press, 1971.

Polishook, Irwin H. *Rhode Island and the Union, 1774–1795*. Evanston, IL: Northwestern University Press, 1969.

Price, Jacob M. *Capital and Credit in British Overseas Trade: The View from the Chesapeake, 1700–1776*. Cambridge, MA: Harvard University Press, 1980.

Puls, Mark. *Henry Knox: Visionary General of the American Revolution*. New York: Palgrave Macmillan, 2008.

Rabushka, Alvin. *Taxation in Colonial America*. Princeton, NJ: Princeton University Press, 2008.

Rakove, Jack. *The Beginnings of National Politics: An Interpretive History of the Continental Congress*. New York: Knopf, 1979.

Rappleye, Charles. *Robert Morris*. New York: Simon and Schuster, 2010.

Ratchford, B. U. *American State Debts*. Durham, NC: Duke University Press, 1941.

Richards, Leonard L. *Shays's Rebellion: The American Revolution's Final Battle*. Philadelphia: University of Pennsylvania Press, 2002.

Ritcheson, Charles R. *Aftermath of Revolution: British Policy toward the United States, 1783–1795*. Dallas, TX: Southern Methodist University Press, 1969.

Robertson, David Brian. *The Constitution and America's Destiny*. Cambridge: Cambridge University Press, 2005.

Rose, J. Holland, A. P. Newton, and E. A. Benians, eds. *The Growth of the New Empire, 1783–1870*. Vol. 2 of *The Cambridge History of the British Empire*. Cambridge: Cambridge University Press, 1940.

———. *The Old Empire: From the Beginnings to 1783*. Vol. 1 of *The Cambridge History of the British Empire*. Cambridge: Cambridge University Press, 1929.

Royster, Charles. *A Revolutionary People at War: The Continental Army and American Character, 1775–1783*. Chapel Hill: University of North Carolina Press, 1979.

Sadosky, Leonard J. *Revolutionary Negotiations: Indians, Empires and Diplomats in the Founding of America*. Charlottesville: University of Virginia Press, 2009.

Saler, Bethel. *The Settlers' Empire: Colonialism and State Formation in America's Old Northwest*. Philadelphia: University of Pennsylvania Press, 2015.

Scott, H. M. *British Foreign Policy in the Age of the American Revolution*. Oxford: Clarendon Press, 1990.

Singer, Charles Gregg. *South Carolina in the Confederation*. Philadelphia: University of Pennsylvania, 1941.

Spaulding, E. Wilder. *New York in the Critical Period, 1783–1789*. New York: Columbia University Press, 1932.

Szatmary, David P. *Shays' Rebellion: The Making of an Agrarian Insurrection*. Amherst: University of Massachusetts Press, 1980.

Van Cleve, George William. *A Slaveholders' Union: Slavery, Politics, and the Constitution in the Early Republic*. Chicago: University of Chicago Press, 2010.

Walton, Gary M., and Hugh Rockoff. *History of the American Economy*. 10th ed. Mason, OH: Thomson South-Western, 2005.

Warren, Charles. *The Making of the Constitution*. Boston: Little, Brown, 1928.

Weigley, Russell Frank, Nicholas B. Wainwright, and Edwin Wolf II, eds. *Philadelphia: A 300 Year History*. New York: Norton, 1982.

Wells, William V. *The Life and Public Services of Samuel Adams . . .* 2nd ed. 3 vols. 1888. Reprint, Freeport, NY: Books for Libraries Press, 1969.

Whitaker, Arthur P. *The Spanish-American Frontier, 1783–1795: The Westward Movement and the Spanish Retreat in the Mississippi Valley.* Boston: Houghton Mifflin, 1927.

Wilentz, Sean. *The Rise of American Democracy: Jefferson to Lincoln.* New York: Norton, 2005.

Withey, Lynne. *Dearest Friend: A Life of Abigail Adams.* New York: Free Press, 1981.

Wood, Gordon S. *The Creation of the American Republic, 1776–1787.* 1969. Reprint, Chapel Hill: University of North Carolina Press, 1998.

———. *Empire of Liberty: A History of the Early Republic, 1789–1815.* Oxford: Oxford University Press, 2009.

Wright, Robert E. *The Origins of Commercial Banking in America, 1750–1800.* Lanham, MD: Rowman and Littlefield, 2001.

BOOK SECTIONS

Adair, Douglass G. "'Experience Must Be Our Only Guide': History, Democratic Theory, and the United States Constitution." In *Fame and the Founding Fathers: Essays by Douglass Adair,* ed. Trevor Colbourn, 107–23. New York: Norton, 1974.

———. "Fame and the Founding Fathers." In *Fame and the Founding Fathers: Essays by Douglass Adair,* ed. Trevor Colbourn, 3–26. New York: Norton, 1974.

———. "'That Politics May Be Reduced to a Science': David Hume, James Madison, and the Tenth Federalist." In *Fame and the Founding Fathers: Essays by Douglass Adair,* ed. Trevor Colbourn, 93–106. New York: Norton, 1974.

Brown, Richard D. "Shays's Rebellion and the Ratification of the Federal Constitution in Massachusetts." In *Beyond Confederation: Origins of the Constitution and American National Identity,* ed. Richard R. Beeman, Stephen Botein, and Edward C. Carter II, 113–27. Chapel Hill: University of North Carolina Press, 1987.

Carrington, Selwyn H. H. "The American Revolution and the British West Indies' Economy." In *British Capitalism and Caribbean Slavery: The Legacy of Eric Williams,* ed. Stanley L. Engerman and Barbara L. Solow, 135–61. 1987. Reprint, Cambridge: Cambridge University Press, 2004.

Conway, Stephen. "Britain and the Revolutionary Crisis, 1763–1791." In *The Oxford History of the British Empire: The Eighteenth Century,* ed. P. J. Marshall, 325–46. Oxford: Oxford University Press, 1998.

DuVal, Kathleen. "Independent for Whom? Expansion and Conflict in the

South and Southwest." In *The World of the Revolutionary American Republic: Land, Labor, and the Conflict for a Continent*, ed. Andrew Shankman, 97–115. New York: Routledge, 2014.

East, Robert Abraham. "The Massachusetts Conservatives in the Critical Period." In *The Era of the American Revolution*, ed. Richard B. Morris, 349–91. New York: Columbia University Press, 1939.

Edling, Max M. "Consolidating a Revolutionary Republic." In *The World of the Revolutionary American Republic: Land, Labor, and the Conflict for a Continent*, ed. Andrew Shankman, 165–94. New York: Routledge, 2014.

Keynes, John Maynard. "Social Consequences of Changes in the Value of Money." In *Essays in Persuasion*, 80–104. New York: Harcourt, Brace and Co., 1932.

Kulikoff, Allan. "'Such Things Ought Not to Be': The American Revolution and the First Great Depression." In *The World of the Revolutionary American Republic: Land, Labor, and the Conflict for a Continent*, ed. Andrew Shankman, 134–64. New York: Routledge, 2014.

McGuire, Robert A. "The Founding Era, 1774–1791." In Price Fishback, Robert Higgs, Gary D. Libecap, John Joseph Wallis, Stanley L. Engerman, Jeffrey Rogers Hummel, Sumner J. La Croix, et al., *Government and the American Economy: A New History*, 56–88. Chicago: University of Chicago Press, 2007.

Miller, Richard G. "The Federal City, 1783–1800." In *Philadelphia: A 300-Year History*, ed. Russell Frank Weigley, Nicholas B. Wainwright, and Edwin Wolf II, 155–207. New York: Norton, 1982.

Morris, Richard B. "Insurrection in Massachusetts." In *America in Crisis*, ed. Daniel Aaron, 21–49. New York: Knopf, 1952.

Rakove, Jack. "The Road to Philadelphia, 1781–1787." In *The Framing and Ratification of the Constitution*, ed. Leonard W. Levy and Dennis J. Mahoney, 98–111. New York: Macmillan, 1987.

Richter, Daniel K. "Native Peoples of North America and the Eighteenth-Century British Empire." In *The Oxford History of the British Empire: The Eighteenth Century*, ed. P. J. Marshall, 347–71. Oxford: Oxford University Press, 1998.

Wood, Gordon S. "Interests and Disinterestedness in the Making of the Constitution." In *Beyond Confederation : Origins of the Constitution and American National Identity*, ed. Richard R. Beeman, Stephen Botein, and Edward C. Carter II, 69–109. Chapel Hill: University of North Carolina Press, 1987.

WORKS IN PERIODICALS

Baack, Ben. "Forging a Nation State: The Continental Congress and the Financing of the War of American Independence." *Economic History Review* 54, no. 4 (2001): 639–56.

Baumann, Roland M. "'Heads I Win, Tails You Lose': The Public Creditors and the Assumption Issue in Pennsylvania, 1790–1802." *Pennsylvania History* 44 (July 1977): 195–232.

Becker, Robert. "Salus Populi Suprema Lex: Public Peace and South Carolina Debtor Relief Laws, 1783–1788." *South Carolina Historical Magazine* 80, no. 1 (1979): 65–75.

Bjork, Gordon C. "The Weaning of the American Economy: Independence, Market Changes, and Economic Development." *Journal of Economic History* 24, no. 4 (1964): 541–60.

Bogin, Ruth. "New Jersey's True Policy: The Radical Republican Vision of Abraham Clark." *William and Mary Quarterly* 35 (January 1978): 100–109.

Bradbury, M. L. "Legal Privilege and the Bank of North America." *Pennsylvania Magazine of History and Biography* 96 (April 1972): 139–66.

Brown, Alan S. "The Role of the Army in Western Settlement: Josiah Harmar's Command, 1785–1790." *Pennsylvania Magazine of History and Biography* 93, no. 2 (1969): 161–78.

Calomiris, Charles W. "Institutional Failure, Monetary Scarcity, and the Depreciation of the Continental." *Journal of Economic History* 48 (March 1988): 47–68.

Davis, Lance, and Stanley Engerman. "The Economy of British North America: Miles Traveled, Miles Still to Go." *William and Mary Quarterly*, 3rd ser., 56, no. 11 (1999): 9–22.

Edling, Max. "'So Immense a Power in the Affairs of War': Alexander Hamilton and the Restoration of Public Credit." *William and Mary Quarterly* 64, no. 2 (2007): 287–326.

Evans, Emory G. "Private Indebtedness and the Revolution in Virginia, 1776 to 1796." *William and Mary Quarterly* 28 (1971): 349–74.

Ferguson, E. James. "State Assumption of the Federal Debt during the Confederation." *Mississippi Valley Historical Review* 38, no. 3 (1951): 403–24.

Goldin, Claudia, and Frank D. Lewis. "The Role of Exports in American Economic Growth during the Napoleonic Wars, 1793–1807." *Explorations in Economic History* 17 (1980): 6–25.

Gross, Robert A. "A Yankee Rebellion? The Regulators, New England, and the New Nation." *New England Quarterly* 82, no. 1 (2009): 112–35.

Harmon, George D. "The Proposed Amendments to the Articles of Confederation." *South Atlantic Quarterly* 24 (October 1925): 411–36.

Holton, Woody. "Abigail Adams: Bond Speculator." *William and Mary Quarterly* 64 (October 2007): 821–38

Hutson, James H. "The Creation of the Constitution: Scholarship at a Standstill." *Reviews in American History* 12, no. 4 (1984): 463–77.

Lienesch, Michael. "Historical Theory and Political Reform: Two Perspectives on Confederation Politics." *Review of Politics* 45, no. 1 (1983): 94–115.

Lindert, Peter H., and Jeffrey G. Williamson. "American Incomes Before and After the Revolution." *Journal of Economic History* 73, no. 3 (2013): 725–65.

Lynd, Staughton. "The Compromise of 1787." *Political Science Quarterly* 81, no. 2 (1966): 225–50.

Main, Gloria L., and Jackson T. Main. "The Red Queen in New England?" *William and Mary Quarterly*, 3rd ser., 56, no. 1 (1999): 121–50.

Main, Jackson T. "Government by the People: The American Revolution and the Democratization of the Legislatures." *William and Mary Quarterly* 23, no. 3 (1966): 391–407.

———. "Sections and Politics in Virginia, 1781–1787." *William and Mary Quarterly*, 3rd ser., 12, no. 1 (1955): 96–112.

Merritt, Eli. "Sectional Conflict and Secret Compromise: The Mississippi River Question and the United States Constitution." *American Journal of Legal History* 35, no. 2 (1991): 117–71.

Michener, Ronald W., and Robert E. Wright. "State 'Currencies' and the Transition to the U.S. Dollar: Clarifying Some Confusions." *American Economic Review* 95, no. 3 (2005): 682–703.

Morris, Richard B. "The Confederation Period and the American Historian." *William and Mary Quarterly*, 3rd ser., 13, no. 2 (1956): 139–56.

Priest, Claire. "Colonial Courts and Secured Credit: Early American Commercial Litigation and Shays' Rebellion." *Yale Law Journal* 108, no. 8 (1999): 2413–50.

Pybus, Cassandra. "Jefferson's Faulty Math: The Question of Slave Defections in the American Revolution." *William and Mary Quarterly* 62, no. 2 (2005): 243–64.

Rothenberg, Winifred B. "A Price Index for Rural Massachusetts, 1750–1855." *Journal of Economic History* 39, no. 4 (1979): 975–1001.

———. "The Emergence of a Capital Market in Rural Massachusetts, 1730–1838." *Journal of Economic History* 45, no. 4 (1985): 781–808.

———. "The Invention of American Capitalism: The Economy of New England in the Federal Period." In *Engines of Enterprise: An Economic History of New England*, ed. Peter Temin, 69–108. Cambridge, MA: Harvard University Press, 2000.

Schweitzer, Mary M. "State-Issued Currency and the Ratification of the U.S. Constitution." *Journal of Economic History* 49 (June 1989): 311–22.

Shepherd, James F., and Gary M. Walton. "Economic Change after the American Revolution: Pre- and Post-war Comparisons of Maritime Shipping and Trade." *Explorations in Economic History* 13 (1976): 397–422.

Sheridan, Richard B. "The British Credit Crisis of 1772 and the American Colonies." *Journal of Economic History* 20, no. 2 (1960): 161–86.

Taylor, Alan. "Divided Ground: Upper Canada, New York, and the Iroquois Six Nations, 1783–1815." *Journal of the Early Republic* 22, no. 1 (2002): 55–75.

Van Cleve, George William. "The Anti-Federalists' Toughest Challenge: Paper Money, Debt Relief, and the Ratification of the Constitution." *Journal of the Early Republic* 34, no. 4 (2014): 529–60.

Warren, Joseph Parker. "The Confederation and the Shays Rebellion." *American Historical Review* 11, no. 1 (1905): 42–67.

Wilson, Janet. "The Bank of North America and Pennsylvania Politics, 1781–1787." *Pennsylvania Magazine of History and Biography* 66 (January 1942): 3–28.

DISSERTATIONS AND THESES

Bjork, Gordon C. "Stagnation and Growth in the American Economy, 1784–1792." Ph.D. diss., University of Washington, 1963.

Calabro, David Joseph. "Consensus for Empire: American Expansionist Thought and Policy, 1763–1789." Ph.D. diss., University of Virginia, 1982.

Forbes, John D. "The Port of Boston, 1783–1815." Ph.D. diss., Harvard University, 1936. (Original now at Small Special Collections Library, University of Virginia, Charlottesville.)

Hall, Arthur Pendleton, II. "State-Issued Bills of Credit and the United States Constitution: The Political Economy of Paper Money in Maryland, New York, Pennsylvania, and South Carolina, 1780–1789." Ph.D. diss., University of Georgia, 1991.

Hatter, Lawrence B. A. "Channeling the Spirit of Enterprise: Commercial Interests and State Formation in the Early American West, 1763–1825." Ph.D. diss., University of Virginia, 2011.

Low, W. Augustus, "Virginia in the Critical Period, 1781–1789," Ph.D. diss., University of Iowa, 1941. (Library of Virginia [Richmond] copy reviewed.)

Warren, Joseph Parker. "The Shays Rebellion: A Study in the History of Massachusetts." Ph.D. diss., Harvard University, 1900.

INDEX